MUIRHEAD LIBRARY OF PHILOSOPHY

An admirable statement of the aims of the Library of Philosophy was provided by the first editor, the later Professor J. H. Muirhead, in his description of the original programme printed in Erdmann's *History of Philosophy* under the date 1890. This was slightly modified in subsequent volumes to take the form of the following statement:

'The Library of Philosophy was designed as a contribution to the History of Modern Philiosophy under the heads: first of different Schools of Thought – Sensationalist, Realist, Idealist, Intuitivist; secondly of different Subjects – Psychology, Ethics, Aesthetics, Political Philosophy, Theology. While much has been done in England in tracing the course of evolution in nature, history, economics, morals and religion, little had been done in tracing the development of thought on these subjects. Yet "the evolution of opinion is part of the whole evolution".

'By the co-operation of different writers in carrying out this plan it was hoped that a thoroughness and completeness of treatment, otherwise unattainable, might be secured. It was believed also that from writers mainly British and American fuller consideration of English Philosophy than it had hitherto received might be looked for. In the earlier series of books containing, among others, Bosanquet's *History of Aesthetic*, Pfleiderer's *Rational Theology since Kant*, Albee's *History of English Utilitarianism*, Bonar's *Philosophy and Political Economy*, Brett's *History of Psychology*, Ritchie's *Natural Rights*, these objects were to a large extent effected.

'In the meantime original work of a high order was being produced both in England and America by such writers as Bradley, Stout, Bertrand Russell, Baldwin, Urban, Montague, and others, and a new interest in foreign works, German, French, and Italian, which had either become classical or were attracting public attention, had developed. The scope of the library thus became extended into something more international, and it is entering on the fifth decade of its existence in the hope that it may contribute to that mutual understanding between countries which is so pressing a need of the present time.'

The need which Professor Muirhead stressed is no less pressing today, and few will deny that philosophy has much to do with enabling us to meet it, although no one, least of all Muirhead himself, would regard that as the sole, or even the main, object of philosophy. In view of Professor Muirhead's long and fruitful association with the Library of Philosophy to which he now also lends the distinction of his name, it seemed not inappropriate to allow him to recall us to these aims in his own words. The emphasis on the history of thought also seemed to me very timely; and the number of important works promised for the Library in the near future augur well for the continued fulfilment in this and other ways, of the expectations of the original editor.

H. D. LEWIS

MUIRHEAD LIBRARY OF PHILOSOPHY

General Editor: H. D. Lewis

Professor of History and Philosophy of Religion in the University of London

Muirhead Library of Philosophy

THE PERSON GOD IS

THE PERSON
GOD IS

BY

PETER A. BERTOCCI

Borden Parker Bowne
Professor of Philosophy at Boston University

LONDON · GEORGE ALLEN & UNWIN LTD
NEW YORK · HUMANITIES PRESS INC

PRINTED IN GREAT BRITAIN
in 11 point Imprint type 1 point leaded
BY W. & J. MACKAY & CO, LTD
CHATHAM, KENT

Dedicated to
my brother
Angelo Philip Bertocci
co-author of many themes
over the years

CONTENTS

INTRODUCTION

What is the nature of the person? The revival of interest in this question in learned circles – literary, philosophical, theological, psychological, sociological, and political – is manifested not only in the range of pertinent knowledge but also in the probing for better methods of studying persons and their mutual relations. This book focuses on the nature of the person, finite and divine.

In that theistic tradition which blends so much in Greek, Jewish, and Christian thought, the Person, God, is required to give structure and meaning to the person, man. To what extent can this tradition be re-confirmed or redefined in a day when the potential of man for good has for some fostered the 'new hope', even as man's new potential for evil has become the 'new despair'? The conviction is abroad that man by prudent self-discipline, guided by imaginative use of scientific method and knowledge, can fathom the secrets of Nature and make it serve his needs. This conviction is accompanied by the pervasive belief that there is no discipline for thinking about, and relating man to God. Thus, in the last fifty years, with some notable exceptions to be sure, it has become customary in learned circles to think of religious belief as the hand-maiden of science, should a handmaiden be required. Several philosophical and theological movements have arisen to fill, or to obviate, the spiritual and ethical vacuum believed to be created by this faith in the scientific spirit and outlook. They in turn have tried to redefine the 'living essence' of a religious view of man and reality.

The essays collected here represent my attempt to deal with matters that, in the last thirty-five years, have been in the forefront of my own philosophical and religious pilgrimage – to live by a faith that needs to repress no major issues in philosophy and philosophical theology. Since a glance at the table of contents will show what some of these issues are, and since each essay is prefaced by remarks that set each chapter in its theoretical context, no further word is needed here.

A brief biographical note may provide some needed background, and in any case provides the opportunity to acknowledge major influences. What will be clear is my debt to Personalistic Idealism, learned at the feet of Edgar S. Brightman in Boston University. This personalistic outlook was invigorated by study at Harvard with Clarence I. Lewis, William E. Hocking, Ralph Barton Perry, and Alfred North Whitehead, deepened by work on a doctoral dissertation guided by F. R. Tennant and W. R. Sorley at the University of Cambridge in 1935, enriched by studies in Italy in 1950 at Croce's *Istituto Storico*, seen in a larger context by the study of Indian philosophy (with emphasis on Radhakrishnan) at the University of Calcutta in 1960–1, and broadened over the years by teaching and study of the psychology of personality (in which the works of James Ward, William James, William McDougall, and Gordon W. Allport were most challenging). I do not even attempt to name living philosophers, theologians, and psychologists who have been part of that inner dialogue that any author knows.

Boston University   *Peter A. Bertocci*

FOR PERMISSIONS

I am indebted to the following publishers for permission to quote the essays printed in this book:

I. 'The Person God Is' in *Talk of God*, ed. by G. N. Vesey (The Macmillan Company, reprinted with the permission of St Martin's Press, Inc., New York), 1969.

II. 'A Temporalistic View of Personal Mind' in *Theories of the Mind*, ed. by Jordan Scher (The Free Press of Glencoe), 1962.

III. 'Foundations of Personalistic Psychology', *Scientific Psychology*, ed. by Benjamin B. Wolman and Ernest Nagel, New York: Basic Books, 1965.

IV. 'The Moral Structure of the Person', *Review of Metaphysics*, Vol. 14 (1961), 369–88.

V. 'The Person, Obligation, and Value', *The Personalist*, Vol. 40 (Spring, 1959), 141–51. Used by permission.

VI. Is There an Ideal of Personality?
Published as 'Education and the Ideal of Personality' in *Philosophy and Education Development*, ed. *George Barnett* (Boston: Houghton Mifflin, 1966).

VII. 'The Logic of Naturalistic Arguments Against Theistic Hypotheses', *The Philosophical Review* (New York: Cornell University Press), January, 1947.

VIII. 'Tennant's Critique of Religious Experience', *Religion in Life*, Vol. 8, (1939), 248–59.

IX. 'The Cosmological Argument – Revisited and Revised', *Proceedings of the American Catholic Philosophical Association* (Washington, D.C.), 1965.

X. 'Can the Goodness of God Be Empirically Grounded?' *The Journal of Bible and Religion* (now *Journal of the American Academy of Religion*), April, 1957, Copyright © by American Academy of Religion; used by permission.

Appendix:
The Goodness of God and Two Conceptions of Value Objectivity, *The Journal of Bible and Religion* (now *Journal of the American Academy of Religion*), July, 1958, Copyright © by American Academy of Religion; used by permission.

XI. 'Toward a Metaphysics of Creation', *The Review of Metaphysics*, Vol. XVII, No. 40, June, 1964.

XII. 'The Logic of Creationism, Advaita, And Visishtadvaita: A Critique.' Presented to Dr T. M. P. Mahadevan, Ganesh and Company (Madras) Private Ltd, 1962.

XIII. 'An Impasse in Philosophical Theology', *International Philosophical Quarterly*, Vol. 5, September, 1965, 379–96.

XIV. 'Free Will, The Creativity of God, and Order', *Current Philosophical Issues*, Essays in Honor of Curt John Ducasse, compiled and edited by Frederick C. Dommeyer (Complements of Charles C. Thomas, Publisher, Springfield, Illinois, 1966).

XV. 'Three Visions of Perfection and Human Freedom', *Psychologia*, Vol. 5, 1962, 59–67.

XVI. 'Religion as the Pursuit of Creativity by God and Man', *Religion as Creative Insecurity*, New York: Association Press, 1958.

XVII. 'The Grace of God as Discovered Through Freedom', New York: Abington Press, 1957.

XVIII. 'What Makes a Philosophy Christian? A Liberal Speaks', *The Christian Scholar*, Vol. 39 (June, 1956) (now *Soundings*).

PART 1

GOD
CREATOR OF CO-CREATORS

CHAPTER I

THE PERSON GOD IS[1]

This essay is a bare outline of a theistic personalism. The remaining essays expand main themes in the argument briefly explored here: what it means to be a person, finite and divine; what the nature of human freedom and creativity involve for man in his relation to other persons and to God; why the Person, God, may be held to be Creator, and why he may be called good.

There are so many historical antecedents to theistic personalism in the history of philosophy and theology that to some it may smack of an unprincipled eclecticism, and to others it may seem to have left out an important part of Plato, Aristotle, Augustine, Aquinas, Descartes, Berkeley, Leibniz, Kant, Schopenhauer, and Hegel.

In twentieth-century America, personalistic idealism, as developed especially by Borden Parker Bowne (1847–1910) and Edgar S. Brightman (1884–1953), re-examined German and British idealism in the conviction that a more reasonable form of idealism and of theism could be developed which would not 'lose' the individual in the Absolute. A similar concern animated the work of Royce, James, Cunningham, Calkins, G. Howison, Boodin, Flewelling (founder and editor of *The Personalist*), and Ernest Hocking. A parallel re-examination went on in England, involving the work of Bradley, Bosanquet, McTaggart, Green, the Cairds, Martineau, Pringle-Pattison, Stout, J. Ward, Sorley, Taylor, Tennant and Temple and C. A. Campbell. Despite differences in emphasis – and without mentioning similar concerns in Germany and France – in such thinkers there is no mistaking the resolve to develop a theory of the person in which rational, moral, and religious experience do not make non-negotiable demands upon each other.

That several of the scholars just mentioned were authors of monumental works in the history of psychology in itself testifies to their interest in the person. And that significant problems about

[1] This essay is from *Talk of God* (Royal Institute Lectures, II), London: Macmillan, 1969.

the person are sooner or later brought back into the arena of philosophical, theological, and psychological discussion is attested on the one hand by several contemporary 'movements' in philosophy with explicit interest in philosophical psychology, and on the other by the establishment, within the American Psychological Association, of a Division of Philosophical Psychology.

The challenges involved in this ferment were not disregarded by E. S. Brightman. In his metaphysics and philosophy of religion one cannot escape the distinctive concern, inspired by a radical experientialism, to keep personalistic theism sensitive to winds of doctrine, whether they emanated from positivist, neo-orthodox, naturalistic, or existentialist and phenomenological sources. In his view a reasonable theologian and philosopher 'takes time seriously', keeps thinking about God in constant relation with what is discovered about man, values, and Nature, and does not play fast and loose with the responsibility for providing a reasonable hypothesis concerning the problem of moral and natural evil. The present essays reflect such concerns, and, if anything, take further steps in the direction of a temporalistic theistic personalism.

In these essays there is little or no reference to a metaphysics of Nature, which for Brightman and Bowne reflected a Berkeleyan emphasis. While I believe that a philosophy of religion ultimately must take its place within a comprehensive and systematic theory of reality, the themes in these essays are developed in a way that does not depend on a final decision between an idealistic and a realistic view of Nature. The approach to thinking about man and God, while profiting especially from the thought of E. S. Brightman, F. R. Tennant, and A. N. Whitehead, expresses my way of coming to terms with issues that may seem to some outmoded, but that that certainly are not unreal. An interest in problems on the borderline between psychology of personality and philosophy has long been a catalyst for my reflection and not the least for the meaning of ethical and religious growth.

I. WHAT IS THE QUESTION OF GOD?

Since my childhood I have given up several conceptions of God. Each time there was quite a wrench, for, in my own limited way, I had been walking with my 'living' God. In my philosophical and theological studies, I have been impressed by the fact that one deep-souled thinker found the living God of another 'dead'. And then I realized that a God is 'living' or 'dead' insofar as 'He' answers questions that are vital to the given believer.

Every believer in God, I am suggesting, lives by some 'model' of God that helps him to live with the practical and theoretical problems he faces from day to day as an actor and a thinker, or, if you will, as a thinker-actor. And he keeps that 'model' of God frequently long after he has begun to realize that it conflicts with the vital evidence as he sees it. He will go on living by it until another view makes more sense to him as a thinker-actor. Sometimes he changes his thought and action with a wrench; sometimes he finds that gradually one view of God died as another came alive. Note, this does not mean that God, granted he exists, died; it means that a given view of God is first challenged by another and then rejected because the other now seems more illuminating. This change of views is no different from what happens every day in our thinking about the world. We are changing our ideas about the moon (and the possibility of life on it) to accord with better evidence.

But the same line of reasoning may be used with regard to the very existence of God. A person may find that any conception of God simply is incoherent with the problems that arise out of his thinking-acting life. Then not only does *a* conception of God die, but the conception that any God at all exists dies. For, it is now held, belief in any God simply does not fit the evidence at hand.

Of course, this matter of what it means to fit the evidence, that is, what our standard of truth requires, is the crucial question. But we shall in this essay assume what has already been implied, that belief in God and belief in a specific kind of God, is a person's thinking-acting response to a conception of God that seems to him more coherent, and that fits in better than any other conception with the evidence.

Any of us who has tried to keep alive to the history of even one great theological-philosophical tradition without losing our sensitivity to the intellectual, religious, and social developments of our own day realizes that a philosophical and theological *aggiornamento* must always be part of our task. Yet – and even here our criterion of truth begins to exert itself – *aggiornamento* must mean bringing the present into challenging relation to the past. The assumption that the 'past' must be brought up to date is as questionable as the assumption that the 'past' can learn nothing from 'the present'. Perhaps, as I think reflection will show, we can, *as thinkers*, forget the labels 'new' and 'old' and ask which idea, hypothesis, which view of God, best illumines the evidence at hand from every source.

If this be granted, then any real dialogue about the nature and existence of God must presuppose a willingness on the part of participants to realize that they cannot hold a fixed view of 'what God must be like' regardless of what the evidence indicates. Great minds, alas, have said: 'There is no God', when all that their argument showed is that a certain view of God is untenable in the light of what they regarded as relevant considerations.

Spinoza, for example, argued (in part) that the Cartesian view of God as Creator was really not God. Why? Because a God who is a Creator is one who presumably would have somehow existed 'in want' until he did create the world and man. This of course is nonsense, but only if the model of God guiding Spinoza is the real God! Again, Tillich argued that God cannot be one being alongside, or among, other beings, for this would not really be God, but some sort of great, yet finite Being. Yet one who knows what Tillich means by truth, and how he believes we come to know it, will see that his view of unconditioned Being is related to the evidence he considers crucial. He may be correct, with Spinoza, but I cannot help wondering why a particular model of God is asserted to be the only being worthy of being called *God*? Obviously, each of us will believe, and should believe that the conception of God which fits the evidence is the true conception of God, but we cannot presuppose what the true God is and then fit the evidence to our view.

To come at last to my purpose here. I know that many have insisted that if God is not a Person he is dead. I see no good reason for such an adamant stand. But because I find it almost fashionable not to know *what considerations led thinkers* to believe that God is a Person, I should like to indicate what it means to say that God is a certain kind of Person. Obviously I cannot speak for all personalistic theists, or for a perspective called classical theism, but only for *a* way of expressing the meaning of God in relation to man and Nature.

II. IF NO PERSON-GOD, THEN NO UNITY AND UNIFORMITY OF NATURE

First, then, what is the essence of the view of person that serves as a guiding model? Any *person* is the kind of being who is a knowing-willing-caring unity in continuity. Let us limit ourselves first to the notion of a person as a unity-in-continuity. The inescapable model is myself as a person. I don't know how it happens, but I cannot escape the fact that I am self-identical as I change. It is as simple and difficult as that! I, as a person, am not a fusion of, or collection of, parts; I am an initial unity which, though changing, nevertheless retains self-identity. Without self-identity there can be no knowing of change. But more, if there were nothing persisting in change we should say not that a being changes, but that one being has been substituted for another (as one actor substitutes for another). This is not all there is to being a person, but it is essential.

Thus, using this model, to say that God is a Person is to assert a Being who, however related to all other beings, is not a unity *of* them; he is self-identical. The question that arises from some who seem to know already what God's nature *must* be, is whether God can, being God, change in any respect. This view of a God who is unchanging Alpha and Omega may be correct. But we need to remind ourselves that to call God *person* is to insist only that God is Unity-Continuity and is unchanging in the unity of his essential being. As a Person he does not change, even if the particular content or quality of his being changes (as when he 'rejoices' when the prodigal son returns).

But why claim that such a being exists at all? What does the Person-God as Unity-Continuity enable us to understand?

Human thought and action are grounded in the regularity and order in the events of the world. To speak of a *universe* is to presuppose beings and events united in such a way that what occurs at one place is connected in an understandable way with what takes place elsewhere. We may not now know how or why one part of the universe is related to the other, but we think and act as if it is not unknowable *in principle*. Order and regularity of some sort constitute 'the way of things'.

Now, such interrelated unity and continuity among the beings and events in the world are illuminated, says the personalistic *theist*, by supposing that there is a Unity-Continuity that creates and sustains all there is, in such a way that basic order, regularity, and connectivity is possible among all the parts.

There are personalistic *pantheists* or monists who would want to assure such ordered connectivity by maintaining that all the beings or events in the world are parts, modes, or centres, of one Absolute Person. Either personalist, theistic or monistic, takes one fundamental stand: no cosmic Unity-Continuant, then no ultimate Ground for the trust we all have in the order of things. (Unless further notice is given, I shall use the word 'personalist' to mean personalistic theist – for whom God is transcendent of, yet immanent in, Nature.) Both pantheistic and theistic personalists argue that we can *reasonably* trust our ventures into the presently unknown only if we can reasonably believe that the unknown is basically continuous with the character of what we do know. And this leads us to the second characteristic of Person, knowing.

III. THE PERSON GOD IS: COSMIC KNOWER

Important as the emphasis on Unity-Continuity is, it is the insistence that Unity-Continuity is most coherent only as it is a knowing Person which gives the personalistic view its name. The personalist holds that the self-sufficient, cosmic Unity-Continuity is, like the finite person, a Knower, a Mind or Spirit.

The storm that has raged around this concept has been caused by the 'model' that controlled the use of the word 'person'. The pre-Socratic Xenophanes wryly exclaimed: The Ethiopains 'make their gods black-haired and flat-nosed, and the Thracians make theirs red-haired and blue-eyed'. What adolescent mind has not sooner or later smartly commented that, after all, men made God after their own image – as if this ended the matter once and for all! Yet, if the world is a universe, and if some Unity-Continuity can be postulated, our thought cannot rest without trying to conceive of what its nature 'must' be in order to fit what we know. And the fundamental fact is that we, as persons, not only ask the questions, but also believe that our human logical questions when supported by human observations will not lead us astray in this universe. Can this universal unity be unlike ours *in principle*?

It is not unsuggestive that Xenophanes, who found no reason for holding that God had blue eyes, did nevertheless say that the nature of Ultimate Being was Thought! That God-intoxicated philosopher Spinoza, de-anthropomorphized God by saying that the One Substance was no more like a finite person than the celestial constellation, 'the Dog', was like a barking dog. But the same Spinoza insisted that, of the infinite number of attributes of Substance, *thought* as well as extension defines the essence of Substance. While Paul Tillich cannot define Unconditioned Being as person, he says: 'The God who is *a* person is transcended by the God who is the Personal-Itself, the ground and abyss of every person.'[1]

---

[1] *Biblical Religion and the Search for the Ultimate Reality* (Chicago, 1952), p. 38.

Any personalistic theist must be sympathetic with every attempt to keep before the believer the realization that no concept of the cosmic Unity will comprehend it completely, that all man's concepts will leak, if for no other reason than that man's knowledge is incomplete. He can also understand why it makes sense to say that no part of the universe, including the human, can, without qualification, describe the cosmic Unity. Yet he urges that it must remain a matter of live debate whether there is any 'model' other than Mind, even as we know ourselves, that will be more helpful to us in defining the *kind* of unity, continuity, and order that will account for the fact that our minds, existing in this world, have been able to fathom its nature progressively.

After all, the basic drift of scientific and philosophical theorizing presupposes that what lies beyond man can be understood by the human mind. This is not to say that man will understand all, but it does mean that the schemes of Nature, however far-flung, are not intrinsically and in principle beyond disciplined human knowing. Indeed, when a person doubts concretely that a particular conclusion in science and philosophy is true, is he not using other considerations, which he believes to be true descriptions of the world, to support his doubting? In the last analysis, we do not believe that the segment of the world we do seem to know will be basically rejected by the rest of the universe we do not now know. The maps we now have will need revision, the models will be fashioned by the very minds that learn from their mistakes and yet press on in the faith that the next map, the next model, will be more illuminating for thought and action.

It is this kind of consideration that leads the personalist to find, expressed in the order of the world, a Mind that in its basic structure is not foreign to his own. If *our* map-making, encouraged and discouraged by the terrain about us, if *our* models suggested by what we know and remodelled in the light of what we encounter, do get us on with the total business of understanding and living in both the microscopic and macroscopic realms, can it be that the total universe as we envision it and interact with it, is alien to our being as persons? To change the figure, if the key 'in our natures' can open the lock of the world to any extent, why is it far-fetched to suppose that the key and the lock do not bespeak a common locksmith? It is easy to scoff at what I believe to be a *legitimate* anthropomorphism. Yet is not the scoffer boasting of his luck if he continues to urge that the way to know what is real is to think

logically, observe thoroughly, hypothesize in the light of evidence
at hand, and act on hypotheses with concerted further thought and
action?

Whenever a personalist, then, hears someone say 'but the
universe is beyond anything the human mind can know', his
rejoinder is insistent. 'This is logically possible. But do you claim
your mind can know *that*? If it can, and if your mind can *know* that,
aren't you asserting that somehow your mind has the secret to its
own impotence? It is one thing to assert that we don't know all: it is
another to say that what we know in ourselves and in the world
provides no good ground for supposing that our progress is helping
us to identify the nature of a cosmic Mind.'

Here the retort may readily be made: But do you mean that the
word 'know' is to be used for God in the same sense as it is used for
man? The answer: Whatever the particular knowing processes in
God are remains open for further discussion. A responsible philosophical theology must be as clear as it can be about the nature of
this knowing. It will not evade such questions as: Is God's knowing
intellectual in the sense in which our logic is syllogistic, or is it
non-discursive and intuitive?

We might at least bear in mind, in passing, that God does not
'speak' either in English or German, or use words – but neither do
animals or the deaf and dumb express their level of awareness in
such ways. More relevant is the suggestion that we seek analogies
within the whole range of human *awareness*, inclusive of aesthetic,
moral, and religious awareness. But the minimum intellective
awareness is knowing similarity and differences in itself and everywhere else. In short, the essential personalistic contention is that,
whatever the 'infinity' of a cosmic Unity entails, we endanger the
Unity if we deny that it is self-conscious and knows the difference
between himself and his world, including persons.

Again, there is a basic problem here. When we stress the
immensity of the universe, the unlimited majesty of God, the
unconditioned nature of his Being, or what have you, do we mean
that no link, no common bond, exists between man and God? Do
we mean to say that what is logical to us would be non-logical or
illogical to that Being? The personalist, while he must speculate
about the nature of the difference between man and God, insists on
the essential continuity between the best in his own experience and
in the universe, including God. Why court mystery here when we
decry impalpable mystery elsewhere? In the name of modesty and

humility we can urge that no human symbols are adequate, but if we take this seriously we belie the amount of success our symbolizing has had, and we tend to foster more scepticism than we intended. At the same time we have disqualified a particular view of God's nature by what are ultimately loaded views of God's ultimacy and perfection.

Again, what does it add to say that God is what we can know *and more*? For if the word 'more' means 'more of the same', it can be granted. But if the 'more' means difference in kind, we simply cannot know what *that* 'more' means even though we seem wise and modest in saying so. What would happen to the construction of computers if we said, for example, that, though the actual process be different, what goes on in the structure of a computer has *no* counterpart in the structure of man, even though, for example, the computer can solve problems it would take ages for man to solve? What would happen to our attempts to understand what goes on in lower animals and in plants if we let our realization that there is 'more than we know in ourselves' stifle reasonable analogy?

Obviously, much needs to be added. It is not incidental, however, to remark that what tends to control thinking here is the model of the finite person we have in mind when we say: God is a Person. If I thought that the person is identical with his brain and body, I would not use the word 'person' for God. In our day there are many who, unwittingly or wittingly, think of a person as some sort of body. But do these same persons think that a person is a male or a female, or are they assigning 'person' to a being, who, however his body is related to him, is *not identical* with that body? Ambiguity courts disaster at these points.

Once more, if, as many in our day hold, the person is a social-biological phenomenon, then the denial that God is a person is understandable. For God's nature, if it is to fit our cosmological evidence, is not the product of learning in some environment (and I say this even though I myself hold that God in some respects does change in response to changes initiated by our persons).[1] For

[1] Indeed, while much of this paper reflects the influence of F. R. Tennant, it is the influence of Edgar S. Brightman, Alfred N. Whitehead, H. Bergson, and Charles Hartshorne that has led me to conceive of change in God in ways similar to Hartshorne's view. At present my main hesitancy stems from the way in which the person is related to God in Whitehead, Bergson, and Hartshorne, for as I now see it the independence of the person is not adequately protected. For example, while the case for personal immortality must be argued, of course, I cannot accept the suggestion that there is wishful thinking and a false sense of values in the desire for personal immortality. On the contrary, if to be a person is

the personalist, however, the word 'person' identifies an agent capable of self-consciousness and of action in the light of rational and moral-aesthetic-religious ideals.

To summarize: in hypothesizing that the cosmic Unity is a Person we are carrying on the same kind of process, of moving from the unknown on the basis of what is known, that activates careful reflection in the other concrete areas of human investigation. If by careful observation, guided as far as possible by scientific method, we discover that our thought-forms do engage us with the world beyond in such a way that one discovery leads to another, on what grounds, consistent with experiential procedures, can we argue that the Being manifest in our world is totally different from our mind-form?

To say that Being or Unity is more than we are is, after all, to say something very innocuous theoretically. This dictum applies not only to God but to everything we know. But, as I suggest, in the actual course of argument, this 'more' in God is often used to disqualify attempts, built on reasoning however inadequate, to see what seems reasonable granted given evidence at least. In every area, the theoretical problem is always one of defining what the nature of 'the more' is. But do we dare move without the reasonably established faith that the more is not unlike what we already know? In a word, the faith of the personalist at this point is, minimally, an extension of the faith that guides all theoretical activity.

IV. THE PERSON GOD IS: LOVING AGENT

We have argued that if God is conceived as a Person, as a unified Knower, then we can the better understand why our thought-forms have succeeded in knowing the interconnected order of Nature. To think of God as a cosmic Person is not to indulge a human whim, but to ground more adequately all of our theoretical ventures, including the scientific. But is God good? Let us ask the same question we asked before. What problem would be solved by this conception?

In answer, we turn again to human experience and ask what the

---

to be a person-in-and-for-oneself I fail to see why, in a universe that presumably conserves and increases value, it is an increase in value to preserve a memory, even in God (in Hartshorne's sense), while personhood ceases to be. Yet, I expect that the nature of creation (see below) and of personal continuity is the bone of contention.

lasting basis of human goodness is. Many factors contribute to human existence and to the growth of quality in human experience. But if the personalist were to be limited to any other one factor, beyond knowing, which makes for *quality* in every area of *human experience in this world*, he would select *loving*. Thinking-loving gives support to thinking-acting; they are the creative matrix in which every other human good is strengthened. Without the other each falters. Accordingly, the personalist argues, thinking-loving is the clue to the best the universe makes possible, as far as we know.

To elaborate: When a person dedicates himself to the growth of other persons in full awareness of their mutual potential for growth, we say that he loves. And he loves unto forgiveness when he does all in his power to enable even those who have purposely abused his love to join the fellowship and community of love. And separation, as Ian Ramsey says, is 'hell'.[1] In a word, in human experience there is no greater good than to be a responsive-responsible member in a community dedicated to mutual growth. This good we call love. Any being whose purposes include the growth of persons-in-community, and who does all in his power to realize this purpose, is loving. The Person God, says the personalist, is good; he is a loving agent. The grounds for this contention may be further elaborated in two steps.

First, is it not experientially sound to say that to the extent to which love is realized in an individual personality, in a family, and in a community, every other value that human beings find worthwhile is enhanced? For the ideal of love-unto-forgiveness (I do not mean sentimentality) is not a dream. It is an actual description of how persons, in relation to other persons, can fulfil themselves in the world as they know it, within themselves, and beyond themselves. Persons are desperate when they feel alienated both from the best in themselves and the best in others. They are more likely to improve and grow if they feel the forgiveness that, looking beyond the harm they have done, draws them into a community of mutual concern. These are requirements for growth in self-fulfilment in community.

Man does not make up these requirements any more than he makes up the laws governing the growth of bodies or the changes in molecules. He finds them – not as he finds the stars or the law of gravitation, however. He finds them in the midst of his very attempt to know what he can best be-in-act. A loving man is a knowing-willing man

[1] See Chapter 13, 'Hell', in *Talk of God* (1969).

developing dimensions of his own being and of other beings, dimensions that come into being *as* he loves. His *knowing in loving is a more comprehensive knowledge* which tells him about himself and his fellow men even as they both *realize* their potential and fulfil each other with a minimum of fruitless conflict.

To put this in a different way: What the personalist is calling to our attention is that men and Nature do not stand in an indifferent relation to each other; they are not juxtaposed. Men are facts about the total world that includes biological and physical beings; but they are also facts for each other in that larger world. For them to understand themselves is for them to become aware of their physical and social environment, in such a way as to keep all of these in a responsive-creative relation to each other. Thus, when a man discovers that mutual respect for another's freedom is the best condition for their mutual personal growth, *he is discovering a fact that the total world, including himself, makes possible.* When he goes on to realize that such freedom – guided by knowledge of self, of others, of Nature – is supported and kept from self-destruction only as it is disciplined by loving, he is also discovering what his life-in-the-world can be.

This first step in the psycho-logic of love encourages a personalist to argue that the same universe which makes it possible for man to know, and to live by that knowledge, is the very universe which makes it impossible for man to perfect that knowledge unless he meets the conditions of love. He must learn to respect both 'the structure and potential of things' for their own sake and the structure and potential of other persons for their own sakes. As long as a man lives in this world, he, given his nature, will not be able to fulfil himself simply for himself; he will not be able to treat either the world or others as if they were meant *only* for him. He will grow without fruitless conflict only as he grows *within* and *for* a community in which persons both respect each other, and co-operate with each other in responsive-responsible growth. It is this fact about the world that best defines what it is and can be in relation to man. Thus, when the personalist says that God is a unity-in-continuity of knowing-willing-caring, he is asserting that the essential constitution of the world and the essential constitution of man are such that the highest good of man is realized in that kind of community in which persons respect and care for each other's growth.

A second step in the personalist's reasoning articulates the first by calling attention to what is involved in the human search for truth. As a matter of actual dynamics within the individual personality and within the community, knowledge grows not merely because the world is knowable. Knowledge grows apace only as it is put to use, and only as it is motivated by respect for other persons and by mutuality in the total venture of knowing. For, in their own way, the community of scholars, the growth of knowledge, the zest for the venture, grow apace as scholars know that their mistaken and misguided efforts will be sympathetically understood, that their errors will be rejected but their efforts encouraged. Thus, in the venture of acquiring and sharing knowledge, without which human existence is inconceivable, love is not an addendum which investigators may disregard.

This point is so simple that its very simplicity allows many to underestimate its importance, and to be parasitic upon what makes for community in the knowledge-venture. Again, the search for knowledge is encouraged by love for more than knowledge; it is sustained by mutual concern for the growth of persons as investigators who find and express themselves in sharing of insights.

Furthermore, truth-seekers in any one community must be free to respond to the lure of truth. But they will feel threatened in their efforts if they believe that the larger community upon which they depend will be intolerant especially when their discoveries challenge the *status quo*, or that the community will judge them only by their failures. Truth-seekers themselves, of course, must be willing to suffer, especially before the intellectual conscience of man. But their courage to seek will be inspired if they can live in the assurance that they will not suffer vindictive punishment.

To summarize: Man, the lover-knower *in* the world, is the lover-knower not threatened by that world but nurtured, challenged, and supported by it as he grows within it. Love has no meaning without such challenge and support, whatever else it involves. Why not then hold that love is the broader principle involved in world-being as we know it? For man's justifiable hope for himself in his world is rooted in his daily discovery that, in disciplining himself by the norms of truth and love, he is part of 'the drift' of things. In knowing-loving he enters into a fuller relationship with a universe that responds to him in his growth as inspired by truth and love. Why not then conceive of the Unity-Continuity of the cosmic Knower as a loving Person? This is the way to say that man's own joy in self-discovery and in mutual growth is no cosmic surprise, for it is grounded in a Universe that responds to man's creative effort as knower and carer.

It should now be clear that a personal God is not one that human beings somehow add to their experience or their world. Personalists do not argue *that* there is a God and then add labels to that Being. They argue that, in the very attempt to discover what they are and can best become in their world, persons find a Person at work with them *in* and *through* their world. For the personalist, the God 'up there' does not exist because he never did, as far as they know. He is always at work in the world and in relation to persons. But this takes us directly to the reasons for saying that God is the Creator of man and the world.

V. THE PERSON GOD IS: COSMIC CREATOR

The finite person, it has been argued, is dependent for his very being and sustenance on God. But finite as the person is, he is free to choose and to create within limits. In the context suggested above, each man, given basic cognitive and conative capacities, is free to choose, within the limits of these capacities, the knowledge ventures and the quality of caring he believes to be best. For this moral development man is himself so responsible that he is a creator.

Such a view of freedom is a minimal requirement for a personalistic view of the person; it is not argued here. But the consequences of this view are crucial for the personalist's thought about man's relation to God. As we have seen, a person is indeed related to his total environment, including God. But a person does not overlap with anything else in the world or with God. His being is his unity-in-continuity of knowing-willing-caring. God in turn, as a person, does not overlap with, or include, any other person.

This whole idea is not easy to conceive, let alone imagine. But it should be clear at the outset that it is the personalist's concern to protect the individuality of the person-man, and of the Person-God, that leads him to propose his doctrine of creation. Unless the context of the doctrine of creation is understood, this doctrine, mysterious enough at best, will be cast aside disdainfully as 'impossible'.

There are two other ways of conceiving God's relation to man and the world other than holding that God creates them 'out of nothing' (*creatio ex nihilo*).

According to the first, which follows suggestions Plato made in the *Timaeus*, God may be likened to a sculptor who creates not 'out of nothing' but out of the material or 'stuff' at hand. This stuff is in itself relatively inchoate, and by itself would never take on any structure or order. While more than one specific order can be introduced into such inchoate being, no pervasive structure is to be found in its formless nature. Yet, because it is an eternal something rather than 'nothing', it will 'respond' to some forms of order better than to others. It may be of some help to think of clay or marble, which will conform to more than one 'idea'; yet clay cannot become exactly what a block of marble can become.

Great philosophers have grappled with the problem of introducing any specific structure – regularity, order, form – into inchoate being which is something (not nothing) and yet in itself almost without any form. They have preferred to postulate some such formless matrix, or 'womb of all becoming', rather than postulate what seemed preposterous – creation '*ex nihilo*', which they translated literally *out of nothing*. Better to suppose that God is somehow co-eternal with such 'material for becoming'; better to hold that God did not create such being and that it could not create him. Better to hold that God and 'matter' are two eternal Principles, two Kinds of Being, both needing each other if anything is to be developed in what is.

Such alternatives all sound so much more picturable and conceivable than 'creation out of nothing' until we ask some other questions. Plato, for example, had to take one more step. For if God is the Sculptor, and the Material (the Receptacle) is that which takes on form, whence the Forms, whence the Ideas or Ideals, that guide the Sculptor in his creative work? There is reason to suppose that Plato believed that they too constituted a realm of their own, co-eternal with 'matter' and God. They are not dependent upon God or upon 'matter' for their existence – in part because as Ideals they are to give form to both God and 'matter'. Hence Plato conceived of God as a cosmic Lover of Forms (Ideas or Ideals) that he did not create. Neither the forms nor the inchoate Being, then, are dependent upon each other. There results a co-eternal trinity of beings in Plato's system at this point. And none of these beings, by definition, is related to the other.

Nevertheless, says Plato, this imperfect, but relatively orderly world can be explained by thinking of God as this cosmic Artist or Demi-urge, who with his eye fixed on the co-eternal Ideals, 'persuades' the co-eternal, inchoate being to take on as much form and order as possible. For Plato, the complex orderly world which man sees about him, and man's own capacity to know and interact with both the world and God, testify to the 'creative' goodness of one member of the co-eternal 'trinity'. Other thinkers decreased the difficulty to be mentioned by moving the Ideals into the mind of God, conceiving of them as the eternal Ideals guiding his will. For them God is still co-eternal with Matter of some sort, and cosmic Trinity gives way to Duality. We need not stop to elaborate on this view, for our concern is to understand why either a co-eternal Two or Three gave way to *creatio ex nihilo*.

It might be urged that any such one-of-two, or one-of-three, view of God was unacceptable to early Christians because it is un-biblical to make God finite. But this only skirts the real difficulty, which is the following. If there are two or three ultimate, co-eternal Being, is it not completely incomprehensible that they should be so complementary? Why should they find that they can interact in a way that does make this kind of orderly world possible? The mystery of mysteries, opaque to our human intelligence because it contravenes what we always assume in our known realms, stuns us. For, when beings are at all related to each other, we assume that, despite their differences, they are not separated by chasms as impassable as these co-eternally different kinds of being must be by definition. Our minds demand that Creator, Ideas, and Stuff (or Creator and Stuff) have something in common if they are to inter-act at all. Indeed, the world as we know it, despite its dissonances and evils, is sufficiently good and sufficiently orderly to suggest that a better marriage actually took place than the one to be expected if both beings are completely independent of each other.

Once more, then, creation 'out of nothing' may be mysterious. But on what grounds may we expect two eternally different principles to be able to interact in such a way as to produce the kind of orderly world we observe? If it offends religious sensitivity, on the one hand, to conceive of God as limited by some co-eternal independent principle, then the theoretical reason cries out, on the other hand, against explaining the kind of orderly world we have by postulating two or three co-eternal, different beings (if we take their independence seriously).

The personalist has no easy task in defending *creatio ex nihilo*. It is only when we become aware of difficulties in *absolute* monism and in *absolute* dualism or pluralism that we see why this difficult alternative became palatable to him. Accordingly, the personalist holds that God, the cosmic Person, *created* the world *ex nihilo*. But this 'out of nothing' is the personalist's way of emphasizing his rejection of any co-eternal, independent factor with which God has to deal. It is not simply that God is rendered finite if there is an independent non-created matter'; it is that we cannot account for the world's being an orderly world at all! Difficult as *creatio ex nihilo* is, it is not so utterly indefensible once one fully understands what is at stake.

The personalist, accordingly, goes on to explain that God's knowledge of all the possibilities and compossibilities guided him in his care to create the orderly world in which persons are sustained. But, more important, the doctrine of *creatio ex nihilo* is also the personalist's way of saying that God is not identical with the world and with persons. Further still, God is not one 'alongside' all the created beings, for they depend ultimately upon his will for whatever independence they have. Without his continuous creation and involvement in accordance with his own being and purpose there would be no 'universe'. The personalist in this doctrine, therefore, seeks to explain the order of the world in a way that preserves differences without endangering the autonomy and perfection of God.

Nevertheless, argue the critics of personalism, the cost of this doctrine is too high. They still find the notion of creation mysterious. The theist would agree that the doctrine is mysterious. But he urges that at worst this doctrine, *if it is exemplified nowhere in* our experience, nevertheless is not contradictory of anything we do find. Furthermore, every metaphysics and theology has some ultimate that is mysterious in that we cannot point to instances of it in the world. But the personalist does advance one other consideration to take the edge off this criticism.

Finally *creatio ex nihilo* does not actually mean that God took 'nothing' and made something out of it. The theist would agree that 'from nothing' nothing can come. Neither God nor man can do what is not even thinkable, make nothing become something! But creation out of nothing does not mean that God 'took nothing and made something out of it'. 'Out of' nothing, nothing comes, to be sure. But the personalist does not start with 'nothing'. He starts with God and says that this Person (far from being nothing himself) is the Creator-Ground of all.

In a word, to say that God creates is to say that beings now exist *that did not exist before.* Finite beings are not made 'out of God' or 'out of some co-eternal being'. They are made, produced, created. There is nothing contradictory in saying that a Creator beings into being what was non-existent without the act of creation; to create means just that!

VI. THE PERSON GOD IS: CREATOR OF CO-CREATORS

Yet before the personalistic theist can persist in this difficult theory of creation, he must explain why he does not find another great vision of God more palatable. Why not say that God is One with all there is, that nature and man are modes of God, or participants in his being who do not have any independent agency of their own?

We must not be casual about this concept of God as The One, for it is proposed by careful monists (Paul Tillich is fresh in mind). They are not saying that everything there is, collectively, is God. This simply renames things as they appear. Nor do such monists say that God is equally in all things that participate in his being. God is indeed the One who is manifest in the many, and the One would not be what he is apart from the many. God is to be found in his different manifestations in different degrees, just as a man is to be found in his varied utterances even though none of them express all that he is.

Again, The One may be said to have many centres of his being. However we express it, on this view the continuity and unity observed among the myriad things in the world manifest, at different levels or in different dimensions, the unity and continuity that God is. While significant exponents of this view – Plotinus, Eckhardt, Spinoza, Tillich – have tended to think of this One as supra-Personal in the sense indicated above, this being has been held to be Mind or Spirit, as in the thought of Hegel, Lotze, Bradley, Royce, and W. E. Hocking.[1]

With such a galaxy of stars gloriously arraigned against him, why does the theistic personalist still maintain his creationist stand? First, he would point out that the *how* of this One-in-many is essentially no clearer than is the how of creation 'out of nothing'. There is no contest here, for it is mysterious to know how the

[1] An essay by Professor H. D. Lewis in Talk of God is an excellent presentation of the issue involved. At the same time Professor Lewis suggests a notion of 'the elusive self' and of interpersonal relations that reinforces the view of personhood suggested here.

infinite can be both infinite and finite, perfect and imperfect. But there is less that is opaque in this mysterious relation than there is in the contention of the dualist and pluralist mentioned earlier. Indeed, many idealistic personalistic theists, such as B. P. Bowne and E. S. Brightman, would even argue that while persons have delegated freedom and independence, beings of a physical and biological nature are direct expressions of the cosmic Person. The main personalistic objection to monism, accordingly, is not that Nature is unified with One but that man is unified with the One. Why?

Persons are not only self-conscious unified beings; they feel themselves to be free, and there is good reason to suppose that this feeling is not a delusion. However, this freedom is not self-instituted nor is this freedom without limits. The freedom of persons is the freedom to choose, within the margins of their own possibilities, in the world that surrounds them. But it is *their* freedom; it underlies their feeling of responsibility for much of what they do. If this is so, then they cannot be part of God, centres of his being. To express this crucial fact, the personalist calls for a doctrine of *creatio*.

It is important to emphasize here that the creationist theist will not allow any theory of the universe and of God to contradict or reduce to delusion the experience of free will. Human freedom, for good or ill, is limited, to be sure. But it is denied only at the cost of making human beings robots. To be sure, the exact scope of human freedom, and related matters, must be debated. But if man's actions are to be his, if they are to define his own individuality, he cannot be said to participate in God in any way that endangers this relative autonomy. If a person is a mode or a centre of another Being, *his* freedom, *his* individuality, is gone. Thus *creatio ex nihilo* now becomes the personalistic theist's way of saying that every attempt to explain how persons can be free and still be *parts* of, or *centres* of, a larger controlling Whole will not do.

There are many who will insist that the doctrine of human freedom is mysterious enough, for they think that a free act simply must mean arbitrary action unlinked to anything else past or present. Why then extend such mystery to horrendous, cosmic proportions, in a doctrine of divine creation of free persons?

The personalist stands firm and replies: If there is to be mystery in any world view, let this be where it is – namely, where it protects human finite unity and freedom, within limits to be determined in each instance. What is basically asserted in the doctrine of creation is that God can make what is not there before his act. This may be hard to imagine or picture, but it is defensible if theory is not to dictate to experienced personal unity and freedom.

Thus man is to be conceived of as a created co-creator. He has delegated responsibility for his own choices and sub-creations in God's world. This means that God is transcendent, for he has a Being for himself. It also means that he is immanent not only by virtue of the dependence of the natural world upon him, but by virtue of his relationship to free persons. For God has created persons endowed with freedom to choose within the limits of their own capacities and of the rest of the world as God made it. It also means that he will join man in creating what is not possible without God and man in mutual response.

Of course this doctrine of the cosmic Person as creator of free persons who, having a place in God's purpose, yet are not *in* or *as* his Being, needs more defence. But since the monistic view of God is often defended on the grounds of the unity felt in mystical experience, one question may be raised here. What is love, or worship, if it does not involve the self-disciplined freedom of man to act in certain ways toward God and man? The personalist would argue that an adequate doctrine of sin, salvation, grace, prayer, worship, and immortality, is not forthcoming unless persons are created, free, co-creators with God.

Finally, is God the Person-Creator in fact arbitrary? The personalist finds no arbitrariness. For (on other grounds) he believes that God in his creating expresses the purposes of love and reason that constitute his intrinsic nature. God, the Creator-Person, creates the finite creator-person in accordance with his purpose that men should be free to choose which way their souls shall go. God's own purpose, as the personalist sees it, calls for a-community-of-responsive-responsible-persons as the norm of creation and history. The kingdom of God, on earth and in heaven, is a community of persons, dedicating themselves to each other as persons. The 'kingdom of heaven' is not the achievement of a benevolent despot; it is the qualitative growth of persons who find in their daily living that their freedom is most constructive and fruitful when it is expressed in creative and forgiving love.

The *Person God is* – he is the Lover-Creator who expresses his love in the order of Nature without which man could not even exist. But the *Person God is* – he is also the Lover-Creator who leaves man free to be a creator. The *Person God is* – he makes it clear in the foundations of Nature and Man that only in mutual love unto forgiveness is there self-fulfilment for God or man. Only in mutual love is there that fellowship-in-creativity-with-God that is God's highest goal for himself and for every man.[1]

[1] See 'Free Will, the Creativity of God, and Order' in *Current Philosophica Issues* (*Essays in Honor of C. J. Ducasse*), ed. F. Dommeyer (Illinois, 1966); Chapter XIV, below.

PART 2

THE HUMAN PERSON AND HIS MORAL STRUCTURE

CHAPTER II

A TEMPORALISTIC VIEW OF PERSONAL MIND[1]

For most of us, who think about the person in the context of biological evolution, the finite person is to be conceived – no matter what – as a certain stage in the evolutionary process. For others of us, the conception of man must fit in with the conviction that he is God's creature. Plato can teach us, I think, an important lesson, even though for this Plato-enthusiast his conclusions leave much to be desired.

The lesson is to keep one's gaze fixed on man himself, and on what his inner growth and decay tell us about him. For Plato each man desires – but as a man and not as an animal or a god! – and he literally lives as a human being at some stage in the pursuit of truth, of goodness, of beauty, and of holiness. Even if Plato had known what is known today about the brain, I think, if we take the *Phaedo* seriously, that he would still have said that the way to think of man is in terms of these life-giving purposes. Whether man is sensing or gratifying his appetites, he knows that in themselves they never yield satisfaction of what constitutes him human. A person, Plato would urge, is a unity that cannot be seen as a collection, or a harmonizing, of elements; he is never a product or by-product of something else, to which he may well, in the last analysis, be related. 'Know thyself' means at least to be aware of what it means to fulfil what one's nature allows.

In the essays in this part, on the finite person, I express what I regard as first order of business in our day, to see the dimensions of the person as he experiences them himself. The person is not to be fit in with some theological, physiological, psychological, and sociological conclusions that for some reason need to be preserved regardless of how the person experiences himself.

Of course, my own analysis may be as full of holes as a sieve. But my fundamental appeal is for a view of the person that is not

---

[1] This essay appears in *Theories of Mind*, edited by Jordan M. Scher (New York: The Free Press of Glencoe, 1962).

motivated by reaction, whether it be against viewing a person as a god or as a thing, against his rationality and in favour of his conative life, against his being observed only by some privileged or private access, against his being divided into mind and body, against his being capricious or predictable in principle, against his having a sense of obligation that is cognitive in some sense, or against his having a religious awareness that is reducible to some other dimensions of his being.

In the essay immediately following, I introduce a temporalistic view of the finite person that is the fundamental to other views in this book. The focus here is on the reasons for not identifying the person with the body as understood by most biologists and naturalistic philosophers. A more complete metaphysics would give an account of the body and of the unconscious in their relation to the conscious person.

The view presented is most consistent with the view that mind and body interact and influence each other in accordance with their own natures; but no more is ventured here. An equally strong conviction is that the temporalistic conscious person is not to be identified with an unchanging soul or self. Here I reluctantly part company, at one important point, not only with the founder of American personalism, Borden Parker Bowne, but with esteemed thinkers like Ward, McTaggart, F. R. Tennant, C. A. Campbell, and H. D. Lewis.

But how, then, is one to conceive of the continuity of person-experience, especially if one cannot agree with the account provided by process philosophers like Whitehead and Hartshorne? The following view may move toward resolving a thorny problem for the temporalist who would escape the difficulties both of soul-psychology and a process-psychology.

I. THE IDENTITY OF MENTAL BEING

If there were no other ground for believing in 'mental being', the fact of cognitive error would force us to postulate its existence. For cognitive error, in any degree, cannot be understood if the knowing process is identified with physiological or chemical-electrical being. Obviously, these assertions need defence, and this will constitute our first point.

Error is a unique kind of occurrence. All forms of it involve the state of affairs in which a statement that was supposed to be true of some other being or event is to some degree not true. Again, very broadly stated, whenever error occurs in any degree, an 'entity' (assertion, image, percept, idea, symbol, sign, experience) is found in some degree not to refer correctly to, not to present, to represent, or to be identical with the state of affairs to be known.

But, and here is the crucial consideration, the error exists, or has a 'locus', for some being, in relation to something else. This erroneous judgment must have an unusual nature. It must itself be a state of affairs referring to another state of being. If no error were ever made, no question would arise about the kind of being an erroneous assertion has. But the assertion: 'That is my book' (when it turns out to be another's) is a state of affairs clearly not identical with or representative of (or in any other way veridical in regard to) the actual situation. And this fact throws the spotlight on what kind of being such assertions involve.

The answer, we suggest, is: Here is a kind of being intended to reflect a state of affairs not itself, a kind of existence whose very nature consists in its being referred beyond itself by a knower. *The judgment as a state of being is not in error. A knower seeking to use this state of being to get beyond it, is in error!*

What can we then say about the nature of the knower? The knower, we suggest, must be the kind of being that can have as part of its being a state of affairs whose very being consists in being referred beyond itself to another state of affairs. The fact, discovered later, that it was referred erroneously, does not change the existence of a judgment, though the error might have led to evil consequences for the existent which 'referred' it. To say that the 'error' no longer exists is not to say that the being in error no longer exists. *The 'being' who is in error thus turns out to be the kind of existent that (a) can have its own existence, (b) be capable of the state of affairs here called 'referring' an attribute to something other than the referring state, and (c) go on entertaining that state without (necessary) vital difference to itself.*

This kind of being also, we contend, is unique. No other being 'makes' errors. One billiard ball striking another, a cell in interchange with the environment, an electrical current which moves in one direction rather than another, all are affecting and being affected, but they cannot be in error. For error has no meaning in terms of interacting events as such. The erroneous being, however engaged in referring, carries on its own business of existing and interchanging, like all other events. But, different from all others, it is undergoing a kind of activity (the experiencing of images, signs, ideas, or symbols), whose very being consists in designating, without being or affecting, the event presumably referred to. This kind of activity is the kind of activity we call cognitive, and it can exist only in the more comprehensive kind of being we are calling *mind*.

To state our contention crisply: If we had no introspective knowledge of mind, if there were no other shred of evidence for mentality, when we try to indicate how error is possible, we find it reasonable to postulate mind as the kind of being which alone can be in error. To summarize our reasoning: Given the fact of error, there must be a being that exists, in error or not. That being, as part of its existence, *can refer*, by way of one phase of its activity upon which its sheer being does not depend, to something other than itself. It is this kind of being which we call *mind* – though mind will turn out to be more than a cognizing being.

To express our first thesis in another way: Assuming that we could define a human being in purely chemical or physical terms, we might regard him as a unique complex of electrochemical changes. Or, perhaps better, assume that we could say that a human being represents a certain emergent phase of evolution from electrochemical being capable of taking on life with its own self-maintaining processes. We then could say that human beings have encounters and undergo changes which destroy their vitality and reduce them to physicochemical events. But this level of description could never yield an account of cognitive error as human beings are involved in it. For it is one kind of being to be hurt, or to become diseased, and another kind of being to exist in cognitive error, though harm might result from error. Why? Because error as error is a unique kind of event demanding for its explanation another kind of existent, emergent or created, namely, *mind*.

To expand our meaning: The processes involved in physical interchange and biological interaction are not the same processes involved in knowing and in erring. The capacity to be in error leads us to invoke a quality or dimension of Being that has no counterpart in the physical or biological realm, and which we might not have invoked had we never been 'in error'. This new being can 'harbour', 'have', 'undergo', states of its own being which exist 'in' it, whether they are true or false, but whose very being consists in their being referred to a state of affairs beyond themselves.

What we have been saying is a long, roundabout way of reaching a point that could be reached easily if we had begged the question and used the psychological language we purposely avoided. We might have said simply: the unique thing about the knowing situation, forced upon our attention by the fact of error, is that in knowing there is an event which exists as psychic but whose very being consists in its being referred beyond itself by the knowing being. This reference beyond itself makes error (and truth) possible, and it distinguishes the being who can 'refer', from every other being we know. One can appreciate H. H. Price's exclamation: 'Let us rather take off our hats to any creature which is clever enough to be caught in a trap. It is the capacity of making mistakes, not the incapacity of it, which is the mark of the higher stages of intelligence.'[1] It would, on the other hand, make no sense to attribute such intelligence to a certain congeries of biological changes or electrical vibrations in the brain, which affect and are affected, but which have no states that 'refer'.

Before passing on, we wish to call attention to the approach we have been following. We did not start with mind, but in *medias res*. Seeking to understand different types of events, we found that the existence of error could not be possible if all events were physicochemical or 'purely' biological. We did not ask, with the rationalistic presuppositions of a Descartes, of what kind of being we could be rationalistically certain, though we would not object to a more carefully guarded statement of Descartes's approach. (For doubt is an amazing kind of existence which forces, we believe, the same kind of conclusion error does.) Nor did we start from some unique datum of introspection called a self or mind – although we were no doubt introspecting as well as inspecting, without, we hope, special psychological or metaphysical bias. All we have said is that if we try to understand the human being as a physicochemical, or biochemical, being, we face, in the possibility of error, a state of affairs which simply has no counterpart or definition in terms of the properties given to such events by experts.

It simply makes no sense to talk about hydrogen being in an erroneous relation to oxygen, for the whole of hydrogen's being is what it is without *reference* to anything, in the sense designated by 'true' or 'false'. While it may make sense to say that an animal makes a behavioural mistake in the sense that some action it takes

[1] H. H. Price, *Thinking and Experience*, Harvard University Press, Cambridge, 1953, p. 87.

brings harm (or misses its instinctive or unlearned goal), such mistakes are hardly cognitive errors. However, let it be carefully noted, we are not tritely saying merely that a man is a knowing-erring being, but we are urging that the possibility of cognitive erring involves us in saying that the erring being (man or animal) has the quality or kind of being we call mentality or awareness in contradistinction to vitality and physicality.

Having thus sustained the contention that error constrains us to believe in mental being, and that the knower is the kind of non-physical and non-biological being that can entertain truth and error, we must now add at least another attribute to such a mind, namely non-cognitive agency (to speak generally).

C. I. Lewis has told us that knowledge, action, and evaluation are 'essentially connected'. It is clear that knowing and evaluating, for human beings at least, exist to guide action into a future that, because it is not-yet, can only 'exist' for an *anticipating* existent. Lewis brings out the difference in being that knowing involves (though this is not his purpose) when he says:

'A creature which did not enter into the process of reality to alter in some part of the future content of it, could apprehend a world only in the sense of intuitive or esthetic contemplation; and such contemplation would not possess the significance of knowledge but only that of enjoying and suffering.'

And he adds:

'For the cognizing mind, something immediately presented – some item of direct experience – is a sign of something else, not so presented but likely to become realized or capable of being realized in further experience.'[1]

We need not commit ourselves to the ensuing theory of knowledge in detail to underscore the central point that knowing and erring involve an *active* being capable of using some of its experience (or undergoing) to refer beyond itself (the enjoyed experience) to another state of affairs. In our own preferred epistemic terminology we should wish to say: A person can experience *objective reference*, which means that he undergoes certain psychological

[1] C. I. Lewis, *An Analysis of Knowledge and Valuation*, The Open Court Publishing Co., La Salle, Ill., 1945, p. 3.

states whose very being consists in being referred beyond themselves by the person to 'something' in the past, present, or future.

II. THE UNITY AND CONTINUITY OF MENTAL BEING

We have already moved from the possibility of error to the existence of mentality as an active being in commerce with 'the world' in both cognitive and non-cognitive manner. It is the existence of memorial capacity that brings us face to face with a special set of problems in defining the nature of mind. We need not remind ourselves that empirical perception, imagination, and thought are impossible without remembering. Nor shall we expand on the fact that objective reference obtains in memorial activity. For remembering is a present experience in which a present object is referred 'back', correctly or incorrectly. This alone, if our argument has been sound, justifies our conclusion that remembering is mental activity – whatever its connection with the nonmental.

The intriguing problem for a theory of mind stems from the fact that retention is not an experience or activity we directly introspect. It is an inference from recognition and recall. From the direct experience of 'againness' that saturates recognition,[1] we infer a past which somehow is linked with the present. But how shall we conceive the nature of mentality whose capacity for retention is not only the basis of empirical knowledge generally but also of its own past? What must mentality be if memorial activity is to be understood? It may help us if we take two steps and ask first: How shall we conceive the nature of any present moment? Second, how shall we conceive of the relation of moment to moment?

First, it seems introspectively clear that any moment of mental existence is never a simple, non-temporal, mathematical point (allowing this description for purpose of contrast). Any mental 'present' is a durational complex unity. It is 'filled' time, or better it is psychic time which can later be abstractly broken into smaller units of 'before' and 'after'. An *erlebt* moment never is a compound of smaller units for it exists *as a temporal span*, or, to use James's special image, it is a 'saddleback' with its own given complexity.

In introspected experience, then, we find nothing more elementary than this Gestalt or *durée*. Whatever other *measures* of time we improvise for different purposes, the segment that is *given* as the

[1] Cf. Price, *op. cit.*, pp. 44 f.

present is not a series of instants and is psychically indivisible. We must avoid the picture-thinking responsible for such expressions as 'one moment of our experience "flowing", into the next', or 'the present *gradually* emerging from the past'. Such pictures might be true if any present were simply the spatial extension of a point being drawn into a longer and longer line. But we cannot spatialize a moment of mental experience, however our words tend to ensnare us into spatial traps. What we actually *experience* is one complex span or moment from which we try analytically to 'carve out' some aspects as 'past', and some as 'future'.

Let us nevertheless, aware of the snares, attempt a closer cross-section view of a moment of our mentality. What we find is a given indivisible complex Gestalt of activities which, after study, we define-wanting-emoting, willing, and oughting. These activities, as undergone, are phases of the experienced whole that is itself a dynamic span, or durée. But our main concern here is to note that within the original, *experiencing-datum*, or *erlebt* moment, a change is felt that we may describe as a thrust into a future 'emerging' from a present. This is simply our way of saying that the present is full, or, in Whitehead's word, pregnant.

In this very burgeoning present, however, we detect two aspects: the relatively unchanging, active *structure* of activities (abilities and capacities) and the changing *content* or quality of the total experience. The activities mentioned above need not be accepted in detail, as a basis for granting our basic distinction between the structure of ability-capacity and any specific content or object of these.

We may use a diagram further to suggest our meaning, but it will be inadequate because, drawn in space, it suggests an atomicity not intended. With this qualification, let us represent a mental moment (Figure 1).

This is one 'filled', growing-waning, passing, moment. The whole figure is a complex dynamic unity, the small circles being used to indicate the multiplicity of contents qualifying the activities (arrow-diagonals). The diagonals also symbolize the fact that as felt, any moment is 'on the go', 'passing', 'growing'. So far as we know, at this stage of analysis, this moment may be a centre of a larger Being, or the conscious development from a Freudian-like unconscious, or of any other being for that matter. As *experienced* it has temporal span, complexity of activities, and each activity may have *a* qualitative object or content which defines its phase at that moment. The point is that this is the complex, unified Gestalt of

activity-structure and content that constitutes one moment of what
we are to call the unified person, or personal self. The activities
may wax and wane, mature and degenerate, but they are relatively
stable from 'moment' to 'moment', while the qualities or contents

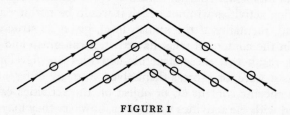

FIGURE I

given in them at any one moment may change (say: pleasure gives
way to pain; 'blue' to 'yellow', one idea to another, one want to
another; but feeling, sensing, conceiving, continue to be qualified
as each allows).

Figure 2 may suggest the manner in which the original unity-
structure grows in response to its environments and yet maintains
its own basic activity-structure. Here, the coiled, expanding, inclusive line is intended to suggest a given structure for mental
being, despite the unevenness of development. (The coiled lines
are not equidistant.) The arrows suggest the active thrust, and the
open end the constant sensitivity to the surrounding world that it
'absorbs' according to its own capacity for intake.

These diagrams of mental present and our discussion thus far
may indicate what we regard as the fundamental nature of mental

FIGURE 2

being, generically speaking. First, the unit of mentality as such is
an original given, the unity being such that, as Leibniz said, it cannot be *created bit by bit* (though it may change gradually). Thus,
for example, the activities of desiring, imagining, conceiving, are
not 'made up', but they are given in their interpenetrating nature

and structure. In the lifetime of a person these may grow into their maturity, and then wane, but the unity of mental being is not a concoction blended in a psychic test tube. For the psychic moment *is* the test tube or matrix; it is what we shall call *the personal self* in one of its moments. And its nature is the original unity of inter-penetrating activities without which it would be nothing at all.

Second, mentality at the human level, given its structure, can change in the content of what its activities can grasp and endure, with the result that these structure-activities can develop them-selves, as it were, or express themselves, in many different ways.[1] But any specific content of, or object of, the activities cannot be identified with the activities themselves, however they may limit or give specific quality to the life of the person. That is, thinking does not consist of, and is not exhausted in, thoughts, nor sensing in the sense-data experienced, nor desiring in the specific or general objects of want.

Yet at any given moment the matrix of structure-activities and quality-content are the matrix of mental being in a complex unity. More activities may develop (as thinking does in the life of the maturing infant and child), and some may be lost (sensing as vision, for example, when one becomes blind), but the life of any mind at any moment will consist (at least) of the way in which the structure-activities have been able to respond, in accordance with their own natures, actual and potential, to the environment. In a word, the activity-structure of mentality remains the same, and changes may occur in the 'capacity' of the activity. But an activity does not become another activity; for example, the activity of thinking does not become the activity of sensing. Yet as long as it exists the activity-structure endures through the various contents which it 'enjoys'. (Much more, of course, should be said at this point about learned dispositions.)

It is this level of complex activity-structure – with its capacities for certain contents and not others – that we call a person, personal mind, or personal self. But crucial to it as mentality is the fact of *unitas multiplex* with enduring capacities and relative flux of con-tent at any moment of its being. So much for the cross-section view of the moment, or the *datum-person*.

More difficult problems face us as we turn to a longitudinal view

---

[1] We shall say that these expressions will constitute the learned *personality* (not *person*), or the unique mode of the person's relatively systematic adjustment to the total environment.

of mentality, that is to successive or serial moments of experience. For our purposes here, once more, we need not commit ourselves to any final ontology of the datum-self. It may be recreated from moment to moment in the light of its past by a cosmic Person, or it may be a centre of an Absolute Being, or it may continually emerge from electrochemical conditions.

Whichever of these, or any other, views may be correct, the data which theorizing must confront is that, as memory indicates, there are *successive* moments, befores and afters, in our conscious experience (to which we are limiting ourselves at the moment). Did the successive moments of consciousness and self-consciousness always follow hard upon each other, as happened during the writing of this last page, the problem of accounting for successive moments that are not identical with each other, would be difficult enough. But the fact is that consciousness may be 'lost' for a shorter or longer interval and then 'return'.

This fact makes the question: 'What makes continuity possible?' all the more important for a theory of mind which takes the fact of *memorial continuity* seriously. Whatever my ontological nature is when consciousness and self-consciousness 'return' after an interval of deep, 'undisturbed' sleep, I immediately recognize my being as memorially continuant with myself as before the intermission. Where 'I' have been I do not know, but that 'I' am in some sense continuing my prior existence is attested to by the fact of memorial continuity. I cannot deny memorial continuity without presupposing some! For to justify denial of my memorial continuity I would have to depend upon my memories of the past to support the denial!

Once more, then, the existence of memory is one of those ineluctable facts of mental being. Whether there be intermittent consciousness or conscious states without interval, there is no denying that personal experience links its presents with its pasts and, in imagination and thought, anticipates its futures. Thus, if anything is central to all personal experience, it is *both* the unity of any 'present' mentality, and also the continuity, cognitively realized, between presents and pasts in remembering. What the ultimate metaphysics of memory is we can decide only after we consider how mentality is related to other existents. Our problem here and now, however, is to consider what we may reasonably say about the nature of personal mind in view of the unity and continuity we find in mentality.

III. THE SUBSTANTIVE SELF VERSUS
THE TEMPORAL SELF

Space will limit us to the analysis of two theories about the self which have been advanced to explain the unity and continuity of the self. The significant fact for any theory to explain is that, as B. P. Bowne put it, an experience of succession is not a succession of experiences! That is, we cannot say that events are in serial order unless something endures from the beginning to the end of the series. The problem is, then: What is it that abides through the succession of unitary moments we have called the person?

The first view we shall consider has a history extending in Western thought back to Plato at least, but the best recent statement is in C. A. Campbell's *On Selfhood and Godhood*.[1] We approach the second view through an analysis of basic contentions in Campbell's theory of selfhood.

Professor Campbell first argues that the activity of knowing 'implies a *subject* that is active'. He goes on to urge: '*that which is* active in activity cannot possibly be the activity itself'.[2] We do not contest the first thesis for we, too, have been arguing that memorial and other cognizing activities are intelligible only as we distinguish, in Campbell's words, 'a cognitive subject distinguishable from, though not of course separable from, particular cognitions'.[3] But there are reasons for doubting the second statement, the grounds for which we must now study cautiously.

If X is the psychical operation of knowing Y, it cannot be that the *activity of apprehending is Y*; and it cannot be that the activity of apprehending is '*that which apprehends*'. 'What is "known" cannot be known *to* the operation of knowing, is not itself *identical with* the knowing.'[4]

Now we should agree that the psychical performance does not exhaust the subject, and that the psychical performance (X) is not the object known (Y). We may definitely affirm (S) subject, (K) psychic activity of cognizing, and (Y) object known. Thus far, with F. R. Tennant[5] and with A. Bowman[6] giving him strong support, Campbell is on firm ground. Our own analysis would force us to agree that cognition of *any* kind – not merely in

[1] New York: Macmillan, 1957.
[2] C. A. Campbell, *On Selfhood and Godhood*, p. 70.   [3] *Ibid.*, p. 70.
[4] *Ibid.*, p. 71.   [5] *Philosophical Theology*, Volume I.
[6] *A Sacramental Universe*, p. 196.

remembering – implies a subject conscious of its own identity in its different apprehensions.[1]

Furthermore, Campbell also urges that, unless the abiding subject is conscious of its own identity through a sequence, there would be no basis for asserting that a sequence is a sequence in 'my' experience. The prerequisite for remembering, and for cognitive awareness generally is not simply an identical subject, but an identical subject aware of that identity. Once more, so far so good.

But it is the next step, the further interpretation of this unity and identity, that gives pause. 'We are led by the argument, apparently, to posit a self which is something "over and above" its particular experiences; something that *has* rather than *is*, its experiences, since its experiences are all different, while *it* somehow remains the same.'[2] Campbell is aware of the avalanche of objections which tumble down against such a substantival view of an 'I' over and above its experience, an 'I' with which we have no acquaintance but only inferential knowledge.[3] Yet, however stiff the resistance to an 'I' that is the same despite its manifestation through differences, Campbell finds alternative views so much more difficult that he retains his own substantival view.

Let us, as Campbell suggests, try to conceive of a self-identifying and self-conscious 'I' as any kind of *relationship between* experiences. What happens? The central fact about the subject-mind, its holding a sequence together as *its* sequence, vanishes among the 'relations'.[4] In the last analysis, Campbell urges, 'self-consciousness . . . is a *fact*, a datum from which we have to start.'

This means not that the substantival self is a Kantian noumenal self about which we can know nothing. For, and this is crucial, the subject self apprehended in self-consciousness is always 'a characterized self'; it is a self characterized by, and 'manifesting *itself* in', operations of thinking, desiring, and feeling. Campbell's view, accordingly, is that though the self is not *reducible to its* experiences, it does, nevertheless, manifest 'its real character (in whole or in part) *in and* through these experiences'.[5]

In order that our succeeding discussion be pointed, let us intervene and state where we believe the issue now is. In so far as Campbell is saying that the self is never a peculiar set of relationships, that it cannot be put together from atomic parts, that it must be conceived as a self-identifying self-consciousness in order

[1] See Campbell, *op. cit.*, p. 75. [2] *Ibid.*, p. 77. [3] Cf. *ibid.*, p. 77.
[4] *Ibid.*, pp. 78–80. [5] *Ibid.*, p. 82.

to make cognition intelligible, we are in hearty agreement. In so far as he urges that the self is not reducible to its experiences, we should concur, for we have insisted on distinguishing the more persistent activity-structures from the flux of content.

But Campbell is going further and is holding to a self which, though irreducible to experiences, is nevertheless manifesting itself, in whole or in part, in and through its experiences. But ambiguity, at least, and real difficulty occur when we try to see what it can mean to distinguish the self *in any way* from its activities. Why must we use the language of 'manifesting itself through' such activities and experiences? Why must we also say: 'The self of which we are conscious in self-consciousness *is* a subject *which in some sense has, rather than is, its different experiences, and is identical* with itself throughout them?'[1]

To be sure, Campbell does not articulate the difference between 'experiences' as activities in our sense, and as 'content' (specific objects of awareness and desire), and we assume it would not make any difference to his essential point, namely, that whether we speak of activities or experiences, the self, though characterized by them, is always more than they and *has* them. Our thesis is to be that the self *is* a continuous unity of its activities which are indeed not reducible to the experienced qualities. And it will be our special burden to give an account of the way in which such a self-identifying agent-knower can be identical from moment to moment and day to day.

Our central difficulty with Campbell's viewpoint may simply involve a lack of insight on our part. But if Campbell holds that the self is not identical with its activities, and if he urges that it is *the same* while all of its experiences change, then no matter how much he says it manifests *itself* through its changing experiences, how can we know that the sameness is manifested? The sameness of the subject must remain other than the changing activities and experiences in which it is supposed to *manifest its* nature in part or whole. To such a charge of self-contradiction and unintelligibility Campbell responds in a way which seems to us adequate in one respect, but inadequate in another, so we must look at it carefully.

The charge of self-contradiction, says Campbell, rests on the assumption that sameness totally excludes difference. Sameness as including difference does indeed involve contradiction on the level of abstract definition, for it is impossible to understand *how* same-

[1] See Campbell, *op. cit.*, pp. 82, 83 (italics mine).

ness can include difference. If we stay at this logical level, it does indeed become unintelligible to say that any entity A includes non-A. But at this level, 'intelligible' means 'capable of being understood' in terms of 'how' the one subject remains itself amid the plurality of changing experiences. And Campbell correctly holds that how things are what they are must be accepted rather than dictated by logical demands. Thinking does not make events or the states of affairs it is trying to understand, and *if* this kind of sameness *is* given, thinking misses its function when it denies a given because it cannot tell *how* it appears. Again, so far so good.

Campbell is safe in distinguishing intelligibility in this how-sense, from 'meaningfulness' in the sense of being able to point in experience to what the non-intelligible event is. We should want to agree that when in self-consciousness we are aware 'that I who now hear the clock strike a second time am the same being who a moment ago heard the clock strike, even though I must have become different in the interval',[1] then we are given a datum in terms of which the claim that the self's sameness includes difference is meaningful (though not intelligible by strictly logical norms).

But while the self's sameness in difference may be given and be meaningful, the *theory* of the self Campbell gives, as a self not reducible to the total of activity and experiences cannot escape either the requirements of logic or, as it seems to us, a more adequate 'meaningfulness' in terms of actual experience! Sameness, at least as required by memorial continuity, cannot be denied despite inability to explain how, but *a particular theory advanced to explain sameness in plurality* had at least better be questioned if it proposes relationships which defy either the demands of logical consistency or of experience. Indeed, it seems to us that the view that the self *has* rather than *is* its activities and experiences itself rests on logical analysis, and not on experience itself. Only in terms of logic *may* one say that *that which is* active in activity cannot possibly be the activity itself, or that the sameness must to some extent not be the different activities.

It may rather be, as we hope our earlier analysis of a moment of experience showed, that what constitutes a datum-person is the unified activity complex rather than a subject *of* activities and experiences, as Campbell suggests. In a word, even to suggest that the sameness of the subject involves a 'that which' that *is* not active

[1] *Ibid.*, p. 83.

but *has* activities is to give a description which might fit abstract logical considerations better than it fits the experienced datum at any moment. If Campbell's *logic* forces him to say that the same self is manifested in its activities (in whole or part), if his logic forces him to say that this self cannot be its activities – any one of them or the whole of them in an original unity – then we may well ask to what *in experience* this theory points.

We agree that any part of an activity-structure cannot be whole activity, but we deny that we have any experienced ground for supposing that there must be something other than activity-unity as experienced to explain the unity. It is the merit of the self-psychology of E. S. Brightman[1] that, in the interest of a radical empiricism, he rejects any shade of a homunculus subject, and simply says that the self is the unity of activities we find in conscious activity and its contents. We shall now put this personalistic self-psychology positively, and then hope to remove some doubts by suggesting an account of the way in which such a self could maintain its identity through differences in successive moments.

IV. THE PERSON AND CONTINUITY THROUGH IMMEDIATE SUCCESSION

Whatever else Being refers to, it includes self-conscious being. But wherever there is self-conscious being the following conscious activities are distinguishable: sensing, feeling, desiring, remembering, thinking, willing, oughting. Some may want to expand, some limit further, this list of activities which in a Gestalt of sameness-difference constitute the irreducible, original, unlearned, unity-in-multiplicity designated the person-datum. At any moment some of these activities are more regnant than others (and in infancy all are not present). The sameness is never other than, or beyond, what these activities are, though it is not reducible to any one of them. Rather do these activities define the nature of mentality at the personal level. The sameness is not the sameness of a logical or mathematical equality, but the very sameness that each of us finds in successive moments of *his* experience. To say '*that which is* active in activity cannot be the *activity itself*' would mean in this view only that the activity of the self is not exhausted in any one of its activities (like thinking). The 'subject' is the unity-sameness which

[1] See Edgar S. Brightman, *Person and Reality*, ed. Peter A. Bertocci, *et al.* New York: Ronald Press, 1958.

is experienced (without 'more-than') in, and only in, these activities at the conscious level.

At any one saddlebacked cross-section, or in any one longitudinal moment, as described above, there is also the particular kind degree of acquired personality-unity which the person-activities have developed to date as a result of maturation and interchange with the environment. We might thus distinguish the *constitutive or ontic person-activities* from the acquired *psychological personality* with its different degrees of integration; but we must remind ourselves that neither ever exists without the other. In the remainder of this paper we shall be concerned not with the important problem of the continuity of personality but with the central problem of continuity of the ontic person.

Thus, we must now ask: Granted that in any one moment unity in difference is given, how can we account for the fact that successive moments in personal history are experienced *as a succession*? Here, like Campbell, we must simply accept fact of unity in any specious present or moment for what it is. But we need some theory to explain the continuity-in-change we remember from moment to moment. The startling fact is not that sameness endures in the momentary differences, but that sameness in difference is required for any succession to be succession in our experience, be it immediate succession or succession after intervals. We must try, therefore, to suggest a conception of the person which may allow first for successive continuity without intermittence and then for continuity despite intervening time-gaps.

The given activity-structure of the person is in interaction, from conception on, with agencies, events, beings, not identical with himself. We are not asking what conditions or causes the person ontologically, but, given his existence at any one moment and given his memorial nature, how may we conceive the process which enables the initial person to maintain continuity and 'self-identity'. We repeat that the fact of activity-identity is undeniable in the sense that any attempt to deny it assumes the very memorial identity denied. Yet, just as clearly, one moment of person-datum is not identical with the next.

How then shall we conceive the essential nature of the continuity-giving process? Our first suggestion is that the person-datum 'maintains' himself as a persistent activity-pattern from moment to moment by being selective in accordance with what his potential up to that point allows in relation to the potential of the environment.

Concretely, I am what I am now because as I enter into each not-yet and constitute it a now, my given activity-nature has been able to accept those elements in my interplay with the not-self which were congruent with my continuance. My activity-identity was evidently 'impermeable' to others. My 'past' is simply the story of what I have been or of what I have succeeded in facing; it exists for me because it was once *me in a certain moment of being which I have succeeded in transcending without losing my nature as affected in that past.*

However, I must *not* make the mistake of picture-thinking my past, and think of myself in memory reaching back to ten minutes ago. For, after all, ten minutes ago is no more; and myself of yesterday and thirty seconds ago are no more. *I am, now*, pregnant with *my* past, and being affected by what is happening to me as my not-yet future is being born. *My* future at this moment is non-existent, and 'exists' only as that which I shall have been able to 'absorb', 'digest', or 'endure' in such a way that I do not lose my activity-identity. In other words, to go back to an earlier diagram (Figure 2), let us assume that self-being began as the original activities in phase (*a*) below, and continued in successive moments to become (*ab*), and (*abc*) (Figure 3).

Figure 3 must not be taken to mean that (*a*) remains as-is in (*ab*) and (*ab*) remains as-is in (*abc*). Rather, my *now* (*abc*) is all I am, but it is what I am now because of my ultimate constitution and what I have become, selectively, in accordance with the nature of (*a*) and (*ab*). In other words, the interval between states (*a*) and

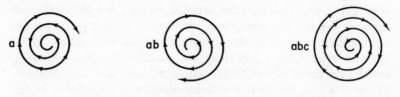

FIGURE 3

(*abc*) is not a gap. Rather is it the case that every (*ab*) and (*abc*) is what (*a*) was capable of becoming in a given environment, and then actually became because of selective interplay with the environment.

Again: 'I' do not 'pass' into a future any more than I 'pass' out of the past. My being is always a 'now' which is said to be older than a 'then', or earlier than a 'later', only because of differentiations which we call memories and anticipations. 'I' do not move through pre-existent time as a ball might roll in space. I *am* my time and the changes which take place 'in' me are discriminated as past, present, and future by virtue of my capacity for remembering and organizing my experience, always in *a* present, as involving a past and anticipating a future.

Thus, while all Being is mysterious or unintelligible from the point of view of our ultimate 'know-how', there is no real problem about explaining the way in which the same of one moment can be identified at a later stage as 'my' self. For I am now able to identify myself with my past because I never moved away from my self, but selected and 'absorbed' the world according to my own subjective aim, to use Whitehead's phrase. Some encounters with the non-self could destroy me, but the fact that I now exist indicates that I have been able to keep myself alive in, and through, and, despite some threatening encounters. There is no passage of 'time', but only the selective experience of a person who maintains the given unity of activity in the course of interchange with the world.

The person, then, is a successive mental unity of activities that in turn persists beyond any particular content created by his interaction with the environment. A unity in any given moment, he is a unity for which there can be succession because (whatever the how), he is able to 'accept' and 'reject' the world which beats in upon him, and he is able to do this in accordance with his own original being and his original potential – which actually is discovered as each experience and activity are enjoyed.

But, we remind ourselves, this view of continuity may do well for continuity which is not interrupted by sleep and 'sheer' unconsciousness. Does this account of continuity enable us to understand the self-identification that exists despite such intervals in conscious experience as sleep and periods of unconsciousness? *Must our theory of mind not introduce a continuant which persists through the intervals?* This might seem all the more likely in view of the fact that some sort of 'work' seems to go on during what we call sleeptime. We refer not so much to the periods of dreaming, in which there is consciousness if not self-consciousness, but to such facts, for example, as our waking up with a solution to the problem that could not be solved the night before. And the very fact that we usually awaken refreshed indicates that change has taken place during the intervals.

V. THE PERSON AND CONTINUITY THROUGH INTERMITTENT SUCCESSION

The problem of identity through intermittency calls for a paper in itself. We are not completely satisfied with the account to be suggested. One must be careful not to assume a metaphysics of continuity at this point; he must require that his theory account for the data. Several general observations may be made in a preliminary way.

The problem of identity through intermittency – when not superficially solved – is no greater obstacle for a temporalistic view of mind than others. In any case what seems clear is that *mind as consciousness*, which did not create itself originally, does have lapses. That is, every *conscious* activity by which we characterize mind is simply non-existent during the lapse. Consciousness continues as these activities reoccur, and to say that mind (as *conscious* mentality of some sort) continues between intervals during which these activities do not occur is to contradict oneself. Once more, to say that I, *defined as a complex of conscious activities*, 'continue' when I am no longer exercising these activities, is to assert a contradiction. Furthermore, a mind that is unconscious – *meaning non-conscious or non-mental* – is a mind that is not a mind in any experienced sense. Reasoned, empirical theory cannot bridge the gap between intervals of conscious experience by asserting that a *non-conscious or non-mental* mind exists during the intervals.

Such considerations will press heavily against many explanations of the unconscious interval, and perhaps even against the view to be suggested below. But no hypothesis should blur the fact that conscious activity (and self-consciousness) does, so far as each of us knows by direct experience, in fact vanish and return (just as the light of an electric bulb vanishes and returns). Does it actually help, for example, to say that a *non-conscious entity* (like the physiological organism), or even an infinite Mind, remain as the basis of continuity between intervals – or does this simply push the problem a step further? The fact *still* remains that during these intervals, no matter how long, there was a lapse in *my* experience as conscious being. A biological continuity at the biological level and not at the level of person-mind. A parallel line of reasoning would hold if we tried to allow the continuity of God's being to bridge the gap, for his continuity is his, not mine. Better remain with no theory than with one which neglects the very facts to be explained.

Let it, however, be clearly understood that we are not denying interaction or some other relation – between the biological realm, or the divine, and our minds. But we cannot think that to say that *they continue* across the gap in 'my' consciousness explains 'my' self-identity through intervals. Whatever other realities may be, and however they are related to my mentality, their existence during my non-existence cannot in any way substitute as much for my being able to identify myself despite intervals.

It would seem, then, that we must look into the nature of the individual person himself for some explanation of the fact that there is self-identification possible despite intervening gaps. The tentative suggestion we now propose – not half-heartedly yet not sure that it would satisfy all the data – requires that we identify a person not only with conscious–self-conscious activity but also with an activity present wherever conscious and self-consciousness exist, namely, *telic* or *purposive* activity. So far as we can see, nothing in what we have said about the unity of mentality or the temporalistic person would be gainsaid. For we are suggesting that mentality at the human level not be *identified only* with conscious–self-conscious phases, but with telic phases of the kind found also at the conscious–self-conscious level. The focus of definition moves, in short, from essentially cognitive activities to essentially conative activities of feeling-emoting-desiring (to speak minimally).

Let us expand our meaning briefly. Cognition itself, be it erroneous or correct, involves telic or purposive processes. Remembering, and forgetting, anticipating, solving problems – or learning and thinking generally – take the course they do because, in good part at least, they are affected by desire or interest. To be a mind is to be a kind of being *in want*, active in a present, whose very nature it is to reach for something it has not yet, and for a state of being it is not yet. In this sense, *conor, ergo sum* tells a more complete story of the human being than *cogito, ergo sum*.[1]

We suggest that the telic strivings involved in our feeling-emotive life – in such states as fear, anger, elation, respect, tenderness, wonder, lust – constitute the womb in which memorial and

---

[1] Incidentally, Descartes, while a rationalist in criterion of truth, did not define *cogito* in intellectualistic terms. Note the sadly neglected passage: 'But what then am I? a thing which thinks. What is a thing which thinks? It is a thing which doubts, understands (conceives), affirms, denies, wills, refuses, which also imagines and feels' (Descartes, *Meditations on First Philosophy*, Meditation II). Thus, the place of the affective-emotional and volitional life in the matrix of *cogito* is undeniable even in Descartes.

intellective activities arise. Such non-intellective urges and stirrings, let alone the sheer thrust of volition, are the power-reservoir
or the dynamo of person. Much in day-dreams and night dreams,
much in the varied manifestations of rationalizing as opposed to
reasoning, and much of what we know about the formation of
prejudice, let alone neurotic maladjustments and psychotic
diseases, testify to the power that feeling-emotive tendencies and
needs have over cognitive functions. Yet, as we have already
suggested, there is no way of extirpating this affective-conative life
from the rest of 'normal' mental functioning. The psychological
analysis of attention, remembering-learning, imagining, perceiving,
and thinking will quickly come upon the selective work of feeling,
emotion, and desire in the processes of cognition. There is a constant
interplay of purposive or telic processes and cognitive activities.
Indeed, it would be better to say that in the unified complexity of
mental life these conative-cognitive processes may be distinguished.

But what we wish now to stress is that telic-conative processes
are broader, though still mental, than the cognitive functions and
persist in them. We do not appeal to any theory, Freudian or any
other, of the unconscious life to substantiate this claim. Indeed, it
is the relationships between conative and cognitive factors in our
conscious life which must, in the last analysis, provide the model-
analogy between conscious and unconscious life generally. It is in
the normal life of awareness that we feel the contrast between the
changing waves of cognition which focus and 'light up' the sea of
conation. There is always that relatively clear focus of awareness
emerging out of the relatively unclear, felt background of seething.

It may help us to distinguish this broader conative matrix if we
can designate three stages or phases of mentality. First, *self-
conscious awareness*, in which one is aware of oneself as the focus of
cognition. Here one is able to contrast self and not-self. The
regnancy of this phase is intermittent. As I write, my awareness is
not focused on myself but on what I am saying; and this is true, we
might say, for most of our workaday awareness.

This first 'self-conscious' phase emerges out of the second stage
of awareness in which I am so absorbed in my task that self-
consciousness all but disappears. This stage of which most of our
awareness consists we have called *consciousness*. Self-consciousness,
as we have said, lights it up, and brings it into a special focus.

The third dimension of mentality we are now postulating involves telic processes such as are not open to but continuous with

their nature as experienced in *consciousness and self-consciousness*. Such telic processes are neither self-conscious nor conscious, in the senses used above, but they are a complex unity of same-difference. They are able to maintain themselves during the intervals when consciousness in the above forms are not experienced. They are never non-existent, nor 'asleep', but they are altered from the individual's birth to death by the processes which they do undergo when they are in the phases of consciousness and unconsciousness.

As we have hinted, a specific account of what these telic processes are would have to be heavily weighted by what is found in consciousness. But in general we may say that, in this phase of mentality, a unity of telic activities is postulated that does not have the 'advantage' of having the directive 'guidance' and differences which they would enjoy in consciousness and self-consciousness. In ordinary conscious experience both the life of desire and the environment are in relatively directed interaction with each other. In this *sub*conscious, not non-conscious or non-mental, state, the nature of conative tendencies as affected through conscious and self-conscious experiences maintain themselves without conscious 'guidance' or 'interference'.

We are suggesting, in short, that mental life in human beings is polar, that it does not lend itself to clear-cut dichotomy between cognition and conation (or other activities), although we postulate a phase in which telic processes go on without consciousness, without losing their mentality. For these telic processes in a conscious phase are present also, we should say, in conscious mentality.

To comment further: There is the phase of my mental life in which feeling-conation seem to be all there is, and another phase in which awareness of the world dominates, with self-consciousness in almost complete abeyance, but to some extent present. As long as we do not make the mistake of *simply adding cognitive* (and volitional, and moral, and aesthetic abilities) to the telic life of conation, or think of the latter as completely non-directed, and waiting for guidance from without, we shall not make serious mistakes.

It will now be clear that we are defining *the essence of mentality at the human level as the range of telic tendency, from unified minimal purposive striving* (in which neither 'self'-focus nor 'world'-focus is clear) *to self-conscious, purposeful organization of telic tendency*. The word *unconscious* (or *subconscious*) in this view would mean not non-conscious, but that pole of mentality in which there is no articulation of self-experience but only individuality of feeling-emoting capable of maintaining itself as it is modified through interchange. The person, therefore, during the deep-sleep (intermittent) period does little more than persist, without disturbance by memory or cognitive activity. But he springs into the various degrees of consciousness required for differential activities, be they dreams or somnambulism, or other phenomena. When the person is 'awake', his feeling-conative life takes on directions and organization which would be impossible without the capacity to remember and think. But there is never an interval in mentality (as purposive striving of a sort to be better defined), but only in consciousness.

There is much more that needs to be done to show that this theory can account for the various types of activity or 'work' which seems to go on through unconscious intervals. In general, we believe that this theory would account for much, since it can appeal to many stages of alteration within the development of individuality. In closing, we may, for example, indicate how it can be related to the Freudian view of the unconscious.

If the unconscious, in the Freudian sense, refers to that phase of conative experience which the patient cannot himself recall and has difficulty in controlling, no serious problem confronts our theory. This 'unconscious' in our theory would be that area of an individual's experience which, owing to conditions in his development, he cannot now recall and control without aid – the psychoanalyst becoming the person who helps him to manipulate his conscious content in a way that will allow such recall and release to take place. But to say that the 'laws' of the unconscious are completely different (as Freud sometimes seems to say) from those discoverable in conscious life seems simply to presuppose a rather superficial and conventionalized analysis of conscious experience.

Once we realize that criticism of the inner and outer world begins with the development of memorial and cognitive functions, that the life of feeling-desire is thus expanded and restricted, there seems to be no basic fact about dream life and dream work, about neurosis or psychosis, that is *in principle* impossible to explain. No particular problem of psychosomatic medicine is solved, obviously, by a general theory of mind.

VI. SUMMARY

The existence of awareness as a unique and irreducible kind of being is rendered highly probable by the fact of error. Cognitive error, involving as it does a kind of existent which has been referred to what does not exist as claimed, is incomprehensible in terms of physics, chemistry, or physiology. Awareness is the kind of being which can exist, can experience and refer ideas (images, symbols, and so on) to a state of affairs beyond themselves which may or may not exist as claimed.

Memorial activity, at the basis of all empirical knowledge, pre-supposes ultimately a complex unified agent which, at the level where logical thought, obligation, and value-choice is possible, we call a person or personal self. This original unity is a *Gestalt* of interpenetrating activities which endure in their basic structure despite changes in content or expression. This agent-unity of activities, either in a given moment or in successive moments, is *durée*.

The theory of a substantive unity of activity beyond, yet mani-fested within, the activities and their contents, though it preserves unity, creates a serious problem which can be avoided if we think of the person as able to endure selectivity in and through its inter-changes with his environments. We have sought to explain con-tinuity despite intermittent consciousness by identifying the person not only with conscious and self-conscious phases of men-tality but also with continuant affective-conative activity ranging from the unconscious to the conscious and self-conscious.

Speaking generally, therefore, telic activity at the feeling-conative level, analogous to the quality of feeling-conation found at the conscious level of activity, may be conceived as maintaining its unity, continuity, and individuality despite discontinuity of consciousness. Throughout all levels of personhood there is original unity in telic agency which is able to maintain itself within the limits of its own varied nature and take on new quality and scope as conscious and self-conscious activities illuminate it in relation to its nurturant and challenging environment.

As a person responds selectively in his interplay with the environment, he can develop personality (or personalities, or relatively systematic modes of adjustment) in order to meet the requirements of his own telic-activity-unity and of the environ-ment. But every varied channel of becoming in which a personal self is involved is possible because of the specific pattern of activity-identity that can maintain itself *in* maturing, learning, and action.

CHAPTER III

FOUNDATIONS OF PERSONALISTIC
PSYCHOLOGY

On the surface, the fact that the ego has 'returned', broadly speaking, to psychology of personality may seem a sign of the durability of a philosophical or theological soul. The mind (the soul, psyche, self, or ego) was unacceptable to an objective psychology because it certainly was not open to public scrutiny and in no sense yielded to experimental probing. But such a soul had already been sent into oblivion by philosophers who, failing to find some circumscribed or encapsulated entity, tried to substitute for it some pattern of psychical elements. Failing in this, they turned to behavioural dispositions which, in the main, could be acquired and observed in a society, and which could be related to, if not identified with, brain processes.

It is especially interesting to note that when Freud brought the ego back he made it a cognitive centre of mental processes which could be located neither in the brain-cells nor among the nerves and their synapses, nor in glandular secretion. If the ego could not be a spark of the divine, it could be a spark that would light up reality enough to keep the unconscious from unnecessary conflict. But the unconscious needed to know not only what 'reality' is, it also needed to find means for avoiding unnecessary conflict and for fulfilling its basic urge for pleasure. Both ego and super-ego, elected to perform such functions, could, and often did, betray the unconscious demand for pleasure.

Thus the ego and the super-ego, a philosopher might reflect, brought back the functions that Plato assigned to the soul, and to its eros, in particular – the search for truth and for the good. But one might well ask: How can the unconscious, consciousness, and conscience be one, or be continuous in a way that provides both the stability and novelty evident in growth of personality?

To generalize: The ego in contemporary and recent psychology symbolizes the need in psychology of personality to clarify the empirical fact that a personality worthy of the name is an organization that is relatively stable and unified. But each personality is unified in a way that provides its present and ongoing dynamic, that is, a focus without which the development and stability of a personality is unintelligible. But any personality with its ego could have been different in its structure had the individual been brought up in a different home and social environment.

Granted, then, that personality is the product of learning. But if the personality, Saul, could become Paul, or if the dissociated Dr Jekyll and Mr Hyde could be healed, we clearly need to ask: Is there not some continuing source of unity and continuity that acquires and is involved in developing these personalities and their egos, and in reorganizing them?

To ask this question is to revive old fears that a homunculus is being postulated that is not publicly observable. So be it – although there are homunculi and homunculi! The question remains for the psychology of personality as it remained for the psychology of the soul: How shall we conceive permanence and change of the sort we find in the ego and the personality it unifies? Entities must not be multiplied unnecessarily, but it is not yet obvious that we can amputate the person from its personality and ego and still understand what it means to talk about ego-identification and ego-crises. In short, the ego and personality take the psychologist back to issues which the philosopher too must re-view without being subservient to his views of the soul or to present fashions and trends in psychology.

It hardly needs to be added that it is impossible today to use the term 'personality', 'ego', and 'self' unambiguously. Nevertheless, in psychology each of these is a name for 'a formation' learned in a given environmental situation. But what does the learning and the uniting that becomes a formation?

Finally, considerations emerging from this discussion lead me to use the word 'person', not 'personality', for God, because 'personality' does clearly refer to what is acquired. Crisply, the basic problem of transcendence and immanence of the person in the personality remains to haunt us in the realm of psychology as the problem of God's relation to the historical process already has in the realm of philosophical theology.

'All books on the psychology of personality are at the same time books on the philosophy of the person.' (G. W. Allport, 1962, p. xi.)

Personalistic thought is unified in metaphysics, in theology, in ethics, and in psychology by one methodological principle, and by one conviction. The principle is: The human being as he experiences himself, as *erlebt*, provides data that all theorizing about him and the world must not disregard or explain away. The conviction is: the human being is a unique unity, to be described, to be interpreted, but not to be dissolved into some other kind of being. This unity cannot be proved if by proof one means that this contention is based on some more fundamental premise. There is no more fundamental fact than the unity of being that constitutes the reasoner himself.

In the attempt to expound and defend this central theme, personalistic philosophers have developed theories of mind, mind-body, and personality that would be relevant to the different facets of human experience: cognition (in all of its ranges), feeling, conation, willing, and moral, aesthetic and religious sensitivity. Thus the psychological *trend* that we are calling 'personalistic' has always been a part of personalistic philosophy.

Recent personalistic psychology has been searching for a *modus vivendi* that will keep it alive both to more speculative philosophical concerns and to scientific data relevant to a balanced understanding of the dimensions of personality. In what follows we shall outline and consider some of the philosophical and psychological developments that have led to and influenced the personalistic perspective in the study of personality.

I

Plato argued in the *Phaedo* and elsewhere that the human soul could never be understood as an additive collection of parts. It is self-moving, irreducible to physiological events, and can fulfil itself only by realizing a structure of values that gives it purpose. A broad stream of successors – Aristotle, Augustine, Aquinas, Descartes, Locke, Berkeley, Leibniz, Kant, Fichte, Lotse, C. Renouvier, R. Eucken, J. McTaggart, G. Howison, J. Ward, F. R. Tennant, W. Temple, B. P. Bowne, W. James, M. W. Calkins, W. McDougall, W. Stern, A. C. Knudson, D. C. Macintosh, R. Niebuhr, J. Maritain, E. Gilson, A. C. Garnett, H. Bergson, P. Weiss, C. Hartshorne, J. Wild, C. A. Campbell, J. Macmurray, A. Castell – whatever their differences, join in battle on three fronts.

First, they defend the individuality, relative autonomy, and unity of the finite mind against absorption into one Absolute by either rational or mystical means. These thinkers are theists, near-theists, and pluralists.

Second, they defend the intrinsic unity, individuality, and continuity of self-existence against atomization by associationist psychology and sensationistic empiricism, without neglecting the influence of learning upon individual development.

Third, they resist the reduction of mental to spatial or material being. Self-consciousness, logical or rational cognition, and moral, aesthetic, or religious sensitivity, cannot, they held, be explained without residue in spatial terms.

In a word, personalists have been so impressed by the active, creative, responsiveness and moral autonomy of the human being that they cannot envision him as a 'pulse-beat of the Absolute', or a concatenation of ideas, feeling, impressions, or brain-events, or as a 'mirror of culture'.

There are methodological issues involved in this personalistic approach. The 'variety of *human* experience', to adapt James's phrase, has kept personalists problem-centred and not method-centred; at every turn they have resisted *methodological imperialism* either in philosophy or psychology. The touchstones of persona-listic investigation – the unity in variety, the continuity despite discontinuity, the uniqueness despite similarity, the purposiveness in the orderly and predictable, the distinctive rational-moral-aesthetic-religious dimensions in the matrix of the alogical, non-moral, brute factors in man – defy any one approach to human nature.

Furthermore, the personalist keeps reminding himself that every perspective a person takes *is taken by a person*, that, in other words, a philosophical and psychological theory must make the activities of the investigator intelligible. The very possibility of a scientific experiment depends on a knower who can survive the time-consuming process, who, having set the experiment up for a purpose, remembers the beginning, middle, and ending of the experiment (Brightman, 1958). Indeed, anything about an experiment is logically dubitable and deniable except the existence of a time-binding observer and his purpose.

Nor can this methodological concern, that theoretical conclusions about human nature be consistent with the presupposition of experiment and theorizing, be left here. Any theory about human beings must not only pay attention to conscious experience and its givens; it must be confirmable by, or consistent with, what is present in consciousness. Theories about the body, or about the unconscious, about any environment, physical, social, or divine, are unacceptable if they distort, slight, or contradict what is phenomenally given in consciousness. The intellectual journey from consciousness starts with data in consciousness, and however far it travels from this home-base, it must return to it and be examined for its capacity to illuminate conscious experience.

For example, there is no denying that 'red' is a datum in consciousness. The explanations of this experience by reference to processes in the physical world, cones in the eye, occipital processes (and so on) are all to the good. But it would be another thing to hold that the 'red' as experienced is 'in' the occipital lobe. The personalist extends the warning against the stimulus-error to the caution: All processes and entities resulting from theorizing – philosophical, scientific, theological – shall not be substituted for the conscious data themselves.

Finally, personalists may disagree with each other about the interpretation of what is immediately given in consciousness. But they agree in principle that *no one type, or aspect of, 'given' conscious experience be allowed to dictate arbitrarily the nature of another*, that the aesthetic experience, for example, be not allowed arbitrarily to determine the nature of interpretation of religious or moral experience. Radical empiricism, synoptic examination as well as analysis – this is the methodology that alone can provide hypotheses which, however far they range, will not lose their anchorage in what is phenomenally given.

We turn now from general methodology to analysis of a basic cleavage among personalists that will serve to throw light on problems being encountered by contemporary psychologies of the 'self'. There is no cleavage about the issue. A person changes. However paradoxical, to say that change takes place, rather than substitution, is to say that change is impossible without permanence. To say that change can be known is to assert at least that a knower exists at the beginning of succession in change and at the end, and knows them as beginning and end. A succession of experiences is not an experience of succession (Bowne, 1910). There can be no series known as a series if the knower is only one member in the series.

To use C. A. Campbell's illustration: When Big Ben strikes the tenth stroke it can be known as tenth only by a knower who exists from stroke one to stroke ten. The kind of unity and continuity that personal experience exhibits simply cannot be an artifact; and it is unintelligible as a collection, or as a series, without that which makes 'collection' and 'series' possible. So urge both philosophical and psychological personalists.

II

But how is the unity to be conceived? Is there a manifest entity that persists through change, binding changes together but itself unchanging? Yes, say the soul-psychologists, or substantialists. What we may call the Platonic wing of personalism in this respect – Plato, Augustine, Descartes, Locke, Leibniz, Kant, Bowne – agree in defining this unchanging unity as non-physiological, and non-spatial. The Aristotelian-Thomistic wing, however, has sought to overcome the chasm between mind and body thus created by Platonic soul-psychologists by conceiving of the soul as the principle or form of life that is not reducible to body. Magda Arnold (1954), for example, has recently sponsored such an Aristotelian-Thomistic view in her argument that man is an irreducible 'compound unity' of hierarchical levels, physical, biological, and psychological (rational-volitional). William McDougall (1920) came close to this when he recognized a relation of mind to body so intimate that 'psychological interaction may be, for all we know, a necessary condition of all consciousness'. But he insisted, nevertheless, that the soul is a 'psychic being', and added that it must not be conceived of as 'a core or substratum underlying and distinct from all attributes of a thing', nor as incapable of growth and change.

William Stern (1938), to state a third alternative, held that the person is 'psycho-physically neutral'. But he distinguished a person from a thing because, despite the plurality of its parts, it 'constitutes a real, unique, and intrinsically valuable unity, and, as such . . . achieves a unitary, purposive self-activity'.

In this sample of differences we note a common concern: to maintain that the mind or self, whatever its relation to body, is engaged in all its activities and yet not to be identified with any one of them. Personalistic thinkers have been haunted by this difficult notion of a self unifying its activities, and yet not to be identified with these changing activities. They have had no little trouble in conceiving such permanence and change together, and have sometimes emphasized one at the expense of the other. The struggle in Borden P. Bowne (1910) is in structure as Franquiz (1942) shows. But C. A. Campbell's recent statement (1957) is an especially revealing example of the psycho-logic of substantive *soul*-psychology.

When I hear the second stroke of Big Ben, *as* the second stroke, Campbell argues, I must not only remember the first but remember *that* I heard it. I am not only a self-identical subject, but conscious of it. All cognition, he concludes, forces us 'to posit a self which is "over and above" its particular experiences; something that *has*, rather than is, its experiences, since its experiences are all different, while *it* somehow remains the same' (Campbell, 1957, p. 77), yet Campbell does not wish to identify his substantival self with John Locke's *je-ne-sais-quoi* or unknowable substratum, or with Kant's 'characterless' ego. His contention is that 'to deny that the self is *reducible* to its experience is by no means to deny that the self manifests its real character (in whole or in part) in and through experiences' (*ibid.*, p. 82).

But is it intelligible to say that the *I* is the same and yet changes? The 'how' of self-unity in change, Campbell agrees, is logically un-intelligible. Nevertheless, what is given in experience is an *I* that in thinking is aware of its identity with the *I* that feels B and desires C, and has other conscious experiences. Can logical demands be allowed to explain away a non-logical given? Self-psychologists will agree with Campbell that demands for a logically intelligible 'how' must not be allowed to dictate what experience must be. But, as we shall see, Brightman, for example, will urge that we can conceive of this psychic unity in more radically empirical terms.

Before leaving Campbell and soul-psychology it will be well to note a distinction he makes that is basic to the way in which both soul- and self-psychology conceive the difference between unity of self or soul and unity of personality.

We must not confuse, says Campbell, the identity of the self, the *I* (that has, but is not its activities) with the personal identity that it develops. The personal identity, that is, the character ('personality' would be the American term), is acquired by the self in the course of its experiences. It is 'a set of relatively stable dispositions to feel, think, and behave in more or less marked ways' (1957, p. 86). A self, in other words, comes to conceive of itself, or to identify itself, with these acquired salient features. When a person says, 'I was not myself when I did that', he is referring to this character.

We might restate this distinction by speaking of the originative *I*, soul, or self, that remembers these stable dispositions as its own, as the *ontic self* or agent. In order to develop, sustain, and identify these dispositions it has to be self-identical. *Its* character and personality tell the story of the particular course the ontic self has taken. In other words, the agent-self always exists in two dimensions – as unlearned sustaining, immanent, unity and as learned unity expressing the nature of interaction between itself and environment. But: 'The self may function when the person[ality] does not, but the person[ality] cannot function when the self does not' (*ibid.*, p. 88). That is, the ontic self can and does function beyond the boundaries of any set of stable dispositions.

The question we shall soon be asking is this: Does psychology of personality require such a self? Whatever the answer may be, the fact is that philosophers like Campbell are concerned lest psychology of personality neglect this distinction between a self-identical self and the personality which it acquires and to which *it* gives unity. Furthermore they would welcome Campbell's exposition as he shows how this distinction can help us to understand both the unity of personality when it does exist and the development of sub-systems that are not harmonious with each other.

For example, let us assume with Campbell, a self, an original psychic unity present in, but not exhausted by, its activities. It starts on its career with native affective-conative tendencies and capacities closely related to a particular body. In interaction with the social and physical environment it develops its person[ality]. In such interaction the self's energies are not, as it were, 'poured without remainder into its functioning as a person[ality]'. This makes it possible for self-identity to be retained both when personality-identity is being developed and also when it is interrupted either through bodily disrepair or through psychological dissociation.

In other words, the same self can develop different sub-systems to serve different functions. In normality the self moves with ease from one to another. But abnormality occurs when conflict between sub-systems is so great that dissociation seems the best way out. However, were the self not identical there could be no felt conflict. And were it not identical and persistent despite the conflicts of the sub-systems into which it had not poured itself completely there could be no healing. Two personalities, if they belonged to two independent spiritual entities, could never be integrated again.

In such a view we can see how a substantive soul-psychology (or a self-psychology), developed to care for certain fundamental epistemic and metaphysical problems, can also throw light on how dissociation and re-integration are possible. In Campbell's view we see a very subtle rendering of the substantive view of selfhood, a dogged determination to avoid 'pure' egos, on the one hand and 'bundle' views of self on the other. F. R. Tennant (1928) would fall in line with this general account of ontic self and personality, but he would deny that the ontic self can be experienced.

Nevertheless, whether one holds with Campbell that the ontic self only reveals itself in part in its activities, or with Tennant that the pure ego is never an object of consciousness, all such substantive or near-substantive views have called forth dissent from personalistic *self*-psychologists on methodological grounds mainly. They have argued that any 'has-but-is-not' view of the self and its activities opens the door to uneconomical multiplication of entities and to possible obscurantism. The only check we have on anything beyond experience is in experience. But what is more, why go beyond experience for unity when it is there in self-experience? Such is the main thesis of philosophical self-psychologists.

To bring the problem into clear focus: The main problem of the *soul*-psychologists is to give an account of the self-identical soul that will be faithful to change and plurality. The problem of the *self*-psychologists is to be faithful to the need for unity. The agonizing of William James with this tension in different stages of his development is fascinating but cannot here be traced in detail. It is Capek's well-defended contention (1953) that, despite appearances and disappearances of the 'I' in James's thought, his final view, most adequately expressed in *A Pluralistic Universe*, confirms the passage in the Principles (pp. 226–7): 'The universal conscious fact is not "feelings and thoughts exist" but "I think" and "I feel". . . It could only be a blunder if the notion of personality meant something essentially different from anything to be found in the mental procession. But if that procession be itself the very "original" of the notion of personality, to personify it cannot possibly be wrong. It is already personified.'

This line of reasoning is developed by the best recent proponent of *self*-psychology, E. S. Brightman (1932, 1958), a more thorough-going empiricist than his teacher, B. P. Bowne, the founder of personalistic idealism in America. The undeniable data for all theorizing are to be found in the undeniable existent, the conscious datum-self. This datum-self is not substantive soul, but a complex unity of conscious experience, it is not a mathematical point, but a 'saddle-back' (James's term), a *durée*, a temporal span with its own complex unity. It is not a unity *in* but a unity *of* interpenetrating or fused sensing, remembering, reasoning, emoting, wanting, willing, feeling, and their modes or 'states', such as sensations, images, ideas, loves, hates, hopes, intentions, volitions. It is this complex, *erlebt* present that is the undeniable *I*. It is this psychic unity that is the only certain model we have of being – a throbbing, temporal, changing, yet self-identical and acting unity of psychic givens. Theorizing starts in *this* reasoning-wanting unity, as it brings its built-in norms of reason to bear in understanding the occurrence, the changes, the sequences, in its present states.

This personal self, this *I*, is not Stern's neutral *unitas multiplex* (1924, 1938), nor Campbell's unity that *has* (but not *is*) its activities. The experiencing self is this temporal, changing, yet self-identical kind of being, and no logic must be allowed to explain it away. An adequate psychology must describe its nature and development; and metaphysics must give the most coherent account possible of its relation to other forms of being. There simply is no experiential evidence, Brightman urges, for an unchanging unity.

However, in every given *I* (or datum-self), there are data that need further explanation. Reasoning about such data leads us to develop theories about the conditions for their being what they are, theories about body, about the unconscious, or, in a word, about *the whole self or person*. We come to realize, for example, that the datum-self is a specious present continuous with its past and moving into a future. But what is important methodologically for Brightman is that no theory of the 'sources of the conscious' – be it Freud's, Jung's, or that of an Absolute Idealist, Theistic Dualist, Materialist or Naturalist – is acceptable if, in the end, it is incoherent with the existence, and complex qualitative nature of, the undeniable datum-self.

We need not linger here, except to note that this account of the personal self, if it were substituted for Campbell's, could account equally well for the acquired dispositions, or any learned systems, that are needed in describing personality. The unity of the knowing-wanting self (to telescope functions) is not poured without residue into particular habits, sentiments, attitudes, traits, or 'personalities' that stabilize the particular 'adjustments' that particular self has made.

III

As we turn to the early decades of the twentieth century, to a period of more explicit conflict between philosophical personalistic psychology and general scientific psychology, we are impressed by the synoptic style, the radical empiricism that persists in the personalistic demand that scientific hypotheses be adequate to the data of consciousness. William James aside, there is no better defender of self-psychology on the scientific level than Mary W. Calkins (1914, 1915).

Calkins was caught with James, Bowne, McDougall, and others, in the advance of psychological movements that were to model the science of psychology on patterns exemplified in the physical sciences. In *A First Book in Psychology*, a text that appeared as a fourth revision in 1914, she argued that 'psychology is a science of self', and the next year she reviewed specific psychological evidence relevant to her thesis that the self cannot be 'bowed out of psychology on the ground that scientific introspection has failed to discover it' (1915).

The self, as Calkins saw it, is self-identical, unique, related to its social and physical environment, but not 'beyond or beside' the experience it has. When the psychologist tries to define the self by making it a member of some broader class, or to isolate it experimentally, it must perforce escape him. For the self is in a class by itself; it is ubiquitous, and cannot be isolated as it might be if it were only a part of experience. It cannot yield itself to experimentation, for it is doing the experimenting; but it can be described by 'controlled introspection'.

Calkins is equally resistant to near-self-psychologists who hold that the self is directly experienced in some experience but not in others (such as perception). A full self-psychology must hold that 'all consciousness is consciousness of self and that the psychologist, therefore, willy-nilly studies the self'. Desirable as it is to know the physiological and physical conditions of introspective phenomena, what is in consciousness must be described for what it is.

Considerations related to Calkins's basic concern that psychological science makes proper allowances for the possible distinctiveness of human self-experience appear in many places. Magda Arnold (1954), for example, points to an anomaly: the willingness of psychologists to disregard data that only human beings can provide, namely, introspective data, especially since they can only finally justify disregard of it by trusting introspection!

Furthermore, she warns, the psychologist ought at least to be aware that he is often presupposing philosophical conclusions, including his philosophy of science, in approaching what is given in personal experience. Thus, to assume a lawful universe that presumably has no place for freedom and purpose in it, or that aesthetic, religious, and moral experience can give no possible evidence about its nature, is to operate *from* a philosophical position and not from observation of what is given in human experience itself. Her stricture is scientifically important because hidden philosophical assumptions have a way not only of restricting one's 'sense of the problem' but also of determining how observed data are interpreted.

Finally, what is given in experience as a whole must be kept before us and not be sacrificed to the convenience of method. Procedures for studying man must be fitted to the problem, not the problem to the Procrustean bed of method. Accordingly, as Allport observes (1947), the psychologist who uses a machine model must be aware that it is drawn not from clinical or social psychology but from the physical sciences. Again, he who uses animal or infantile models should be aware that they 'lack the long range orientation that is the essence of morality'.

A. Maslow joins Allport in concern lest the higher ranges of human experience be treated on the premature assumption that the higher is simply an extension of the lower. Maslow (1954, 1962) in particular urges that self-actualizing persons and 'peak experiences' be seen not as deviations from 'the normal' but as fulfilments without which 'the average' and 'the lower' may be seriously understood.

Such methodological cautions are developments of the broader philosophical method we have seen to characterize personalistic philosophy. Thus, speaking methodologically, we can summarize: Personalistic psychology is problem-centred and not model-method-centred, be the model or method drawn from 'successes' in physics, biology, logic, or theology. Models can help if we do not forget that we are using them, but neither man the sinner, nor man the robot or feed-back idol can be given arbitrary priority.

The psychologist of personality cannot afford to disregard continuity or discontinuity with the subhuman, cannot de-emphasize similarity for the sake of uniqueness, the lower for the sake of the higher, or be unaware of philosophies and theologies relevant to the interpretation of man. Facts – for every source, ticketed with the method by which they were obtained – and values, individual or universal, high or low, labelled so that they may be observed in experience – are grist for the personalistic psychologist's intent to understand relationships among the varieties of human experience.

IV

The evolution of Gordon W. Allport's probing and theorizing is not only guided by such basic methodological considerations as we have reviewed, but it is also a revealing commentary on the movements and problems that we have outlined. We centre attention on Allport's psychology of personality because it is the most systematic psychological account of human experience that reflects a personalistic frame of mind.

If James, like Calkins and Ward, lived in the adolescent stage of psychology's rejection of its philosophical parent, Allport lived in the young adulthood that fathered behaviourism, objective psychology, Gestalt and depth psychologies, tests and other statistical techniques for describing personality. If 'objective' psychologies waged war on consciousness and introspection and sought 'positive' laws of behaviour, depth psychologies, less firmly rooted in physiology, set the conscious personality uncertainly on generic unconscious energies – with the common result that no account was given of the uniqueness that characterizes personality. Allport found support in Gestalt psychology against atomism and over-reliance on unconscious mechanisms, and in favour of a phenomenalistic approach to conscious phenomena.

But there is one point at which Allport stands alongside all other academic psychologies, namely, against philosophical interpretations – such as that of Personalistic Idealism and Absolute Idealism – that seem to favour the conscious at the expense of the unconscious and question the bodily integumentation of the person (Allport, 1953). Allport sets out, therefore, as a psychologist not with a substantive soul or a self-psychology, but with descriptive, naturalistic presuppositions. This is to say that his naturalism is not doctrinaire. He sees the human being as a biological creature, whose personality is 'a unique creation of the forces of nature' (1961, p. 4), whose development can be conceived in terms 'neither exclusively mental nor exclusively neural (physical)' (1961, p. 28). The new-born babe lacks 'the characteristic organization of psychological systems', has 'a *potential* personality' that develops 'within the skin'. The givens of personality are an idiographic complex of physique, temperament, and intelligence, motivated in infancy by essentially biological and nutritional drives. As the infant matures and interacts with the social and physical environment, he develops a personality. Once beyond the infantile state, this personality cannot be understood in terms of biological motives alone. It is the post-infantile development with its transformation of beginnings and its growing individual pattern that captivates Allport's attention and finally brings him to focus attention not on self-psychology but on psychology of 'self'.

Before considering the factors in Allport's own thought that call for a 'self', it will be well to take note of a trend in the investigation of personality that resulted in the reappearance of terms like 'self', 'ego', 'self-actualization' – a development that Allport has influenced and by which he in turn was influenced. The contributors to this trend are many – such investigators as M. Arnold, H. Ansbacher, R. Assagioli, N. Brown, C. Bühler, H. Cantril, A. Combs, M. C. D'Arcy, F. Deutsch, H. Erikson, V. Frankl, H. Hartmann, K. Goldstein, S. Jourard, P. Lecky, K. Horney, E. Fromm, K. Moustakas, O. Mowrer, G. Murphy, H. Murray, C. Rogers, P. M. Symonds, A. L. Van Kaam, R. White, and C. Wilson – but despite their variety A. H. Maslow (1962) suggests that they might constitute a kind of 'third force' in contemporary psychology. What impresses us is that there emerges from members of this group, who, like Allport, set aside souls, selves, and mind-body problems, observations and reflections that refocus attention on problems in psychology of personality similar to those faced by philosophical personalists when they confronted the variety and unity, continuity and discontinuity of human experience. A thumbnail sketch of the reappearance of what might be called the *psychological* self or ego must suffice.

Freud, having hypothesized the unconscious because of resistance in consciousness exhibited by his patients, developed, in turn, a theory of the conscious ego and then of a largely unconscious superego to explain the specific directions of individual personality-formations. In the thought of Jung and Adler persistent and unique organizations of response, at once influencing and expressing the conscious and unconscious givens of life in their interaction with the environment, were distinguished as the *persona* and 'style of life' respectively. And when individual development was seen in the context of mental health (the fulfilment of potential or self-actualization), as in the thought of Karen Horney (1950), Erich Fromm (1951), and A. Maslow (1954, 1962), the 'self' reappears as the 'authentic' or 'real' being. The intrinsic needs of the self, such psychologists urge, must find adequate expression throughout the different phases of life if the individual is to escape mediocrity and illness.

On these views, so far as the writer can tell, the self is a kind of being whose qualitative demands, for responsible freedom, for authentic individuality, for self-actualization, will be felt as a kind of inner guide to preferences. As Fromm and Maslow put it, 'one *ought* to become what he *is*' (1951). No created image of the divine, nor introjected demands of a culture, are envisaged in their portrait of man; he is an insistent-potential self that cannot be lastingly frustrated without illness. What seems to have happened is that among these psychologists the description of personality has moved from 'public' physiological categories to hypotheses of at least non-localizable capacities and functions related 'somehow' to the physiological – and called by terms – *ego, self, style of life* – intended to emphasize the individuality of needs, responsiveness and creative direction.

The psychological self was also to emerge from another area of investigation, in learning and theory of perception especially, and once again as a dynamic influence in what was selected and retained. Thus, Gestaltists pointed out that the psychological or behavioural environment, the inner space of the individual, however stimulated by the geographical environment, reflected the nature of the wholistic tendencies in the perceiver. Phenomenologists like Combs and Snygg (1959) emphasized that the world of the individual could not be understood without understanding his frame of reference. Transactional psychologists, like Hadley Cantril (1950, 1959), observed that what the individual perceives has no one-to-one correspondence with the external world but reflects a transaction responsive to the individual's own organization as well as the 'objective' state of affairs.

The basic conclusions emerging from these investigations is that what a person knows and perceives will be a function of the degree and nature of his self-involvement, of his conception of himself. Theories of learning that make repetition, reinforcement, and tension-reduction central fail to explain the selectivity and the permanence of learning that seem clearly to be not a function of repetition, re-enforcement, and tension-reduction. The human learner and perceiver respond to an immediate stimulus-situation not simply in the light of the past but in the light of long-range goals, persistent frames of reference, or concept of self. Nor can the emphasis be placed on the underlying, universal needs or motives; it must be shifted to contemporary ego-structure.

It is dangerous to ascribe too much unity in what are mainly trends away from emphasis on the objective past or the objective present. We are more concerned here to point to the ferment which is part of the 'environment' in which Allport's system is a constructive, sensitive response. And since we are talking about the reappearance of the self, we must note the kinds of cautions and disclaimers that often accompany talk about the self.

First, while Cantril claims, 'it is only through the life-setting and participation that meaning and continuity are given to the 'self', he warns against the mistake of 'positing an abstract self' of 'ego' that can 'somehow be isolated, pointed to, analysed, or experienced apart from any social contact' (1959, p. 133).

Second, Carl Rogers points out that the reorganization of the self is late in coming, that it resists change unless it is non-directively encouraged. He acknowledges that his thinking about the self is close to G. H. Mead's 'I' and 'me', and associates himself with Lewin, Angyal, and Allport with the remark that the self is 'an organizer of experience and to some extent an architect of self' (1959, p. 7).

The integrative function of the self as it arises from, and transforms, the social matrix is thus emphasized by both Cantril and Rogers (and others). But the question must arise: Is the self that organizes experience, that is said to be an architect of 'self', identical with the initiating self? Is the organizing self itself a product of a confluent environment? If so, do the 'environmental influences' simply fall into a unity, or is a unified selective 'architect' being assumed unwittingly? Social theories of self, we suggest, seem to make the self a 'crossroads' of interacting factors, and thus provoke two questions: Why should the result not be a collective 'omnibus' self rather than an architect? And why, in view of new arrivals at the crossroads, does unity and pattern survive, especially since there is no selective traffic officer present, presumably? These are the concerns that come to mind as one also reads Hilgard's recent Presidential Address (1949). But the interchange between Snygg and Combs (1959) and M. Brewster Smith (1959) is unusually relevant to this whole problem of the ambiguous status or double role of the self.

Snygg contends that 'the fundamental need in a phenomenological system appears to be the preservation of the organization and integrity of the phenomenological field and especially of that part of the field which is the phenomenal self, whence our tendency to remain unaware of, or to reject with emotion, data inconsistent with our own beliefs' (1959, p. 13). He explains in a footnote that 'the self we are trying to preserve is the phenomenal self, that is to say, our own picture of ourselves'. On this view what is meant by 'preservation' is the preservation of this phenomenal self, the self that stands for self-respect, self-esteem, status, and cognate concepts. And we would ask: what develops and preserves this phenomenal self?

Hence we concur when M. Brewster Smith wonders whether one term, 'self', is not being asked to perform two tasks. For the self, hypothesized as a phenomena/entity to account for perceptual organization and the self-identity involved in the phenomenological field, can hardly be the same as the developer of the self, and the self-concept. 'Can a phenomenal self consider perceptions and reintegrate itself [see Rogers above]; can a threatened phenomenal self deny perceptions, or is this rather a doubletalk resulting from the attempt to make one good concept do the work of two?' If he is to be coherent, the phenomenologist must smuggle in 'a second hidden concept', or 'organizing selective processes in the personality which are somehow guided by the nature and status of the self (among other things) and somehow, in turn, have an influence in its nature and status' (1959, p. 251).

What does Snygg reply to this? His answer is methodological. The assumption of 'a hidden organizer . . . neither necessary nor helpful'; at best is a 'second order construct' set up to 'explain . . . by a greater mystery' (1959, p. 276). He urges rather: 'When organization is found it does not need to be explained in order to be used in prediction' (1959, p. 226).

The issue seems fairly clear. Snygg hesitates to appeal to 'a hidden organizer', because he is interested in prediction. Now, no philosopher or psychologist would hold that so ubiquitous an agency as the (organizing) self has specific predictive value – except that it is important to know whether the organizing agency at age seven can be banked on to be using the same logical principles and making similar basic demands at fifteen and twenty-five.

But what seems clearly to be dodged here is the issue: Shall the psychologist in the name of predictability, and what *may be* mystery from the point of view of predictability, allow himself to be unaware of his presuppositions, and to double-talk? Can we remain content when a phenomenological psychologist says: 'the essential characteristic of any organized field is its tendency to maintain its organization in the face of intruding forces' (Snygg, 1959, p. 276)? Or do the data show that the organization maintained can so radically change, and yet remain self-identical, that we should wonder how the organized field can maintain its organization in the face of intruding forces. We fear that the double-talk persists.

v

We return to Allport, then, with the problem of the critical factors in the organization of personality uppermost, and ask: Why does the problem of the self become important for him? In what sense is a doctrine of self 'fruitful' or 'a greater mystery'? What are his concerns about such a doctrine?

The Allportian challenge to psychological science and to psychology of personality in particular is that it confronts and develops the techniques and theory for understanding individuality With Bergsonian fervour, Allport keeps hammering away at the ineptitude of generic concepts for growing uniqueness in personality organization. There is pattern, there is growth, there is order in both pattern and growth, and these invite the construction of theoretical concepts that will not allow the idiographic to escape. No preconceived notion of what science 'must be' keeps him from trying to understand the individual order of change.

To come closer, for Allport, personality is a living system, a system from which we, to use Hegelian language, can abstract different dimensions – but should not forget that we abstracted them! The true personality is the whole, 'a total functioning structure' albeit 'an incomplete system, manifesting varying degrees of order and disorder' (1961, p. 566). Allport's faith, if you will, is that if we view the personality as an open-ended system, interacting with, but not a function of, society or environment, there is hope that, without losing track of strands that can up to a point be nomothetically described, we can see them as they are, interwoven aspects of a dynamic organic system.

It is hard to label Allport's system neatly for this very reason. Gough has recently (1962) urged that the term 'psychomorphology' might do justice to the 'dynamics and morphogenesis of structure' in Allport's emphasis on the unified complexity of personality. It is our contention that not only does his system actually fall more clearly into the personalistic framework of self-psychology, but that without an adequate articulation of self-psychology the actual system he expounds leaves unanswered questions and faces unnecessary difficulties. Let us see why.

Allport, we have said, wishes to draw 'special attention to those laws and principles that tell how uniqueness comes about' (1962, p. 572). Uniqueness in motivation is simply inexplicable if we start with any one generic drive (like the id), with propensities (as proposed by McDougall), or even with the very flexible instinctoid needs of Maslow. Psychologists should give up what has been a fruitless, age-long struggle to substantiate any list of universal drives, and realize that such commonness as there is in motivation can be accounted for on the basis of learning in similar environments (1940). In any case, no list of inborn needs, however channelized and directed, can actually account for the 'qualitative differences between infant and adult (e.g. the emergent motives of social responsibility), and also for the extraordinary diversity of adult motives unique in each particular personality' (1962, p. 203). Furthermore, while the fact is that 'human beings are busy living their lives into the future,' such theories of motivation are 'busy tracing these lives backward into the past' (1962, p. 206); and they treat the person as a reactive agent rather than the progressive, proactive being that he feels himself to be.

Allport accordingly advances his well-known doctrine of the functional autonomy of motives to explain the undeniable data: 'Adult motives are infinitely varied, self-sustaining, *contemporary* systems. They are not fossils' (1961, p. 211). Whatever their historical connection with past motives may be – and it is one thing to say that they are reducible to 'underlying' unchanging drives and another to prove it – the present 'go' of motivation is autonomous. For people, the motives after twenty-five years of marriage are a transformation of the motives that led to marriage in the first place; and they are self-sustaining.

There are many important empirical and theoretical issues at stake here (Bertocci, 1940), but we focus on a critical one. Instinctive and drive theories, for all their difficulties, did manage to account for continuity in change. The more flexible the universal motives were held to be, the more did they seem to allow, in view of differences in ability and environment, for diversity between persons and for differences within a life history as well as for continuity.

If Allport gives up the continuity in striving that doctrines of persisting motives provide, if he substitutes a doctrine of motives that stresses the discontinuity of present motivational structures with the past, he is faced with the formidable problem of accounting for the inner, long-range, complex variety and continuity of personality. At a deeper metaphysical level, Allport's doctrine of functional autonomy of motives is a doctrine of emergence (nutritional needs aside). But metaphysical theories of emergence explain variety, novelty, plurality always at the possible expense of systematic unity, so, if the discussion is pushed to a deeper level, the same problem of accounting for unity despite discontinuity needs to be faced.

Staying, however, at the psychological level, what is to hold a personality (not its bodily aspect alone) together if motives, being functionally autonomous, have no continuous inner bonds with each other or with pervasive motives? On the face of it, there is no ground for assuming either continuity or unity of aim if functional autonomy, the emergence of new motives, the supplanting of old, is taken seriously. Yet it is the complex unity of the unique system that Allport makes the obstinate empirical datum of personality theory.

In *Becoming* (1956), and more elaborately in *Pattern and Growth in Personality* (1961), Allport develops his conception of the '*proprium*' or propriate striving, in order to describe the dynamic continuity discoverable in personality after the infantile stage. For as partially formed interest systems develop we can distinguish 'the central' and 'warm' portion of personality from portions that are on the rim of one's being. The child is developing a sense of 'self' and his interests fit into 'self-system' (1961, p. 107). In other words, in some learning activities he is more ego-involved than in others. 'Whatever is ego-relevant is absorbed and retained' (p. 107).

The facts of growth and patterning in personality demand that we 'allow adequately for coherence and self relevance' in a way not possible on quasi-mechanical and intellectualistic theories of learn-ing. Propriate striving gives us the kind of concept we need if we are to understand the 'evolving sense of self'.

Allport outlines several aspects of this 'evolving sense', each in-volving a dimension of the complex unity: the movement from unorganized sensori-motor experiences at birth to the fixing of recurrent bodily sensations into a 'bodily me', which 'while not the whole of one's self' continues to be 'a lifelong anchor for our self-awareness' (1962, p. 114); the achievement of continuous self-identity made possible especially by language and one's own name; the self-esteem that reflects others' evaluation of him; the extension of self and of his self-image as the growing individual tries to discover his place among others and his vocation, and his life-goal. What is crucial is that as the individual develops into adolescence and adulthood, 'long-range purposes and distant goals add a new dimension to the sense of selfhood' (1961, p. 126). Since each of these dimensions involves 'matters of importance to the organized emotional life of the individual', they are best united or fused under 'a fresher and broader label', *proprium* (1961, p. 127).

This proprium, then, is Allport's suggestion for fusing 'selves' and 'egos' as advanced by other psychologists, and it serves to provide the continuity in organization that is so vital for under-standing his theory of personality and its uniqueness. This propriate self we also learn is *'the self "as object" of knowledge and feeling'* (1961, p. 127, italics added). It is this self 'of which we are immediately aware' and of which we think as 'the warm, central region of life'. Furthermore, as such a warm, central region, 'it plays a crucial part in our consciousness' (a concept broader than self), in our personality (a concept broader than consciousness). Thus it is some kind of core in our being. And yet [he hastens to add] 'it is not a constant core', for it sometimes takes command 'of all our behaviour and consciousness' and sometimes seems to go 'completely offstage, leaving us with no awareness whatsoever of self' (1961, p. 110).

In epistemic terms, Allport obviously is talking about the empirical, the phenomenal and phenomenological self, of which 'each of us has an acute awareness' (p. 111). It is this self which the 'presumably conscious infant', who 'lacks self-consciousness com-pletely, gradually distinguishes from the world and becomes 'the pivot of later life' (1961, p. 111). And it is this self, the growing, long-range, dynamic, forward-thinking motivational core, which is the matrix of contemporaneous motives. In a word, while contemporary motives are functionally autonomous of antecedent motives they are never functionally autonomous of the proprium that is developing and expressing in these different ways the relatively systematic 'go' of personality, 'sometimes consciously, but often unconsciously' (1961, p. 129).

One can readily see why Allport believes that he has solved the problem of continuity and discontinuity in motivation. And the case is all the more plausible when Allport develops the distinction that his theory of the propriate self as the 'object known' forces upon him. Thus Allport purposely asks: 'Who is the I who knows the bodily me, who has an image of myself and sense of identity over time, who knows that I have propriate strivings? I know all these things, and what is more, I know that I know them' (1961, p. 128). Some knowing subject or self is required, Allport now contends, as a continuant 'somehow' from infancy to death.

But when it comes to determining 'the nature of' the knowing 'I' Allport has serious qualms, and of the sort we have already encountered in the case of the self-psychologist against the soul-psychologist, and of the sort we have seen Snygg advance against Brewster.

VI

We conclude our study, therefore, by noting Allport's hesitations against *self*-psychology in particular, and asking whether a self-psychology is not actually what will give greater coherence to his theory of the propriate self and this development of personality.

In favour of self-psychology Allport grants that to hold that the self is a knowing, striving, willing agency in personality would indeed properly focus, as he has, 'on the unity and coherence that mark the propriate functions of personality' (1961, p. 129). But 'from the scientific point of view' he suggests: 'If we admit the self as a separate agent that knows, wills, wants, and so on, are we not in danger of creating a personality within a personality?' We seem to be postulating 'a little man within the breast' (1961, p. 129). And, furthermore, we keep on begging the question, or 'passing the buck' to such a 'little man', if we say 'the self does this or that' and so forth.

Allport accordingly concludes: 'It is my position that in the structure of *personality*, if rightly understood – including, of course, the propriate structure – we shall find the explanations we seek. It is unwise to assign our problem to an inner agent who pulls the strings.' And he urges that, whatever philosophical purposes might justify regarding the self as a continuing entity, 'in psychology we do well to avoid the sharp separation of the self "as agent" from the functioning of propriate systems within the personality' (1961, p. 130).

Allport later returns to the same problem from another angle. In actual life, he says, 'a fusion of the propriate states is the rule'. But behind these experienced stages of selfhood, he adds, 'you catch indirect glimpses of yourself as "knower". And he asks: 'Who is the self that knows these self-functions?' The question is especially important because 'we are not only aware of what is peculiarly ours, but we are also aware that we are aware' (1961, pp. 137, 138).

Thus Allport rejects not only the postulation of a transcendental knower, but also a combined knower-wanter-striver-willer. Why? Because it sets up 'a master co-ordinating agent within the personality' that pulls the strings. Where, then, does this leave him? A knower he needs – and accepts – a knower each of us presumably catches a glimpse of – but he cannot allow it to be conceived as something beyond the stream of patterned experience. But the creative-volitinoal nature gets different treatment! 'It seems on the whole sounder to regard the propriate function of wanting, striving, willing as interlocked within the total personality structure' (1961, p. 138).

To readers of this chapter it will be clear that Allport's objections to some unempirical, hidden homunculus are grounded in the same radical empiricism that inspired self-psychology in its rejection of soul-psychology. Allport's strictures against an agent pulling the strings, but not revealed, in conscious experience or in personality, cannot be ignored by any philosophy, let alone psychology, that would ground logically intelligible hypotheses without remainder in terms of experience. Indeed, this is the very reason for Brightman's beginning with the unity *in* and *of* conscious experience as given and for his building hypotheses about the whole self, including the body and the unconscious, on evidence provided by conscious experience. Any personalist must tread cautiously where experiential data (in the broader sense or as confined to consciousness) are scanty. What remains to be shown is that the logic or psychologic or personalistic theory must take us beyond, not 'the scientific viewpoint' but the very quandary in which Allport seems to leave us.

To be specific, if the 'self' or *proprium* of personality is acquired, and as a part of the personality that is also acquired, then a continuant that begins the learning, moves from one learned solution to another as it recognizes and responds to new problems, must be involved to play the 'integrative' role in behaviour. There is a self-identity of the knower without which to talk of personality as a learned system is meaningless. No system – especially if it is a growing structure – without a systematizer. Nor need the systematizer be a homunculus. At every stage from birth to death it is engaged in the differentiations and interpretations that make *this* as opposed to another possible personality actual. It is never disengaged from any actual phase in the growth of personality or *proprium*.

In other words, what experience seems to tell us at every stage is that the knowing being, active at one moment *in* perceiving and thinking about the road ahead as he drives, is nevertheless not exhausted in these specific modal activities, for he can turn his attention to other matters, thus using other activities, and then come back to these. What we must do is to begin with the *kind* of being also who is actively knowing and involved in the ways he expresses his needs at a given stage in his development, and in a given environment. This kind of being is not a puller of strings but pulling, pushing, and aiming in response to problems in a given way now; he is *now becoming* the pulling-pushing-aiming-self-in-personality. Nevertheless this self cannot be identified, or interlocked exclusively, with any particular stage in the development of personality, for its activities are potentially broader than any one personality in which its activities are being expressed. Were this not so, were it completely exhausted in any one personality, it could not guide the changes that take place in personality.

There is no analogy for the kind of relation between any unified, active, changing, knowing self and *its* personality; we must try to grasp this dynamic relation without giving in to substantive modes of thought. This self is not an agency that might invest itself, as a person might invest his capital in different banks, but remain unchanged and uninvolved in directing the changes that take place. *The personal self cannot delegate powers to his personality!* At any moment a personality *is* the knowing self's relatively variable way of dealing with the intentional-internal pressures; it will never be exactly the same self again because of this experience. But it will continue to function as a knower, wanter, willer, fertilized by its past and present, and now giving birth to a new future. This self is indeed 'interlocked' with its total personality structure, but not exhausted in its basic activity-potential by the personality it has developed in a given environment. I am the personality that my self, given its needs and capacities, has been able to acquire in America. Had I been born and brought up in China, my knowing, wanting, willing, feeling (agent-knower) would have taken different forms, but they would not be different capacities.

Does not what Allport says about propriate striving and the *proprium* fit neatly in this scheme? All the more neatly, we suggest, for now we have a discriminating agent-knower forging its empirical self-identity, a self-identity that affects its further acting-knowing, but sensible to keep it from varying the content of its proprium (within limits).

In relation to the *appropriated self*, or proprium, indeed, contemporary motives may be autonomous. But a question that would take us further into motivation theory than we can go here would still need to be asked. Granted that the *proprium* is acquired but relatively enduring, the fact is that it, too, is subject to change. Must not the knower from the very beginning to the end of its existence also be a wanter, with enduring though flexible needs? Any propriate self is the solution *thus far* to the individual wanter's struggle for autonomy and identity in a given growth-environmental situation. The fact that the *proprium* can be changed, that what is now propriate may become peripheral and vice-versa, calls for both wanting and knowing in a unified continuant.

If our reasoning is correct, then, a self, understood as the unity of its intrinsic activities, is engaged in discovering and realizing its own potential in a challenging-nurturant environment. In seeking to fulfil itself, in learning to transact successive proprium-personality systems, it is always engaged in the selective process of taking and giving. It is always discriminating and developing what we might call the warmer and colder aspects of adjustment in accordance with unrealized potential that is making itself felt. The self is never without *some* personality, but *which* personality is a by-product of its interaction with the environment in the light of the maturation-learning processes and activities that define its being at any one time.

If our reasoning is correct, we cannot accept Allport's suggestion and interlock the propriate function of wanting, striving and willing within the personality of structure while the knower remains disengaged from the proprium. Indeed, how shall we understand the statement that propriate functions are 'felt as self-relevant' if there is no want or need for whose gratification they are relevant? If, as we assume, there is no knowing without interest (of various sorts), the knowing self must also be a knowing-wanting unity (or a *unitas multiplex* of knowing-feeling-wanting-willing-oughting activities, as we would propose). Knowing in all of its dimensions – from sensory perception to logical, aesthetic, moral, and religious valuation and action takes place as one phase of a unified matrix that is also feeling and wanting (at least).

To be sure, a theory of motivation must indeed meet Allport's strictures against unchanging needs and unchanging souls or selves. But, once more, if the agent-self is conceived as a concrete original unity of activities (a unity in which different activities may be discriminated but not abstracted out), and if among these activities may be discerned generic dynamic tendencies that demand expression and gratification (but can be expressed and gratified in different ways), one can keep the dynamism and the future-orientation Allport rightly wants as integral to the very being of a unified self (see Bertocci and Millard, 1963). At the same time one can explain why some sets of propriate strivings, why some habits, attitudes, sentiments, traits, intentions and even styles of life do in fact give way to others. For while these are developed as part of, or along with, propriate strivings, they must ultimately meet the requirements of the active-potential self's knowing-wanting nature. It should be clear that on this view there are not generic goals first, and then channelizing into specific motives. There is only a continuant knowing-wanting unity that is a 'fighter for ends', seeking satisfaction for its maturing and challenged potential, seeking to sustain itself from moment to moment in the light of the transactions it undergoes and of its conception of itself and the total environment.

Thus, unique and unified initially, living in an environment its own given nature and life-history makes eligible for it, the self acquires its own characteristic, more or less systematic mode of adjustment (personality); it continues to live from the vantage-point and achievement of that personality until further change is forced upon it or selected, or both. But as it grows and learns it is this knowing-wanting self that discriminates the near and the far, the possible and the impossible, the convenient and the necessary. In this process the valuable and the disvaluable *to it*, the proprium or warm centre of its adjustment, is acquired, enhanced, and sustained against attack, until it proves to be so inadequate that new adjustments are made. The self that was Saul becomes Paul, and Paul, no doubt, was the Paul that Saul *could* develop in view of Saul's past. But it could not become Paul without giving expression and direction to unused and unrealized potential.

Perhaps enough has been said to indicate that Allport's qualms about self-psychology can be met, and at the same time bring greater coherence into the interpretation of the growth and pattern in personality. While such a self-psychology would lead to no specific prediction it does provide greater theoretical foundation for the order in uniqueness without which prediction is hard to explain.

Personalistic philosophy and psychology can move, if you will, at different levels of description and interpretation, with full awareness of the interpenetration of the two. But the personalist, of all philosophers and psychologists, does not stop being a philosopher and start being a psychologist, or vice-versa, especially when the understanding of personal development is at stake. As he tries to understand the nature of the person, his personality and his *proprium*, he bends every means of penetrating the unknown. Above all, he insists that the person be not lost in the artificial battle of disciplines; for he realizes that there are in the last analysis different ways which persons have developed in order to understand themselves and the world in which they live.

BIOGRAPHICAL NOTES

Allport, G. W., 'Motivation in Personality – Reply to Mr Bertocci', *Psychological Review*, 1940, 47, 533–54.

Allport, G. W., 'The Ego in Contemporary Psychology', *Psychological Review*, 1943, 50, 451–78.

Allport G. W., 'Scientific Models and Human Morals', *Psychological Review*, 1947; reprinted in G. W. Allport, *Personality and Social Encounter: Selected Essays*.

Allport, G. W., 'The Psychological Nature of Personality', *The Personalist*, 1953; reprinted in *Personality and Social Encounter: Selected Essays*, Boston: Beacon Press, 1960.

Allport, G. W., *Becoming*, New Haven: Yale University Press, 1955.

Allport, G. W., *Pattern and Growth in Personality*, New York: Rinehart, Holt and Winston, 1961.

Bertocci, Peter A., 'A Critique of G. W. Allport's Theory of Motivation', *Psychological Review*, 1940, 47, 501–32.

Bertocci, Peter A., *An Introduction to Philosophy of Religion*, New York: Prentice-Hall, 1952, Chapters 8, 9.

Bertocci, Peter A., and R. M. Millard, *Personality and the Good: Psychological and Ethical Perspectives*, New York: David McKay Co., Chapters 7 and 8.

Bowne, Borden P., *Theory of Thought and Knowledge*, New York: Harper and Brothers, 1897, Chapter 3.

Bowne, Borden P., *Metaphysics*, New York: American Book Co., 1910.

Brightman, Edgar S., 'The Finite Self', in C. I. Barrett, *Contemporary Idealism in America*, New York: The Macmillan Co., 1932. Chapter 8.

Brightman, Edgar S., *Person and Reality* (An Introduction to Metaphysics), (ed. Peter A. Bertocci *et al.*), New York: The Ronald Press, 1958, Chapters 2, 3, 4, 14.

Calkins, Mary W., *A First Book in Psychology*, 4th rev., New York: The Macmillan Co., 1914.

Calkins, Mary W., 'The Self in Scientific Psychology', *American Journal of Psychology*, 1915, 26, 455–524; 495.

Campbell, C. A., *On Selfhood and Godhood*, New York: Macmillan, 1950.

Cantril, Hadley, *The 'Why' of Man's Experience*, New York: Macmillan, 1950.

Cantril, Hadley, 'Perception and Interpersonal Relations' in *The Phenomenological Problem* (ed. A. E. Kuenzli) New York: Harper, 1959, 182–99.

Capek, Milic, 'The Reappearance of the Self in James', *Philosophical Review*, 1953, 42, 533.

Combs, A., and Snygg, D., *Individual Behaviour*, Harper, 1959.

Franquiz, Jose A., *Borden Parker Bowne's Treatment of the Problem of Change and Identity*, Rio Piedras, University of Puerto Rico, 1942.

Fromm, Erich, *The Sane Society*, New York: Rinehart, 1955.

Gough, Harrison O., 'Review of G. W. Allport's Pattern and Growth in Personality' in *Contemporary Psychology*, 1962, 7, 313–15.

Hilgard, Ernest R., 'Human Motives and the Concept of the Self', *American Psychology*, 1949, 4, 374–82.

Maslow, A. H., *Motivation and Personality*, New York: Harper, 1954.

Maslow, A. H., *Toward a Psychology of Being*, New York: Van Nostrand, 1962.

McDougall, William, *Body and Mind*, New York: The Macmillan Co., 1920, 364, 365, 372.

Rogers, C., 'Some Observations on the Organization of Personality' in *The Phenomenological Problem* (ed. A. E. Kuenzli) New York: Harper, 1959, pp. 49–76.

Smith, M. Brewster, ''The Phenomenological Approach in Personality Theory: Some Critical Remarks', in *The Phenomenological Problem* (ed. A. C. Kuenzli), New York: Harper, 1959, 253–68.

Snygg, Donald, 'The Need for a Phenomenological System of Psychology' in *The Phenomenological Problem* (ed. A. E. Kuenzli), New York: Harper, 1959, 3-li, and see pp. 268–80.

Stern, William, *Person und Sache*, I, 1924, p. 16 as quoted in A. C. Knudson, *Philosophy of Personalism*, New York: Abingdon Press, 1927.

Stern, William, *General Psychology from the Personalistic Standpoint* (trans. by H. D. Spoerl), New York: Macmillan, 1938, p. 70.

Tennant, F. R., *Philosophical Theology*, Vol. I, Cambridge University Press, 1928.

CHAPTER IV

THE MORAL STRUCTURE OF
THE PERSON

A *personality* is learned as a *person* interacts with other persons. More exactly, a person's personality is his more or less systematic mode of response to himself, to others, and to his total environment in the light of what he believes them to be, and what they actually are. I have argued that to identify person and personality is to confuse the continuing agent (who is at work selectively expressing his needs and abilities in and through his personality), with this personality – which may not be all he would prefer. The more established the personality is, the more does the person find his future responses affected by the habits, sentiments, attitudes, traits, style(s) of life and self-concept that are 'segments' of his personality.

Indeed, some thinkers hold that whatever freedom a person has, and whatever choices he makes, are to be understood entirely in terms of 'character', or relatively fixed formations, in his personality. On some views, both a person's freedom, and his sense of obligation, are confined within the possibilities allowed by this present total organization of personality. Thus the word 'will' has all but disappeared from the vocabulary of psychologists particularly. In turn, 'ought' and 'obligation' are derivatives of formations, both conscious and unconscious, in the personality.

The contention of the following essay[1] is that those views simply misconstrue the person's experience of will and obligation. Yet no adequate theory of will and obligation can disregard the influence of learned formations in personality.

I. THE NATURE AND SCOPE OF PERSONAL WILL

(a) The Person as the Matrix of Choice

The following discussion of free will and moral obligation presupposes certain other convictions about the nature of a person. I shall, therefore, first sketch briefly what I mean by 'person'.

[1] Essay appeared in *Review of Metaphysics*, Volume 14, March 1961, 369–88.

1. A person is a unique, indivisible, but complex unity of sensing, feeling, desiring, remembering, imagining, thinking (and willing and oughting). These interpenetrating activities are phases of a self-identifying agent capable of self-consciousness. There is also a subconscious phase of this continuant agent or personal self.

2. This personal agent, though not identical with bodily events, interacts with its body. Many qualities in mental experience are affected by bodily events; if psychosomatic medicine is to be taken seriously, the quality of bodily function is affected by the quality of mental demands.[1] The personal agent interacts with the space-time world by way of its body, but the interpretation and evaluation of any event is, in the last analysis, dependent on the appraisal made by the thinking person. Here begins the drama of the life of choice.

3. The moral life begins with reflective conflict. It does not begin at the point where desires conflict. For desires do not, as such, conflict. They simply exist, just as the appearances of the different colours do. Desires can create a maelstrom of conative traffic in consciousness. But they conflict only for an agent who, remembering past involvements and consequences, now interprets the course of their action as leading to ends which he does not approve. Only a self-conscious being can experience conflict and face the problem of deciding what to do about it.

4. Any decision or choice, furthermore, takes place within a complex personal matrix that includes *unchosen givens*. There are, for example, sensory qualia and the order of these qualia. They set the stage for learned perceptual significance. But there are also unlearned, *given* affective-conative qualia and their order.

Imagine three castaways in a lifeboat, in the throes of thirst, hunger and fear. They cannot do anything about the psychic tone and trend in their emotional states. In their watery environment they will find themselves unusually sensitive to certain qualia and sequences and their affective-conative 'sets' will influence the perceptual patterns they experience. Hastings reports, for example, that 'individuals who give evidence of being relatively insecure tend, when placed in an ambiguous perceptual situation, to see objects closer to them'.[2]

---

[1] Paul Weiss says that since each self is part of a man, who has a body as well, it will be 'biased toward a particular body'. Weiss recognizes that the self 'enhances all possibilities', but can have its vision distorted by those of its own body. He urges, accordingly, that 'when a man acts he must rectify this distortion or fail to act wholly as he ought'. *Man's Freedom*, New Haven, 1950, pp. 201–2.

[2] See George Boas, *The Inquiring Mind*, LaSalle, Ill., 1959, p. 329.

A choice, therefore, never means that the person is *making up* the underlying qualia or the sequence in sensory and affectional-conative responses. We do not *think* or *will* basic emotional qualia and their thrusts or trends into being any more than we think or will sensory qualia and their sequences into being. Any possible choice does not *constitute* but is *affected* by what the person has learned about these qualia and the way they may be interrelated or woven into the fabric of his life.

The matrix of choice, we conclude, is an agent who (1) is aware of what is now going on in him, (2) interprets what is happening in the light of what he believes has happened, and (3) anticipates what may happen in the future as *he* appraises the situation *now*.

5. We have no grounds for supposing that the person at any given point is his development uses all of his hereditary capacity in every way. His tomorrow will no doubt be affected by his today and yesterday. But can we say that at any specific moment he has used all that his nature allows (although this may be the case with regard to some specific problem)?

A *person*, as a Gestalt of activities, is not exhausted in his *personality*, that is, in the acquired, dynamic, and relatively systematic mode of response he has developed thus far. Yet a person's action at any specific point in his career will be affected by the personality-structure he has acquired to date. However, the fact that his personality can and does change means that, given his capacities, he can alter the modes of adjustment he has made in the past.

This does not mean that the person is a *homunculus* behind and within the acquired, developing personality. It means that the personality does not develop itself. The personality takes the shape made possible by the native powers of the person as he seeks to express himself in interaction with the total nurturant and challenging environment. The main point is that the person is not simply a cross-roads or centre of converging activities; he is himself a unified agent cutting across streams of events around him, coming to know what his own potential is, and trying to maintain himself within the concurrent events that constitute the world. There would be no problem of choice for him if he could not be self-conscious, think about his experience, and propose some lines of action among the many that are open to him in some degree.

(b) The Nature of Will-Agency

It is exactly at this point, where thinking is involved, that analysis of personal free will can begin. By thinking, I do not mean psychological association. I mean the process of relating ideas to each other to answer questions, or to solve problems in accordance with logical norms and some accepted criterion of truth. Concretely, the psychological process of remembering and associating are, at any one moment, filling my consciousness with images and ideas which are there before I can do anything about them. These trains of images and ideas provide much of the raw material for, but do not, strictly speaking, constitute thinking.

The distinction between thinking and associating is critical for understanding what is involved in personal willing. For the switch from associating to thinking involves what I shall call 'effort' or 'will-agency'. To illustrate: I am given some news about my son which, if true, places his scholastic success in jeopardy and opens him to serious social reproach. My protective sentiments are aroused and my ego is threatened. In a psychological situation like this I am invaded by all sorts of associations and, *effortlessly*, provide myself with all sorts of alternatives which would exonerate him and protect my ego. I find myself *wanting* to believe anything but that my son is guilty of the shameful deed. Indeed, I do not *want* to *think*! And, if I do start gathering the facts, I find myself favouring those which can be used for exonerating my son.

The situation is serious. If my son is exonerated, another's son will be almost certainly blamed. What is required in this situation if I am going to do any more than allow myself to take the most wanted conclusion? I command: Think! But to think I must (1) avoid logical error, carefully collect and organize all the relevant data, and (2) no matter how much I dislike each new unfavourable fact, I must develop an hypothesis which is most consistent with the data, whether it be consistent with my psychological yearnings or not.

It is here that the possibility of free will becomes critical. To be free *in* this psychological battlefield is to become sufficiently free *from* my warring affective-conative dispositions to be free *to* think. Is my conclusion to be the result of *my* relating evidence to hypotheses as impartially as possible; or is it to be a conclusion at the end of a gruelling battle between the affective-conative tendencies in my life?

In such situations I sometimes find myself *thinking* about possible ways in which the data can be interpreted.[1] Then, as the

[1] There may be times when the forces at work are such that the *thinking*

thinking process goes on and the conclusion becomes harder to accept emotionally, but easier to accept intellectually, I still find it difficult to keep on thinking. And here is the moment at which I find myself capable of effort, of will-agency (or of an experience of 'fiat' were we to use James's term).

I do not know all that goes on in me when I will to go on thinking. But in will-agency, that is, in the effortful, willing act, I am not wanting, or oughting, or thinking. Will-agency is an activity with a qualitative psychic tone of its own which makes a difference in my total awareness when it is present. In this instance, when I want both to stop associating and continue thinking, to exert effort makes it possible for me to continue the activity of thinking beyond the point where, were my battlefield left to itself, I would stop thinking. Two further comments may serve to clarify the activity of will-agency.

First, during this continuing process, I may not be able to control the data which psychological processes and environmental interaction at any moment catapult into my consciousness. And often, try as I will, I cannot bring the word that is on the tip of my tongue into consciousness. Will-agency works within the matrix of my total being at a given point of development. Nevertheless, assuming that much passage in my consciousness is beyond my agency, and that my total ability and dispositional development will control *what* I can think about, nothing can determine *for me* what I shall *think of* what is passing. C. I. Lewis says: 'What we shall think about is partly within our control and partly not; but what we shall think of it is our full responsibility.'[1] Again, I may not determine what happens to me, and anything that happens to me will call forth many affective-conative responses, and many associations, but my belief about what happens to me depends on what I think *of* what is happening.

Second, the possibility of arriving at a *truthful conclusion*, as opposed to a *dénouement*, depends on my being able to sustain the process of relating data to conclusions. In emotionally charged situations, my effort or agency has to be sustained every step of the way to the conclusion. Yet, assuming that I have arrived at a truthful verdict, there is no assurance that I shall take the action

---

process never gets started, and if all instances were like this there would be no basis for argument.

[1] C. I. Lewis, *The Ground and Nature of the Right*, New York, 1955, p. 26.

consistent with it. The exertion of agency will have to continue in the resultant matrix from moment to moment.

It is clear, then, that will-agency exists, and, as such, alters the problem-matrix in a way that would not occur did it not exist. But will-agency may not in fact have the *power* (will-power) needed either to continue the thinking-process to an evidence-warranted conclusion, or to put the conclusion into action.

We shall need to say more about the distinction between will-agency and will-power. Here we emphasize what seems an undeniable, *prima facie* datum of experience, which constitutes the basis for our conviction that we are *free within limits* to make a difference in what will occur to us, although we cannot be sure at any one time how much difference our agency can make.

The amount of effect that agency can have, the power of our will-agency, must not decide, however, the question whether we have any agency or freedom. For we cannot tell how much effect our agency can have until we have initiated the sustaining action or tried to initiate a new process, as when one tries, say, to break a habit. To will at all is to be free from and to be able to be free to make some effect. To will at all is to will freely, but my will-power is the degree of efficacy in a given situation. Will-power is a joint-product of my will-agency and all the factors psychological and otherwise in the choice-matrix. Paul Weiss says: 'No man is so fixed and solid in nature that he can be sure just how much *strength of will* he will exhibit later.'[1]

We must stop to examine a very interesting passage by Professor Blanshard. He grants that 'no amount of dialectic seems to shake our feeling of being free to perform either of two proposed acts'. But he explains this stubborn intuition thus:

> The first reason is that when we are making a choice our faces are always turned toward the future, toward the consequences that one act or the other will bring us, never toward the past with its possible sources of constraint. Hence these sources are not noticed. Hence we remain unaware that we are under constraint at all. Hence we feel free from such constraint. The case is almost as simple as that. When you consider buying a new typewriter your thought is fixed on the pleasure and advantage you would gain from it, or the drain it would make on your budget. You are not delving into the causes that led to your

[1] Paul Weiss, *op. cit.*, p. 230. (Italics added.)

taking pleasure in the prospect of owning a typewriter or to your having a complex about expenditure. You are too much preoccupied with the ends to which the choice would be a means to give any attention to the causes of which your choice may be an effect. But that is no reason for thinking that if you did pre-occupy yourself with these causes you would not find them at work.[1]

But I must demur even against so clear-headed a thinker as Blanshard. This fact (that in making a choice I am always facing toward a future, and that I am not aware, therefore, of the stealthy constraints actually bearing down upon me) might suffice to explain *a belief* that I am free *from* and *to*. But, if my description is correct, it does not describe *the experience* of *effort*. Nor will it explain away the *fait primitif*, the actual experience of effort.[2] The feeling of agency is not reducible to 'the feeling of an open future as regards the choice itself', as Blanshard seems to imply.[3] No doubt the agent *believes* that the future is somewhat open, but to say that our experience of free agency is possible '*because* we are not aware of the forces acting upon us'[4] is to infer too much from that the fact that 'the chooser's face is always turned forward'.[5]

Again, whether or not my present choice 'emerges out of deep shadow',[6] whether there are physiological or subconscious forces pulling upon me, can I explain my experience of agency here and now by such facts? Is it simply because other pulls from present and past, conscious and unconscious, are not strong enough that I now, facing the future, feel the quality of experience I call effort?

Is it not a presumptive kind of reasoning which explains my admitted experience of will-agency by the fact that I am not paying attention to the factors which supposedly are forcing the choice? The presumption is that if I could, at the moment I felt free, turn my eye backward and bring 'constraining factors to light' I would no longer feel free. Granted that if I knew the factors preceding my choice to be constraining, I could not justify my belief in freedom. But, surely, whatever I feel or know about the past can-not change my actual present experience (which, indeed, could be

[1] Brand Blanshard, 'The Case for Determinism' in *Determinism and Freedom*, ed. Sidney Hook, New York, 1958, pp. 5–6.
[2] See the very interesting treatment of this whole problem in Phillip Hallie's *Maine de Biran*, Cambridge, 1958, especially Chapters 2 and 3.
[3] Blanshard, *op. cit.*, p. 5.   [4] *Ibid.*, p. 6.
[5] *Ibid.*, pp. 6–7.   [6] *Ibid.*, p. 7.

used to case doubt on the power of the constraint). Whatever the antecedents of the experience of will-agency, I cannot gainsay the experience itself which I hold to be the basis for belief in it. Will-agency as experienced is the making of some difference here and now to the emerging future! It is both freedom to and freedom from.

(c) Will-Agency as the Condition of Truth-Finding

I continue with the strongest theoretical factor which should tip the scales in favour of belief in free will, even if other things were equal. I should not advance this argument if there were no experience of agency, but given the experience of agency briefly described above, it can now take the centre of the stage.

On what grounds can the denier of free will ask us to believe in his conclusion? Not surely because it is *his*, but because he believes he has been adequately assessing the evidence – that certain evidence, regardless of his past predilections or present preferences, is determining his conclusion. But can this be if his feeling of freedom is no more than the fact that he faces the future without being aware of sources of constraint? Can he trust his conclusions – and can we – if he has not been free to *keep thinking*, to keep relating evidence to hypotheses, even when to do so went against his grain?

Any rational faith in the reflective life is baseless unless human beings can plough through difficulties, interpret data and develop hypotheses in the way which makes all the difference between rationalizing and reasoning. If thinking is going to be more than having ideas flit through one's mind, lighting up this emotion and that impulse; if thinking is to be the more orderly process of logically connecting ideas with each other, with the data, and with the problem to be solved, then there must be sufficient will-agency to initiate and continue the process of organizing varied data in accordance with the demands of experiential growing coherence.[1] C. I. Lewis says, we can trust neither ourselves nor others unless we believe that as persons we can develop the virtue of being 'willing to give as much weight to what the opposition may put in evidence as to what we advance ourselves'.[2]

Such conclusions have special relevance to the theory and practice of psychotherapy. Why should we, for example, trust

---

[1] For further discussion see my *Free Will, Responsibility and Grace*, New York, 1958, pp. 24–5.

[2] C. I. Lewis, *op. cit.*, p. 33.

Freud's conclusions if we cannot believe that he was able to free himself sufficiently from his own upbringing and his own hopes to develop hypotheses which illuminated *the data*? And unless any psychotherapist has the freedom to listen patiently to his client, to develop a particular theory about his client, relevant to the facts spread before him by the client, and not by his own theoretical predilections alone, on what rational grounds can the client trust his psychotherapist's conclusions?

Furthermore, what value is his therapy if the patient himself, armed with new insight, and freed from unnecessary ignorance and misinterpretations and 'blocks', still has no freedom to see situations *as they are*, but only as they will appear to him in the light of the strongest psychic forces prevailing in him as he emerges from the therapeutic analysis? Unless both therapist and client are sufficiently free from their pasts, *to* listen, *to* think, and then *to* act, and to do so in accordance with the situation as it unfolds before them in theory and practice, the therapeutic process is merely one of juxtaposing psychic forces, and not one of discovering either the truth or what is best for the patient.

(d) Will-Agency and Will-Power
A person who initiates an *approved* process (in our example, the act of thinking) invariably finds the path to success cluttered by many internal and external obstacles. To focus on the inner, these may be dispositions and habits much stronger than anticipated, and the person may find himself fighting a delaying action, a kind of moral Dunkirk. In a word, whatever free-agency a person has is never agency which operates (1) outside the basic unlearned capacities of the person, or (2) outside the particular engagement of such capacities in the more or less stable dispositions of the personality thus far developed.

For this reason, the changes in development owing to free-agency are not usually a matter of radical discontinuity with the past. A person, in will-agency, works to reorganize patterns of dispositions available to him in his total nature at a specific point of maturation and learning. He does not deploy something called 'will' in the place of emotive (or other) activities. In will-agency he may favour some developed skills and habits more than others; and he may initiate the process of developing new skills and habits. But the person does not put something called 'will' in the place of habit.

Will-agency, then, is the activity of the person operating to initiate new (or redirect or continue old) dispositions. The irritable individual becomes less irritable not simply because will-agency keeps him from it, but because he develops other attitudes which, by the alchemy of psychic process, discourage irritableness. Will-agency becomes a holding action, or an initiating action, at points where the approved goal has not enough support in the present dispositions of personality.

For any point of initiation or holding, there is no guarantee how far will-agency can go in achieving its objective. I can at a given moment control my anger from moving into action, but then suddenly discover that I can 'hold it in' no longer. Clearly I had will-agency with a certain amount of will-power, yet enough power in that situation to produce more than a delaying action. But there are times when much to my own surprise more headway is made against obstacles than I would have thought possible; more discontinuity with my past was possible than I realized.

The distinction (not separation) between will-agency and will-power reminds us that belief in free-will does not relieve us in concrete situations from deciding whether, and to what extent, a given action is free. This should dispel the concern of many that free will jeopardizes the stability of character and moral growth. We are asked: What is the use of teaching one's children to be honest if 'some arbitrary act of will' can destroy this habit by one stroke? The answer is that when such radical discontinuity is observed we must accept the fact in the context of that personality. Yet, as we know, even the most radical moral or religious conversion does not have easy going in changing the personality 'overnight'. The fear that will-agency could be capricious neglects the fact that will-agency always has the *power* open to it at a particular psychosomatic stage of development in a given environment.

This distinction between will-agency and will-power has relevance to the problem of fair assessment of moral responsibility, and especially where unconscious motives are involved. Thus John Hospers has written recently:

I am only saying that frequently persons we think responsible are not properly to be called so; we mistakenly think them responsible because we assume they are like those in whom no unconscious drive (toward this type of behaviour) is present, and that their behaviour can be changed by reasoning, exhorting, or threatening.[1]

Now, if the analysis above is right, since we never know *how much* will-power a person will have, we can never be certain *how much* responsibility is his. Moral judgment must always be cautious and tentative. Furthermore, the way in which we can seek to change a person will have to depend upon knowledge of the dynamics of his life. I never know whether an act that I am fairly free to do is one my neighbour can do equally freely, for I do not know enough about either his conscious or his unconscious pattern of motivation.

But does the addition of unconscious to conscious forces to the choice-matrix essentially change the way in which the individual feels his responsibility? Unless we dogmatically presuppose that the unconscious controls the conscious life, any person at *his* choice-points will still be faced with the question: What can I in this situation do to achieve my goal? He may never get to the end of the thinking process. He may get to the end of it and then find that he simply cannot, in action, overcome emotional disposition developed earlier. Nevertheless, he feels responsible for what is still open to him in his specific choice-matrix.

In other words, I grant that, in any present struggle, tensions and dispositions, whose fuses extend back into my childhood experiences, may explode their charges in my face. I cannot neglect such factors in my assessment of my own future, and certainly not in assessing the behaviour of others. But the introduction of underground psychic dynamics, complicating as it does the problem of assessment, does not alter the fact of responsibility. And while I may not be held responsible, or even hold myself responsible, for a given bit of behaviour, I may be to some extent responsible for the groundwork from which this present action emerged.

A criminal, a neurotic, or a saint is not made all at once or once for all. There are choice-points or junctures all along the road; new growth from within, new environmental demands from without, and at most points there is the opportunity to decide what a person shall now do about what is given to him. Just as the physically maimed still have choices to make all along their path, so the emotionally handicapped have difficult choices open to them, but open nevertheless within the context of their whole lives. At some point the battle can go on, if the person decides to battle.

[1] See *Determinism and Freedom*, 1958, p. 115.

II. THE NATURE OF MORAL OBLIGATION

(a) Obligation as Experienced

In the first part of this essay I avoided considering the nature of obligation. The experience of will-agency needed first to be described in its own right, and now its relation with obligation can be brought out. I begin with direct exposition about the experience of obligation.

I shall use the verb 'oughting' for the *erlebt* experience of obligation. Oughting, like willing, thinking, sensing, does not exist except as a focus or phase of the person. It is distinguished from *what I ought*, just as I distinguish thinking from thoughts – although, as there is no experience of thinking without thoughts, so there is no oughting without *oughts*.

I never experience oughting when I am convinced that there is nothing I can do about a situation. I have frequently been incorrect about whether I could alter a situation, but I never feel obligated to do what I think is impossible for me to do. I do not feel any obligation to fly, to walk on my hands, to change my pigmentation, though I feel obligation, despite uncertainties and risks, to take planes, to develop a good gait, to keep a healthy colour. Whenever some act is beyond my envisioned range of ability to control, I feel no obligation even to try to perform it.

The other side of this experiential shield is that when I am oughting, I never experience compulsion (must) to do anything about what it is that I feel obligated to. The word 'compulsion' must be used carefully here. There are three kinds of 'musts' or constraints I do not feel when I am oughting.

First, 'I ought' does not mean I must in the *logical* or near-logical sense of 'constraint'.

Second, when I feel *I ought* I do not feel the kind of constraint 'forced' upon me when I am thrown off-balance by a greater physical power. In such situations to say 'I am under compulsion' means 'I cannot escape the conditions imposed on me by a given form of existence once I am involved in that form'. Thus, if I am to think, I must note relationships; if I am *in* a moving automobile, I must move as it moves. Such 'compulsion' I call 'physical constraint'. When I feel I ought I may be aware of physical constraints, but to feel ought is not to feel such constraints.

Third, I ought, as felt, is not affective-conative constraint. Some would say that the experience of 'oughting' is reducible to strong affective-conative constraint. But when I experience an 'I ought', this experience *feels* different from the constraint I feel when, for example, 'I couldn't help being afraid'. Nor is it the kind of constraint that occurs when I find, for example, that no sooner have I put that melody I was singing 'out of my head' than I am humming it again.

If, when I feel I ought, the experience is not one of logical or physical or conative constraint, what is it?

When I feel I *ought*, I experience a unique kind of authority. It is not the authority of power or force, though, in a phrase of Butler's, it 'magisterially exerts itself'.[1] Bishop Butler further says: 'Had it strength, as it has right; had it power, as it has manifest authority, it would absolutely govern the world.'[2]

Kant, we also recall, urged that the moral law created respect in a person. In his analysis of respect, Kant points to a unique psychic tone in 'oughting'. 'Respect,' he says, 'is a feeling [that] differs specifically from all feelings . . . which may be referred either to inclination or fear . . . though . . . it has something analogous to both.'[3] Our feelings and inclinations, we may approve or even love, but moral obligation has an *imperative* quality that must be experienced to be understood. Along with Butler, Kant would urge that the power of obligation is neither fear nor love. Still it has 'authority'.

(b) Is the Experience of Obligation Cognitive?

Yet both Butler and Kant, and other intuitionistic ethicists, think this ought delivers some knowledge to us. To experience obligation was to be aware of some rational or non-rational value-datum or duty. The result historically is that the fate of the experience of obligation has been tied to theories about the nature of what I ought to do. When value-data have been conceived as irreducible and unlearned givens, then the person has been endowed with a 'moral consciousness' which was at once an *experience* of obligatoriness and a cognition of some duty, value, or moral principle. When, on the other hand, values have been conceived to be derived from desires and feelings as affected by the process of learning, the moral consciousness has been dethroned, and oughting has become a

---

[1] Butler, *Five Sermons*, New York, 1950, Section II.
[2] *Ibid.*, p. 41.
[3] Kant, *Fundamental Principles of the Metaphysics of Morals*, New York, 1949, p. 19.

by-product of acculturation. What some had considered *vox dei* or *vox mei*, now became the introjected *vox populi*.

But why should the experience of obligation rest upon a conclusion about the way in which values are cognized, or what values are cognized, or even what the final nature of value-experience is? It may be as Weiss, for example, holds, that there is 'an absolute 'ought to be' of which all other possibilities are fragments and specializations', and that it is of man's essence to sustain the absolute good as relevant to all that is.[1] But, the *prima facie* structure of obligation is independent of any particular theory of value-cognition. I must return to the experiential context in which obligation is felt to justify this view.

To state the conclusion first: my experience of obligation is to 'the best I know', whatever that best turns out to be. For, if I am correct so far, I feel obligation only in situations in which I believe there are alternatives I can do something about. But this is the *occasion* for my experience of obligation, not the *condition*. I do not feel obligation because there are alternatives, or to alternatives as such. Yet the moment I come to a decision that one alternative is better than another, at the moment I feel obligated to that 'better' alternative. I never feel obligated to do what I do not believe is the better alternative. This is an ineluctable psychological fact about human nature at choice-points, where some decision (for whatever reason) has been made about *what* is better.

I am urging, if you please, that the kind of condition obtains here psychologically which obtains when one gives assent to the understood conclusion in a logical situation. One cannot realize that a conclusion follows from certain premises without saying, intellectually, *yes*! So, if one is convinced that A is better than B, he cannot withhold the non-intellective unique response: 'I ought to do A.' This does not mean that he *must* do A, or that, if he does *will* A, he will succeed. It means: A *ought* to be done by me, as far as possible, whether I like to, or want to, or not.

A simple moral situation may clarify the psychological matrix of obligation. Let us assume that I am offered a chocolate sundae. (A) I want the sundae, but (B) I also want to lose weight. Assume also that (for whatever reasons) I decide that want B is better than want A. I immediately experience: 'I ought to do B.' I do not stop wanting the sundae, and it may be that I shall not be able to refuse

[1] Weiss, *Man's Freedom, op. cit.*, pp. 203 ff. And see *Modes of Being*, Carbondale, Ill., 1958, pp. 95 ff.

it. But as long as I believe B is better than A, I feel obligation to B.

Never, however trivial or critical the alternatives before me may be, do I feel obligated to what in that situation I believe to be less than the best. Oughting is not an unwavering cognition of the best, but it is an unwavering magnetic thrust authoritatively demanding that the best in all choice-situations be realized.

To conceptualize this unaltering cry for quality in the choice-situation, I therefore suggest: *I ought* means 'I ought to do the best I know'. One does not introspect and intuit 'I ought to do the best I know', but this is a generalization about the situations in which obligatoriness is felt.

Before passing, let us relate this view of obligation to competing views. On this view, for example, the contention of the ethical realist or intuitionist, that obligation is irreducible to desire, is upheld. But it is not embarrassed by the objection, levelled by opponents of intuitionism, that moral intuitions differ both in the life of the growing person and between persons. For oughting is not tied once and for all to any specific value-datum, but to what is deemed best in every choice-situation.

At the same time, our view accounts for the fact that our sense of obligation is no less resolute because we have changed our verdicts about the best. Thus, the person who moves from a non-pacifist position to that of a nuclear pacifist feels equally obligated to his new conviction. 'I ought to do the best I know' preserves the integrity of moral heroes, without minimizing their disagreement about moral issues.

In sum, the imperative to the best is absolute, whatever the best turns out to be. Obligatoriness does not depend on the will of God or of society, but it is a person's response to his decision that a given alternative is the best or better in the conceived situation. What the theistic absolutist, social relativist, naturalist, or emotivistic views of obligation never explain adequately is the imperative felt by the individual toward what *he* believes is the best even when it does jar with what is, or has been deemed to be, the will of God, the nature of man, or the cultural norm.

(c) Is Obligatoriness Acquired?

We must now face the contention that the feeling of obligation may well be the psychological residue of the accommodation of an individual to his culture. This matter has been discussed elsewhere,[1] but the brunt of my psychological objection to this view can be put in the form of a question. Can a million introjections of 'you must, if' into the life of the most suggestible child ever produce an iota of ought? Any theory of identification, introjection, or conditioning, whereby the demands of parents and society become the interiorized censor of a person who by definition has no feeling of obligation – any such theory explains the emotional constraint or release one feels when he has obeyed or discharged these fixed demands. But do such theories explain 'ought', with its peculiar psychic (non-must, non-want) tone? I am not denying that musts and external sanctions are interiorized, and that they form important constituents in personality. But I ask: By what psychological miracle or alchemy do such musts become not specific oughts, but oughting?

Our meaning will be clearer as we call attention to the emotional states which accompany oughting-experiences in contrast to must-experiences. For if I disobey the dictate of my interiorized conscience – assuming now that it became fixed in me without critical approval or disapproval – I may indeed experience the lurking anxiety that the interiorization was to avoid. But anxiety is not guilt. Feel the psychic tones of the two. The essential components in anxiety are fear and uncertainty in fusion. But when I feel guilty, do I feel anxious? Is the experience of guilt any blend of fear? For myself I can only say that the psychic distance between fear and guilt is so great that I wonder how acute thinkers could have confused the two and used the terms 'anxiety' and 'guilt' interchangeably. It is true that I can experience both guilt and anxiety together, but it is also true that I can experience anxiety without guilt, and guilt without anxiety!

For example: If I were condemned to prison or to death for an action which I did not do, or for one which I did but believed to be right, I would certainly feel anxiety. But I would not feel guilty. Social and legal disapproval would stir up many disturbing affective-conative states which would keep me reconsidering my grounds for what I felt to be right. But social disapproval is different from that gnawing feeling of guilt that, often far from tumultuous, grinds away and makes it hard for me to live with myself. When I decide I ought to do it, and then do not do what I can about it, there comes that feeling of having let myself down, whether I have

[1] See my 'A Reinterpretation of Moral Obligation,' in *Philosophy and Phenomenological Research* VI, 1945.

let others down or not. One may feel miserable, but not necessarily guilty, about the hurt he may have caused others. Moral guilt has an ache much different from the agony of anxiety. In sum, anxiety is not guilt; anxiety may stem from many internal affective-conative learned dispositions. Guilt springs alive the moment I do not try to do what I decided was best.

Conversely, 'moral approval' is not 'social approval', though it may be compresent with it. How often a man has the approval of even those he admires and yet does not feel that inner 'self-approval' which comes only when he has done what he thinks is right. There is one thing neither God nor man can give or take away, as Job so well knew – that feeling which comes when one knows he is doing all he can to realize what he believes to be right. The results for himself and for others may leave much to be desired. His may be the tortured spirit of one who knows that what he is doing is hurting loved ones who might suffer less, or not at all, if he ceased his own struggle for right. The path of duty is a self-*righteousness* that can always be accused of *self*-righteousness.

III. CONCLUSIONS

It is now time for us to pull together the strands which compose the essential moral structure of the person. Starting where we have finished, we may see that structure revealed as a person confronts a situation in which, of wants (or values) seen to be conflicting, he decides that A is better than B (according to whatever theory of value he holds). The moment he decides that A is better than B, he feels the obligation to do A. B may have social approval and even be the alternative to which his own personality up to this point has been predisposed. The making of the decision and the enacting of it involves initiatory will-agency, which may or may not have the power needed to make the proper changes.

Let us say, for example, that the religious convictions of one's childhood and of the family circle are at stake. His parents will be bitterly disappointed if he breaks with his past, and many deep affections will be threatened. So strong is the pull of the past upon him, and so much does he hate to have his parents hurt, that he has a difficult time thinking straight, and holding himself to the careful sifting of relevant factors. At no point is he sure that he is correct, but, we assume, he believes that a reasoned decision, however incomplete, is better than any other. Hence, he feels the obligation to think, and wills to think and continue thinking despite the affective-conative dispositions that make it difficult to assess the evidence before him. If he stops thinking, if he knowingly allows his conclusion to be improperly influenced by his predispositions, he will feel guilty, though snug in his sense of parental approval. If he wills to think, he will need to do battle with the anxieties that well up within him.

Let us assume that his will-agency does find the power to think through to an intellectual verdict contrary to that of his childhood. Shall he tell his parents, shall he affiliate with a church closest to his present convictions, shall he take the new moral stances publicly, and shall he now start the reconstruction of habits and building of virtues hitherto foreign to him? If he believes that all these actions are to any extent within his power and that they are consistent with the new value-pattern now accepted, he feels obligated to act; there can be no other 'line of duty'.

The future is indeed 'open' to him, but the experience he feels, as he begins to will the best he knows, is one of generating, or bringing into being. In this instance his oughting and his willing are in harmony. He does not know whether his will-agency does indeed have the power, given the configuration of conflicting forces within and the patterns of power that will emerge as he proceeds, but he knows that he ought to will the best, as far as possible. There will be disappointment and sorrow as some cherished goods must go, and there will be the torture that since he may not be right, he perhaps might hurt others. But there will be also, in the midst of this tumult and anxiety, that sense of moral approval that comes only to those who will the best they know as far as is possible to them. He may not in fact have the will-power that he had hoped he had, and he will now experience inner disappointment. Yet even in the midst of such failure, having lost a moral battle, he will feel *blessed*, though not content or happy.

Thus reflective thinking, willing, and obligation always stand at the broken and ragged edges of the moral battle-line in the development of personality. The person coming to reflect on givens, native and acquired, in his life, finds that he does not know how far he can go both in thinking and in conscientious action. But the moral magnetic needle keeps pointing to the best, though it alone can move him not. At this point the person wills to effectuate the best; and his only sense of achievement may come in knowing that for him, if failure must come, it shall at least come here.

CHAPTER V

THE PERSON, OBLIGATION, AND VALUE

Obligation, I have proposed, is neither the voice of God, nor the voice of society, nor the voice of a person's basic needs and abilities as re-formed in his personality. 'Oughting' is that imperative to the best which a person experiences at choice point, once he reflects on the alternatives he believes are open to him. The experience of obligation is neither a cognition of some irreducible value-data, or *prima facie*, or *a priori* obligations; nor is it an emotive response symptomatic of the person's affective-conative preferences.

'Oughting' has its own magisterial authority, as Bishop Butler said. Yet Butler and the cognitivists, or ethical realists, do not take into account adequately the fact that 'cognitions' of the best do change while obligation to the best does not. Nor do they adequately see that needs and wants, learned and acquired, are the raw material for choice and do influence the range of actual preferences in the person's moral horizon. In the present chapter, I indicate how the authority of oughting is related to the person's decisions about what he ought to become as he analyses the welter of claims and counter-claims that confront him as a caring person.

The Personalist, Vol. 40 (Spring, 1959), 141–151.

It is the theme of this paper that a more adequate account of moral obligation and value may be given if the experiences of obligation and of value are seen as distinct, though complementary, phases within the matrix of personal self-experience. It is to be suggested that 'obligatoriness' is not an attribute of any value-object *per se*, but a *sui generis* quality of personal experience. Value-experiences, on the other hand, become norms for persons, not because they are non-natural, but because, critically selected, they become guides to creative fulfilment. On such a view the emphasis of the deontologists on irreducible obligatoriness is granted, but is re-located as a unique quality of personal non-cognitive experiencing in choice situations. At the same time, value may be defined in terms of experienced preference, or preferred experience, and located in the person as he interacts with the environment. These suggestions may be briefly amplified as follows:

1. Whatever final metaphysical status is attributed to a person – whether, for example, he be a composition of electrical charges from which conscious states emerge, whether he be a focus or centre of unconditional Being or of an Absolute Spirit, whether he be a 'substance' created with delegated spontaneity by God – his existence as a knowing-agent is presupposed in hypothesizing any theory about his metaphysical status. Human knowing cannot go on – that is, sense-data cannot be interpreted, logical and mathematical relations clarified, a perceptual world organized, comparisons and contrasts drawn, conceptions entertained, and experiences evaluated – unless remembering and constant present undergoing or experien*cing* are inseparate aspects of the knowing process (H. H. Price, Bowne, Brightman, Tennant). Thus, to be a person is, minimally, to be an active-timebinding unity of experiencing. Experiencing is used here to embrace that kind of *durée* or process which can be stipulatively or ostensively defined as a *unitas multiplex* (W. Stern) or sensing, remembering, thinking, feeling, willing, wanting, and, as we shall see, oughting. It is a person who develops theories about himself upon the basis – of what else but experiencing? Finally, if a person knows that, wherever there is cognitive experiencing, what goes on is a mental process of connecting and relating; if he knows that this process is distinguishable from sensing, and that both thinking and sensing are distinguishable from emotive and wanting processes, it is because, as experienced, these activities have qualitatively different psychic tones – for want of better words! Yet, so far as we know, each experiential process is embedded inextricably in the unified matrix of the kind we call a person. This largely phenomenological description of personal experience must suffice as a background for the analysis of moral obligation and value.

2. Among my experiences as a person I note a peculiar experience of obligation. This experience has been described in different ways and in terms which seem not to do justice to the phenomenology of the experience. The experience of obligation has suffered by being interpreted, rather than described, in its own experienc*ed* light. For example, Freudians, materialists, naturalists, and others

have interpreted it in the context of what it might be expected to be if the remainder of their theories of human nature were to dictate. In their hands the experience 'I ought' becomes, generally speaking, a consolidated complex of desires, especially of fear and approval, conditioned in a cultural milieu to specific or general permissions and prohibitions. On such views, however, the experience of obligatoriness, of *oughting*, if I may coin the appropriate verb, turns out, on analysis, to be totally explained by understanding what pressures in each case were brought to form this monitor or censor.

Many theists (Butler, Kant, J. Baillie, A. C. Garnett), on the other hand, have interpreted the experience of obligation as ultimately a moral cognition of God's norms for men. On either 'naturalistic' or theistic views, the experience of oughting ends up as the experience in man of specific or general imperatives originating beyond the individual experient's nature.

But do not such accounts, though logically possible as theories, run contrary to what a person actually feels when he experiences obligation? I am not denying that conditioning is present in the total personality, nor am I denying the possibility of God's existence and effects in man's life. But, to limit myself here to the naturalistic social theory of obligation, I must question whether ought, as experienced, is essentially the introjection of social pressures and approvals. There is nothing coercive, or permissive, in a strict sense, in the experience of felt obligation. The different degrees of psychological compulsion I may feel are not that which is present in oughting as such. I can never fairly substitute the words 'I must', or 'I may', 'I fear', 'I am anxious', as a description of what takes place when I feel 'I ought'.

Again, *prima facie*, when 'I ought' is felt, social disapproval or approval may accompany it, together with felt desires, fears, and anxieties. But, *prima facie*, oughting is not felt as what is required by pressures of desire from within or demands from others. For it itself is not felt as a conative urge. ('I want'), or as compulsion ('I must'). *Oughting* has its own peculiar tone, its own kind of appeal or urgency, within the context of wants, fears, and feeling-emotive tensions. When I say, 'I ought to do X', the X may be what others approve or disapprove, but I never feel I *ought* in connection with X unless I believe that what others approve or disapprove is the best standard for me also. Let the reader ask himself: 'Do I feel "I ought" about a command or demand which

I myself in no sense approve? On the other hand, if the command or demand is deemed by me to be the best possible in this situation, or most consistent with what I believe to be the best, do I not feel *I ought* in connection with it, even if, in fact, I then fail to will it?' In brief, the suggestion here is that the experience of obligation is felt about any alternative or option approved by the person (whatever his criterion of the good or the best may be).

We cannot consider here the genesis of the experience, but must remind ourselves that *prima facie* facts must be explained by genetic psychology and must not be explained away. It is such a far cry from 'I must', or 'I want', to 'I ought', that this writer would hold that the experience of obligation is as primitive and irreducible as the experience of wanting or thinking, and that it appears in the maturing person at that point when he begins to contemplate and compare alternatives. Oughting seems clearly to be present in adult experience when a choice-point is confronted, and when the person judges which alternative is best. The moment he decides which alternative is best, he feels: I ought to do it. Thus we may conceptualize the experience of oughting in the words, 'I ought to do the best I know'.

Persons may differ, owing to innate sensitivity or perceptivity, owing to differences in personal learning and cultural influences, owing to whatever the factors may turn out to be which influence the final decision as to what is best. But is there ever a choice situation in which a person does not feel obligated to the best as he sees it? A theory of value-experience is, to be sure, crucial in the final decision about what is best, but the contention here is twofold: (*a*) that whatever the theory of the value-object or objective by which one determines the best, at choice-points a persistent, continuous obligation to the conceived best is felt by the person. This is as much a part of his unlearned nature as thinking is, though neither is present at birth. Furthermore, whatever the structure of value, or of the universe may be – whether, for example, there be a good God or not – 'I ought to do the best I know'. As a person grows and reflects, the meaning of 'the best' may change, but the inner imperative to the best possible is unwavering. This is not one ought among other *prima facie* oughts (W. D. Ross), but the underlying and common thrust of every other selected best or specific 'ought to do'. (*b*) This experience of obligation, as such, cannot be conceived as a by-product of the pressures of society, of the world, or of the rest of a person's nature upon him. The 'ought to will the best I know' is as irreducible at the level of choice as, say, the 'will to live' is at the level of sheer psychobiological conation.

Thus we are simply not describing the personal structure of experience adequately without adding such 'oughting' to the distinguishable list of human capacities. What is considered best may vary with maturity and learning, just as the thoughts one thinks vary; 'oughting to do the best' is as unwavering as a magnetic needle toward the best in choice situations, even though it must await decision rather than itself assert some intuition of the best.

This account of the uniqueness of obligation may be buttressed by calling attention to what a person feels when he obeys his 'ought to the best' despite the fact that stern social reprisals or personal disappointments ensue! He may indeed feel fear and anxiety because of what may happen to him, yet he still can 'look himself in the mirror', as we say, and feel what, for want of other words, we may call moral approval. The surgeon who has done his very best to save a patient when all was in vain, feels miserable indeed. But he feels, together with disappointment, a 'moral approval'. The prophet may feel anxiety, but he still feels, and is exalted by, the unique moral approval of: 'I can do no other.'

What happens on the other hand, if a person does not will his chosen ought-objective? He may feel social approval, and he may feel that other ends are now secure – but he also feels moral guilt. To feel guilty is not to feel anxiety (though one may accompany the other), and it is anomalous that so much psychology identifies the two. But there is, to say the least, a component of fear in anxiety which is never present in guilt as such. Anxiety may be produced by social pressure, but guilt never. A professor may feel anxious lest he lose his position owing to the publication of his investigations, but does he feel guilty if he believes that publication is for the best? To take the surgeon again. If his patient gets well despite an avoidable surgical error, he may not feel the pointing finger of social disapproval. But on coolly contemplating his avoidable actions, he will feel guilt – and may try to wipe these feelings away by rationalization. For such reasons, then, we may contend that moral approval and moral guilt are misconstrued if reduced, respectively, to social approval and socially conditioned anxiety.

It will be noted that this analysis of obligation so far could be classified as agreeing with deontologists like Ross, against utilitarian, 'emotivist', Freudian, and many psychosociological reductions of personal-social interaction. But it seems to me that deontologists, while properly insisting on obligations as an impregnable 'given' in human experience, have erred, together with moral intuitionists like Butler or Hartmann. They have committed the cognitive fallacy in regard to the experience of obligation. For 'oughting' is no more a cognitive experience than are 'wanting' or logical thinking as such. The 'object' of oughting is its 'objective' (the best), which may vary from situation to situation in specific content, as a person decides what value is the best. The 'ought' imperative to 'the best I know' is absolute and unwavering. But there are no specific values, or 'rights' which are found by its nature to be 'the best', apart from learning or moral experimentation. Even W. D. Ross grants this basic thesis by saying that his special obligations are *prima facie* only, and in need of further criticism; and he gives greater authority to the obligation to optimize the good than to his other special obligations. At any rate, as Mandelbaum has reminded the deontologists, 'the phenomenon of obligation is not merely a matter of action-accordingly-to-rule'.[1]

3. How, then, on this view does one come to know what values constitute the best? The suggestion to be made is indebted to nonintuitionists in value-theory – and especially Dewey, R. B. Perry, F. R. Tennant, and E. S. Brightman. Here the emphasis is placed on the fact that what is deemed the best value depends on the

[1] M. Mandelbaum, *The Phenomenology of Moral Experience*, Glencoe, Ill.: The Free Press, 1955, p. 52. I am glad to note many parallel developments to basic contentions in this paper in Mandelbaum's excellent and original treatment. Thus the view of obligation here has much in common with Mandelbaum's, though there is more 'perceptual intuitionism' in his conception of 'the fitting' than there is here in the 'ought to the best'. I would contend that the 'fitting' which he makes the object of obligation consists of a judgment, 'This is more fitting than that', in the phenomenological situation confronting the deciding person. There is a tendency in Mandelbaum's thought to assimilate the moral situation of choice to the aesthetic situation or 'Gestalt' in which there is 'demand' without choice. Moral obligation, as I see it, presupposes not merely an apprehended relation of fittingness, but the reflective decision that one line of action will be more 'fitting' than any other in the totally envisioned situation (though this would seem to be granted in some passages) (cf. pp. 69–70, 81). Nor am I clear that it is the condition of a feeling of obligation that the value (objective) 'must appear as independent of our inclinations or desires' (p. 85). What I experience as the 'condition of obligation' is simply that one alternative, be it desired or anything else, is deemed better than any other; but 'oughting' is not geared even as a *prima facie* tendency (Ross) to a specific right, or to any specific perception of what is fitting.

careful organization and systematic criticism of actual value-under-
going on the part of persons, with a view to discovering which ideal
of personality and society will protect the widest range and the
highest quality of values open to man as he interacts with his total
environment. In a word, 'the best' is not some one quality or value
independent of any enjoyed experience of desire or interest, nor is
it definable *a priori* or independently of *experienced* and *experience-
able* values. In every choice situation, 'the best' refers to some
desired experience or experiences, critically conceived (after comparison with other desired experiences, and after assessment of
foreseeable consequences), to the total value-complex of which
persons are deemed capable. Once a desired experience is judged
'the best' in a given situation, it immediately becomes the object of
obligation, until some other alternative takes its place. Thus, once
more, obligation to the best is invariable and unwavering, but
what constitutes the best may vary as the person's insight into
values and their conditions grows.

To explicate: 'Value', to begin with, is the name for any desired
human experience; 'disvalue' for any undesired or unwanted
human experience. In this sense, there are no values or disvalues
of any kind without persons undergoing experiences which are then
deemed wanted or unwanted. As experienced, the 'value' is always
at least a wanted state of a person undergoing the experience. The
wanting does not have to precede the experiencing, for a person
often finds himself experiencing a state which he then wants to
continue or discontinue. The 'problem of value' in a given life is
always the problem of deciding which of desired states (or undesired states) is to be chosen when there is a conflict between the
human states desired or undesired. In view of the fact that persons
grow and situations change, no assessment of value-experience is
intrinsically beyond question – no matter how convinced, psychologically, a person may be about the asserted *prima facie* value of
'fittingness' of any experience. It is more cautious to say that we
all begin with *prima facie* value-claims, and that the problem is to
decide which 'claims' are trustworthy.

What does the word trustworthy mean in a value-situation?
Where are the controls to be sought? Within the person? Outside
the person? The answer involves both. First, a person has a fundamental structure common to other persons, together with differences which constitute him a unique person among other unique
persons. No person knows exactly what he is and what he can

become. Second, every person interacts with other persons in a non-human world, whose exact nature is not exactly known. Nevertheless, within his own nature he discovers more dependable 'structures' or tendencies and abilities which he himself cannot constitute or create as such, though they may be amenable to change within hard-to-define limits. And he finds himself among other persons who bring him up amid the values which they believe to be trustworthy for their natures in the world as they conceive it.

Two considerations emerge as crucial to an adequate theory of human valuation. (a) While human valuations are aspects of human experience, they represent one's own interaction, on the basis of one's own given ability and sensitivity, with value-schemes and natures of other persons in this kind of not-man-made world. (b) A value-claim, accordingly, is a joint-product, for whatever its final worth, of the total nature of the person, as developed to a given point, and of the total nature of the nurturant environment, as it impinges upon him.

Put differently: In making a value-claim, a person is making a claim about what he believes at least possible to human experience in a given social situation in a given world up to this time. In claiming certain experiences to be valuable for him, he is also, until he is brought up short by brute experience and reflection, suggesting that this experience is valuable for others also. The stress here is on the fact that in saying that values are related to persons and their structure and growth-potential, we are not asserting that values are relative to the individual in the sense that no standards at all can be found for judging which value-claims are to be preferred to which other value-claims. For the controls are fixed (but not all, or finally, known) within the potentialities of human nature for wide varieties of value-experience and within the possibilities allowed to human experience by the non-human world.[1]

Value-experience, then, is indeed man-made in the sense that man can 'make' or 'unmake' any value-experience (and its consequences) as he wants. The biological, psychic, and spiritual potentialities in his nature do not operate helter-skelter in their growth and fulfilment; nor are they fulfilled without the encouragement, discouragement, or nurturance and sustenance, by the actualities and possibilities open to human nature in the world

---

[1] I am glad to note at this point and at others, agreement in B. Blanshard's Howison Lecture, *The Impasse in Ethics and a Way Out* (Berkeley, University of California Press, 1954).

within which man lives. It is this world which 'allows' that vast experiences which are human responses to it. It is this world which constitutes a realm of value-eligibility and non-eligibility, for it demands responses adequate to its nature. Value-claims are man-made, but neither man nor the total environment is by any means totally man-made.

To come back, then, to the problem of value-selection. Assessment of value-claims is forced by the plethora of possible value-claims and the actual conflicts which ensue if certain values are pursued and not others. By what are we, or can we be, guided in value-selection? By the initial *prima facie* quality of a value-experience, by the sequences and consequences found as a result of actual human experimentation in value-realization, by the interrrelation of value-experiences with each other, and by as careful an assessment as we can make of what further value-experience may still be possible if certain selections and not others are made. Each of these considerations involves us in making 'factual' statements about what is happening, has happened, and may happen to human beings, given their nature, as so far known, in the kind of universe, as so far understood, responded to, and appreciated. The resulting criticized 'real' values are statements of what is most coherently believed to be possible in the light of what has been possible to persons in this kind of world!

What we actually do as we proceed to criticize value-claims is to take each value-claim and criticize it by other claims of our own and in relation to the claims of others. We judge each by its supportive, enhancing, or undermining relation to other value-claims.

The verification of a value-judgment (whether it refers to biological, social, intellectual, aesthetic, or religious value-claims), consists in understanding its relation to other value-experiences and their probable relation to the developing potentialities of human nature in the total environment. 'The best', concretely defined, will, accordingly, consist of some interrelated system of value-experiences deemed to protect creative growth in value-realization open to persons in this kind of world. Thus, any theory of 'the best' is also a theory of what persons can and ought to be in this kind of universe.

4. To suggest the outcome of these brief reflections: The obligation is being experienced when the person is confronted by a choice-situation in which wanted (and unwanted) experiences are in competition. The total situation, in minimal terms, may be

characterized thus: I want A, but I also want B (and possibly other conflicting wants). I cannot have both. As I reflect upon these varied value-claims in the light of all I know about myself and others in the world as I conceive it, as I reflect upon the quality and the foreseeable consequences of these value-claims, I decide (let us assume) that A is better than B. As soon as the judgment is made, I feel: I ought to will A and not B. If I will A and find unforeseen disagreeable consequences and disapprovals, I am disappointed and even anxious, but I do not feel guilty. If I will B (less than the best I know), I may find unforeseen good consequences and approvals which gratify me, but I feel guilty. But always my choice of the best is guided by growing knowledge of the optimum-maximum range of values which for ever constitute the obligatory, and of human development. A person is morally good to the extent that he consistently wills the best he knows. But he can be morally good without being happy or 'fulfilled' (*summum bonum*). He approaches fulfilment in so far as he creatively realizes and coherently orchestrates those values which bring the total potential of his human nature into creative interaction with the activities, achievements, and possibilities of other human beings and of the total environment. Thus, both the moral good and the *summum bonum* involve creative growth of persons, and the kind of good which they can achieve is a fact to be properly assessed in any adequate theory of the universe.

The limitations of space forbid a consideration of the metaphysics of value and of the relation of values to God – indeed, too much of what has been said must sound too dogmatic, though the hope is that it will be taken as programmatic. But until we know what we mean by the word 'good' and what the ideal of human existence is, we cannot think clearly about the existence and, especially, the goodness of God. On the other hand, as the writer has suggested elsewhere, if knowledge-seeking and finding, if creative moral fulfilment in compassionate love and forgiveness, if the poignant joys and 'peak-experiences' open to us in aesthetic and religious experiences are to be taken as any part of the evidence for an adequate metaphysics, then we may indeed find in the very possibility that persons can enjoy and incarnate such values grounds for reasonable faith in the goodness of God.[1]

[1] See the author's 'Can the Goodness of God be Empirically Grounded?' in *The Journal of Bible and Religion*, Volume 25, April 1957, pp. 99–105.

CHAPTER VI

IS THERE AN IDEAL OF PERSONALITY?

Plato in his ideal of justice as the goal of person and society, and Aristotle in his analysis of the moral and non-moral ingredients in happiness, set out basic directions in an ideal of personality. The Judeo-Christian and other religious traditions often seem more intent on analysing what it is that God requires of man. They find little ground for hope in man's own nature independent of the power available to it in God's grace.

Some philosophers, who have been unable to accept the religious consciousness as an independent and self-sufficient way of knowing, have sought to establish the authority of man's ideals in the experience of autonomous obligation. Psychologists, making a new start on frankly naturalistic foundations, have considered such a view unscientific. But they have largely disregarded or neglected both the experience of God or the authority of an irreducible moral sense.

Nevertheless, in their search for natural roots for mental health and 'productive' personalities, they have been close to the Platonic and Aristotelian orientation, although they have substituted 'scientific' reasons for 'reason' as Plato and Aristotle conceived it. They have, to be sure, been far from agreement on the natural sources of good and evil, as revealed in their widely differing views of motivation and emotion. Nevertheless, this has not dampened their increasing interest in the traits and orientations of a healthy personality, or their assurance that an ideal is to be found that can guide growth in personality and the formation of social and political theory. It is in this context that the following proposal is made.

A paper on the ideal of personality belongs in the middle of a treatise on ethics or on the philosophy of education, for it presupposes the answer to other critical questions. Plato's *Republic* remains the classic example of this fact. As Plato saw, without some conception of the dynamics of human nature and society, and of man's possible relation to the structure of the universe, discussion about the ideal of personality and the aims of education can be irrelevant to the human situation. Irrelevance to the individual and social concerns of man in this kind of world is the one mistake that ethics and education must avoid at all costs. What man can become and what he ought to become – these are the magnetic questions in ethics, each pulling relevant data to themselves and each posing new fields of enquiry for the ethicist and the educator. Hence, before turning to the considerations of the ideal of personality, we must consider briefly three preliminary questions related to this search for an ideal, questions to which my own orientation needs to be clear.[1]

I. OBLIGATION IN HUMAN EXPERIENCE

The first question is: Why ought I to choose one ideal rather than another?

A human being is always partly satisfied and partly dissatisfied. Some of his needs or wants are gratified, but he is also 'in want'; he is always desiring something else, if no more than a change. But a man does not simply experience need or desire; he makes judgments about his needs and desires, judgments that are accompanied by feeling some *ought* or *ought not* about their realization. We must not let any specific theory either about the ought or about human wants, 'to' blind us to, or allow us to oversimplify this complex situation in which a human being usually finds himself.

In the simplest terms, we can say that what a man is and what he wants is always challenged by what he feels he ought to be, do, or want. We cannot disregard either what man is, or what man ought to be, and still claim that we are dealing with concrete human beings. In a word, the ought is the ought *of* man and *for* man and not the ought of some dog or some angel; what *man* ought to do can only make claims on what man is and can become. I am about to propose an ideal of personality which all men ought to realize as soon as possible, and I shall try to show that this ideal is rooted in a critical analysis and synthesis of the value-experiences persons have undergone and, as far as we know, can experience if, as I shall argue, they are to actualize their full potential.

[1] The actual tracing of the pattern of values in the ideal of personality begins with Section III below. Some readers may prefer to begin there.

But I may be asked: Why ought I to realize my full potential, as opposed to a partial potential? What is it about your ideal of personality that ought to have a hold on me? Or, more generally, Why ought I to choose any one ideal in preference to any other?

I reply: Because part of what it means for you to be a person is to experience *obligation* (not compulsion) to choose what *you* think is best. As a human being, I suggest, you do not simply feel wants and desires. When you, at some choice-point, reflect on the presumable choices before you, do you ever say: I ought to choose X rather than Y, if you believe that X is not better than Y? It is Y, that choice which seems to you to offer the closest approximation to the best, that immediately calls for your allegiance. If you later change your mind, and, and think that X and not Y is in fact the closest approximation to the best, you find yourself *oughting* X and no longer *oughting* Y. Indeed, you are asking me to defend what I suggest is the ideal of personality because you are in the grip of some ideal of truth you acknowledge. You believe you ought to accept the best theory possible, as you see it; and you do so because you believe you *ought* to think and choose the best you know.

Elsewhere I have discussed the nature of obligation at some length,[1] but here I may summarize by saying that *oughting* does not develop out of some *is*, human or divine. *Oughting* is a kind of experience – imperative experience, not affective-conative, not volitional experience – that human beings undergo along with sensory, conative, reflective, and appreciative experiences. *Ought*, in other words, is not an adjective intrinsic to some value that is presumably irreducible to desire or want. Again, a value is not obligatory merely because it is the will of God, or the will of my conqueror, or of my society. *Ought* is not a quality of any value *as* such. *Ought* is an abstraction from *oughting*, a quality of human experience, an activity persons undergo in relation to those experiences which they claim to be better than others (that is, to be 'the best' according to some criterion they discover in their experiences of themselves, and with each other, in this kind of a world).

That is, on this view the 'is-ought' issue is 'resolved' by locating the imperative (ought) not in some experienc*ed* values or *cognized*

---

[1] See Peter A. Bertocci and Richard M. Millard *Personality and the Good*, New York: D. McKay and Co., 1963, Chapter 9. In this book, which we have called an essay in psycho-ethics, there is more elaborate discussion of what is suggested in this paper. See also Peter A. Bertocci, 'The Moral Structure of the Person', *Review of Metaphysics*, Volume 14, March 1961, 369–88.

value, but in the matrix of personal being. *Oughting* is a kind of experienc*ing* or activity, along with think*ing*, want*ing*, sens*ing*, will*ing*, appreciat*ing*. It differs from them by being that activity which, irreducible to any of them, 'gives' the person the feeling of obligation, or an imperative *Erlebnis*. When expressed in words, that *Erlebnis* is translatable into: I ought to do the best I know (in a choice-situation). *Ought* attaches to some value, to some preference, because it is judged to be the best by a person who experiences oughting, the imperative to the best. In other words, I find inadequate both the view that *oughting* is either the derivative of wanting or thinking, and the view that some specific obligation (I ought to be just!) is obligatory simply because it is the introjection of social norms or *vox populi*, or *vox dei*.

Much more, of course, needs to be said to defend such a position, but in this context a specific answer emerges to the question: Why *ought* I to realize *my full* potential if, for example, I now do not *want* to? The answer is: If you can be convinced or convince yourself that it is best to realize full rather than partial potential, then you will find yourself feeling that *you ought to do so*. Why? Because you are *you*. Because this *is* your response to your own choice-situations. 'You ought', is an ought and not a *must*; you are not compelled to do what *you* feel *obligation to* as the best, but you cannot deny (I should argue) that you do feel obligation when you reflectively say: This alternative is better than that. Again, I cannot change your feeling of oughting, but, should I be able to persuade you as to what the best is, I shall find that you too feel obligation to the ideal or to the best in the total situation as we see it. Neither of us may will as we ought, for we are free not to, but this does not change our feeling of ought to the best. Oughting has authority, but not power in itself.

One further note may help to confirm this contention that 'oughting to the best in a choice-situation' is universal. If you disagree with my *ought*, that is, this *present* ought, you do so because you feel that this *ought* is not the best (toward which you feel obligation); you are choosing in accordance with your felt imperative to the best. We both always fly from one ought to the another on the wings of 'oughting the best I know'. Hence, in answer to the original question: Why ought you, or I, to choose any particular value? The answer is: Because we are the kind of beings that we are, feeling inevitably an imperative to the best as we know it.

The second preliminary question is: Why try to articulate an ideal of personality?

One preliminary comment may help. While they have not been using these words, many psychologists have, for reasons we need not pursue here, found themselves urging that persons ought to be 'integrated', 'mature', 'healthy', or that they ought to gain insight into themselves, face reality, be creative, be loving, live authentically. But when we ask: Exactly what do these 'injunctions' mean, that is, where do we go from *here*, we are left high and dry. Or – to take a philosophic moralist by whom I have been much influenced – Immanuel Kant tells us on good grounds, I think, to treat persons as ends in themselves and never as means only. But what does it mean to respect personality in myself and in others? Surely I cannot do this without guiding myself by some ideal of what a personality ought to become (because it can so become).

The same concern applies to the injunction of John Dewey: Be intelligent! Be democratic! – injunctions that have been so influential in guiding educational philosophy. I still ask: What kind of a human being am I aiming for when I am intelligent, when I am democratic?

Again, in respected circles of Christian ethics, I am told that the ultimate good is to love God and my neighbour as myself, that I am to go to my neighbour's side. But what do I do when I get there? I must guide myself, must I not, by some ideal of what my neighbour can be and ought to be, as I see him?

To generalize: in so much ethical, psychological, and religious thought we have become so fearful lest we become 'casuistic', 'moralistic', 'impositionistic', that if we ask what I wish to ask: 'What kind of personalities are we trying to produce?' we are left with generalities that are not, I should say, relevant enough; we are left with 'ideals' that actually have guiding power simply because they do presuppose some hidden conception of the ideal person, or at least of what evils we must avoid. Alas, such general injunctions have also left a vacuum that was all too readily filled by adherence to some socially accepted code when it came to specifics.

There are serious hazards in the way of my journey back to, but not restricted to, the Platonic and Aristotelian search for an ideal of the kind of personalities human beings *ought* to develop, and which can help to guide our thinking about an ideal society. A philosophy of education seems to me ultimately irrelevant without some such goal.

The third preliminary question involves another far-reaching question in philosophy of personality: Can we define human needs in abstraction from value-claims?

A questionable and sometimes unwitting assumption is often made by psychologists of personality, clinical and otherwise. The motivational *givens* of personality are described without reference to the value-experience of persons, on the assumption that knowledge of basic needs and interests should guide theorizing about the nature of the good for man. In an adequate psycho-ethics, there can be no adequate theory of value that disregards or miscontrues both underlying and important acquired needs or motives of men. The contention here is that if we are to avoid reducing human needs to presumably overarching and overriding implacable biological needs, or to infantile stages of human life, it is necessary to guide one's analysis of need-structures by keeping value-structures themselves in mind. Furthermore, values cannot be selected or guided in accordance with a theoretical need-theory or motivational theory alone. For how do we know that values are simple derivatives of a need-theory unless we also carefully inspect the *varied dimensions of human value* on their terms. Values, in other words, are not addenda to a need-theory. On the contrary, values as experienced may provide important guidelines or clues to basic needs. The ends of human life may throw light back on the beginnings. In sum: we can be satisfied with nothing less than a sensitive interrelating of needs to each other, to abilities and to environmental demands and opportunities.

In these three preliminary questions we are surrounded by many thorny problems. But our orientation may now be clear. An adequate psycho-ethics needs to be aware of both beginnings and fruitions as the operative conception of man itself is further scrutinized. Neither ethics nor a philosophy of personality must be regarded, even unwittingly, as an adjunct either to materialistic, naturalistic, or to a theological psychology of personality. Our data must remain the variety of values human beings experience in their total situation. In a word, since a theory of ethical value and a philosophy of education is a theory of what human beings can and ought to become in the world as they conceive it, we must accept the task of defining our final view of man and of analysing value-experience on the way to discovering whether any pattern of values constitutes at least the core of an ideal personality.

II. EVALUATING VALUES

A value is always an experience of a person: 'value' is a term used when a person refers to an *experience he wants* ('disvalue' to an experience he does not want). What is valued (or disvalued) is always the experience, the experience of eating a pear, the experience of hearing (experien*cing*) Bach, the experience of friendliness. 'Value' and 'disvalue', in other words, refer to some personal undergoing, to some personal *Erlebnis*; no person, no values or disvalues.

The experiencing of value, however, is not the evaluation of the experiencing. When we *evaluate* we are analysing and relating immediate value-experiences to each other. Furthermore, in human experience we never start in a value-vacuum, from zero value-experience. We do not begin evaluating by some point of reference beyond the experiences themselves. Evaluating finds us already predisposed toward some values and value-patterns. Before we start reflecting about value-experience, before we start purposeful evaluation, our psycho-physiological natures have already been in the business of reaching for, preserving, and avoiding some experiences.

Accordingly, we do not, when we evaluate, create the value-experiencings; we ask questions about them from within our experiences simply because we find that the value-experiencings have different qualities, that they conflict with each other, or converge with each other. Thus, when we evaluate we grade value-experiences in relation to each other, not only in terms of their felt-qualities, or patterns of felt-qualities, but in relation to their mutual support or non-support of each other. For example, a man may enjoy the quality of Camels-smoking, and the sociality of smoking with other persons. Let us assume, on the one hand, that he now comes to enjoy the quality 'smoking-a-cool-cigarette' without decreasing the sociability, although he still prefers Camels. On the other hand, he finds that he does not enjoy the image of himself as a chain-smoker, since he abhors the possibility of cancer. Should another cigarette be marketed that does not yield the same immediate quality of enjoyment (for instance, does not taste so good) but preserves health, he may switch from Camels. His analysis, note, is of actual experiences and of foreseeable consequences for further immediate experiences of value.

The further point to note here, however, is that grading value-experiences, or evaluating them, forces the person to move beyond the experiences themselves to equally obstinate facts about his physiological and psychological nature in relation to what creates these value-and-disvalue-experiences – in this case, taste, sociality, the effects of chain-smoking on his health, his cigarette-addiction, the sacrifice of other values. In other words, the evaluating of value-experiences takes us rapidly beyond their immediately 'enjoyed' quality to an understanding of the conditions *within* the person and *beyond* him that produce them. Again, to evaluate is to become aware of the causal relations that (*a*) exist among the experiences of man themselves and (*b*) of man's interaction with his environment.

It may now be clearer why I hinted earlier that theory of value will force us to raise questions about the nature of man and of the world, and at the same time reflect conclusions to these questions. If there is a pattern of values that we can affirm as mutually supportive, this will result not only from the fact of the experienced quality of the values but also from the relations they have to each other in the context of human experience in this kind of world.

Thus, a value-pattern is a description about the world *with man left in it*; it is a consequence of his relating himself in thought and action to his own nature, and to his total environment. Values and value-patterns are experiences of man; they *relate* him to his world. To say this is not to court relativ*ism* in value-theory, for man's value-patterns are not the product of his whims or desires, but joint-products of his nature (actual and potential) in interaction with the total nurturant environment. In so far as values are *adjectival* of persons in their interchange with the environment as it comes home to them, values are also statements about a world that challenges, threatens, and nurtures, some of man's choices of value-experience more than others. At the same time, it is hazardous to *assume* that one stage in human development is the criterion for all others.

There is no point in arguing this matter further here, for, in the last analysis, anyone who rejects relativ*ism* must sooner or later suggest some universal value, or pattern of values, actually related to man-in-the-world without being relativistic. Hence, I shall proceed directly to outline a core-pattern of values as normative for all human beings, beings who, experiencing 'ought to the best', can never disregard their given needs and abilities, who can never neglect the interchange that destroys or fulfils, impedes or supports

their value-experiencing. I shall also make such comments relevant
to educational policy as time will allow.

III. EXISTENCE, HEALTH, AND TRUTH VALUES

Persons prefer life to death; there would be no problem about the
ethics of suicide, murder, or immortality were this not so. Being
and staying alive is the necessary but not sufficient condition for all
other values. Yet to be alive, to exist, is already to be engaged in
enjoying or suffering value-and-disvalue-experiences. Our question, then, is: What values are mutually enhancing and sustaining?
For a human being who can be aware of himself, who can
remember, and plan, 'the purpose of life', as Socrates said, 'is not
to live, but to live well'.

There will probably be no objection to the statement that healthy
existence and survival-with-health is to be preferred to mere existence and mere survival. *Physiological health* is existence-value enhanced by qualities that not only increase the likelihood of survival
but give vigour and tone to day-by-day existence. If the only choice
were between sheer existence and physical health there would be
no problem, for the experience of health is intrinsically preferable
to that of physical weakness or illness.

But the outline of the patterning of values begins right here. The
necessity of knowing about our bodies, and of the many factors that
affect health, makes us immediately aware of the fact that health-
values depend upon other values, the pursuit of which may often
endanger health itself. These values are truth-values, that is, all the
values involved in searching for, and discovering, what the nature
of man is in his relation to his total environment. We need minimal
existence, not full health, to discover truths that will guide us in
our desires for more healthy survival. But the healthiest person
may be destroyed by his ignorance of some survival-relationship
between himself and his world.

I would not waste your time with such obvious remarks were it
not that we tend to overlook a very important consequence for
explicit education theory. We often talk as if the most important
thing is the health of our children, whether we are talking about
their life at home, at school, or elsewhere. The stress can be on
excellent buildings, proper food and exercise, and schedules that
build up the body – we succumb to an oversimplified generalization that a strong body is the condition for a sound mind. The

American standard of living is frequently applauded when the core of the standard seems to be freedom from hunger, from pain, or relative disease and from discomfort – *as if these are the conditions for, and not in large part the consequences of, the search and discovery of relevant truths in the environment*. Hence much more attention is concentrated on the number and costs of schools, on comparative salaries of teachers, than on the kind of teachers, the educative process, and the other conditions for becoming sensitive and creative in the search for truth in this kind of world.

Socrates pointed to the actual relation between truth-finding and the achievement of health, when he said that the unexamined life is not worth living. Socrates would have agreed, of course, that men have died, that millions have lived in ill health, when more knowledge might have saved them. For human beings, clearly, the dependence of both existence and health on discovery of truth is so great that we might be tempted to claim that, given existence, *the value upon which all other values depend is the discovery of truth*. And, while more argument is needed for adequate defence, this surely forms much of the ground for the contention that the one thing the school at every level must do for human beings is to fulfil the human need for truth.

Yet Socrates would have defended the search for truth by saying that the actual experience of sensitive knowing, from perception through empirical generalization to abstract reasoning and speculation, has a quality *as* experienced that is preferable to physical health as such. Who prefers to be a healthy idiot, a moron, or an uninformed and dull person to a curious, problem-posing, problem-solving, reflective person? To paraphrase John Stuart Mill, it is better to be Socrates unsatisfied than a healthy person who has no experience of thinking and truth-seeking. In any case, the healthy person will soon need to depend on the person whose life is not only healthy but aware of truths relevant to protecting health.

We have hardly started in our search for the pattern of the good life. Yet, we have already discovered that while value-experiences are different from each other qualitatively they do not exist in separate compartments but are mutually related or interpenetrating phases in the experience of persons. *To exist as a human being is to seek health and truth both for their own sakes and for each other. And we know this by observing the qualities of the experiences themselves and the causal web within which they exist.* Each supports the other and furthers the other, and each could be used to destroy the possibility of the other, but the realization of one cannot survive without the actualizing of the other. To this extent, then, our knowledge of the pattern of value consists in our being aware of what actually happens and is possible in human experience.

IV. TRUTH-VALUES AND CHARACTER-VALUES

But the moment we note that truth and health are interrelated, we realize that they are also tied to other value-experiences. We have been talking as if existence and a modicum of health were the only conditions for truth-finding, and as if 'knowledge is virtue'. But neither knowledge nor virtue are forthcoming for persons who are unwilling to discipline themselves. Virtue presupposes knowledge, but knowledge alone certainly is not virtue, but presupposes what may be called 'character'. *Character* is the willingness to discipline oneself by one's own ideals; in relation to truth-finding it is the willingness to sacrifice for the ideal of knowledge to which one adheres.

We can immediately see the relevance of character both to health and to truth values, and, looking ahead, to every other value in the pattern we shall find. For there are obstacles on the path to truth, and the control of appetites that can create illness calls for self-discipline in accordance with such knowledge as we have. One can provide another with free medical aid, one can see to it that food and housing is adequate for him, but one cannot supply another with the self-discipline he needs in order to avail himself of these goods even when they are within his reach. For so many human beings the problem of health is not the problem of knowledge but the problem of character. Knowledge and health aids are available; what is lacking is what these persons alone can provide if they are not simply to know the truth but do it. Knowledge by itself does not guarantee other virtues; nor is it likely to come to those without self-discipline.

We have been stressing that the search for truth puts a special premium on character; but other values and virtues (*moral* values) cannot be overlooked even in passing. One may seek the truth in order to eat or to become healthy; one may eat in order to think; our human experience shows that we must think in order to eat. But it also tells us that often those who pursue the truth are required themselves and make sacrifices not only because the discovery of truth requires self-discipline, but because they are living with others who believe they will be inconvenienced or hurt by new discoveries. Persons equally concerned about the truth may jealously throw road-blocks in the way of any one truth-seeker; they pile scorn upon him, and they add to his need to discipline himself by his own ideal of truth. We often underestimate how much the freedom of any one scholar and inventor is dependent on the tolerance of others, and especially in the forbearance of equally learned scholars. Truth-seeking calls for social self-discipline, for a sense of humour, and deep-rooted humility on the part of both truth-finder and of the community in which he lives. In short, the discovery of truth presupposes sufficient individual freedom of will on the part of the scholar as he disciplines himself by ideals of evidence and not by wishes; and it also presupposes sufficient social and political tolerance to enable him to pursue that course. At the same time, he who pursues the truth must be willing to be censured and to be criticized; he cannot proceed unless he has the will to discipline himself within the total context of social and political freedom.

Once more we note one of the instances where value-theory posits questions about human nature. We can do little more here than emphasize that the centrality of character in the pattern of values forces us to ask questions about the conditions in human nature (such as needs and human freedom) that make character possible. But *character* as used here seems to be a monolithic virtue when in fact it is a trend that exists only in the development of virtues. Were we to turn our attention to the structure of character, we would find, I think, a pattern of virtues related to the pattern of values we are here proposing.[1]

But here we must restrict ourselves to underscoring an understandable but nevertheless egregious error of omission in educational theory at this point – an error stemming in part from a theoretical, psychological climate that did not favour talking about the will, or to the nature of character itself. The error consists in a de-emphasis on character (in this sense) in favour of conduct and 'behaviour'. The omission is understandable. For we cannot give, we cannot teach, character, by itself, to anyone. Self-discipline by nature rests with the individual, in the last analysis. Yet, while we often pay 'the need for character' lip-service, have we integrated it into the aims of education? Have we in educational and social practice created the atmosphere or climate in which character can be encouraged without turning into self-flagellation? Granted that

[1] See *Personality and the Good*, Chapters 16, 17.

in teaching we cannot communicate character – even in ethics classes or social studies – yet have we built an educational community with the need for this ingredient in personality explicitly in mind? Or have we actually assumed that this phase of human development was based on a mythological account of man, and an outworn ethic? Have we gone so far in demanding that we must 'make the material interesting', that 'we must involve the individual as participant in the learning process', and so forth, that our students have justified themselves for not learning what is not 'interesting' or what does not immediately involve them? I suspect that we have actually expected them to exert more self-discipline than our theories of volition allowed.

In any case, we can learn from Immanuel Kant at this point. He said, we recall, that: 'Nothing in the world – indeed nothing even beyond the world – can possibly be conceived which could be called good without qualification except a good will!' Kant saw that the good will is 'the indispensable condition of even worthiness to be happy', as well as the condition for the development of other values. And with unerring insight he also saw that the experience of good will, 'the summoning of all the means in our power' to do what seems best, 'would sparkle like a jewel with its own light as something that had its full worth in itself'.[1]

Indeed, we are now not talking about the enjoyment of physical health; nor are we talking about the joys of truth-finding and contemplation. We are talking about another phase of human experience that does not exclusively depend upon other values for its existence. As Kant says, even when our good will does not achieve what it wills, we realize that it is better to have hewn to the line than to have yielded to inclination. The character, the will to discipline oneself by one's ideal, is not the complete good or the sole good even for Kant, but it is a good that enriches every other good and yet, in the final count-down, depends on the individual's own decision to sacrifice whatever need be for the sake of what some existentialists today are calling 'authenticity'.

In emphasizing character in the pattern of ideals we are saying no less than this: a human being finds an irreducible satisfaction in living not *by* impulse, not *from* impulse or desire, but from his

---

[1] *Foundation of the Metaphysics of Morals*, First Section, Lewis White Beck, editor and translator; Immanuel Kant, *Critique of Practical Reason and Other Writings in Moral Philosophy*, Chicago: University of Chicago Press, 1949, pp. 55, 56.

reflective decision about what is worth while inclusive of his desires and needs. This experience of 'character' in turn helps to define what it can mean to be human. A human being who has little or no character may be biologically healthy; he may live by truths that others have discovered, but he never knows that 'peak' experience (to borrow Abraham Maslow's term) of setting and working his own way toward an approved goal, despite hardship, inconvenience, and risk of failure. A person of character has gone beyond being interactive with, and responsive to, his world; he now is responsive-responsible; he is active and not simply re-active; he lives from within his decisions even as the stimuli from the outside world and the alluring appetites make themselves felt in his development.

If this Stoic, Judeo-Christian, and Kantian teaching is at all true, this stress on character as the core of the pattern of human values must make us more sensitive to its development in the total educational programme. As I have already hinted, we tend to exclude from our teaching and programmes what we cannot put into a programme as subject-matter. So much teaching, both in college and in secondary schools, can become a kind of psycho-logical manoeuvring of the individual student, a kind of manage-ment of learning, that we develop a model of the person that fits our strategy. But such strategy, and such a thermometer or com-puter model of the person, neglects the fact that all the learning in the world cannot replace the value experienced by the person who knows that he can manage his own life within limits, that he can take his own risks, that he can accept responsibility for his own becoming and its effect upon others.

If we could do nothing else, we could remember that we are teaching not subject-matter but persons. I for one need to keep reminding myself that I am not teaching philosophy; I am teaching persons. I am, hopefully, teaching them the ways, the problems, and answers they do well to be responsive to as they become philosophically responsible. The pattern of values cannot, in the last analysis, be stronger than the value that at once defines each human venture in goodness, enables the person to overcome obstacles in actualizing values, and yet it can never be completely determined by such achievements. No character – then no zest, no creativity in the ethical life, and in education.

Not for a moment, then, will I take back the contention that character is the moral crucible for the creation of values. But to insist on this is not enough. He who makes character central to the realization of values must insist equally that character unguided by truth makes for fanaticism. Indeed, the de-emphasis upon character in explicit, ethical and educational reflection is probably due, in part, to the fact that 'the road to hell', to paraphrase William James, 'is paved by good will'. Crisply put: Character without other values is blind; other values without character are threatened with early death if they are born at all. Why?

V. TRUTH, CHARACTER, AND AFFILIATIVE VALUES

Consider what we would have before us if a personality is strong in the values of health, truth, and character, but is very weak in the value of *affiliation*. (I purposely do not say *love*, since I reserve the word 'love' for a total style of life and not for one type of value.) By *affiliation* I mean the capacity to be responsive to the needs and wants of others, and to enter into non-parasitic, appreciative relationships. Obviously, we are here running close to the ethical problems of justice or altruism. But whatever the final definition and justification for these, all that is initially in mind here is that a human being has a wanted experience, nay, an intrinsically worthwhile experience, when he knows the quality of affiliation in his relation to others. The person who cannot emotionally care about anyone else, who treats other persons as if they were as incapable of response to him as things are, who finds that he cannot willingly accept any responsibility for other persons – that person may have physical health, he may be strong-willed, and he may enjoy his lonely search for truth, but he is a poverty-stricken human being.

Here again, if we knew nothing else about the psychology of personality and the nature of persons, we should be justified in asking psychologists and philosophers to keep in mind that persons do intrinsically enjoy experiences of affiliation and that their theories of the person must take full account of the qualitative experience, affiliation. This unique, irreducible quality of fellow-feeling must guide further analysis into the dynamics and ramifications of the experience in personal and social experience.

Here we need only note how deeply interrelated is the value of affiliation with the creation, conservation, and increase of all the other values. Because persons are born dependent for health, growth, and understanding upon adults, their opportunity for character-development is affected by the willingness of other persons to discipline their own wants so that from the beginning the growing person can make his choices with freedom guided by insight. In a broader context, as we have noted, a person's search for truth is impeded by the unwillingness of others to allow the truth-seeker freely to pursue his investigations and then to public-ize his conclusions. The quality of conversation, the development of science, art, industry, the family, church, state – these all depend in large degree on the course affiliation takes in the lives of persons. Indeed, so many of the values of life are created in, and enhanced by, mutual sharing and enjoyment, that we need not labour the importance of affiliation.

Yet, here again we cannot forget that affiliation, including friendship and romantic love, can become sentimental unless they are dedicated to the realization of other values. The great seduction in the area of romantic love stems from the failure to realize that affection becomes shallow and insipid when it is not invested in pursuits that keep both persons growing. There is all the difference in the world between: 'I like you', and 'I love you'. To be together is to be together not merely in space, not in body alone, but in the creation and mutual enjoyment of other values. And is it not a dominant fact of experience, for all of our frequent blindness to it, that often the profoundest fellowship, creative of new dimensions in a relationship, is born of mutual sacrifice, of loyalty in suffering?

Indeed, none of the creative dimensions of affiliation are possible without the self-discipline we have called character. At the same time, often the greatest social injustice is the product of affiliative tendencies that are not guided by, or disciplined by, truth. In the name of 'our' family, 'our' community, 'our' country, 'our' God, hatred of others and war has been justified. Hell is let loose by persons who will not allow the truth-claims and the value-claims of others to live with their own in a creative compromise. And when narrow affiliation is linked with strong character, but not linked with enough truth, violence to others, and ultimately to self, results. Once more the interpenetration, the patterning, of values is inescapable.

If a person could develop no other values, but could experience health, truth, character, and affiliation, he would already have a personality that could not only resist evil but create further values. Hence we are tempted, having arrived thus far, to say that these are the critical value-centres of personality. If no other realm of value could be added, our hypothesis that a pattern of values can define the ideal of personality would be well on the way to reasonable verification. For this pattern so far expresses both needs and satisfactions of men in the everyday rounds of life: fulfilment of the need-value 'health' is the enduring foundation of economic and industrial activity; the need-value, affiliation (and its protection in family and in social and political institutions as well as in the search for truth), would operate in a vacuum apart from economic and social life. Meanwhile, the development of character, as we have realized, is reflected in and influences the creation and increase of these values.

Before passing on, let it be noted that we have been keeping one eye on the *experienced quality* of the values themselves, and another on the *interrelation* that exists between values by virtue of the fact that these experiences have their being in and for persons. Hence, these values and their interrelation have been contributing to our knowledge of what human nature can become in the light of a certain psycho-logic of value.

VI. VOCATION AS VALUE-EXPERIENCE

Our growing pattern of values takes on an even deeper dimension as we make an addition that at once reflects and inspires achievements in the realms of health, character, truth, and affiliative values. I have in mind the value of *vocation*. I am not thinking of vocation as a job, that is, in terms of all its instrumental, economic, and affiliative values. The job one has, the work one does 'for a living', may well take its place alongside of family-experience as the arena in which most persons develop their personalities in association with others. But without wishing to dissociate what I am calling the value-experiencing of vocation from the work one does as part of the economic-socio-political structure, the stress *in value as vocation is on the qualitative satisfaction one experiences when his energies and activities are focused on a task that is large enough to express and challenge his own becoming.* A man's work, and its value in a community may indeed be his economic and social capital; it may evoke admiration, respect, and praise from others, and thus be a source of many social and economic values. It can, accordingly, support and express the values of health, truth, character, and affiliation.

Yet all of these values will be enhanced, and the individual will experience creativity in a unique way, if he has a sense of vocation in his life. A vocation is the pivot that gives direction to life in terms of the individual's own total abilities and potentialities; and, to indicate interpenetration once more, his sense of vocation will be affected by his capacity to discipline himself in truth and affiliation.

Long ago Plato argued that each man ought to do what he can do best, that only thus could he be just to himself and to his fellow men. Plato did not seem to be troubled about whether the distribution of talents, in relation to the actual needs of men in a given environment, would so interlock that the highest good of all would thus be harmoniously assured. We need not assume that such pre-established harmony would be the case, especially in our society, in order for us to take Plato's basic point more seriously in education. Every person must distinguish between 'making a living', or having a job by which he will support himself economically, and having a vocation that does bring out the best in him. He is very fortunate if vocation and job are consistent with each other. But it will be fatal to his long-run sense of well-being if he does not, with the help of his schooling, begin to develop insight into the meaning of this distinction for himself.

Educational policy certainly cannot gear itself mainly to preparing persons for the jobs that need to be filled. While the person must be free to select the job-preparation he wished, educational policy cannot be content with less than the provision of graded and diversified programmes that will help the person to discover his competencies and the areas that bring him high qualitative satisfaction – and mainly because he feels that his own unique constellation of wants and abilities are best fulfilled therein. The fact is that too many people who 'are making good money' are bored with life; they are mediocre as persons because their lives have lost the direction and deeper focus that a sense of vocation can give. On the other hand, many persons, especially in an economic world in which automation is spreading, will need to find their sense of vocation outside the purely economic sphere. Persons who do not feel fulfilment somewhere in their everyday concerns are likely to develop a spiritual vacuum, or a psychic disease, that cannot be overcome by activities which give temporary, symptomatic relief only. Will the educational programme, especially for adults, not need to provide opportunities for fulfilment rather than for preparation? In the last analysis, must not education for personal, vocational fulfilment supplement the concept of education as job-preparation?

VII. AESTHETIC VALUES

And here we are already bordering on another realm of values that
consists essentially not in 'coping with life', but in expressing oneself creatively. I mean, of course, aesthetic values – and recreational
values in so far as they involve aesthetic orientation. By *aesthetic
value* I mean the goal-directed experience of expression and
appreciation undergone or 'enjoyed' for its own sake.

This is the place to re-emphasize that the realms of value are not
compartments of life but moments of experience that live together
in the complex of personal existence. Even the most utilitarian
pursuits can have their aesthetic moments or phases; the moral
ventures of life can express and be enhanced by aesthetic meaning
('the good deed done gracefully'). However, while the setting aside
of an hour for aesthetic experience is as ridiculous as setting an hour
aside for moral experience, or for worship, the fact remains that we
find our lives richer because we can 'take time out' to appreciate
aesthetic performance and to express ourselves artistically.

Once again we note that in any attempt to define aesthetic values
we are defining ranges of qualitative experience that the psychologist and philosopher must not neglect in their descriptions and
theorizing about the nature of man. The aesthetic components in
human experience, the whole range of the arts, invade every nook
and cranny of life and lift it into a perspective that makes the
experience of it more meaningful for the whole of life because of
the aesthetic ingredient. The aesthetic experience and the arts are
not incidental luxuries that may be added casually to the main
course of existence. The aesthetically sensitive person who enjoys
and suffers dimensions of being, along with the other dimensions
of life, finds quality not open to other human beings and feels the
better for both.

For example, imagine what a human life becomes that is dead
to the experience of song and music, that makes no response to
drama and the visual arts, to whom nothing in nature is thrilling,
to whom the comic and the tragic, the beautiful, the ugly, and the
sublime make no difference, and you have before you a human
being who may sense, feel, and even think and be socially responsive – and yet know no resonance. At the same time, let a person
give himself to the disciplines of aesthetic control in every area of
life and he will find a kind of growth that cannot be measured in
terms of physical, moral, or intellectual strength alone.

We are aware once more of the plurality of value-experiences on one hand, and the network that binds them together in the person. In seeking the pattern of values, we have been scanning human experience for moments and movements that have been found highly satisfying; we have been impressed by the ways in which they express different facets of personal being and, at the same time, create problems of growth and harmony. If we can draw any conclusion at all from this brief outline, it is this: *The problem of life in the areas of value-experience is to learn how to orchestrate the values so that each may contribute to the whole without losing distinctiveness.*

Before proceeding further, let us suggest a diagram that emphasizes the interpenetration of values in the 'pattern'. This diagram does not illustrate the 'symphonic' dynamism now to be stressed.

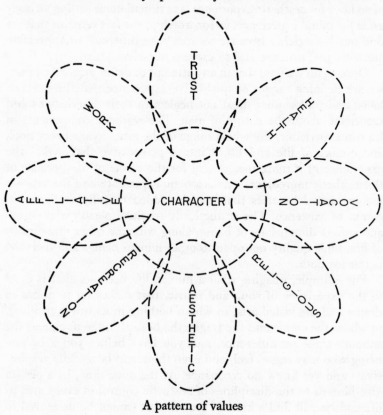

A pattern of values

FIGURE 4

I find the expression 'symphony of values' more meaningful than 'pattern of values' because it suggests this dynamic development of different motifs or movements which receive attention, but not exclusive attention, from the point of view of the whole. Which orchestration as each life moves from infancy to old age, which orchestration as each life faces the opportunities and exigencies of its existence in physical and social environment, will allow greatest mutual value-enhancement and support? The death of quality comes if we simply make sure that everything is tasted once, in a cheap democracy of values; at the same time, while specialization in one area of values will be difficult, such concentrations as intellectualism, aestheticism, and moralism warn us of what can happen to warp life by sacrificing too many other value-considerations to high hopes of proficiency in one area.

Abstractly put, the problem is how to achieve optimum quality without sacrificing variety. Three things are certain: first, tension, conflict, and challenge cannot be avoided in creating, conserving, and increasing values. Second, as is suggested by the notion of symphony, at any one point in the development of a pattern, the problem is to keep the themes of value in a relationship that will be mutually enhancing. Phrases like 'nothing too much', 'creative counterpoise', 'dialectic of values' are different ways of indicating that the human search for quality in value-experience always faces some concrete problem of selection for the sake of ultimate range and unity; risk is integral to the search, and 'peace of mind' is inimical to growth.

Concretely put, the problem for any human being in his own life, and for the educator who would help a person to find himself, is to orchestrate value-experience in accordance with that individual's stage of development. Just as every personality is unique, so will the specific ways in which values are realized in a given personality be unique. We are not presenting, as it were, a fixed pattern of personality which becomes a kind of harness to which one fits himself. More in mind is a 'mobile' that keeps its inner dynamics, is responsive to its environment, and yet, to change the figure, creates its responses with the pattern in mind.

We have been showing that the pattern of values is adjectival, is related to the nature of human need, ability, and sensitivity in the nurturant-challenging environment without becoming thereby relativistic. We would all the more insist that each person, in his stage of growth, in his situation, relate to himself, and relate himself to, this pattern not because it is imposed upon him willy-nilly, but because it offers him a regulative guide, growing out of basic human experience, by which his own pilgrimage in value-experience may be lured. The task of self-education is the task of finding where one is, and how far one can go, in relation to the total human venture in value-realization.

VIII. RELIGIOUS VALUES AND PHILOSOPHICAL ORIENTATION

Every dimension of value deserves much more discussion than it has been afforded here, but nowhere do we feel the restriction more than when we seek to place the religious and philosophical dimensions of life. How are the two dimensions related, to each other and to the other dimensions of value-experiencing? The history of the discussion of faith and reason, of home, of church and state, of religious and philosophical education in the schools, tempts one to be silent at this final stage of our discussion. But no ethicist, metaphysician, philosophical theologian, or educational philosopher can drop this many-sided problem. For the fundamental issue remains that of being adequately sensitive to the role which each does and can play in a human pattern of values. I can only intimate the approach that seems fair to me.

The seeker – for health, for truth, for creative control (character), for aesthetic expression, for affiliation – inevitably asks whether man is alone in his concern for value-realization. How is man's search for value related to whatever the structure of the world, in itself as it were, is? More specifically: Is there a Being for whom man in his search for values is a value? Historically these questions have purely theoretical roots as well as purely religious roots. Here we shall confine ourselves largely to the religious.

Whatever the validity of the human religious quest, it would dry up, as religious, were it not freshened by the continuing experiences, not only of religious 'experts' like the mystics in every culture and nation, but also by the testimony of millions who are not religious seers or prophets. At the moment I care not how we finally interpret what I am here calling the experience of the holy. I soberly record the fact that those human beings who have experienced 'the holy' have felt that this experience was at least as significant for them in their search for value as any other – indeed, they have felt both challenged and supported by it, and it has given them power, they testify, to do what they believe they would not have done otherwise.

Again, human history is simply unintelligible apart from what I am here calling the experience of 'the holy'. Around it religious creeds and religious communities have been built; much philosophical speculation has stemmed from the attempt to understand and relate this human experience to the rest of what men have undergone. Often, the inspiring theme for the orchestration of myriad human lives has ultimately depended on a particular interpretation of this religious experience.

Let me put this point in another way. Man, in view of his religious experience, has been called a worshipping animal. What he has worshipped has become the source of unity and power in his life – his vocation. The object of worship has fascinated him, gripped him, and claimed his allegiance. In its name he has lived and died; in its name he has been willing to sacrifice all other values; in its name he has been willing to extend himself unrelentingly in the search for truth, beauty, and goodness for himself and others; in its name he has also hurt himself and others.

If such an analysis is at all true, it will be clear that no search for a pattern of values can possibly disregard the experience of the holy and of worship; for it can destroy a symphony of values or it can be its dominating creative theme. No responsible educator, therefore, can minimize the importance of the search for, or neglect the task of interpreting, the meaning of religious experience. Not, at least, if he is interested in the dynamics of the orchestration of values. If at every stage in education there is concern for, appreciation of, and responsibility for, both part and whole, then education that discourages the experience of, and critique of, an experience that has such creative and destructive possibilities in a life is simply halting, truncated education. For education to be unwilling to educate the sense of awe – even as it educates the aesthetic and moral ecstasies – is for education to be willing to neglect the experience that sets the whole of life on fire – for good or evil.

It will be noted that I have not been speaking of religious cults and denominations, which historically have both produced their prophets as well as persecuted and killed them. My concern is more far-reaching, especially in a day when religious and philosophical dogmatism of the right and of the left seem bent on spilling the wine that does not fit their bottles. The school is neither the home nor the church. But a philosophy of education that is a philosophy of education, and not simply the rationalization for any social, domestic, or religious structure, must keep its attention focused on the dimensions of personality and demand that they be scrutinized with a view to the development of the person as a whole.

The specific problem the philosopher of education faces with regard to religious experience – and which every individual faces with regard to his religious experience – is a certain authoritarian claim that so readily grows out of the power of the religious experience. This claim is that religious experience (and what is claimed to be revealed in it and delivered through it), be given logical, ethical, and metaphysical priority, or, better, any autonomy which would relegate other dimensions of experience to it in servile fashion. Yet, whatever one's own final conviction about the validity of a specific religious revelation or interpretation, any person within any religious tradition must be cognizant of the difference in the meaning assigned to the religious experience within his tradition, let alone within his own life; he must face the fact that the quality and meaning or interpretation of religious experience has varied and in fact been affected by its conceived conflict and harmony with the other facets of life.

For the writer, the psychologist of personality, Professor Gordon W. Allport, has expressed the ideal in his description of a mature religious sentiment. Recognizing the need for a unifying philosophy of life, on the one hand, and aware, on the other hand, that an immature religious sentiment may keep a personality from growing and promote rigidity, he urges that a mature religious sentiment, in orienting and committing a person to *what he regards as permanent or central in the nature of things*,[1] will not dam up the main stream of personal experience by unstructured ecstasies. Indeed, because it is part of the individual's search for meaning, the mature religious sentiment will be more than 'just emotional', more than 'cold reason'; it will encourage the person not to allow his life to run off into little rivulets by confronting him with the demand that he take seriously the integrity and the possible integration of his values with an Ultimate Ground of being. The mature religious personality will indeed know that since he cannot know all he must remain in uncertainty even as he 'learns to act wholeheartedly even without absolute certainty'.[2]

[1] G. W. Allport, *The Individual and His Religion*, New York: Macmillan Co., p. 56.
[2] *Ibid.*, p. 72.

What else have we been pleading for in the above other than *philosophical perspective* both on religious experience and every other dimension of life? Obviously a conception of philosophical experiencing is being presupposed – although it has been partially illustrated in the above. For philosophy means philosophizing; it is a never-ending search – fraught with the challenges, the discouragements, and the zest discovered in every realm of value-experiencing – for connections that are as ranging and deep as human beings can understand. The person who is philosophically alive is not necessarily 'the philosopher'; he is the person who knows what it is, in his life at his stage of development, to examine each facet of life for what it is, to see it in larger context without losing its uniqueness. There is an intellectual creativity in such an experience, there is a quality of satisfaction regardless of the specific outcome of the reflections. What else could have justified Socrates' dictum – the unexamined life is not worth living?

A final note: There can be no symphony of values, no patterning of ideals, for a person who is not willing to be at once attached and detached in his pursuit of values. On the ideal of personality presented here, the overriding sin is to pursue one set of values as if it were the end-all and be-all of a life. Philosophizing is the attempt to conduct the orchestrating by a score that is created by experimentation with values within a given life, and in human community. Philosophizing does not take the place of living, or of any other values; it is the systematic attempt to connect every fact and value in one's life so that the person will know his connections and act thereby.

PART 3

GOD, THE COSMIC PERSON AND HIS GOODNESS

CHAPTER VII

NATURALISTIC ARGUMENTS AGAINST
THEISTIC HYPOTHESES

I introduce Part III with this discussion of the logic of naturalistic objections to theism because the possibilities of empirical argument still remain a bone of contention in philosophy of religion and philosophical theology. The naturalist, extending the logic of such empiricism as is successful in science, canonizes the verifiability principle and argues that one cannot move from man and nature to God. Curiously enough, he is joined in this conclusion by revelational, orthodox, neo-orthodox, and existential theologies – which maintain that any attempt to find the God of religion through the course of nature and history is bound to fail if unaided by religious experience. Thus much of the problem in philosophy of religion and philosophical theology centres around the method of argument and the criterion of truth.

If the naturalist elevates the logic of scientific empiricism into a methodological imperialism, and if the supernaturalist already knows what God's nature must be and thus makes only polite gestures of hospitality to its guest, natural theology, there is no communication possible between scientific empiricism and 'the dictates of religious experience'. In this and other essays in this Part, there unfolds another view of empirical method and of an empirical criterion of truth.

In this method there is a synoptic appeal to every facet or dimension of human experience; in this criterion there is a demand for the most probable systematic interrelation of hypothesis and experience. This view of reason and experience has a longer historical lineage than sense-bound empiricism or revelational empiricism. It finds classic expression in Hegel's dictum that the truth is the whole, but it is committed in advance to more than the concern that any hypothesis be seen in the light of experience in its concrete variety and possible togetherness. No logical coherence this, but an experiential growing coherence which requires that the hypothesis which is more harmonious than any other hypothesis be accepted as true until new evidence leads to its reconsideration. It is this criterion of truth, problem-centred and rooted in the variety of experience, which is the foundation for reasoning about any hypothesis regarding God – even as it is the underlying foundation of our reasoning about man and his values.

I

In 'Naturalism and Religion'[1] Professor Sterling P. Lamprecht throws into relief some fundamental objections to theism from the standpoint of naturalism. What is at stake, however, is not only the validity of theistic hypotheses but the nature of philosophical methodology. For the attack on theistic hypotheses does not spring from animosity to religion but from dissatisfaction with philosophical procedures used historically and recently in arriving at religious conclusions. We are here concerned to evaluate this naturalistic approach to religion as a part of a total philosophical programme.

Naturalism comes on to the philosophical stage as the sponsor of philosophical urbanity and freedom from theological dogmatism and moral impositionism. In this mood it is the philosophic censor keen to sift the chaff of wishful thinking from the wheat of well-founded religious truth. In this mood, the naturalistic protest against orthodoxy is directed not so much against religion as against pontificating about the nature of one realm of being by deductions from a totally different sphere. In so far as the naturalist thus insists on an open philosophical court in which evidence from the natural world receives a careful hearing, he enlists and deserves the support of all who believe in the philosophic mission.

But this is not the whole story. Naturalism in another mood would have more than its day in court; it would rule the court. It pontificates as to the possibilities and limitations of religious truth. In this mood, it, like the orthodoxies, is most conscious of method in achieving truth and emphasizes the ascetic requirements of *strict* empiricism. Naturalism would thus seem to expose itself to the very mistake which it finds in the exponents of supernaturalism. That it succumbs to this error of impositionism we shall now see as we follow the logic of the naturalistic case against the existence of God.

[1] Chapter II in *Naturalism and the Human Spirit*, ed. Y. H. Krikorian, New York: Columbia University Press, 1944. All references will be to this book.

II

'Naturalism', Professor Lamprecht tells us, 'means a philosophical position, empirical in method, that regards everything that exists or occurs to be conditioned in its existence or occurrence by causal factors within one all-encompassing system of nature', however "spiritual" or purposeful or rational some of these things and events may in their functions and values proves to be'. Professor Lamprecht also says that though 'Naturalism does not stand or fall with rejection of the arguments for the existence of God', it does stand or fall with its acceptance of a strictly empirical method and its refusal to believe a matter of great moment when no evidence can be found.

In the name of 'strictly empirical procedure', therefore, the naturalist criticizes a type of argument for God developed by thinkers like Pringle-Pattison, Ward, Sorley, Taylor, Tennant, and Temple in England, and by Hocking, Macintosh, Brightman, Hartshorne, Calhoun, Montague, and Lyman in this country. In general, these thinkers develop hypotheses about God which coherently embrace both the data of existence and the data of value; they deny priority to any one realm of experience, be it scientific or religious. One may find that these thinkers and others are not equally cogent or faithful to the total experiential data, but their methodology is unmistakably empirical as they develop hypotheses which interrelate the various aspects of human experience. But Lamprecht chides: 'Some philosophers, seemingly intrigued by the prestige which the empirical tradition today enjoys, want to call themselves empiricists merely because they consent to reject those beliefs that can be shown to contradict ascertained facts.' Naturalists, however, 'take the empirical method more seriously', for they seek 'to distinguish the varying degrees of probability which ideas seem to have, to accept as beliefs only those ideas that are well accredited, and to entertain any further ideas only as hypotheses or hopes or fancies. They reject satisfaction as a requisite test for truth, except such satisfaction as is found in the discovery of strict conformity of idea to ascertained fact.' In other words, the naturalist, in accordance with strict empirical procedure, refuses to espouse the existence of God unless there is direct evidence of Him within the realm of fact. Only one type of 'satisfaction' is philosophically legitimate. An idea of God *consistent with* the facts, *implied by* the facts, *suggested by* the facts, even if it renders the facts more intelligible or life more satisfactory, is not tenable, *for there is no direct testimony*; at best it remains an interesting and momentous hope or hypothesis.

But when we ask the naturalist: '*Is empirical procedure the criterion or norm for the facts* to which ideas must conform?' we discover that a fusion has surreptitiously taken place between the *method* of truth-finding and the *criterion* of truth. Empirical method is now more than the method of solving problems by hypotheses consistent with experience. Empirical method is now the *scientific method* or *criterion* of truth. It has become the method of solving problems by developing hypotheses which are not only consistent with sensory experience, but which can sooner or later make specific sensory differences. However, when empirical method is thus *restricted*, it is no longer the method for finding truth about *any* possible realm of being, but the method which *restricts the realm* of being to what can be known by that procedure. Professor Sidney Hook may say: 'As for decreeing what does or can *exist*, there is no scientific method that *forbids* anything to exist. It concerns itself only with the responsibility of the assertions that proclaim the existence of anything.' But if the responsibility of assertions is to be judged by the capacity of those assertions to guide the kind of operations which the physical and social sciences rely upon, then scientific method *does forbid* the assertion of any being which cannot be ascertained by operations involving public perceptual observation. If the only responsible assertions we can make are those which are in accordance with a method which was adapted to sensory reality, then it is clear that this method, *strictly applied*, does indeed legislate for all reality. The hook which efficiently caught medium-sized fish in the ocean of reality is now being used as the criterion for all life in the ocean; what can't be caught by that hook cannot be.

Thus to attack naturalism is not to attack scientific method or 'to be free to believe whatever voice speaks to us'. There can be no serious objection to establishing a method for the physical realm and then extending that method to *equivalent* aspects in the biological, psychological, and social realms. If the naturalist, basing his plea on past achievements, asks for more time to acquire the data and hypotheses to deal more adequately with the problem of mind and values, then both naturalist and non-naturalist can pursue their problems peacefully.

But the naturalist is asking for more than this. Bewailing our 'failure of nerve', he rules out all past religious hypotheses because they do not fit the requirements he now lays down as he extends his method-criterion for a given area to all areas. And he objects when some who resist this extension call themselves empiricists.

Such thinkers, who come to believe in God by way of empirical method, consider themselves empiricists because they, in accordance with the empirical tradition in philosophy, are not willing to accept any *a priori*, religious or rationalistic, as an adequate basis for knowledge about God. They insist that any ideas of God square with human experience *as a whole*, whether organized (as in science) or not yet organized. They are unwilling that any one aspect of human experience be given priority. For this reason they reject not scientific findings but the findings of naturalists who seem to dictate one pathway to reality and at the same time to have such questions as the purpose of the world unanswered simply because the answers can't possibly conform to the requirements of their specific version of empiricism. Religious empiricists such as those mentioned would be the first to grant that their results do not have the same degree of probable truth as most of the findings of science. But they would also claim that their hypotheses do greater justice to experience in all of its aspects, sense-data, values, 'intuitions', and hopes. With the Platonic Socrates they pray for insight as they enter territory which seems to be mined against philosophical advance, but move they must with their hunches and with their knowledge of the world and man.

When naturalists point out the difficulties with specific religious hypotheses, they are performing a useful function (as when Lamprecht states his dissatisfaction with the ambiguity in theistic accounts of God's relation to man). But when the naturalists point out that theism is untenable because it doesn't fit the requirements of a restricted empirical method, there simply cannot be a meeting of minds. A reductive dogmatism, as dogmatic as ancient orthodoxy, bars the way. The following specific objections to the God-hypothesis which Lamprecht raises support this conclusion.

III

The traditional ontological argument cannot stand in the face of any empirical critique. But the naturalist finds the cosmological argument also untenable because it rests on a 'supposition for which there is no empirical evidence' namely, 'that where there is order there is manifestation of mind'.

Now I submit that if there is no empirical evidence for the generalization that where there is order there is mind, it is only because 'empirical' means 'checkable-by-sense'. There may be other types of order than order-instituted-by-mind, but that mind, as we know it, is an ordering agent cannot be denied except by a materialistic and deterministic philosophy which itself has to admit the *prima facie* mental teleology which it explains away. And that the order which constitutes 'Nature' resembles an order characteristic of mind at its best is a hypothesis which is closer to the facts as we know them than any other hypothetical explanation of order.

There are difficulties in the cosmological argument, but to object to it on the ground that there is *no* supporting empirical evidence is to reveal an underlying bias which outlaws it and the question which it is supposed to answer, namely: Is there any independent, self-sufficient cause? One may answer that question in the negative, but one may not by-pass it with the answer: There can't be, because we can't find one with our method.

The teleological argument is meant to make clear that the causal order is ultimately an expression of the means-to-end order which characterizes mind-order at its best. Both the older and the newer teleological arguments call specifically for a mind-order which fights for ends, using a stable order of causal means! Whatever their weaknesses the teleological arguments certainly united into one argument the moral, aesthetic, and religious values envisioned in the ontological argument, and the causal sequences of the cosmological. For Lamprecht to say, with Hume and Kant, that the teleological argument depends on the cosmological, and to reject it for their reasons, is to invoke once more a sense-bound empiricism and its legislation for reality.[1]

But the naturalistic exposé of the weakness of theistic arguments

---

[1] To add that the teleological argument rests on a 'fundamental confusion between two quite different meanings of "purpose" – purpose as design or intent or plan, and purpose as utility or harmony or adaptation', is to suggest that the latter is a better interpretation when that is the point at issue. Does harmony or utility or adaptation lend itself to a simpler and less forced interpretation than that of mind as fighter for ends? The theist holds that what is called purposeless harmony in the world is of such a nature that it is most adequately interpreted as the display of a Mind capable of grander rational themes and moral-aesthetic aims than is the finite fighter for ends. It may be suggested that Kant might have been fairer to all the data, both teleological and dysteleological, had he been willing to follow a suggestion of Hume's Cleanthes and accept the God to which the teleological argument pointed. Some religious empiricists, like Montague and Brightman, have argued for a finite God. See the essay below in Chapter 9 and 10 especially.

reveals its own reductive bias most clearly as it deals with another issue. Thinkers like Aquinas, A. E. Taylor, and Whitehead have found it possible to believe that from the contingency in the space-time world one could infer a self-sufficient Deity. Lamprecht argues that 'to go from existence and events that are contingent to an entire world that is contingent seems difficult and may be an instance of the fallacy of composition'. It *may* indeed. The problem is real and the field is open for hypotheses.

Now, the hypothesis of a timeless, self-sufficient God reflects the conviction that it is less coherent to suppose that contingency is the final truth about the world as we know it or the universe as a whole. The hypothesis forces us to expand our intellectual horizon and the horizon of the world by suggesting that contingency stands as a part or phase of a total cosmos which is itself not contingent. It holds that the physical world is *not* to be considered a 'world-as-a-whole'; that it is incoherent to conceive of it thus except for certain non-philosophical purposes.

The naturalist, however, holds that 'it seems questionable whether the world-as-a-whole can ever be the subject of empirically verifiable propositions'. This contention is once more based on the Humean analysis that since cause and effect are categories which apply to relationships within the world, the statement: 'The world-as-a-whole is an effect' is meaningless. As long as the word 'cause' is used in the very same sense for the Agent or Being on whom the world-as-a-whole is said to depend, then there is no answer to this objection. But while the word 'cause' appears in 'First Cause', the definition of this Being as self-sufficient or *causa sui*, should not have misled us into the supposition that the same sort of sequential relation was meant, despite resemblances.

Furthermore, the plausibility of this naturalistic objection, let alone its strength, rests, let it be remembered, on Humean postulates. Of course it will be impossible to verify 'empirically' the world-as-a-whole. However, what the theist contends in this argument is that the world-as-a-whole as defined by the scientist and the sense-bound empiricist is not the whole of being. If the naturalistic world-as-a-whole suggested no further questions, one's mind might rest there, but questions can be asked. Suggestive hypotheses are forthcoming from philosophers who are quite aware that their more comprehensive hypotheses cannot in the nature of the case have the degree of probability credited to scientific hypotheses. But what their hypotheses cannot receive in the way of accurate verification they make up for in importance for the meaning both of existence and knowledge, as Lamprecht grants. If man, nature, and value can be grounded in the structure of reality, if the heroic struggle which naturalism espouses can be considered to have the conscious support of God, then nothing in the way of critical knowledge and careful living need be lost, and much may be gained.

CHAPTER VIII

TENNANT'S CRITIQUE OF RELIGIOUS EXPERIENCE

It would be difficult to find a more sustained and systematic philosophical theology, especially in the 'empirical' tradition, than F. R. Tennant's two volumes, *Philosophical Theology*. It was the author's privilege to have Tennant as one of his guides as he worked out his dissertation, later published as *The Empirical Argument for God in Late British Thought* (Harvard, 1938; Kraus, 1970). The present essay was written in an almost desperate attempt to reduce the misunderstanding of Tennant's reasoning about the way in which religious experience enters the argument for God. Too many persons in his own day, and since, simply put Tennant down as one 'who does not believe in religious experience'.

The truth in the claim is that Tennant's analysis of the phenomenology and epistemology of religious experience leads him to maintain that religious experience cannot be a self-sufficient source of religious knowledge. Tennant's view, to be sure, would not satisfy those who hold that in revelation (or faith, or 'religious' experience) there is not only an indubitable awareness of God but also knowledge of God's attributes, and of his relation to man and the world. Adherents of this view can claim that there is a science of theology that needs neither basic defence nor aid from the rest of human experience, scientific or otherwise. This view becomes the counter-thesis to the humanistic and naturalistic thesis that Nature and man can be understood scientifically without the aid of theology.

Tennant's whole effort is to show that neither of these claims to independence or self-sufficiency adequately interpret the place of sensory and non-sensory experience in the total economy of human existence. He would deny that anyone can write 'The Future of an Illusion' – for either religion or science. Yet neither religion nor science must surrender to a demand for certainty; for experience yields only the probability which is the guide of life.

This essay attempts no original contribution to the philosophy of

religion. Its purpose will be realized if it can free from misunderstanding one of the keenest critiques of the evidential value of
religious experience – a critique never more needed than in the
present day when the primacy of feeling is again being advocated
in many quarters. Indeed, seldom in contemporary theological
literature does one find more cautious theoretical procedure, more
painstaking and acute delineation of the problems involved in
religious belief, and more pregnant insights, free from dogmatism
and irrelevance, than in the work of F. R. Tennant. It is, therefore,
all the more desirable to lift his critique of religious experience into
such relief that this aspect of his work may be subjected to a more
understanding evaluation both by exponents and critics of Tennant's
views.

For one cannot escape the conclusion, after oral discussion and
an examination of the literature, that, in his critique of religious
experience, Tennant is often misinterpreted even by his admirers.[1]
It is Tennant's conclusions from his examination of the evidential
value of religious experience which have disappointed many, who,
jubilant at Tennant's vindication of the reasonableness of theism,
and confident in the strength of the positive teleological argument
which he constructed to support theism, have been not a little
puzzled and even ruffled by his refusal to admit that religious
experience is a primary source of evidence for the existence of God.
In the excitement, few seem to have pursued a careful study of
what Tennant did allow concerning religious experience. Instead,
his critique of religious experience has been torn from the context
of his total philosophy and represented as completely hostile to any
of the values of that experience.[2] A painstaking study might have
revealed, however, that Tennant has not denied that there is
rapport between God and man in religious experience, but rather
found it necessary to inquire wherein lay its value for *philosophy*,
for an intelligible and coherent understanding of the world, and for
the description of God. There are few people who can love and yet
criticize the implications of their love with a view to understanding
exactly what love as such contributes to their experience; there
seem to be correspondingly few who, having had the religious

[1] For this reason, this exposition has been submitted to Tennant himself and
is fortunate to have obtained his approval as a statement of his convictions.

[2] Even as understanding a critic as G. F. Thomas, for example, implies that
Tennant draws the 'extreme conclusion' that 'religious experience is of no value
in establishing religious knowledge'. *The Nature of Religious Experience*, Essays
in honour of D. C. Macintosh, Harper and Bros., N.Y., 1937, pp. 50, 51.

experience of love and commitment to God, can test the *cognitive value* of the experience *per se*.

Hence, it is necessary to indicate at the outset, even before reviewing Tennant's actual analysis, that Tennant is challenging *conclusions* which he believes have been drawn too hastily from religious experience by the mystics, on the one hand, and by such thinkers as Schleiermacher, Rudolf Otto, and John Oman. His main interest has been to propose issues which his opponents must meet if they would fairly insist that religious experience in and of itself gives *knowledge* of God's existence and nature. He does not deny the value of religious experience from the viewpoint of emotional conviction and inspiration; nor does he assert categorically that *no* knowledge about God can be derived from it. But he is concerned to point out, with the ultimate view of founding theism upon unimpeachable evidence, that conclusions drawn from religious experience frequently overlook the epistemological importance of the fact that such experience is interpretative.[1] In other words, Tennant has never denied that religious experience may be communion with God (how strange that would be in a man who had spent his early years as a pastor in intimate contact with the problems of his flock!); but he has criticized a certain view of it eventuating in a specific type of theology.

I

The view Tennant opposes maintains that there can be a science of theology, as self-contained as any other science, whose independence derives from the fact that a unique datum is given in religious experience which is irreducible to any of the data provided by the other sciences. This datum is as ultimate as sense-impression and reveals in immediate experience a supersensible, spiritual environment. Such a position has, for instance, been quite recently presented by H. H. Farmer in *The World and God* and reviewed by Tennant.[2] According to Mr Farmer, religious experience involves direct, non-inferential apprehension, 'living awareness' of a personal reality, distinct from ideal objects or abstracts validities. If such a contention can be rendered a reasonable probability, it does

[1] As Dean A. C. Knudson has so well said, 'All experience is interpreted experience . . . Interpretation inheres in the very nature of religious experience, as it does in a different way in that of articulate experience in general.' *The Validity of Religious Experience*, New York: The Abingdon Press, 1937, p. 28.

[2] *Mind*, Volume 45, 1936, pp. 241–6.

indeed serve to give theology a place apart, relatively indifferent to the discoveries made in other sciences, and confident of the reality revealed by its systematized data.

In striking contrast Tennant indicates his own position: 'I have represented that the unique data, so-called, of religious experience are not the pure data, for which they have been taken – that is, are not pure in the qualified sense in which data that are *recepta* ever can be pure – but are data overlaid with explicated, interpretative ideas.'[1] The presence of these interpretative ideas is minimized or camouflaged by applying the word 'immediate' or referring to the intuitional 'flash' seemingly present in religious experience. Tennant insists that those accepting Farmer's views should realize that a 'living awareness' may well be an outcome of a 'synthesis issuing in synopsis, or involuntary fusion of "awareness" in a sort of intuitional flash'. 'There is no doubt that immediacy, in the temporal sense of rapidity of intake, attaches to such intuition; but that, of course, does not guarantee the truth of the synoptic judgment, since it may rest on faulty presuppositions or be a synthesis of unverified or erroneous opinions'[2] Nor does Tennant deny that such immediacy frequently carries with it a deep conviction as to the reality of the objective content of that experience. But he does demand that we take account of the distinction between the two kinds of certainty, namely, a state of mind – personal convincedness, which may have important consequences – and an objective characteristic of some propositions, which alone is relevant to the question of validity. 'Convincedness, however, is a matter of personal biography', say Tennant, 'while philosophies are concerned with public truth; and sanguine convincedness as to *credenda* is compatible – as in the case of Bishop Butler – with recognition that, in respect of logical grounding, they are but probable.'[3]

Tennant's first word of caution, therefore, is a reminder that the theologian keep distinct the psychological motivation-value of an experience and its epistemological status. A similar related caution will occupy us later, but this *fallacy of specious immediacy*,[4] as it might be called, cannot be overemphasized in view of the common disregard of it in recent religious thought. The self-evidence of such religious intuition, the genetic and analytic psychologist reminds us, is due to a confusion of psychological and epistemological imme-

---

[1] *Mind*, Volume 45, 1936, p. 245.   [2] *Ibid.*, p. 243.   [3] *Ibid.*, p. 243.
[4] Tennant, *Philosophy of the Sciences*, Cambridge University Press, 1932, p. 174.

diacy. The latter is a characteristic of very few types of cognition, and guarantees indubitableness, while propositions having the former kind of immediacy are always doubtful, since any interpretation of the psychologically immediate datum may be incorrect. How frequently we find that the meaning of the emotional expression on a friend's face, which we are sure we *read off* in immediate comprehension, is a misinterpretation and therefore a meaning which we found in his facial expression only because we had surreptitiously put it there! Such 'immediate' knowledge is not immediate, but unconsciously mediated, interpreted according to the apperceptive mass of the individual and the psychological set of the moment. That which seems to be self-evident has the self-evidence of the habitual and familiar, not of the immediately (epistemological and cognitive) given. To this extent, therefore, Tennant cannot be gainsaid. The 'immediacy' of religious experience is no guarantee of its truth.

II

But the crux of the problem lies in the question as to whether there is present in religious experience a datum, unique and irreducible, the immediate cognition of which reveals the nature of God. Tennant is quite ready to grant that there is no *a priori* impossibility of this, but, once more, he demands a careful consideration of this contention. His own examination leaves him sceptical about maintaining that in religious experience, which is effect, there is a special *cognition* of a (noumenal) cause which renders the experience possible. Though recognizing the peculiarity of the *response*, Tennant, nevertheless, is doubtful about concluding that a similar peculiarity exists on the stimulus (cause) side. For, to say the least, one must distinguish between the religious valuation made by the experient and the metaphysical cause which supposedly evoked that valuation. In other words, from numinous or religious valuation we must not, nay, we cannot, infer as hastily as has been done, (*a*) that there is a numen, or religious object proper, and (*b*) that we have acquaintance-knowledge of it similar to that which we indubitably possess in sensory experience. So far, it seems, Tennant is again methodologically correct, for, given a certain effect, the nature of the cause is a subject for investigation.

And Tennant's caution is all the more warranted after an examination of the so-called religious datum. This object is certainly unlike the sensory object, for it has no specific quality. A sense-datum, such as blue, is irreducible, but what religious object is analogously irreducible in its specificity? At this point Tennant's reader must pause and recall that, as a result of previous psychological analysis, Tennant had concluded that the primary data of the profane sciences are sensory perceptions, that 'our percepts and their simpler relations are the sources of our ideas and universals, at least in the sense of being the occasions of our obtaining them'. Hence, when one realizes that for Tennant 'sense-given-ness is the sole original certificate of actuality',[1] that for him even value is due not to the perception of a value-object but to feelings evoked by sensory and ideal data, he sees the theoretical basis for Tennant's scepticism about a specifically religious datum, and for his conclusion that 'theology must be an outgrowth from ordinary knowledge of the world and man'.[2] But to imply, as some have done, that these logically prior conclusions are the basis for Tennant's blindness to or 'dismissal' of unique religious knowledge is to overlook his lengthy examination of the proposals of his opponents. If some theologians are to set out from data equally objective and immediate, though of different species from the sensory, and equally provident of fresh knowledge-contact with the ontal, then it is for them to point out some specific and indubitable quality of a sensory or non-sensory nature.[3] But, as Tennant finds, some such unique quality is not forthcoming, because the numinous object is 'characterized only by its agency, which is not an object of immediate apprehension, in causing or evoking a specific kind of valuation or subjective attitude'.[4] If then God is present in religious experience, his presence is not 'directly apprehended', but is inferred, as is any metaphysical (as opposed to phenomenal) being, or transcendent cause; and consequently his presence is not necessarily to be inferred, *unless* it can be shown that the subjective response cannot be caused or evoked by any other type of stimulus, imaginary or real. If the religious response has some common, unique factor in it, incapable of being reduced to the imaginal or any other source

[1] Tennant, *Philosophy of the Sciences*, Cambridge University Press, 1932, p. 168.

[2] *Ibid.*, p. 168.

[3] To say, as Thomas does, that it is obvious that experience of God can 'never take the form of apprehension of a specific quale such as a colour, for God is not a sensible quale nor indeed a quale of any kind' (*The Nature of Religious Experience*, p. 51), is to overlook what seems to be the necessary condition of all immediate cognition of the existent, as distinct from the subsistent or relational.

[4] Tennant, *op. cit.*, p. 171.

in human experience, then there would be grounds for supposing
that this unique factor is evoked by a source of which the religious
experience is an index (in the same way as the experience of blue is
an index of the kind of thing the physical world can produce in a
human being). How much could be ascribed on the basis of this
factor alone to the independent causal Being would, however, be
still a question. Nor let it be forgotten as Tennant observes further,
that, if God *were* an object of direct acquaintance, there should be
no error in the cognition of deity and no basis for the variety of
religious opinion which has been characteristic of religious progress.

It is, in fact, his very search for this common factor or unique
datum that Tennant is forced to pronounce fruitless. As he says,
'It would seem that the numinous object, constitutive of religious
experience, throughout its many stages of refinement, cannot be a
quasi-perceptual datum, of the same order of underivedness as the
sensory. Its vagueness and lack of quality, in virtue of which it can
figure . . . in all kinds of religious experience, mystical or normal,
bespeak its identity with the generic image or with the concept
reached by abstraction or idealization, rather than its affinity with
objects of firsthand apprehension or acquaintance.'[1] Again, 'the
numinous Real is indeterminate enough to enter equally well into
a multitude of diverse mythologies and religions: . . . its abstract-
ness, qualitylessness, commonness to a variety of phenomena,
etcetera, render precarious and apparently groundless, the assertion
that it is apprehended in the concrete and with immediacy'.[2]

In all this, then, Tennant's attitude will be seen as less than
dogmatic denial of religious experience; it is rather the hunger of a
critical spirit for real knowledge. What is it, exactly, in religious
experience which gives such knowledge? To say, with Thomas, that
'prophets and poets are right in believing that intuition gives us an
initial, if not a complete and infallible insight into moral and

---

[1] *Ibid.*, p. 173.

[2] *Philosophical Theology*, Volume I, p. 309. Knudson also states: 'Indeed, the
objectivity of religious experience is not only as dubious as that of sense experience; it is psychologically much less compelling. Our sense impressions, no
matter how misleading they may be, usually carry conviction with them. As
Zeno put it, they "take hold of one by the hairs of one's head and drag one to
assent". This could hardly be said of ordinary religious experiences. The fact is
that there are no concrete religious percepts such as we have in sense experience.
Our religious impressions are as a rule vague in character and only dimly apprehend the more-than-human object.' *Validity of Religious Experience*, p. 90.
Cf. also, pp. 31, 54, 99, 100.

spiritual reality',[1] and that this 'creative' intuition reveals 'insights' which 'can never be completely stated in philosophical terms'[2] and yet not indicate what that common element is in the psychological object of the intuition, is to turn Tennant down without an answer. For the objection still persists that such speech refers only to something indeterminate and abstract though fused with a highly emotional experience. To go on and add that 'faith springs from need for a higher life, . . . from an intuition of the existence of a spiritual nature struggling to realize itself in our lives',[3] is certainly to be guilty both of the fallacy that the indeterminate or the abstract can be immediately given, and of the fallacy of specious immediacy (in the use of the word 'intuition' for what seems clearly to be an interpretative process). Indeed, for Thomas to add: 'Since this spiritual nature meets with resistance at whatever cost, we know that it is no mere ideal of our imagination, but a creative force rising out of the depths of our nature',[4] is clearly to indicate the inferential process involved in placing the causal agency. The problem still remains: What is given? Is it a value? If so, what value? Is it a spirit, and, if so, what are its reliable witnesses in our experience? To say: 'For as the anguish of *inquietude* or guilt betokens the alienation of the soul from its spiritual destiny, so joy bears witness to the presence of God, the fulfilment of religious longing',[5] is not to enlighten us, especially if we are seeking that touch of God in our experience which reveals unmistakably *his* nature, not ours.

Unable to discover any distinctive and controlling object in religious expereince, Tennant is forced to conclude that religious valuation is not the product of a unique datum, but rather of 'a derived and mediate image or conception which is interpretatively read into perceptual or ideal objects, as the case may be. It is *thought* to be there, or is suppositionally assigned as the *unapprehended* cause of mental states, such as emotions or sentiments, upliftings, and so forth, which are immediately apprehensible in introspection.'[6] In religious experience, he insists, we are immediately aware of an interfusion of the emotional, imaginal, and conative, but not of a *sui generis* datum in itself revelatory of an extra-human realm. The experience, however, is so unusual, as *erlebt*, and in its consequences for our lives, that we are ready to explain it by inferring a cause independent of us. This latter tendency is

---

[1] Thomas, *op. cit.*, p. 53.   [2] *Ibid.*, p. 54.   [3] *Ibid.*, p. 63.   [4] *Ibid.*, p. 63.
[5] *Ibid.*, p. 63.   [6] *Philosophy of the Sciences*, p. 174.

understandable enough particularly in human beings who, having accustomed themselves to a certain tenor of life, naturally regard a singular break in this routine as externally and especially provoked by a Reality whose existence has, in fact, already been postulated critically or uncritically to explain other mundane experiences. Yet, however spontaneous such religious experience may be assumed to be, to establish its objectivity in any exact sense is a matter of more rigorous evidence than has been available. And it must be remembered that the burden of proof lies on the shoulders, not of Tennant, but of those who contend that God is immediately recognized in religious experience.

III

Thinkers who are not yet impressed with the force or plausibility of Tennant's contentions must bear in mind still another possibility which, if disregarded, leads to confusion and the loading of religious experience with elements really extraneous to it as such. The religious response, like any other experience of an affective or cognitive nature, 'is undoubtedly rapport with an object',[1] but this psychological objectivity is not to be accepted without further argument as an indication of the metaphysical existence of the Object or God. Furthermore, it is undoubtedly true that the person who believes that the object of his cognition is 'the Holy' may well issue from that experience a changed man. Nevertheless, the presence of inspirational emotions or cognitive states is not enough to justify the influence of a causal metaphysical reality. For, Tennant reminds us, not only does the psychologically objective include the imaginal and the ideal (for example, 'the centaur and the Euclidean line'),[2] but these 'when they are believed to be actual, can evoke feelings and sentiments as profound, intense, inspiring and practically fruitful, as those excited by perceptual or actual things: and imaginary persons count for quite as much as real ones in the lives of most people'.[3] Hence, the conception of God which the individual uses for the interpretation of his experience, thereby constituting it 'religious experience', may well determine the course of religious life, once it has been initiated. It may also be conceded that one might issue from such experience with a 'hunch' about God to be tested by the rest of his experience, but a 'hunch' is still not knowledge. Nor is it denied that such

[1] *Ibid.*, p. 176.   [2] *Ibid.*, p. 176.   [3] *Ibid.*, p. 176.

emotional experiences have led men to make fruitful hypotheses about God (except that most men would be inclined dogmatically to assert the reality rather than philosophize about hypotheses, especially when deeply emotional experiences have been theirs). But from the content of religious experience alone, even the least critical cannot come to a full-orbed conception of God.[1]

IV

The question as to whether there is a real 'counter-part' to the objects indubitably present in religious experience now begs an answer. But curiously enough, according to our philosopher, 'that question cannot be answered by religious experience itself'.[2] If Tennant is correct as to there being no underived and peculiarly religious datum, it would seem that the uniqueness of religious experience can only be accounted for 'by attributing it to the introduced interpretative idea of God, or of the numen'.[3] It is this idea of God, derived not *from* the religious experience but from reasoning about the world and man, which 'permeates the other data or analytica [of the experience], and it alone bestows upon them the capacity to evoke emotional response of a peculiar kind. Previously to the acquisition and the causal or interpretative use of this derived emotion, experiences such as were destined to become religious could not be religious: they could only be regarded as natural, not as super-natural – whether aesthetic, moral, or of other types'.[4] The knowledge which, supposedly, we got *out* of religious experience is exactly what we brought to non-religious experience, thereby constituting it religious. Certainly, ideas of God's unity, of his love, of his causality and creativity are not read off in religious experience! Would R. Otto, for example, have interpreted the numinous experience in terms of creature-feeling apart from his previous idea of God as creator? The very fact that the interpretation of the nature of God has kept step with moral and intellectual changes instead of surging ahead on the waves of religious experi-

---

[1] It is for this reason and for the admitted fallibility of religious intuition that Thomas commends Tennant's teleological argument. 'For religious experience and faith alone can never yield adequate knowledge of a God who has revealed Himself in the natural creation as well as in the spirit of man.' (*Op. cit.*, p. 55.) Hence the title of his article: 'A Reasoned Faith', and the conclusion that 'while religious faith is intuitive in origin it must be developed and supported by philosophical analysis of nature and man'. (*Ibid.*, pp. 64, 65, and cf. p. 67.)

[2] Tennant, *The Philosophy of the Sciences*, p. 177.

[3] *Ibid.*, p. 177.   [4] *Ibid.*, p. 177.

ence as such is another fact with which critics must cope. Furthermore, for what reason should we be more able to obtain direct knowledge of God than we can of other persons?

Thus, it would seem that when the Christian asserts his immediate sense of the indwelling Christ, he is imposing a learned causal interpretation on immediately introspected experiences of peace or joy and strengthening of resolve, 'and he would not be able to extract that dogmatic content out of his present experiences had it not been first interpretatively read into them'.[1] To this Tennant adds, significantly: 'This dogmatic content may of course be true, but it is not matter of direct experience in the sense that joy and peace are.'[1]

V

The 'religiousness of religious experience' is due, then, to the saturation' of the experience by the idea of God otherwise derived. It is for this reason that Tennant does not include an appeal to religious experience as part of his cumulative teleological argument for God in the fourth chapter of *Philosophical Theology*, Vol. II. This omission has been interpreted by some perhaps to corroborate the contention that Tennant does not take adequate account of religious experience, but it is now intelligible and the contention correspondingly loses force.[2] For, as Tennant says, the psychology and epistemology of religious experience must be philosophically 'atheous' (not 'atheistic') as far as the constructive case *leading* to the probability of God is concerned. After the theistic position has been rendered more probable than others 'by a more circuitous path than the short-cut of alleged immediacy' (that is, by inference from the nature of the world and its relation to man), then, and

[1] Tennant, *The Philosophy of the Sciences*, p. 180.
[2] A recent letter from Tennant, dated November 12, 1937, applies to this point. 'As to the omission of reference to religious experience along with morality, etcetera, in my teleological argument, I may say that the only connection in which it could be mentioned is as indicating, along with human rationality and morality, the purpose or goal of the design exhibited in the cosmos; religious experience having been represented to be the *outcome* of rationality and morality, I did not feel it essential to emphasize it explicitly in that context, but rather supposed the reader would take it to be implied. Its place, in my exposition, can only be in the description of theism and its corollaries after theism have been arrived at.' Speaking of his contention 'that religious experience itself gives no *proof* of Deity because already presupposing such belief', he adds: 'But this has no value for life, or that it is illusory, provided *other* grounds for theism are sound.'

then only, can the strongest theoretical base be put under the
religious experience as it is re-expounded. Tennant would not, of
course, deny that the data of religious experience as uncritically
interpreted provide phenomena with which the philosopher must
deal 'on the way up'. Indeed, this is exactly why Tennant himself
examined its claims in Chapter 12 of the first volume of *Philosophical Theology* which precedes the actual argument for theism in the
second volume. But, if his own analysis is correct, the 'intimations'
of religious experience must, for the critical, indeed be meagre
sources of divine *information* and inspiration, unless the existence
and attributes of God can be inferred from broader and more
public data. Indeed, if God's existence can be rendered probable
on other grounds, religious experience, not as a source of philosophical knowledge, but as a source of intellectual, moral, and aesthetic
inspiration, may be a final confirmation of a total argument for God
which finds its coping-stone in the moral, and *its final affirmation*
in the religious, experience. No one who has carefully read
Tennant's work can say that Tennant's God is not immanent in
natural process and in the life of man with all due respect for man's
freedom of will. The bone of contention has been the evidential
value of religious experience. And it would seem that the theolo-
gican cannot find a short-cut to knowledge of God *via* religious
experience. To be sure, the mystic and the man of faith may be
bored and left cold by a long series of arguments to prove the
existence of God, and it may be as Ritschl and Troeltsch insisted,
that 'it is impossible to reach what faith designates as "God" by
the simple expedient of pushing scientific or metaphysical explanation a little further'.[1] It may also seem that 'to transpose faith into
the key of philosophy would change its very nature . . . bleed
faith white and drain out the vital elements of mystery since
speculative constructions as such are hypothetical, whereas the
hidden life of faith is certainty'.[2] But perhaps the task of the
philosopher is to render the absolute commitment and the 'spirit
of trust'[3] which characterize religion as a living sentiment a
reasonable thing (a reasonable irrational fact), if such it can be. In
any case, to revert to our first point, Tennant is not denying
personal convincedness and moral significance to the religious
experience; he is testing its *evidential*, epistemological value as an

[1] H. R. Mackintosh, *Types of Modern Theology*, New York: Scribner's, 1937,
p. 193.
[2] *Loc. cit.*   [3] Thomas, *op. cit.*, p. 66.

argument *on the way to God*, especially as an independent approach to discoveries in other fields. It is only as the cosmos, including man in his moral struggle, suggests with great probability that it is ordered 'for the realization of moral and other values' that we have a 'reasonable guarantee' for belief in God which neither ethical nor religious experience 'alone can provide'.[1] Hence, the conclusion: 'Theology explicates what the other departments and sciences suggest; and they supply it with a basis, in facts and in generalization, for a faith such as is but a further stage, in that venture to believe where we cannot rigidly prove, which we have found to be inevitable in all that we are wont to call knowledge of actuality'.[2] Personal convincedness may therefore in a reasonable life be interfused with philosopical probability.

[1] Tennant, *The Philosophy of the Sciences*, p. 184.
[2] *Ibid.*, p. 187.

CHAPTER IX

THE COSMOLOGICAL ARGUMENT – REVISITED AND REVISED

It is one thing to indicate the weaknesses in naturalism and humanism; it is another to show that a better – a more inclusive and therefore more reasonable – hypothesis is forthcoming.

The present essay is an attempt to elucidate what might happen if we realize that we cannot first assume a view of Nature and then add 'God' to it. This is no more acceptable than to assume a certain view of God and then fit 'Nature' into it. There are certain cosmological questions that thorough thinking about our human experience raises and that require some sort of answer from persons who are more concerned about solving problems than hugging their methodological heads and puristically 'pass by on the other side'.

This is the place to say that, as I see it now, should cosmological contentions such as those discussed in this chapter fail (not in certainty but in most reasonable probability), then teleological, moral, and religious evidence go begging for interrelation with our experience of Nature. In any case, as the other chapters in this Section suggest, I think the time is overripe to give up talking about the different arguments for God and to review each as we evaluate what it can contribute to one comprehensive argument for God. Too often in philosophical theology we have sought short-cuts to a preconceived idea of God rather than asking what kind of world-view is most consistent with our actual and varied evidence.

I

The contention in this paper is severely limited. It is that there are considerations in the cosmological argument for God that should not be overlooked by any philosophical cosmologist or by any thinker who believes that the question of God's existence involves a metaphysical issue and is not an autonomous or independent theological problem. Therefore, instead of assuming that the cosmological argument is valuable only if a certain kind of God is proved by it, we shall consider what question is central to the cosmological argument and what the nature of the answer is. We shall indicate that while the cosmological argument itself does not adequately justify belief in the traditional God of theism, it does lay the groundwork for hypotheses which philosophical theology, in particular, may explore further in the light of additional considerations. Once the epistemic, metaphysical, and religious stances in the ontological argument are set aside by a thinker, he still needs to ask the questions involved in the cosmological, teleological, moral, and mystical approaches to the nature of existence with a view to discovering which hypothesis they render reasonably tenable if not demonstrable.

The question here, accordingly, is: How far does the cosmological argument get us in our thinking about the nature of existence, once we leave the question open as to what the nature of God is? Since Kant's critique of the cosmological argument has been so influential, we begin by analysing his frame of mind regarding it.

II

Kant summarized the traditional cosmological argument in one sentence: 'If anything exists, therefore an absolutely necessary being exists'.[1] By an absolutely necessary being Kant assumed the traditional meaning of '*ens realissimum*', a union of being and perfection.

His rejection of the cosmological argument is actually based on one main contention. There is no way of knowing, he argued, what kind of a being a necessarily existing being is, if the existents from which you argue have no particular properties.

It should be noted that Kant is denying only that the specific attributes of a necessary being must remain without content if all we start with is 'anything exists'. One need not deny that a necessary being exists, but only that we can argue what kind of a being it is from mere existents of any kind. Since Kant assumed that a necessary being had to be a perfect being, he went right on to press the contention that we certainly cannot move from an imperfect existent world to a being complete in the absolutistic sense of perfection. Thus Kant says:

[1] Immanuel Kant, *The Critique of Pure Reason*, ed. Norman K. Smith, London: Macmillan, 1930, A405, B633.

The transcendental idea of a necessary and all-sufficient being is overwhelmingly great, so high above everything empirical, the latter being always conditioned, that it leaves us at a loss, partly because we can never find in experience material sufficient to satisfy such a concept, and partly because it is always in the sphere of the conditioned that we carry out our search, seeking there ever vainly for the unconditioned. . . .[1]

Kant's basic argument, then, is this: There is no way of gaining insight into what the unconditioned can be if we seek clues in the realm of the conditioned. Why? Because the idea of the unconditioned, necessary, and all-sufficient being is, as Kant sees it, 'so high above everything empirical' that in vain do we look for some clues to it in the conditioned.

Two assumptions were operative in Kant's thought. First, as we have just seen, that necessity and the 'overwhelmingly great all-sufficiency' were synonymous. Second, that proof of God had to be demonstrable, or capable of absolute certainty.

But what would happen if one did not grant Kant either the assumption that knowledge of God needs to be apodictic or that the necessity of God's being must carry with it a particular kind of 'all-sufficient perfection'? Presumably we could then postulate the existence of a necessary Being, worthy of worship but not perfect in the classical, absolutistic sense. Such a Being might well be required to make such existence, knowledge, and values as we have reasonably, if not apodictically, intelligible. Indeed, Kant himself suggested that one might 'postulate the existence of an all-sufficient being, as the cause of all possible effects'.[2] But Kant succumbed to the demands of the traditional ontological argument, not for a probable hypothesis, but for logical certainty regarding perfection. This demand for certainty in knowledge, wedded to the notion of all-sufficient necessity, exerted final control over Kant's thought. It is all the more fascinating, therefore, to watch him play with another tantalizing alternative that he gave up in the end.

Thus when Kant does consider the specific content of the observable world he is so impressed by 'variety and beauty' that he exclaims: 'all speech loses its force', and, 'our judgment of the whole resolves itself into an amazement which is speechless, and only the more eloquent on that account'.[3] And he soon adds:

[1] Immanuel Kant, *The Critique of Pure Reason*, ed. Norman K. Smith London: Macmillan, 1930, A621, B645, italics added.
[2] *Ibid.*, A612, B634, italics added.   [3] *Ibid.*, A622, B650.

Reason, constantly upheld by this ever-increasing evidence, which though empirical is yet so powerful, cannot be so depressed by doubts suggested by subtle and abtruse specula-tion, that it is not at once aroused from the indecision of all melancholy reflection, as from a dream, by one glance at the wonders of nature and the majesty of the universe – ascending from height to height up to the all-highest, from the conditioned to its conditions, up to supreme and unconditioned Author (of all conditioned being).[1]

But why did Kant not pursue this empirical vein in his reason-ing, that is, why did he not pursue a teleological approach which, as he himself said, is 'best suited to the ordinary human reason'?[2] Because he was convinced that it would lead only to 'an architect of the world who is always very much hampered by the adaptability of the material in which he works, not a creator of the world to whose idea everything is subject'.[3]

To summarize: for Kant the cosmological argument will not do, because reason faces a 'veritable abyss' in trying to move from any conditioned to the unconditioned; and the teleological argument falls short because it cannot yield more than a conditioned Author or Architect. When Kant is tempted to move from nature to God, he is halted by a controlling idea of the kind of being God must be. Yet with this absolutistic conception of God before him, he is con-vinced that nothing in the world can ever give it apodictic theoret-ical support.

Suppose, however, we remove from our eyes the blinders that kept Kant from a calm appraisal of the evidence before him. Suppose we favour what Kant called 'ordinary human reason' or what Butler called the 'probability that is the guide of life', – and move 'from the conditioned to its conditions', to what extent can we realize 'the lofty purpose which we have before our eyes, namely, the proof of an all-sufficient primordial being'.[4]

III

We shall take as a point of departure a passage Kant himself wrote in cosmological vein. This passage actually summarizes, we suggest, the basic thrust in the cosmological argument once we get away

---

[1] *Ibid.*, A624, B652, italics added.   [2] *Ibid.*, A624, B652.
[3] *Ibid.*, A627, B656.   [4] *Ibid.*, A627, B655.

from preconceptions of what knowledge must be and what God's nature must involve.

> The whole universe must thus sink into the abyss of nothingness, unless, over and above this infinite chain of contingencies, we assume something to support it – something which is original and independently self-subsistent, and which as the case of the origin of the universe secures also at the same time its continuance. What magnitude are we to ascribe to this supreme cause. . . ?[1]

The only unfortunate thing about this statement is that it might lend itself to an imagery in which God is as it were added on to a contingent series; but it should be clear from the whole that a much more intimate relation is involved. What does come out clearly in this passage are the questions which the proponent of the cosmological argument (hereafter called the cosmologist) seeks to answer. Let us look at them.

Granted that there is nothing in the observable, existent world as man knows it that depends upon itself for its existence or for its continuance. Is there nothing, nothing, nothing, whose very essence it is to be the being it is? Indeed, can we give a reasonable account of the existence, continuance, and basic interconnections or interactions of contingent beings, without postulating some unconditioned Being?

These, of course, are not rhetorical questions; nor are they restricted to persons who are trying to give reasons for a particular religious belief. Philosophers in the East and in the West – religious and non-religious – have asked the same questions. In a changing world in which things come into being and pass away, where similarity and difference in beings and events persist in such a way as to suggest structure in change, the question will not down: Is there a sustaining structure to which order-in-change is related? Once a thinker could move beyond agnosticism or scepticism, the answer took a basic form: something (or some things) eternal there must be – whether it be Water, Air, The Indefinite, Fire Changing in Fixed Measure, Thought, Four Roots (Earth, Air, Fire, and Water), or Atoms and Empty Space, Ideas, The Good, Prime Mover Unmoved. Hylozoist, Rationalist, Realist, Materialist, Idealist, metaphysical Monist, Dualist, or Pluralist – all agree that

[1] *Ibid.*, A623, B651.

observable changing things cannot be adequately understood because their very being and any specific order in their change require a supportive unchanging structure or a network of events to explain the continuity in changing existents.

If a thinker can go this far, he is not required to hold that eternal being is perfect. But two other conclusions are required by the thrust of the argument. First, eternal being depends upon nothing else for its being what it is; it is self-sufficient or *causa sui*. Second, eternal being must be such in its relation to observable changing things and events that what is observable, far from being denied, becomes more intelligible.

When one speaks this way, he is of course aware that there are different kinds of intelligibility, serving different human purposes. But one becomes aware of the kind of intelligibility illustrated by the cosmologist when he tries the following theoretical gambit. 'There is nothing about me that insures that I exist or continue to exist. There are certain relationships that I must acknowledge as affecting my existence and the quality of its continuance. These relationships do not depend upon me for their being – for example, that I was born of parents, and cannot stay alive without air. It is, therefore, entirely conceivable that I should not exist: and, come to think of it, that these other events should not exist, since in their own way their existence is not guaranteed by their essence. And this reasoning can be extended to every thing, to all the beings and the events that I call Nature. If no part of Nature must exist, that is, if this world need not exist in any of its parts or events, then can it be that Nature itself as a whole need not exist?'

The answer is clearly: 'Nature as a whole need not exist, if none of its parts need not exist.' This, we take it, is the point of Kant's own sentence: 'The whole universe must thus sink into the abyss of nothingness unless, over and above this infinite chain of contingencies, we assume something to support it.'

For our passion to understand as much as possible will not readily accept a conclusion that follows once we say that neither the events or entities in what we call Nature, nor Nature as a whole, must exist. The conclusion is that there could be nothing at all, or that some kind of being need not exist. If there is any conception before which, as it were, our minds faint, it is the proposition: No world at all, no being at all, has to be!

Ask a mind to think that everything could ever be or become nothing, or that everything should come from nothing, and it simply gags: it has nowhere to go; or better it just cannot move. The mind can think that this world need not be, but it simply finds no ground for supposing that no-world-at-all need not be. Hence, it concludes, there is Something whose very nature is such that it could never become nothing. Something is, that could never come from nothing, whose very nature it is to be, some such eternal being there must be. Again, why? Because we should otherwise need to suppose that since being-or-events in Nature are contingent none of them need to be, and hence neither the 'realm of Nature' we know, nor any other similar realm of contingent events, has to be.

We have thus come to the first basic conclusion at the heart of the cosmological argument. It is not that a certain kind of God, or a certain kind of necessity must exist, but only that, in Kant's terms, if anything contingent exists some absolutely necessary being exists. Necessary being does not in itself require it to be perfect being.

But what kind of being can Necessary Being be? It is at this point that we can learn from the impasse[1] which occurs if we insist that it is absolutistically perfect. For Kant is correct that we cannot know what this Necessary Being is from reflection on imperfect beings. But if we ask what it probably is, what its nature may be by reasonable postulation, we need not be stopped in our tracks; we can, for example, call it Supreme Being (as Kant hinted) and articulate the nature that it needs to have in order to keep our known, or any other contingent, world from possibly sinking into the abyss of nothingness. We are free now to develop an hypothesis that is more coherent with the total observable evidence than any other, an hypothesis that is experiential because it takes its cues from the order of beings, events, and values discoverable in the realm of nature and man. It may not turn out to be the classical theistic God, but this cannot be the cosmologist's first concern.

IV

We must pause, however, to consider two objections raised by Milton K. Munitz in a very comprehensive critique of the traditional cosmological argument. Because the cosmological argument has been stated and interpreted in so many ways, one must always

[1] Peter A. Bertocci, 'An Impasse in Philosophical Theology', *International Philosophical Quarterly*, V ,1965, 379–96.

be careful to state the particular interpretation he is considering. That Professor Munitz includes the form set out above is clear in his own summary:

> For if there were only contingent things in existence, and these have the possibility of not existing, then, we could envisage a situation in which there would be nothing at all in existence . . . But then it would have been impossible for anything to come into existence. For in order to do so, there must already be something in existence (since nothing can come into existence of itself). The fact is, however, there are things in existence. We must, consequently, surrender our original assumption that the only things that exist are contingent beings. There must be a Necessary Being, one that neither comes into existence nor can not exist. This necessary Being (God) confers existence on all other things, while being itself uncaused.[1]

As Professor Munitz sees it, 'the crucial step is that in which the argument proceeds to make a judgment of the same type about the world, as it makes about any individual object or event within it, namely, that the world, too, is contingent. It is this step that is open to serious doubt'.[2] He concludes, the part of the cosmological argument we have been examining 'commits the fallacy of composition. We cannot say that, since every event or object in ordinary experience is contingent, therefore, the entire world is also contingent'.[3]

But does the cosmological argument in this respect actually commit the fallacy of composition, if by the world (or Nature) we do mean the series of beings and events that are related in such a way as to allow them temporally or spatially, at least, to be interrelated? The issue, as we shall note in a moment, may actually turn out to be what we mean by the 'world', but if, as Munitz himself dissentingly realizes, the world is regarded as an all-inclusive class or totality, it is hard to see why in this instance the fallacy of composition is necessarily committed.[4] If the argument had to be that,

[1] Milton K. Munitz, *The Mystery of Existence*, New York: Appleton-Century-Crofts, 1965, pp. 116, 117. See W. I. Matson, *The Existence of God*, Ithaca: Cornell University Press, 1965, p. 57 and pp. 56–86, for a good statement and critique of what he justly calls this 'subtle form of cosmological argument'.

[2] *Ibid.*, p. 117.

[3] *Ibid.*, p. 119. See also Munitz, *ibid.*, pp. 78–83.

[4] It is indeed logically possible to conceive of the world as made up of 'temporally overlapping events' such that the going-out-of existence of each

in view of the fact that all beings and events in the world are contingent, we draw the conclusion directly that a non-contingent Being exists, the fallacy would indeed be committed. But if, as we would wish to put it, every event included in the existence of a world (or some sort of complex organization of the being and events) is contingent, then we fail to see what has been illogically or unempirically added in the conclusion that the world as a whole is contingent. For, as contingent, even if the world is said to be an everlasting series of overlapping contingent events, it still remains valid to say that the world at any one point and as a whole is contingent.

It is true that wherever attributes are attributed to wholes composed of relatively discrete parts we do need to take a second look at the conclusion about the whole, but the burden of proof still rests on him who argues that the whole is characterized by other than what characterizes every part. In the case of this form of the cosmological argument, we may deny that a fallacy necessarily exists.

It is also true that we are forced back to asking what we mean by world, but then a whole battery of other questions needs to be asked that would take us beyond our purpose here – and Professor Munitz's views would deserve careful critique in this consideration. But we cannot assume that some other view of the world is correct in debating the cosmologist's contentions.[1]

Nevertheless it is important to bring out what the cosmologist is contending. The central question for the traditional cosmologist, as for Munitz, is indeed whether it makes sense to say that the world might not have existed.[2]

---

individual event will occupy some finite temporal interval. 'If, then, the beginning of one event depends causally on the ending of another', and 'if we have an infinite time in the past throughout which to trace the causal sequence of relative beginnings and endings in finite events . . . there is no point in the past where absolutely nothing exists' (*Ibid.*, 119). But without pressing the question of the possible reification of 'infinite time' in this case, so that it does the unifying work of God, the cosmologist could grant that there might well not be a point where absolutely nothing exists without denying that the totality of things is still a totality of contingent beings, if now an everlasting series. Everlasting contingency is still contingency. The issue remains: Would everlasting contingency be a more likely explanation of the being and order we observe than eternal Being which is such as to account for the order of contingent beings known (everlasting or not)?

[1] This, alas, is what critics of the argument assume: They show with plausibility that there are 'cracks in the structure of the argument' (cf. Matson, *ibid.*, p. 78), but they assume that the theory of the world from which they are operating has no cracks.

[2] Munitz, *ibid.*, p. 120.

Without entering a prolonged debate on what we mean by world, we would return to the minimal contention that to speak of 'world' is to mean the beings and events so related to each other in space and time, whatever the discontinuity, that they are believed to be a whole with some degree of mutual interdependence. It is true, as Munitz says, that world must not be defined in such a way as to presuppose that God exists, but it is also true that it must not be so defined in such a way as to rule out the existence of God. What is increasingly clear, and what the cosmologist may be said to be urging, is that the problem of God and the problem of the world are interconnected! We cannot assume that we already are so clear and decisive about the kind of world we are in that to talk about God is simply to talk about an 'additive' that is not needed.

Thus, Munitz seems to have misconstrued the problem when he concludes:

> In short, we cannot say that we need, simply, to start from the realization that the world is contingent, and that we should then come to recognize that its existence is dependent upon God; to have characterized the world as contingent, as something that might not have existed, and whose existence is dependent on some being independent of itself, is already to use the concept of God.[1]

For it is not assumed that the world as a whole is contingent – as Munitz's own critique of the argument as involving the fallacy of composition shows. But it is argued that unless we can show that any being or event in the world involves its own existence then we must indeed ask the question: If no event or being depends upon itself for its own existence, and if, as far as we understand it, every event or being is found to he dependably related to other beings which are themselves not dependent upon themselves, can we understand the dependable order that enables us to call it a world, including ourselves, without raising the question of order-in-change? It does not follow deductively, as Munitz is seduced into thinking by some expositions and defences of the cosmological argument,[2] that contingency must mean Necessary Being or a Creator (as atomists have showed). Neither does it follow deductively that the world-as-a-whole is in some sense self-existent.

[1] Munitz, *ibid.*, p. 120.   [2] *Ibid.*, pp. 121–5.

What is fundamentally posed by the cosmologist is this, and we beg to repeat the above thesis: If the world is defined as changing beings and events in and among which orderly structures are observable in the succession of beings and events, is it reasonable to suppose that those beings and events, and the orders they display, are themselves related to, or the effect of, a Being which is expressed or involved in them, but not exhausted in them? It may be that a world can be so defined that appeal to such an hypothesis is otiose or incoherent; but it cannot, surely, be assumed that such a substitute view is true and therefore can be used against the cosmological argument. Let one metaphysics vie with another, but let no metaphysical view, theistic or non-theistic, be taken for granted as an account of what 'the world' seems 'clearly to be'.

What further needs to be emphasized is that the cosmologist is not trying to supplant a scientific description of the world; indeed, he would argue that if he is correct it is more understandable that scientific disciplines should be as fertile as they have been.[1] He is not trying to add a new law to scientific laws, or to add a new being to those already discovered scientifically. He is rather asking whether a world, of the sort the human mind in its scientific enterprise understands as an orderly word of beings and events, is not better understood if it is seen as related to a structure of Being whose own intrinsic being and order is the ground for such order and being as we have. Again the cosmologist's question is: In what way can we think of the world, including man, so that we

---

[1] While, alas, some proponents of the cosmological (and other arguments for God) sometime open themselves to this accusation, it is hardly relevant for Matson to argue:

> Suppose word were flashed to all the laboratories of the world that it has at last been proved, beyond any peradventure of a doubt, that an infinite Being, though sufficient reason for the world, exists: what help could this conceivably be for any research in progress? If the bulletin announced instead the definitive triumph of atheism, would any project have to be abandoned? Individual scientists might be elated or depressed at either report; that is all. (*Ibid.*, p. 78.)

But could the same thing not be said about a bulletin announcing the certainty, (or dethronement) of, the postulate of the uniformity of Nature or the universality of causal connections of some sort? The theoretical issue is: Do both theory and practice more reasonably cohere with the belief that basic principles observable to operate in one part of the world may be trusted to operate in any other part? Are not Scientists who believe in the uniformity and universality of causal law not encouraged to seek causal explanations when such seem difficult to come by, even as believers in the goodness of God are encouraged to seek the possible good in evil? In both instances respectively the issue is: What are the theoretical grounds for believing that there is a universe of a certain kind of order or of a certain kind of goodness.

are not unreasonably surprised that it should have the pervasive orders of being and events that enable us to call it 'a world'. To 'better understand' means: to answer questions that are raised by the human mind when it moves from the task of describing the world with a view of prediction to the task of explaining what is presupposed by the fact that such description is possible.

Let us, then, be explicit about what the cosmologist finds it unreasonable to believe. First, that the observed world as an ordinary sequence of events is adequately understandable on its own terms. The cosmologist is not disposed to quarrel with the assumptions that physicists, for example, make about the physical order of events for their own purposes. But if, for example, a physicist postulates the uniformity of nature as a practical working principle to guide his own investigations, the cosmologist does ask: On what grounds do you, on your view of order as regularity, justify your belief that if a sequence *ab* is followed by *c* in one part of your world it is expected to follow everywhere else in the world, especially if you hold that no being or event in the world is self-existent or that no relationship is self-existent? It may seem to suffice for you as a physicist to say that the principle of uniformity has been and is a fruitful working principle that also encourages research. But this restricted assumption that enables you to get on with your work will not suffice when we ask why this human assumption is so pervasively successful. We need to probe why your practice is so successful when on your own terms one would have no good reason to suppose that any specific event or pattern of events should be similar or repeated. You are marching bravely from station to station, but we develop a theoretical limp when we ask why the next station should be basically consistent with your theoretical and practical needs. Why not reconceive the framework of the world in its parts and as a whole so that the regularity rather than being surprising is to be expected? You need not give up an iota of what you find empirically, if you postulate a Uniform Being so related to the order of beings and events as you see them that their pervasive and persistent order is what you may expect because its nature and structure is the sustaining ground of that 'world'.

V

In the preceding discussion we have purposely assumed that the changes or beings in the world are not internally related, for the view that they are is in itself a cosmological answer, on a monistic ontological model, to the problem of an orderly many-in-one. But since the cosmological argument is historically connected with theistic arguments, we shall deliberately not pursue this alternative, once we have granted that the theistic view needs to confront this other theoretical alternative. Yet the theistic and monistic views of 'the world' are united against any basic pluralistic views which so atomize the world that the order we observe is a constant surprise. If what we observe about us is a realm of dependably predictable, determinate changes, then, if there is no Self-Sufficient Unified Structure in some way controlling-sustaining the order we observe, we seem to be courting rather than cornering mystery. For now many substance-causes (to collapse 'beings' and 'events'), each *ab initio* intrinsically independent of each other, presumably interacted in a fashion that produced and will go on to produce a dependable togetherness that is unreasonably expected if they indeed were initially unrelated to, and constitutionally independent, of, each other. Ultimate Pluralism is always hard put to explain order. For if there is a dependable order among the events or beings that make up what we call the world, why make that order difficult to understand by postulating beings that presumably are independent completely of each other? Hence both theistic and monistic cosmologists are united against any view of the world that makes the order itself a constant anomaly, given pluralistic presuppositions.

Restricting ourselves to a theistic alternative we must ask how the Ground of the world is related to events in the world and their order. On any theistic view the dependent substance-causes are created, which is to say basically that they are neither part of the Ground nor emanations from it. They are 'posited', 'planted-out', to use F. R. Tennant's terms. But any cosmological theist must disabuse himself and others of the view that the Ground is a First Cause in a temporal sense – some cosmic Watch-maker who makes the parts of the watch, then the watch, and finally, perhaps, leaves it alone while he goes about other business. For what the world calls for, if it calls for any Ground at all, is a Ground that is at every moment related to each contingent being and relation just because every moment, as we know it, is not self-dependent. Any First Cause cannot be merely a Self-Sufficient Being that creates a time-series which then runs presumably by derived power.

If there is any Productive Ground at all, it is not First Temporal

Cause but Creator and Recreator or Continuer persistently and contemporaneously involved in the very existence and interrelations of the beings that we know as 'the world'. The notion of cause as merely regular sequence is to be given up because regularity could not be adequately conceived as 'residing' in the substance-cuases as such or in their different relations. A particular view of the Productive Ground cannot be justified without reference to considerations not given so far and we cannot present them here. For our main concern is to indicate the kind of alternative which cosmological reasoning finds reasonable for explaining the dependent substance-causes-in-their-relations. The Productive or Creative Cause that replaces a supposed First Temporal Cause fulfils its theoretical function only if it is contemporary with every substance-cause and relation in the world.

In a word, to rephrase and expound Kant, the cosmological arguments runs: 'If any being and event exists as contingent, then a Contemporaneous Creator-Ground of its being, continuity, and interrelations, exists as its cause. What a doctrine of creation calls for further is the subject of another paper'.[1] The argument will indeed founder if such a doctrine cannot be shown to be reasonable. But to tide us over for the time being, the notion of contemporaneous Creator can be imperfectly illustrated in this way.

The words I speak are not created by me in such a way that they can be said to produce their own sequence (as a listener might be tempted to suppose). Were they heard on a phonograph record it would seem easy to think that they and their sequence needed no source beyond themselves. But actually when they were first uttered I, the Thinker-Speaker-Producer, was contemporaneous with them and their sequence reflected a Purpose I had in mind. The words did not exhaust the fullness of my being, and I could go on to produce other sentences that indeed reflect the import of those I already uttered. But I transcend the order of speech in which as contemporaneous Cause I am immanent. Other persons, especially if they were listening to a phonograph record of my creation, need not, as they listen keep my-being-myself in mind (as the physicist need not keep the Creator-Source in mind), but the fact nevertheless exists that the uniformity of meaning discovered depends on unobserved Presence – because I am present in different ways in all that I uttered. This brief suggestion may suffice with due

[1] Peter A. Bertocci, 'Towards a Metaphysics of Creation', *The Review of Metaphysics*, *XVII*, 1964, 493–510.

apologies for the personalizing of the Creator, for it is not evident from the evidence adduced so far that the Creator is a Mind; the Ground is creative Being.

VI

We must now take another step and remove the blinders that restricted Kant's vision, as well as that of most traditional or classical cosmologists. If the Creator Ground is a Necessary Being, but is also contemporaneous with the temporal world, it is hardly consistent with the evidence to assert that it is non-temporal, or unchanging in every respect. The facts about the world are that the continuity is a continuity-in-change. The Creator cannot be in the world and not of the world in the sense that 'he' escapes change; at the same time the continuity-in-order of change among substance-causes bespeaks unchanging 'structure'. Given the experiential evidence he has, therefore, the cosmologist will do well to urge that there is a Self-Sufficient Creator-Unity (a Cosmic Substance-Cause) and go on to insist that this Creator-Ground is not impervious to the changes that reflect its nature. The writer believes that other considerations, not here advanced and not part of the cosmological argument being considered, would justify belief in the Creator-Ground as Creator-Person. He could then assert that as Person the Creator-Ground primordially and omnitemporally is unchanging even as the 'context' of his being would alter the quality of his experience; but that is another story.

What our discussion seems to indicate is that if we take the cosmological argument by itself, it does not take us to the classical God of the ontological argument. But neither can its basic thrust be disregarded. For it asks us to undertand that the orderly world as we observe it is incompletely understood until we see it as the involvement of a Creator-Ground, the nature of whose unity and uniformity is at least to some extent expressed in the world. Is the Ground a Person and is it perfect in the classical sense? Kant was correct as far as he went. But rather than give up the argument he should have followed the evidence where it took him once he gave up a preconceived notion of what God's nature has to be and what knowledge of him must be. Kant might then have discovered, as the writer believes we have, that cosmological considerations, far from depending on the ontological for a model of God, need to be amplified by such as those adduced in the teleological argument.

What may be called the cosmo-teleological argument for God, would allow reason to be constantly upheld by this ever-increasing qualitative evidence and moved from height to height not only to the supreme and unconditioned Contemporaneous Creator-Ground but also a Creator-Person that is good and worthy of worship.

CHAPTER X

CAN THE GOODNESS OF GOD BE
EMPIRICALLY GROUNDED?

APPENDIX: THE TWO CONCEPTIONS OF GOD AND TWO CONCEPTIONS OF VALUE-OBJECTIVITY

In Chapter 4, 5, and 6, I sketched a view of the moral structure of man and of his values. (This view has been presented in systematic detail in a book, of which Richard M. Millard, Jr, was co-author, *Personality and the Good*, New York: David McKay, 1963.) This essay and its appendix need four introductory comments.

First, I have been challenging the all too easy assumptions that first we know either Nature or God and then we know how to think about man, his experience of obligation, and his values. The nature of man and of his actual experiments with value are involved in man's interpretation of what he believes to be Nature and God. At least it should not be assumed that man's experience is to be judged by norms that have no anchorage in his own nature and experience.

Second, both the moral argument for God and the argument from religious experience have, each in its own way, urged that there are unique, irreducible value-data. (Consider, for example, the 'ought-to-be' in N. Hartmann's *Ethics* and in W. R. Sorley's *Moral Values and the Idea of God*, and the holy in R. Otto's *Idea of the Holy*.) Such arguments for God from the objectivity of the moral and of the religious consciousness are impressive, and not to be dismissed lightly, and I hope I have not. My hesitation about their independent validity stems from one basic root. Even granting that love, for example, were an irreducible, experienc*ed*, imperative, I could not know what is meant by love apart from the analysis of the rest of my nature and experience.

My underlying contention is that the independence of any moral or religious insight cannot be assumed to be self-sufficient, any more than can the claims of sensory-perceptual experience; each dimension of experience must become witness before the court of experience as a whole, interpreted as coherently or reasonably as possible. In other words, I find it reasonable to deny such objectivity of the sensory, moral, and religious life as would enable each of these areas to be a stronghold from whose secure vantage-point it can claim independence of the others, or demand that the others be rendered consistent with its own presumed authority.

Third, one can see why it would seem that I am reduced to some form of subjectivity in value theory. Subjectivity, yes, if the only kind of objectivity is that demanded by the epistemic realist in each area – specifically, that reality is as experienced through the avenues of sense, obligation, and religious experience. But not subjectivity if it is realized that on the view here presented, man's experience and knowledge – hallucinations and delusions excepted – are not his own outright creation but the by-product of the interplay of his nature with the nature of the world. And by 'world' I mean experienced and hypothesized beings and animals, other persons and their organization, and the God who may well be influencing man directly and indirectly in ways of which he is not aware.

Fourth, while broad ranges and patterns of ethical value are obligatory whether there be a God or not, the contention I press is that the autonomy of ethical values does not mean that their full import in human life can be understood without relating them to the sensory, aesthetic, and religious life. Just as I have argued that God is not an addendum to a natural world already completely known, so I would argue that He is not an addition to a moral realm already completely interpreted. At the same time, what it means to say that the Creator-Person is good cannot be understood apart from understanding what 'good' means in human life independent of man's belief in God.

I

The existence of a cosmic Mind is not to be argued in this paper. I believe that both the existence and attributes of a cosmic Mind can be ascertained by coherently organizing the variegated data which are at hand in the sensory, logical, aesthetic, moral, religious experience of the race. I take it as basic methodology that no one has a right either to believe or disbelieve in God, or any proposed attributes, unless his hypothesis allows more of the data of experience to become intelligible than does any other view.

It follows that no data of human experience can arbitrarily be kept from the witness stand in a reasonable court of investigation. It follows, also, that neither narrow religious empiricism nor scientific or positivistic empiricism are acceptable. Further more, no adequate natural theology is possible and no adequate revealed theology is possible, but only a theology which seeks to give a reasoned account of the data in what were demarcated as natural and revealed realms. In what follows, I hope to illustrate what can be done by applying this criterion of empirical coherence, based on a synoptic methodology, to the most important of the attributes for God, his goodness.

II

On what ground, then, can we say that a cosmic Mind is good? Can we say that the goodness of God is revealed in some moment of illumination or revelation? There is nothing intrinsically impossible about this, but it is highly improbable. Why? Because the goodness of any being can hardly be revealed in any one act, as if it were a sense-quality like red, or a factual sensation. The goodness of a human being, for example, is not something we can be assured of in one moment of insight. 'Good' seems to be a word we use for any agent whom we conceive to be responsible for our values. Unless we know what our values are, we cannot define the action of any agent as good. The goodness of God, then, cannot be defined as some attribute we reach by contemplation of his existence alone; it must be a conclusion we come to as we specifically see the relation of his existence to what we deem good for us as human beings. A mother is good not merely because she is a mother, but because her existence is related to that of the child in a way to improve the values in her child. Similarly, God to be considered good must be *good for* man and *to* man in the light of what man finds good. God as an existent Being, or even as the Creator of all being, is not by that very fact good; he is good by virtue of the fact that other existents find him supportive of their good or values.

Perhaps this general thesis can be made clearer by referring to the more specific attribute of love which dominates the Christian conception of the goodness of God. For a Christian to say that God loves man is to say that God is that agent who creates, sustains, lures, and forgives in a way which allows man to reach the highest fulfilment open to him as a finite creature. But can the fufilment open to man be known by consulting the nature of God as an existent? Must it not be known by understanding the nature of man *in act* and *in potentiality*, and then relating the very nature of man and his fulfilment to the existence of God?

This, more concretely, is to say that even if one claims that man knows the love of God by intuition, or by revelation, then that intuition or revelation could only stand as an hypothesis to be tested, and not as a characteristic 'read off' once and for all. For even if the love of God were known in some such way, would it be possible to know what it means to say that God loves unless we have unconsciously assumed the very values in man's nature which man presumably could not realize without God? As a matter of fact, has the history of concrete Judeo-Christian thought been more than specific clarification of what God's love for man is? And I submit that the answers have not come by analysing God's nature alone, but by analysing man's experiments in living in his total world, including his experiments in living with God.

It has been urged that we cannot first know that God is good and then deduce from that what the good life is for man, without consulting man's actual experience, and criticizing his own many and varied values. Let us take an example. If, assuming the existence of God, one felt that he experienced a direct command of God to kill an innocent child, what would the response be to such a God? Would it not be that, however powerful such a Being were, he would certainly not be good? If the interpretation of one's experiences leads a man to believe that any human being – a Herod, let us say – is wicked because he demands that innocent children be destroyed simply to protect his own status, would he not level the judgment 'wicked' toward an omnipotent Being who demanded the same?

Again, if an Abraham believes that God demands the death of his innocent son, Isaac, can he legitimately say that God is good in making such a demand if he would consider a Herod wicked? He would indeed be suspending his ethics, to use Kierkegaard's phrase, and the question now asked is: On what grounds does Abraham do it? Is it because he is a 'knight of faith', as Kierkegaard calls him? One may doubt if he is a knight at all, if he is willing to save his own soul by destroying an innocent boy's life. The point I would make by reference to this story of God, Abraham, and Isaac is that it is quite possible, contrary to many interpretations, that Abraham does not suspend his own ethics. For the Abraham who responds to God responds to a God whom he already believes to have been good to him, who has already given him Sarah, and Isaac. His act of faith in the goodness of God is not one in a vacuum of value-experience; it is not a suspension of a rational ethics, but rather a reasonable extension of his moral experience.

Let me be bold enough to suggest further the line of inarticulated reason that a man in Abraham's situation, believing that he has intuited the will of God, may well presuppose. 'The God who has already been so good to me, and on whom I gratefully depend for all that is good, now demands of me that which I would ordinarily condemn as a hideous act, namely, the sacrifice of my innocent son. This offends my reason, but let me consider whether more is not involved than appears on first inspection. If I believe that God is good, and if I believe that this is his will, this may still be a situation which will bring goods I cannot now foresee. From my past I have learned that the moral life over and over again demands a sacrifice of a good in hand to a good which I believe will come. I am now faced with the question of whether I would be willing to give the life of my son, more precious to me than my own, to what I believe must be a greater good. For I cannot believe that what God, who has been good, now commands is really evil.' To repeat, Abraham is not suspending reason but extending the logic of his past life-situation to this one.

III

I have now completed the first part of my task. This was to show that even the supposed intuition of God's goodness is hardly a revelation independent of the actually experienced values in human existence. The remainder of this paper must pursue a more positive course and suggest the lines along which God's goodness can be empirically established. Here the greatest obstacle in a brief paper confronts us. The definition of goodness and the good life is nothing to dogmatize about in a few pages. Here, again, I am guided by the conviction that, whatever the source of value-judgments, their truth must be tested by their capacity to protect a maximum-optimum of value-experience in as many value-bearers, or persons, as possible.

Where, then, are the values which, if experienced, are not only most satisfying but also support the maximum of other values and, at the same time, encourage the creation of value? The answer must be found not by looking beyond man's action and enjoyment but into the quality and structure of his experience. This means, as C. I. Lewis has recently put it, that 'the ground of validity of imperatives must somehow lie in human nature'.[1] Indeed, the very word 'satisfying' cannot be given any meaning except in terms of needs, trends, and capacities of human life in transit. There would be no problem of choice, no problem of ethics, unless human beings were changing, knew that they were changing, and sought those changes which they might effectuate profitably in themselves or in their total environment, or both.

As it is, human beings find themselves to be highly complicated beings in a total environment of things, animals, persons, and hypothecated entities (be they atoms, unconscious tendencies, angels, or God), and they live by impulse, by deliberation, by calculated risk, by leaps of almost blind faith, each type of experience bringing specific qualities of experience into their lives which they could not have predicted. Many experiences are forced upon them, but these too bring out qualities of experiences which they might not have sought by themselves, but which, once experienced, reveal to them what their human nature can be as it interacts with the environment. How much of the unexpected yet enlightening potentiality of human life is brought out as a man responds to the environing beauty and ugliness, pain-causing and destructive cancers of body, blinding winds and ruinous tornadoes, loving nurture of mother and father, succourance of friendly compassion, patience of dedicated persons, torturing suspicion and contempt of prejudiced minds, and the calculated abuse of power-loving and greedy persons! The point is that the myriad qualities of experience, be they sought after or gratuitous, do not simply happen *to* man and *for* man, but they happen *in* man and modify or inflect his nature, producing different results he in his ignorance could not have predicted, but which he as a reflective creature evaluates. It is in these experiences, products of his *interaction* with the total environment, or, better, *joint-products* of his nature in commerce with the total environment, that man finds himself, because he is what he is, wishing to preserve and wishing to avoid.

Again, this is not the place to develop a particular theory of value and valuation, but the underlying insistence is that no man ever has something outside upon which to model himself strictly, though each man may compare himself to other men, and his experiments

[1] C. I. Lewis, *The Ground and Nature of the Right*, New York: Columbia University Press, 1955, pp. 85–6.

in living with theirs. Even then the only being whose existence and experience would give relevant guidance to his own experiments would be a creature of similar flesh and psyche, of similar need and capacity, tempted as he is tempted, delighted as he is delighted, sorrowing as he sorrows. But if he cannot model himself upon something unlike himself, neither can be simply feel his own pulse and narcissistically glut in his own image as if he were something he could lastingly produce and alter at will. For his values and his disvalues are the working in him of co-making factors in the total environment. For him to look at himself at any given moment, as well as at long range, is to get a partial glimpse, at least, of what *the whole of his environment, or some part of it, is becoming in and for him!* To adapt something James Ward once so effectively said: A man eats because he has a stomach, but after he eats he has a different stomach to eat with, a stomach stronger or weaker because of what he ate. Man finds himself enjoying and suffering what he does because he has a nature whose potentialities-for-value-and-disvalue he did not create any more than he created the possibilities for value and disvalue in the nurturant and resistant environment. The facts in the human situation are that man does not create either the value-possibilities in the world around him, the value-potentialities within him, or the actual kinds of mutual support and reciprocal hostility between the values and disvalues he experiences.

To summarize, the laws of human value and disvalue, that is, the regular sequences which man finds between his values, given his nature and given his total environment, are no more a creation of his than are the sequences which he discovers between the heat of fire and the volume of water, or the effect of carbon monoxide on the human body. These laws of value are no doubt much more difficult to trace, but the sequences are there in the structure if interaction. Man's values are his values, to be sure, but they are not his outright creations; they are the responses of his nature, given its potentialities, to the possibilities pressing upon him and awaiting realization in the context of his nature. Man's choice, in so far as it exists, is between sequences which he has learned; and in making this choice all he has to go by are the patterns of value which have been exemplified in human living before his time and in his own experience.

In a word, a theory of the good life for man is at the same time a theory of what is deemed possible and worth while for man to accomplish in this kind of universe as so far understood. A theory of the good life is a statement, an hypothesis, about the best which man can realize, with a nature he did not create, in a world he did not create, if he will take full advantage of both. Thus, whatever other arguments there be for a theory of the universe in which man lives, that theory cannot include all the facts unless it treats, as part of the evidence, man and his struggle for, and experience with, values. An inclusive theory of the universe must leave man in, even as it must not arbitrarily exclude the possibility to start with, that his existence is not significant evidence.

IV

We turn, then, to what we may suggest as the basic principles and values by which man can best optimize other values, decrease the disvalues of his existence, without discouraging new ventures in value experience.

These are (a) impartiality in all efforts to discover truth and value, (b) creativity in concern for value, and (c) love in sharing one's values with all those capable of appreciating and enhancing them – objectivity toward all bearers and creators of value. Other principles, a system of values, and a system of virtues, would be required to begin to do justice to the complexity of human existence, but for our purposes here the following comments must suffice.[1]

First, the principle of impartiality draws attention to the fact that the only reliable way to come to a conclusion on any matter of existence and value is to take account of all the given and available evidence, no matter what its *prima facie* source, and connect it, without logical error, with the problem to be solved. This calls for openmindedness and the willingness to subject the clamour of desires, pet hopes, and favourite antipathies, to the data. The traits or virtues especially required for, and related to, impartiality are patience, honesty, and courage. No man has justified a conclusion without developing these virtues as he sifts facts and values with a view to understanding their relationship to each other.

The principle of creativity in concern for value calls attention to

[1] Readers of E. S. Brightman's neglected *Moral Laws* will find these in a form of four (out of a larger number of) moral laws, namely, the laws of autonomy, the axiological law, the law of altruism, and of the ideal of personality. Readers of C. I. Lewis's little gem, *The Ground and Nature of the Right*, will recognize the influence of his Law of Objectivity, Law of Compassion, and Law of Moral Equality. See *Personality and the Good* for elaboration.

the fact that the purpose of knowing truth and goodness is to enhance the quality of life. There is no point in a reasonable conclusion, for example, that knowledge is better than ignorance, that the 'Passion of St Matthew' is better than 'Dixie', that having a family is better than remaining single, unless one commits all in his power (the Kantian good will) to the realization of it. One's actual creativity may never extend beyond his determination to achieve certain approved foreseeable consequences. Yet, unless he turns his mind and will to create, at least in his own life as far as possible, the patterns of values which his critical investigation approves, he can never approximate what he takes to be the ideal person.

I pause to emphasize that the actual experience of creativity seems to me to be that which ennobles and sanctifies human existence. None of the highest ranges of human experience, work as opposed to sleep, working out a project as opposed to drudgery, a job to do as opposed to being busy, playing a game rather than passively watching it, being a friend rather than taking others for granted, solving a problem rather than memorizing, creating a picture or modelling a sculpture rather than taking photographs, cultivating a field and reaping a harvest rather than owning it, loving rather than being loved – nay, all of the tip-toe experiences of life in which one seeks to increase the values he already has by using them as a basis for creating new values, yes, all of them, involve creativity. There are, indeed, evils in life; there is pain and suffering, there is torture and contempt, there is the long siege of cramping pain and agonizing uncertainty – and none of us who does not know the trials of Job had better be glib about them – but however we finally evaluate evils, the thesis hazarded here is that they are most poignant when creative possibility is strangled by them.

I have sometimes asked those of my students who idolized a hedonistic paradise, in which there would be neither pain nor danger, whether they would choose unadulterated pleasure if they had to give up the possibility of creativity. I have pictured a state in which one's nerve endings, as it were, might be played upon by stimuli creating sequences of delicious ecstasy. The price to pay for such ecstasy, however, would be one's never being able to do anything about it himself. I can only speak for one, but without for a moment castigating many of the joys in a qualitative hedonistic paradise, I would not be willing to pay that price. For, as I see it, the deepest pleasures of life, if pleasure be the word, would have to be left out, for these all involve creativity.

So much for our first two principles, for impartiality and creativity. The person we have now before us is one who has been coherent in his choice of values, not stingy and unimaginative in exploring the routes of value-experience, and creative in his determination to increase the value-potential in his life. But, the third principle, that of altruism, calls attention to the fact that no person, sensitive to the facts about human nature from which values spring, would go far in his exploration without realizing that the largest number of man's most cherished values involve appreciative and co-operative association with other persons. Not only is man social in his need-structure, but others are involved in the discovery of truth, in the creation and enjoyment of economic, educational, aesthetic, social, recreational, and religious values. And one fact, if he is objective, he must face. In so far as any other person is able to be hurt and to be helped by the experiences he has samples of in his own life, he must respect that person's need and place the same value on that person's values as his own, other things being equal. This means that the objectivity and creativity he enjoys in his own life are to be respected in the life of other sentient beings.

A person will find it no easy matter to respect properly the values of others, especially since there are so many other persons and since the lines of value-creation and preservation are hard to trace. Yet if he is to be both objective and creative, he cannot but respect their claims to value, or in short, to respect them as persons in their own right as bearers and creators of value, and never as mere means to his own ends. This Kantian development of the categorical imperative, this more explicit statement of the intent of the Golden Rule, Lewis calls the Law of Compassion.[1] One cannot promote values for himself, or encourage others to create values for themselves, without full consideration of the consequences on all beings affected by the action.

The examination of human experience leads us to emphasize what may well be considered an extension of altruism, or the Law of Compassion, namely, the Law of Forgiveness or the Law of Love.

It is an undeniable fact of human experience that each of us not only fails to live up to his ideal for himself or for others, but we purposely hurt each other and abuse each other often. Whatever the mixture of motives and causes which enter into our choice to

[1] C. I. Lewis, *The Ground and Nature of the Right*, pp. 90, 92.

take advantage of others or to use them simply as a means to our own ends, there is no doubting the road-blocks which are created in human affairs when we destroy another's good, actual or possible, in order to feather our own nests. But such action not only hurts the victims; it endangers the mutuality which is necessary for the growth of both agent and injured. It separates the doer of evil from the sufferer of it, and inspires fear and distrust.

Little wonder is it that there is no more difficult act for a human being to perform than that of forgiving another person who has selfishly hurt him. More than kindness is called for here. Kindness binds the wounds of the helpless weak; it shares the suffering for the innocently hurt. It is easy to will compared to the act of forgiveness in which one says to him who has purposely hurt him: 'In forgiving you, I wish to do all in my power to help you overcome the weakness which has led to your destructive acts. While I condemn the acts, and you in so far as you are responsible for them, my concern is not to hurt you in return but to share humbly with you in the persistent attempt to nullify the evil and build the good.'

It is so easy for us to say that we are all sinners against each other, and so easy to become sentimental about redeeming the wrong, that we often do not trace out the fundamental fact that without redemption we actually allow the roots and fruits of evil to flourish and discourage the growth of good already accomplished. Forgiveness which redeems life is forgiveness which understands evil-doer and evil-sufferer; it uproots the evil as far as possible and fosters good in the evil-doer. Forgiveness is not an act of supererogation in the development of worthy persons; it is not a virtue we benevolently and somewhat proudly indulge in. It is the very condition of re-growth, of re-creation, of inspiring effort in the process of human fellowship. Some say that forgiveness is an intuition of the will of God, but if it were only this, if its value in human life, impartially inspected, was not supported by the actual facts of growth in human personality, would we be justified in holding it to be the will of God?

V

I come, at long last, to the conclusion upon which these varied reflections converge. The human situation seems to be one in which a large variety of values and disvalues are possible within the framework of physical, biological, psychological, and social existence. Man can stay alive, merely exist, for a span of years if he is able to meet certain conditions imposed upon him. But the quality of his existence is left, within limits, to his own willingness to discipline his needs and abilities. His profoundest experiences involve creativity as this is expressed in the pursuit, contemplation, and use of truth, in the creation and appreciation of beauty, and in the responsibility for the widest and richest development of the possibilities in personality. Freedom, disciplined by truth, developed by beauty, dignified by the mutual love which encourages growth of personality, – these are the experiences and goals which give human life fullest significance.

But these also are the experiences which simply would not be without the supporting order of the physical, biological, and psychological structures on which man depends and which man's cognitive equipment, however limited, can reliably know. In a word, man's yearning for value-realization, which he finds within his nature, can be fulfilled within the total nurturant environment that made his existence possible, but only on condition that *he* decides to be creative. If this is so, if his bodily, psychological, and spiritual needs take shape within a larger structure, and if they are transformed by his own creative use of the means at his disposal, may he not call his universe good? Indeed, can he, in his search for understanding himself, in his relation to his fellow men and nature, come to any more reasonable conclusion?

I have purposely in this exposition tried to steer clear of the terminology of the religious life. For my contention is that to call God good is to say that the universe is such that certain values and not others, certain patterns of living and not others, are integral to the structure of the cosmos. We mean by saying that a cosmic Mind is good that this Mind does not simply foster and condone any kind of existence, but that he labours for the creation, preservation, and increase of all the values which make of every disciplined life a new creation from day to day. To say that one loves God without saying that one is dedicated to the creation and continuance of the values which nurture the growth in personality is to make religion sheer sentimentality. To say that one loves God is to say that one gratefully and humbly enters into a mutual fellowship of concern, of tender care, to use Whitehead's phrase, that nothing of value be lost.

Religion, in the last analysis, is, in this sense, the most creative of human values for it involves total consecration of one's being to the goodness of God. Religious dedication brings the human life involved to a boiling-point at which a new quality of being is made possible by the creative interaction between man and God.

APPENDIX

In the April 1957 issue of this journal my article 'Can the Goodness of God be Empirically Grounded?' appeared. Daryl E. Williams in the October issue asks: 'Can't the *Goodness* of God Be More Empirically Grounded?' Professor Williams wonders whether I have not returned to the moral argument for God which I found it reasonable to reject in earlier writings. I think I see why Williams, quite understandably, was led astray by the April article. I hope I can explain the source of confusion and also state my relation to other questions he raises.

I

The context of the April article should have been clearer. I was there trying to refute the contention of some Christian theists, that the goodness of God cannot be grounded on *reasoned* inferences from human experience in value-realization. Many Christian theists hold that while the existence of some kind of cosmic Power might be asserted, the goodness of God cannot be grounded apart from some form of direct revelation, or apart from man's criticized, though intuitive, awareness of moral values whose nature and validity do not rest on man's experience of them. I believe that both of these approaches to grounding the goodness of God are inadequate. But, in order to argue about this attribute of God alone, I said, in that article, that I was assuming the existence of God. I should have emphasized that this was an artificial experiment for the sake of argument, for I believe that one cannot first assume the existence of God and then argue for his goodness. In accordance with my synoptic methodology and the criterion of truth as experiential coherence, I hold that until we examine all the available evidence, as forthcoming in logical, scientific, ethical, aesthetic, and religious data, we cannot draw reasonable conclusions about either the existence or the nature of God. We may make provisional assumptions (as I was doing) to get on with study of a particular problem – in this case the goodness of God – but conclusions drawn from any segment of human experience and knowledge may need to be altered when seen in the light of other segments.

I can understand why Williams wondered whether I was still

arguing with myself about the moral argument for God in links three to five in the wider teleological argument for God as presented in my *Introduction to the Philosophy of Religion*, and why he thought I might be returning to a form of it in the April article. But to rephrase one of his sentences (311), while I would insist that the area of moral experience be examined quite distinctly apart from a search for general teleology, I would urge methodologically that conclusions from any one realm of human experience stand in review of conclusions from other realms as we seek the hypothesis which will be fairest to the varied data as a whole. I find, when I do this, that a wider teleology is discernible in which God and man are creatively interactive in different ways in different areas of experience, and that the creativity we find in human love of man and of God is the ultimate, illuminating goal in the teleology.

II

This general statement may clarify the confusions I unwittingly created. But it does not touch what seems to me both a misunderstanding of, and disagreement with, the theory of value-experience which I have proposed. Williams is quite correct in saying that I hold that the *experience* of moral obligation (expressed in the words, 'I ought to do the best I know') is cognitively innocent. Here I am trying to state a fact about human nature – whatever else may be true about values or the universe. A human being, confronting alternatives of choice, say between A and B, cannot consciously judge A to be better than B without feeling the moral imperative to enact A to the best of his ability. He may not in fact, owing to free will, try to enact A, but if he does not, he feels moral guilt. I believe Williams is quite clear about my view this far, but now both misunderstanding and disagreement set in.

Williams does not believe that objectivity of values is possible on my view of value-experience and judgment. I may, of course, be vulnerable, but I doubt that 'either Bertocci does not have objectivity [of moral standards] or that he introduces it surreptitiously somehow', I do not have the *kind* of objectivity Williams claims to be a better kind, but if there is any possible uniqueness in my view it is in the way the 'objectivity' of value is defined, which I am not quite sure Williams understands. A brief statement here can hardly sound more dogmatic, but I must indicate the kind of objectivity I have in mind.

Having rejected any *cognitive* independence and validity in 'the moral consciousness' as such, I turn to an analysis of how we come to know 'the best' to which we find ourselves obligated in moral experience. I find that we have many experiences which we desire. This constitutes them value-claims for us. Value-experiences are ongoings or processes in our natures; they are not 'glimpses' of any realm of values independent of us and valid for us. While we may, at the moment of experiencing them, feel that these desired experiences (or undesired experiences) are completely trustworthy, better or worse than other experiences, our actual experimenting with our value-experiences shows us that our first 'valuations' or 'prima facie' values cannot be accepted at face value. Such experiences may be 'psychologically objective' or 'convincing', but in themselves they are not trustworthy signs of what is 'truly' valuable for our natures in their interaction with the striving and abilities of other sentient and conscious beings in the common matrix we call 'the world'.

To the first phase of value-experience, then, the 'psychologically objective', we cannot grant epistemological Objectivity; nor can we say that the 'value' thus experienced has ontological or metaphysical objectivity. By 'epistemological Objectivity' I mean (following Kant as extended by Tennant) the Objectivity which is not a state of affairs metaphysically independent of the knower. It is the state of affairs which results when knowers, each confronting their psychologically objective experiences, find themselves able to come to substantial agreement about what value-experiences, or patterns of value-experience, it would be worthwhile for men to pursue in their intercourse with each other and with 'the world'. Such Objectivity is not, I hold, a copy of, or identical with, a metaphysically objective realm of values or norms (in God or not). Such Objectivity is a rendering or interpreting of their value-experiences by human beings in which there is sufficient agreement or universality to ground further thought and action. Such Objectivity reaches for the *common to man* in intersubjective interaction with 'the world' in which their efforts are both supported and discouraged.

But such Objectivity *is* to be trusted because it does grow from human beings (*who did not create their own natures*) *in interaction with forces beyond them which they did not create either*. There can be such common-to-man Objectivity simply because, *despite* differences among men, in their perceptions, conceptions, and value-experiences, common factors are discernible which would be impossible to explain if each person created his own nature and values or *lived in* a purely private world. Thus, in trusting his Objective construction of what values are worth further pursuit, of what value-organizations and value-scales are to be considered 'the best' to which he feels obligated, man is thus trusting not simply himself but also 'the world' which brought him into being and which sustains, discourages, and inspires him. This 'Objectivity' is, indeed, humanized or 'anthropic', but it is not relativistic as the 'psychologically objective' may well be.

To be *related to man* is not to be 'relative' to man, unless we can show that man depends only upon himself for his being, continuity, and all value-experiences. As things stand, man's coherently criticized, psychologically objective value-experiences are believed to be Objective in the sense that they are reasonable hypotheses, at any one stage of human development, of what the *value-possibilities* in the nature of things (metaphysically) are as these are related to the *value-potentialities* in man (metaphysically).

Thus I reach the conclusion that there are non-man-made *value-possibilities* in the structure of things and *value-potentilaities* in human nature because the Objective value-patterns I do discover, as a result of value-experiencing and value-experimenting, are the *joint-product* of human nature and the world beyond it. Let it be noted that 'values' on this view can be indices to the structure of things simply because they are in fact effects of man and world in interaction. The values man experiences tell about his nature and the nature of the world which allows him to be and sustains him in his search for greater value.

There is, therefore, a vast difference between the contention that there exists 'a realm of values' independent of man and this view in which value-experiences and their Objectivity are not existent except as they are expressions of what man's nature may be as he interacts with 'the world'. This kind of Objectivity, related to metaphysical objectivity, may not be the kind Williams can accept, but the point to be debated is whether, in moral experience at least, any other kind of objectivity is available.

III

Much more, of course, needs to be said, but this may suffice to suggest why I proposed 'that the coherent organization of value-claims, in the light of all the knowledge we have, can lead us to hypotheses about true-value which are relevant to human existence *because true-values come to life in the very struggle of human beings to sort out their experiences and to live up to the obligation to the best they know at every stage in their development'*. The difference between the Objectivity I have in mind and the objectivity Williams has in mind comes out in the comment he makes upon this passage. 'One wonders', he says, 'why Bertocci did not write "because true-values come to *light* in life" and hence frankly admit the possibility of objective value norms.' For here it is clear that Williams thinks of true-values as already real (metaphysically objective) in some sense and of man's moral consciousness as bringing them to light. Indeed, he adds 'unless some glimpse of God's structured intent is possible, it is hard to make moral sense out of Bertocci's moral man'.

It is here that the earlier methodological point must be re-emphasized. For 'God's structured intent' is not glimpsed, as I see it, especially at this stage in the argument, in any moral intuition. On my view, *both* the existence of God and his goodness are at stake in the interpretation of the true-values which come to life in man's experience. I cannot assume from value-experience as such that there is a God or a good God, and that is why I cannot admit 'a wider moral argument', as Williams suggests, but only a 'wider teleological argument' – within which, indeed, human value-experience in the world becomes the coping-stone in the argument for the existence and goodness of God.

The intent *of God* is indeed structured, I believe; it is, however, not 'glimpsed', but inferred from the nature of our true value-experience which in turn, I repeat, is the joint-product of the inter-action between man's given nature and the given structure of things. Thus I would have to reject Williams's statement: 'A man may produce *his* values, but not his *values*.' For if man's values are *his* values, it is not because *he* has made the value-potential in his nature or the value-possibility in the world whose coming together brings value-as-experience into being. The same values cannot be *experiences* in man and in God at the same time, although God may intend that man should have such values when he creates and sustains the value-possibilities in the world and the value-potential in man's nature.

It is for this reason that, following Brightman at this point, I speak of *values* in man's experience and *norms* of value in God's experience and purpose. For God to intend love, justice, loyalty, courage as human beings experience these is not for God to experience these as human beings do. What is metaphysically objective then is the 'structured intent' of God, norms of his value-experience and purpose, and the expression of these in the value-possibilities and value-potential in 'the world' and man respectively. If God did not exist with these norms there would be no adequate accounting for the fact that man, with his given potential for value-realization, exists in a world whose value-possibilities are the constant source of the kind of values *he* can experience. God, on my view, does indeed know truth and beauty and goodness long before I know them, as Williams suggests, but to think of my knowledge-values, aesthetic-values and moral-values as 'glimpses' of the truth, beauty, and goodness which God experiences is to fuse and confuse human experience with divine experience.

It is, then, one thing to say that God is the ultimate and sustaining Ground of value-possibilities in the world and of value-potentials in man, and thus the ultimate Ground of man's value-experience. It is another thing to say that our values are dim reflections of his value. To say that God is the ultimate Ground of man's value-experience is to say that God *is* in interaction with man, but the exact nature of that interaction calls for an adequate doctrine of general and special grace, which must remain beyond the confines of this rejoinder.[1]

I am sorry that I cannot do justice to the specific alternative which is expressed in Williams's article, but I hope it will be soon developed at greater length. I am grateful to him and to the Editors of *Journal of the American Academy of Religion* for providing this opportunity at least to sharpen the issues.

[1] See the author's *Free Will, Responsibility, and Grace*, New York: Abingdon Press, 1957.

CHAPTER XI

TOWARD A METAPHYSICS OF CREATION[1]

This essay directly supplements the analysis of the cosmological way of thinking about reality. If there is a God, or an Ultimate Being of any worth, the question arises: How is this Being related to beings that are not ultimate?

In this essay I attempt to understand the metaphysical problem which the notion of *creatio ex nihilo* was intended to relieve. In pre-Socratic philosophy, when Thales argued that Water is ultimate, he bequeathed to philosophers the question: How shall we understand the fact that one limited kind of thing becomes other limited beings? To answer, as did Anaximander, that the only way we could understand the relation of the Ultimate to finite beings is to consider the ultimate to be the Indefinite, was to raise the question as to what it means to say that what is nothing in particular can become specific! Understandably, Anaximenes hastened back to an ultimate Definite, Air!

While much metaphysical water flowed under the bridge, the essential issue had been raised: Spinoza's answer to Descartes and Leibniz's to Spinoza grappled with the same basic issue. And we shall see that in Indian philosophy the underlying struggle goes on. The appeal of some naturalists to emergence, and of other thinkers to creativity, does little more, as far as I can see, than re-name the issue. It seems that here we have a mystery not of technique, which could be resolved by improved know-how, but a mystery faced by every philosophical perspective. For it concerns the way in which whatever it is that does not come and go, and is in that sense self-sufficient, is related to what does come and go but not in any which way. Our next three essays deal with this question.

In this paper I am assuming that a good case can be made for the existence of God. I shall defend the thesis that creative change

[1] The Presidential Address, delivered at the fifteenth annual meeting of the Metaphysical Society of America, Georgetown University, March 20, 1964.

characterizes the nature of God. I shall suggest that such a view of God can be supported by a temporalistic view of such personal being as we find in ourselves, and I shall finally argue that a temporalistic form of personalistic theism (not pantheism, not panentheism) can reasonably illuminate what we actually do find in human experience and the world. On such matters, of course, we can expect, as Plato reminded us, no more than probability – the probability that Bishop Butler saw as the guide of life.

However, in proposing such theses I am aware that the challenge is to great traditions in metaphysical and religious thought. Accordingly, I begin with a brief statement of what I take to be the strongest and basic motifs for the contention that ultimate Being must be perfect in the absolutistic sense that nothing could conceivably be added or subtracted from its existence.

I

One main motif surely is the epistemic demand for intelligibility. Here the model of intelligibility is logical implication. When this model is operative, only those existents are considered real that are parts of a *logically* coherent whole. In such a logical whole there can be no question of anything's being or becoming other than what it is, of something's becoming in some sense what it now is not. Creative change in particular is unintelligible since it involves novelty not reducible to what already is. Reality, therefore, must be conceived as a unified non-temporal whole, as metaphysical monists like Parmenides, Spinoza, Shankara and Bradley held.

I am too firm a believer in the importance of consistency to the very life of mind to wish to treat this view of intelligibility lightly. Without logical connections the mind may associate but can never understand. To neglect the search for logical connections is to court chaos in thought and action. Could I convince myself that thought, experience and action must yield inevitably to the demands of logical intelligibility, I should be happy, in my search for understanding, to find rest in this alluring ideal.

But I cannot forget that the logical ideal of intelligibility is one model only of the cognitive ideal, however elegantly expressed in logical and mathematical systems. This ideal of logical necessity I do not find incarnate necessarily in other systems or types of being; indeed the attempt to see it as the ideal form of their existence cramps important aspects of their natures.

It is no accident, therefore, that metaphysical systems developed in the light of this logical ideal are defended at critical points by claiming that, if only we knew more than we do, we should find that a logical network would extend to all of being. The critical point invariably is felt when the grit of individuality – when some alogical experience of desire, or obligation, or will – begins to grind in the smooth functioning of the machinery of this logic; or the critical point may arrive when sets of events occur that defy logical connection with all else simply because, in the light of what is already known or expected, they surprise by their novelty.

Such considerations are even *prima facie* grounds for suggesting that, without giving up the aid of logical consistency, we seek another model for understanding what we experience and observe. The demand for logical intelligibility must not be permitted, however suavely, to take the change out of changing being, let alone creative being.

II

Such epistemic misgivings almost fade into triviality, however, when I confront the second, and metaphysical argument for denying that change can be ultimate. If one attributes any passing-away to the Ultimate, it is said, he must explain what happened to that which ceased to be. And if coming-to-be means addition in some sense to the Ultimate, whence does the addition come? This is no verbal matter. Even at the finite level we may ask: When the acorn becomes the oak, whence comes the stuff that produces increase in size, shape, and colour, and what happens to the old size, shape, and colour? If the new colour *is*, and if it is *now*, what was it before? Whence did it come? It had to have some being or we should have to say it came from nothing.

We here begin to see the reason for saying that in the last analysis what is *is*, and what is not, is *not*, and there can be no change from one to the other. For to say that an addition to what is comes from nothing is to speak utter nonsense. No addition to being can come from sheer non-being. Furthermore, the logical contradition of urging that being can become non-being aside, what can the state of sheer non-being possibly be? Surely no decrease of being can entail sheer non-being. Yet these absurdities seem to be forced upon us if we say that the evil man becomes good, the seed becomes a tomato, the boy both loses his ignorance and becomes wiser in a certain respect. Be it change in virtue, change in being, or change in knowledge, we simply cannot countenance the contention that something that *is not* or that *was not*, in any sense, can come into being. Similar considerations hold for ceasing-to-be.

I beg your indulgence in this rehearsal of pre-Aristotelian metaphysics, but in essentials the old conflict still confronts those of us who today insist that what is ultimate can be changing, or that something can come into being that was not 'there' in some sense. Coming to be and passing away – I seem so sure of these as real, until I ask: But how can one add even an iota to all that is, especially since I cannot tell whence the iota would come? And what can it mean to say that one iota is utterly removed? At such times I can hardly resist either one of two conclusions: There is one unchanging reality, and the changing is 'opinion' or appearance; or there are many unchanging realities and whatever changes there are involve only different organizations of what is, and not alterations in the nature of the ultimate elements. Something eternal, something unchanging there must be, not only because knowledge is impossible if all is change, but also because no one can either imagine or understand whence the change can come, if creative change involves coming into being of a difference that did not exist until the change took place.

The argument appears all the more powerful because it seems to rest on something incontrovertible: From nothing, nothing can come. And so great is the power of this seemingly self-evident and indubitable truth that in traditional philosophy whenever 'the really real' was defined – be it Democritean atoms, Platonic God, Aristotelian Prime Mover Unmoved, Spinozistic Substance, Cartesian or Berkeleyan God, or Hegelian Spirit – change was excluded from the definition.

An escape, or at least an easement, might be thought to be in an Aristotelian doctrine of potentiality. Now, though potentiality, as I should hold, is a category of reality, it will not supply a metaphysics of creation. Not without point do we note that Aristotle used the action of potentiality to ease the understanding of change, but only at the finite level of contingent being – from acorn to oak. When he came to define the really real, he could allow it no potentiality – any more than could classical theists in the Judeo-Christian tradition assign potentiality to their Creator-God.

Since potentiality, then, consists of some sort of being and not of sheer non-being, it may seem to ease the problem of creative becoming at the finite level. But attribute potentiality to infinite Being and you feel the ancient metaphysical horror of thinking that ultimate Being could ever be in any sense less than complete or actual being. Why? Because potential being is potential and *not* actual. When it becomes actual, something takes place – something is added that was not before it became actual. The unmusical boy becomes musical; something is added – whence? And when the unmusical boy becomes musical his unmusicality goes out of being – where?

Yet that horror we must face! When the potential becomes actual, either we have one actuality taking the place of another actuality – in which case we have not change but juxtaposition – or the dreadful alternatives of something's becoming nothing, or an increment added from what-was-not comes back to plague us. Were this not the situation, I doubt that Aristotle would have insisted that the Prime Mover is Pure Act, and that the classical Judeo-Christian theist and pantheist would have argued that God is the unchanging Perfection.

III

One who has faced the epistemic and metaphysical reasons for holding that the Ultimate or God cannot change in any respect understands all the more readily the religious motif – and it needs only mention here. In the name of 'the religious consciousness' many hold that God's nature is so majestic and inclusive in range and content that nothing could possibly be added to make it richer or more complete in any sense. Such a being has no motive for change, since it already has all that is worth having. What happens in the world cannot be interpreted as adding to or subtracting from the perfection of God's being.

Thus, the logical ideal of mutual implication has no place in it for change; the metaphysical difficulty, confronted when we see that change or creation involve in some sense addition to being from non-being, throws us back to the conviction that the ultimate must be unchanging; and a kind of religious *a priori* will harbour no Being as worthy of worship who is not perfect in the sense that nothing can be added or subtracted in the nature or quality of his Being.

As an alternative I now propose to indicate a view that, drawing upon legitimate concerns in the logical, metaphysical, and religious ideals, hopefully is not subject to their experiential embarrassment, and escapes the horrendous consequences of allowing creative changes to characterize ultimate Being. I shall first suggest a different model of reason and then outline a concept of personal being that may help us to see why creative change can be attributed to reality.

IV

I have already urged that the logical ideal is not itself logically mandatory as a model for reality. Indeed, for this model the very appearance of coming-into-being and passing-away remain mysterious. One might argue that an element of mystery will have to be involved in any metaphysical system, but the mystery here seems to be created by the very ideal proposed to rid us of theoretical difficulty. Whenever this happens it is time to make a new start.

However, what is left to us if we reject logical imperialism and yet try to understand what we observe and experience? I suggest that we now follow what might be called the wider relational life of reason, of which, indeed, logic may be considered a phase. Reason in this sense is the complex cognitive activity in the life of a person that, sensitive to the qualitative differences and similarities in the content of experience, follows connections or links – such as time, space, causality, purpose, unity, valuational differences – which experiences themselves suggest. On this view, reason seeks to discover hypotheses suggested by experience that may enable it to grasp patterns of life and existence but never at the cost of rejecting what is given and found in experience. It will be noted that on this conception of reason, logic is still at home; no contradictory statements or hypotheses are allowed. But the emphasis is on another demand, another ideal of reason. The speculative and constructive interweaving of hypothesis and experience satisfies the cognitive demand that some pattern be discovered, if at all possible, *in* experience and observation. Our demand is for as much *experiential coherence* as may be discovered, as the shuttle of reasoning weaves the materials of form and content into a pattern that may round out what is given within experience but may never explain away or minimize what is given.

With such a criteriological note in mind, I present a model of being as I think we find it in ourselves as personal experients, a model that may well serve as a reasonable analogical base for understanding creative change at the cosmic, metaphysical level.

V

Whatever else personal existence is, as lived, it consists in a unity of activities – sensory, memorial, perceptual, reasoning, emotive, volitional, moral, and appreciative (aesthetic and religious). These activities mark distinctions within a unity. The unity is not a collection of faculties or functions; it is not a fusion of contents; nor is it a mathematical unity. It is an irreducible, active matrix, a complex unity of activities defined by their capacity to undergo or enjoy qualitative 'contents' – sensory, ideational, imaginary, volitional, affective, and valuational. For example, in this complex unity the activities of logic and reasoning are present; but so are the concrete feelings or 'contents' of personal activities – the memories and the sensory-emotive-volitional-appreciative undergoings without which reasoning would have no content.

To repeat and expand, in personal existence, unity is found not as a mathematical one, nor as a collective many; it is found as a variegated unity. Were this unity not original or primitive, were it a series of activities, or a mere route of occasions, or a grouping of 'contents', there would be no seamless stitching of the parts into a unity, nor would there be awareness of the interpenetrating texture of activities and of contents at any one point. For another characteristic of this unity is that it is proprietary and 'owned'; this active, throbbing fact of unity is *my* unity – it is changing in some way or other and yet recognizes itself as changing – I'm changing; the change is *my* change. Again, this unity does not feel like an unchanging being; and yet it knows its activities and its changes of content as belonging to it. It is aware of the changing 'faces' within its experience, the shift from figure to ground, as it were, that marks them as belonging to it.

To put this more intimately – for me to be is to be active, to be different and make a difference, to become what in some sense I was not, and yet to keep my 'ownership' of my changes. This is what I mean by saying that I am self-identical in succeeding myself. While it is tempting to think of this self-identity as an unchanging string – some sort of soul-substance – which collects the successive beads of varied hue, this is not what I experience. The fact seems simply to be that my very experience of succeeding myself and of noting succession *among my* experiences constitutes what I mean by myself as the kind of complex unity of activity I am.

Again, if I try to explain this feeling of unity by using some pattern that is not within my experience, I am tempted, as so many respected thinkers have been, to conceive of, or to interpret, this unity-in-change as a substantive unity underlying change but not itself changing, or as a unity that has, but is not, its activities. It is both of these conceptions (and other near-neighbours) that I would replace, for I think that they are motivated by logical concerns of the sort I have criticized. Furthermore, they create the mystery of accounting for the fact that an unchanging being can be connected with change and be still unchanged by this logical relationship. Faced by this artificial mystery – one created by the ideal – I return to a model of unity in change, of one in many, at the very point where I contend it is given; I locate the mystery where indeed we might expect mystery to haunt us – at the point where we experience our own givenness.

I have been urging as a highly probable if not undeniable fact, that in self-experience we have a kind of unity whose nature it is to be self-identical in change. I am now further suggesting that we take this fact, unity-in-change, as primitive and not allow it to be lost from sight as we consider our relation to our past. Thus, what does it mean to say that it is my very nature *to be in change and know myself as changing*? It means that *I* realize that some discontinuity exists between *my* present, *my* past, and *my* emerging future. The fact seems to be that my past is remembered in my present and my future is anticipated in my present. It is my present unity in multiplicity that survives as it discriminates its waning and waxing, its continuity-discontinuity.

Some philosophers would explain this continuity-discontinuity by suggesting that the past is preserved in the present, that the present is pregnant with the past as it changes into its future. I suggest caution in interpreting the metaphor. I grant that the past influences the present and that the present will influence the future. Yet I would urge that such continuity as I have would be ungrounded experientially if we simply assert that my present is pregnant with the past, without emphasizing that my present is its own unique unity.

Indeed, the datum is never a past becoming present. What I seem unable to deny empirically is that something in my *now* refers to a past that is no longer existent, that is no longer making its full impact upon me, and therefore, to some extent at least, has no longer any being. I am the one who was the coward I am not now; I am the one who was the child I am no more. Something I now only remember has ceased being. It is nothing in itself; it is remembered only. Again, something that was mine in my past is no longer mine in the same way, and has to that extent ceased being. This seems to be the clear fact. Yet when I try to understand what this ceasing-to-be can be, my imagination blanks and I gag intellectually. I cannot imagine something going completely out of being, and my logical sense will not stand for it. But if that past does not go out of being in the sense that it is no longer making full impact, then my past is not distinct from my present. This surely cannot be. Pastness involves discontinuity just because something has been lost. The ideas I was thinking two pages back are remembered, and as remembered they are influencing my thinking in my *now*; but they do not have the same force of influence as the ideas that dominate my present thought-matrix, and to that extent something has ceased to be.

This point is crucial, and two consequences need to be made explicit. First, I am suggesting that the notion that *everything* experienced is conserved, has no actual experiential support. For my past can *be* for me only because something about it is no longer. I suspect that we have been able to hold that *everything* is in some sense conserved only by a linear or spatial view of time. Only a linear or spatial view of the past can see the present simply as extending or being added to the past. But if our human experience is to guide us, there is *no* ontological past 'behind us' by which our present is guided. And there is no future to be added to our present. Our present unity is crescent and concrescent; it is what we are now because we have lost something and because we now, in response to our total environment, are growing into *our* future which will soon be *our* present and then *our* past, because something is gained and something lost in our crescent-decrescent experience. (See pp. 56 to 64 above.)

Second, if these observations are at all valid, why not use them in vigorous challenge to the assumption that nothing can go out of being either in us or in the universe? Indeed, what actual fact is left unexplained if we say that our *nows*, our present selves, are selectively 'pregnant' with that portion of our pasts that survived our interchange with our total environment? At every moment we are as we are, unities maintaining ourselves 'crescently and con-crescently' in commerce with our total environment – losing here, gaining there, in the light of our present concerns in a given environmental situation. *We are not a present added to a past, or a present passing to the future.* We are present active unities who find ourselves able to maintain self-identity even as we respond to *our* lingering past, *our* concrescent present, and *our* anticipated future. On this view, so far as I can see, we have lost nothing – except the seemingly comforting thought that nothing is lost. Perhaps nothing is lost *completely*, but to say *nothing* is lost is to say too much. Coming into being and passing away, I conclude, can be taken seriously if we adhere to the radical experientialism of personal being.

We cannot avoid this conclusion by urging that what is lost to us is not lost ultimately since it remains in the eternal total present of God. For what is lost to us is lost to *our* experience, whatever it may be for God; that is, *our* experience does not in fact have what God presumably now has all to himself, as it were. Our own specific loss is irreplaceable, and there is no way round it. Some events cease to be – and that is all!

Similarly, some events come into being – period! When I will a certain moral quality, that I now do not have, into being, *I become* kind, let us say, for the first time; or *I become* courageous, in situa-tions where I was formerly cowardly. And thus a new trait begins to grow, begins to be added, or rather accrue, to my personality. Something has come into being that was not. This means that the kind of being I am, given my abilities in certain situations, can create what would not have been a part of my life without my wilful action. My courage may indeed be related to my abilities, to my other traits, to the demands of the situation, but *that act* of courage, the initiation of *that* trait of fortitude, is a new fact in *my* nature. Whatever preceding and concomitant circumstances may be re-ferred to, the fact is that this courage is none of them; and no abracadabra can be invoked to say that it came *from them*. A new event, a new formation in personality has now been initiated into whatever else constitutes all being.

If these observations are correct, we begin to see a model of being in which continuity and discontinuity live together, by which creation and cessation are shorn of horrendous metaphysical con-sequences. For we find given in ourselves a kind of being, personal being, which, thanks to its unified nature, can bring something into its own being that could not be found in its earlier nature or, as such, anywhere else. And a personal being can lose what was once in his experience because he goes on being. Again, in this kind of being there is unity that is continuity; not a mathematical unit, it survives subtraction from, and addition to, its experiences and nature. A person loses his cowardice and he creates courage, and yet he is self-identical in this dynamic sense. *His nature is what it is because there is ceasing-to-be and coming-to-be.* Indeed, in a literal sense we can say, therefore, that he creates *ex nihilo*.

Lest this clause, 'creates *ex nihilo*', awaken old prejudices, let us note again exactly what is being asserted here. Courage did not pre-exist in the person's nature; nor did it emanate from his nature. In so far as it is new in his development as willed by him we say that it is his creation. Nevertheless, it is created by a person with a given structure responding to his own total present. I am saying that what is given in his structure, as part of his capacity, is the fact that he can create under certain circumstances. *Creatio ex nihilo*, in this finite context, in other words, is the way of saying that a given existent, with the kind of unified structure a person has, can create what was not already present as such in his being and in the universe. An actual person can bring into being what, *after the fact*, we may hold to be 'consistent' with his nature and his past. An actual person can bring into being what, *before the fact*, could at most have been a possibility known to an omniscient mind, and, *at least*, an envisioned end in his own consciousness.

It is at this point, faced with this view – that the finite creator can create *ex nihilo* – that a critic will be tempted to decrease the shock of discontinuity by some doctrine of potential being. But while appeal to potential being may seem to bridge the chasm between being and non-being, I must again warn against the seductions of such a view. The doctrine of potential being does not render the supposedly obnoxious '*ex nihilo*' unnecessary. For potential being, if it be potential, is not actual being. *Creatio* still takes place in the transition from potentiality to actuality. Potential being may seem to relieve the need to extend a bridge from the old to the new, but in fact, as long as it is potential being and not pre-existent being, it cannot form the desired bridge – for it is the very growth, the *new* being, involved when the potential becomes actual, that is at issue.

In a word, I am far from denying that for the explanation of change a doctrine of potential being is required; but I do deny that increase and decrease of being, creative change, can be fully accounted for by a doctrine of potentiality. In our experience we do find the kind of actual being who, given a unified structure of activities and their potentialities in relation to the total environment, can create in certain circumstances whatever the difference is between his actual-potential being and the new quality of being achieved.

VI

Can this model of the person and creation be illuminating at the cosmic level? On the classical theistic view, radical novelty is possible to a finite person, if at all, only because he and all other finite existents and events, in the last analysis, depend on a cosmic, non-temporal Person. But in this eternal Person there is no potentiality, no change; and *creatio ex nihilo* must be so defined that not an iota shall be added or subtracted from the fullness of his Being.

Advocates of this view have historically not been insensitive to the difficulties of maintaining that a transcendent, non-temporal Person (or Being) created and sustained relatively free persons in an orderly, changing world while remaining himself, nevertheless, qualitatively unaffected by that freedom and change. I shall suggest that the classical view suffers less embarrassment if it can be modified along the lines of the temporalistic view of personal being that we have been considering.

However, there are four emphases in the classical view of creation which must be incorporated into any view that takes the person and *creatio ex nihilo* seriously. First, God does not create in Platonic fashion, as a demi-urge, from co-eternal stuff external to him. The classical creationist realized that from mutually independent co-eternal beings the harmony we observe in the world-order is hardly forthcoming.

Second, creation, if it exists at all, is as much a brute fact as ultimate Being itself; the *how* of creation is beyond conceptualization. Furthermore, in asserting that God created neither *from* himself, nor *from* something imposed upon him, the classical theist avoided creating more mystery than existence itself exhibits.

Third, we cannot disclaim entirely a third classical contention, that creation involves a Creator who persists through the activities and processes of creative change. Classical theism insisted that change presupposed some unchanging Ground of creation. In so doing, it articulated the fundamental truth of which every school of philosophy takes cognizance in some form or other, that in the universe there is something eternal, some unchanging structure. An eternal Being creates. *'Creatio ex nihilo' does not mean that from nothing at all something comes.* And this 'self-caused' Being creates neither out of nothing, nor from nothing; it creates what *was not.* There is no understanding of the doctrine of *creatio ex nihilo,* or *ab nihilo,* if we forget that the universe does not 'begin with nothing' but for ever expresses the eternal nature of God.

Fourth, classical theism was correct in maintaining a critical analogy between God and the finite person. Classical theism, however, failed, if our argument is correct, in the doctrine of the finite person and its conception of the interchange between creative beings.

In what follows, then, I would wish to profit from the classical contention that *creatio ex nihilo* is the creation by an uncreated ontic Person who knows what he is doing, and has power to create in realizing the ultimate goals he envisions. It is no weakness to insist that the act of creation is always irreducible, and that the *how* of it is beyond human comprehension, if our actual experience indicates that creation is never reducible simply to recombination of what already existed.

But, as suggested above, theoretical incoherence and irrelevance or opposition to experienced data enter the picture when certain rationalistic and religious motifs are allowed to dictate the model of what the ultimate Person must be. In particular, it is theoretically incoherent to say that a completely unchanging Being can be the source and sustaining ground of changing being, can be the contemporaneous Creator of orderly change and novelty, and yet be itself not a whit changed by what was created. For if what is created has no effect on the Creator, in what possible sense does it exist (and is not merely possible) for him? That which has no effect on anything is nothing. I am assuming, clearly, that to exist *at all* is to act and to be acted upon; it involves making a difference to, and being influenced. If created beings have no effect at all on God, then they are as nothing to him either in being or value.

VII

The following four tenets in a personalistic temporalism may be suggestive.

1. God, the Ground of all existents, is in essence a unified Person. He never was, nor will ever be ontically divisible. He will never be other than a Person. Nor will the ultimate goals that give normative structure to his creation change. In this respect God is unchanging. To be a *person* at any level is to be a complex unity whose will is capable of guidance by reason and love. (I am not concerned here to outline differentiations of the subhuman and superhuman.) The first tenet, therefore, is that the cosmic Person is unchanging in the structural or essential form of his personal Being.

2. The cosmic Person is unchanging as Person but not in the quality of his experience. The content of God's experience changes in accordance with his varied activity in creating and re-creating with a view to enhancing every opportunity for value in the total universe at any one stage of its development. If God has created co-creators, then the concrete undergoing that is his Being, and the working out of his aims, are influenced by their relatively free activities and the consequences of them in man and nature.

Obviously, I am assuming here that our universe is one in which the orders of thought and value do not constitute a little oasis without connection with the rest of being. Indeed, such interconnectedness as there is provides, as I see it, the reasonable ground for postulating a cosmic Person as the metaphysical Unity in whose nature and purpose the created orders we know are grounded. But granted a cosmic Person who grounds the basic structure of the known world, why not follow the dynamics of creative involvement in which creator and created affect each other selectively?

If our analysis of personal being is correct, it is not true experientially that creative change presupposes an entity unchanging in every respect. Our finite model exhibits the fact that change does not defy, nor lie outside of, continuity of unified structure. Thus, my thoughts change, but my laws of thinking and organizing do not. The fact seems to be that my thinking is not exhausted in any stream of thoughts, that while specific thoughts come into existence as I think them, and go out of existence when I stop thinking them, *I go* on thinking other thoughts in accordance with the same laws.

Why not hold, then, that the Ground of the changing-orderly world keeps its essential structure and norms with it in changing? Why reject such a model on the cosmic level when to do so creates the same kind of theoretical difficulties we encounter in the soul-substance psychology at the finite level? The world as we know it changes and yet exhibits a continuous structure in so doing. Why not then say that the cosmic Person will never be less than personal Being, and that concrete coming-into-being and going-out-of being do not change his personal structure but do affect the specific qualitative undergoings and tasks his Being confronts? No finite situation will express adequately what happens at the cosmic level, but will the following example help? Beethoven is Beethoven in his Fifth and in his Ninth Symphonies, but the qualitative undergoing and enjoyment are not the same in the Fifth as in his Ninth Symphony. Each Symphony may bring Beethoven's crescence to fulfilment in that respect, but there can be greater fulfilment yet, without his losing his essential personal structure. The cosmic Creator is always at work somewhere and everywhere on some level of creation without exhausting his personal Being anywhere.

3. God as a cosmic Person creates in accordance with his purpose – assumed here to be the creation and support of (at least) persons who can be co-creators within limits. The activity of creation is an activity intrinsic to the constitution of the cosmic Person; the coming into being of other unities-of-activity (finite persons), the changes in them, their limited creations, would be impossible without God's contemporaneous creation.

Here again I agree with the classical absolutistic tradition as I understand it. But the truth about God is not – as the absolutistic view puts it – that he is an unchanging Creator in every respect. For in creating, he directly introduces changes in the quality and extent of his own experience. Every child that is born is a new fact for God, a new object of tender care; but it is also a new creative agent adding its new influence to the divine experience. To be sure, what the final effect of his children upon him will be depends upon what he himself chooses to do in relation to the new situation with which these created-creators confront him.

To say this is not to shake the foundations of the universe. It is to reconceive the nature of the foundations. For in marrying the unity-continuity of the cosmic Person to the increase and decrease in his qualitative experience, we have in fact disregarded nothing we know. We have not undermined the creativity in, or the kinds of unity-continuity that we know in ourselves and the world-order. For God is self-identical as a cosmic Person, whatever his involvement in the specificities of existence. The virtue of our personal model is to exemplify for us the kind of dynamic unity of cognition, power, and love that is involved in its specific aims and contents, without being so thoroughly transformed by them that its being can neither resist nor affect the influences that rain upon it.

At the same time, God is not a cosmic co-ordinator or manipulator who is indifferent to the ways in which particular created beings affect themselves, each other, and him. He is responsible to all that is and is becoming, whether he approves or not; he keeps on making the contribution that is fitting to his purpose at any given point of individual and cosmic advance. And, as I would want to argue further, the 'guile' of his reason and love in all creative activity is selectively to serve the potentialities for growth and creativity at every level of existence, and for all beings constructively and compossibly. No disappointment is so great that he hurls his thunderbolts in anger; no pain is so small that he does not feel the effect directly and indirectly; no disaster leaves him unwilling to quarantine the evil and develop any latent value to the utmost, consistent with his aims of protecting as much co-responsiveness and community as possible.

4. Finally – and here we stress the difference from panentheism – created persons are no part of God, and God is no part of them. God has his own uncreated, indestructible, unity-continuity of self-experience. Finite persons do not create themselves or ontically sustain themselves. But they are created, 'posited', 'planted out' with limited autonomy. As co-creators they are relatively free to respond to the basic conditions for creativity that depend on God's purpose in creation. In this paper, I have purposely refrained from considering the much-too-large problem of God's relation to the subhuman realm of being. I have concentrated only on the construction of a different model for the relationship between the cosmic Creator and personal co-creators.

The part-whole relation between persons and God must be set aside, and likewise the kind of pluralism in which God is *primus inter pares*. God is the Creator-Continuant upon whom all persons depend for their existence, and for the conditions of order and value that enable them to grow in ontic interaction with each other, the world, and God. But persons have too much autonomy, and God has too much autonomy, in 'essence' and 'content', to fit into a part-whole model, either in the 'organic' sense or the panentheistic. On the other hand, finite persons, albeit creators, are too dependent in essence and in content upon the creativity of God to justify metaphysical pluralism or pre-established harmony. Such unity as we find is better conceived in terms of a community of

purposers. What is called for is a model in which there is co-responsiveness and co-responsibility in the pattern of interaction.

No analogy will do exactly, but what might be called a *symphonic pluralism*, suggested by the model of the relation of the conductor to the members of his orchestra, may be helpful. To be
sure, at the human level the conductor does not create the players;
nor does he create the score, as God does. Let us then assume that
the Conductor is also Composer. Let us also say that the players
would not be playing what they play, and in the way they are
playing, without the Conductor-Composer's creation and guidance.
Each member is playing his instrument and responding to the score
and to the Conductor-Composer as he sees and understands and
feels them. But each member is responsive and creative in the light
of his own interpretative interaction with the created score, and
with the Conductor-Composer.

We should also imagine that no one of the players is playing his
part as the Conductor-Composer could or would. But the purpose
of the Conductor-Composer in creating the score was not simply
to have the players follow the score slavishly. His ultimate aim was
to help the members to enter creatively into the total value-
meanings that he himself experienced. He is creating anew as he
conducts *this* orchestra. And he in turn undergoes a new moral-
aesthetic experience as he responds creatively to the performance
of each of these players and to the performance as a whole.

To the extent that the players in their creative response 'catch
the spirit' of the Conductor and remain sensitive to each other's
performance in their attempt to create for themselves and for each
other the optimum aesthetic value, they, together with their Conductor-Composer, create a new symphony never before heard or
experienced. The human creator can be creative because the conditions of creativity have been provided. But the orchestra's creation is *their creation*, or better, *their co-creation* with God, just as
his creative response, seeking to take advantage of every good, is
his response. The metaphysics of creation, in short, involves
Creator and co-creators in the ebb and flow of a responsive- responsible cosmic community in which the sensitivity of free spirits to
each other and to their Creator is reflected in every moment of
human and divine history.

CHAPTER XII

THE LOGIC OF CREATIONISM, ADVAITA, AND VISISHTADVAITA: A CRITIQUE

Any believer in *creatio ex nihilo* must be given pause by the fact that the most influential – not to say entire – trend of philosophical thinking the world around, ancient and modern, has not favoured outright creation. Any mystery seemed more palatable than that of *creatio ex nihilo*. And, as we have seen, even creationists cannot accept what is probably the greatest objection to *creatio*, if it is taken, as I think it must, to mean some alteration in the being of God. The objection is: If whatever is considered ultimate, be it God or Space, changes, what would cause the alteration? An ultimate, after all, is introduced to give final intelligibility to all observed change.

Nevertheless, the believer in some unchanging Absolute still accepts responsibility for an account of time and change. In the present essay, I consider both the way in which a distinguished contemporary Indian Advaita philosopher and mystic, T. M. P. Mahadevan (University of Madras), grapples with the problem of time and eternity, and also the critique of this Advaita view by Ramanuja and his followers. Incidentally, this debate, reminds one of the discussion among eternalist theists in the West, and should serve to dissipate the exaggeration of basic differences in 'Eastern' and 'Western' thought.

It is, notwithstanding, my concern to press the question on both Advaitin and Visishtadvaitin: Why not reconceive the perfection of God so that good and evil, truth and error, progress and decay, can affect the qualitative manner in which God experiences himself and the world, and in a way consistent with his omnitemporal unity and continuity?

How is Brahman or God related to the world of Nature and especially to finite persons? There is one answer to this question to which astute Indian religious and philosophical minds resolutely object, and that is creation 'out of nothing'. In this rejection, of course, they enjoy unanimous support of ancient Greek philosophy. Furthermore, there are many Western thinkers, ancient, modern and contemporary, who chime in on the chorus. Indeed, we have been singularly impressed by a kind of intellectual impatience with the doctrine, and the not always subtle suggestion that a philosophically sophisticated mind would no sooner look at it than give it up.

In this essay we shall first expound the main line of thought involved in theistic creationism (Absolute Theism), Advaita (nondualist Monism or Absolutism), Visishtadvaita (Qualified Absolutistic Monism). We shall then try to show that, contrary to the assumption usually made by Advaitins and Visishtadvaitins, the rejection of the theory that God created man *ex* or *ab nihilo* leaves them with problems at least as serious as those they wished to avoid by rejecting creationism. In the last section, we shall consider a weakness which pervades all three perspectives and suggest another approach. We begin by reviewing the background for creationism so that we can better appreciate the problems all three perspectives are attempting to solve.

I

We have said that the Greek mind did not even suggest a doctrine of radical, metaphysical creation. The exact ontological relation of Aristotle's Prime Mover Unmoved to the world and man is certainly not clear, but it is not creationism. Plato's valiant struggle with the problems of the relation of the Ideas, or the Good, to the World of Appearance is a matter of record. As we interpret Plato's struggle, the early Plato, who had seriously considered that the changing world was an imperfect copy or imitation of the Ideas, who had also held that things 'participate' in the Ideas, gave way to the doctrine of the middle Plato's *Republic*, that the Good is the Source of the world's being and being known. The later Plato saw such difficulties in these earlier views that he was willing to consider a radically different view in the *Timaeus*. There an infinitely Good but not infinitely powerful God, with his eyes 'fixed' upon the co-eternal ideas, strove to 'persuade' the co-eternal Ananké of the Receptacle to take on as much of the perfect as possible.

We can learn from Plato that the metaphysician cannot allow his philosophical imagination to be restricted arbitrarily by impositions of revealed or conventional religious dogma. But we can also learn from this great mind's 'sense of the problem' that, on such ultimate issues, the metaphysician must not impose his own desire for certainty, but realize that perhaps he will only be able to reach what at best will be the most probable account. Thus, Plato's own reflections led him, tentatively at least, to suggest an alternative which, for all its tantalizing qualities, poses insuperable obstacles to philosophical understanding.

For in this *Timaeus* account, as we said, the imperfect beings in the changing world are the product of the cosmic Demi-Urge's effort to conform the 'womb of all becoming' to the requirements of the eternally independent Ideas. No outright creation is contemplated. Plato envisages three independent and co-eternal metaphysical ultimates: the Demi-Urge, Eternal Forms, and the Receptacle. Interaction between them produces the world of time and space.

But the deadly fault in this theory is one that, once realized, forces a thinker to some form of metaphysical monism or creationism. For, if, by definition, co-eternal entities A, B, and C are not responsible in any way for each other's being and Nature, since no common factor other than 'self-existence' can be assumed, one is left to ponder. On what grounds could we expect such beings (*a*) to affect, or be affected by, each other to begin with, (*b*) to combine and give the degree of order and goodness we actually find in existence?

There are difficulties in Absolute Monism, in Qualified Monism, and in Creationism, but they certainly are not as harsh as those faced by posing ultimate plural entities – be they two, three, or infinite in number – for though metaphysically independent and primitively indifferent to each other, the Entities somehow came together to create the dominant order of the finite world. Until one has faced this difficulty, decided that it simply will not do, he will not be appreciative of the alternative views which, whatever mystery they still involve, escape this one.

This is the time for us to realize that exponents of theism and absolutistic monism are not proposing that all mystery is dispelled on their views of the relation of the finite world to God. They agree with Whitehead that the problem of philosophy is not to solve all mystery, but 'to corner it'. Hence, if a thinker has decided that metaphysical dualism and pluralism render mystery more mysterious, he may ask how well Creationism, or Advaita or Visishtadvaita (to which we are restricting ourselves) 'corner' the mystery.

We have given the context in which the creationist advances the view that God created the world 'out of nothing'. He *means to deny that God depended on, or created 'out of', something other than his own being, independent of his being, and co-eternal with it.* To escape the shoals of metaphysical pluralism is one fundamental motive. The other is his desire, usually, to protect the self-sufficiency and infinity of God.

The creationist is ready to admit that he does not know the technical 'how' by which an infinite Being creates the finite world. He confesses that this remains a mystery, but he reminds us that as created beings we should expect to fail in understanding *this* 'how'. He does not mean, however, that God, as it were, takes 'nothing', zero-being, and makes 'something' out of it. To repeat, the creationist does not know what the process of actual creation is, and he has no final confidence in analogies drawn from the finite world, for both imagination and conception run dry at this point. In the doctrine of creation he wishes to affirm one basic and to him all-important conviction: that nothing other than God's own nature and purpose is intrinsically responsible for the existence of finite persons. (We might have said 'finite Nature and persons', but since theistic idealists would maintain that Nature does not exist independent of God's own being, we have limited ourselves and shall continue in this essay to do so, to the relation of the ultimate to finite persons.)

Whatever differences a creationist theist might have with other creationists, as to the nature of relation of the physical and organic world to God, his crucial insistence is that finite persons, however intimately related to and dependent upon, God, are no parts of his being, or no modes of his being, or any kind of 'filaments' thereof. Convinced that the finite person cannot exist for a moment without being dependent upon God, his creator, recreator, sustainer, the creationist steadfastly maintains that the person cannot be ontologically one with, or 'any part of', or an emanation from, or effulgeration of, or a transformation for God's being.

Why does the creationist theist hold so tenaciously to such relative ontological independence or dependence-independence for persons? There are two main reasons, especially in the Judeo-Christian tradition. He believes that the person's experience of (limited) free will, his responsibility for moral good and evil, would be in fact annulled in any monistic view. He simply cannot see how the person's actions can be in any degree his own if his total being

THE PERSON GOD IS

is identical with, or non-different from, God's being, or if he is regarded as part of God's nature. Only creationism can, he believes, be fair to the limited autonomy or freedom of the human person.

Similarly, cognitive error, the abuse of reason, is man's responsibility, and has its locus in man's mind. The creationist cannot understand how an Absolute Consciousness can be said to know at the same time the limited perspective and errors of finite minds and the truth. For an infinite Mind who knows 'error and delusion' for what it is does not really know what it is to *experience the erroneousness*, the taking of something to be what it is not! If error, illusion, and delusion exist for finite minds, it will not do, therefore, to say that they can exist in an Infinite Mind who 'sees through' them and is not led astray by them.

Again, the very objection to error is that one does not know at the time that he is in error. Where is this 'not knowing at the time' going to be lodged if a finite mind is not, to use F. R. Tennant's terms, 'planted out', 'posited', with 'delegated' spontaneity and autonomy? Thus, to anticipate a moment, if the Visishtadvaitin, taking his lead from Ramanuja, thinks that 'creation is explained as the self-differentiation of the Absolute which Brahman wills to be the many',[1] the creationist theist wonders whether the Visishtadvaitin can, if pushed, consistently maintain what is central to Ramanuja's own rebellion against Sankara and the Advaitins, namely: 'Every person is primarily responsible for his conduct and it is morally unjustifiable to throw the blame on supernatural agencies or on the highest Lord.'[2]

We have purposely introduced the Visishtadvaitin into the discussion at this point, for it is, among other things, his central insistence on the moral responsibility of the (limitedly) free person that leads him to join forces with the 'western' theist against Advaita. For we must note that, however much the case against the Advaitin is based on the contention that 'existence of a plurality of selves is a fact of experience in all its levels',[3] all three positions are equally insistent that the Ultimate be protected from any possible imputation of imperfection. Furthermore, each perspective grounds its conviction about the perfections of God's nature on what are claimed to be revelations of religious and mystical experience. But

---

[1] See P. N. Srinivasachari, *The Philosophy of Viśiṣṭādvaita*, second edition. Adyar: The Adyar Library, 1946, p. 203. See also A. C. Das, *A Modern Incarnation of God*, Chapter VIII. Calcutta: General Printers and Publishers, 1958.
[2] Srinivasachari, *ibid.*, p. 268.   [3] *Ibid.*, p. 301.

we must realize, before passing on, that because each side will resort to religious 'faith' and 'realization' to ground its conviction about the necessary perfection of God's being, this appeal cannot give advantage to anyone perspective over the others.

II

The rational case against creationism consists mainly in pressing home to the creationist the consequences of even his relative pluralism for the nature of God. The trouble with the creationist, says the monist, is that while he properly realizes that pluralism is untenable, he does not seem to realize that creationism, in conceiving of a created world and persons as independent of God, involves an externalism in the relation between God and his creation which finitizes God. For God is now limited by the creation, which stands over against him; he still remains One over against the Other or Others. Such metaphysical remoteness not only limits God's omnipotence, but also jeopardizes the intimacy attested to and needed for religious experience and confidence.[1]

Furthermore, does not creationism mean that God existed for an inestimable period without the world and man? Why would an all-knowing, all-good, and all-powerful Being be without his creation, even assuming that the idea of a God without any world is plausible?

The first type of objection need not bother the Judeo-Christian theist who has granted the mystery of the *how* of creation. For his view is that God is both immanent in creation and transcendent; ontologically, God sustains his world and even the delegated autonomy of finite persons is supported by his continued recreation.

But it is the second question that gives the creationist real pause. He knows that as long as it is suggested that the temporal process, as a whole or in any part, is said to affect or influence God, the unchanging nature and infinite qualities of God's being are threatened. Furthermore, the traditional creationist theist is at one with the Advaitin and Visishtadvaitin in what he believes to be the inexorable theoretical and religious demand that the Ultimate be self-sufficient in every respect. This means that however related the Absolute Being is to time, the vagaries and influences of the

---

[1] Cf. T. M. P. Mahadevan's critique in *Time and the Timeless* (Madras: Upanishad Vihar, 1953), pp. 63–6.

temporal process cannot contribute to, or take away from, the self-sufficiency of this Ultimate Being.

There are, of course, independent theoretical arguments, such as those advanced by Sankara, Spinoza, Hegel, and Bradley, which conclude that the notions of change and time, and of externally related monadistic entities influencing each other, are riddled with contradictions. These arguments have impressed great minds too much to be considered less than formidable. At root one wonders whether they are not in the last analysis different ways of stating a hoary, haunting question: How can that which is ever become what it is not? How can one add to all that is, as creationism seems to require? Whence could such addition be acquired? Can any of the changes which would then result be intelligibly conceived unless there were a pervasive, unchanging Being to support, direct, and sustain the Process? Nay, whatever importance we give to time or to changes in time, we make time itself unintelligible and we lose any rational ground for trust in what happens in time unless time is undergirded by Eternity. Better to hold to some inscrutable fact about Being which, while recognizing time, keeps it from infecting Reality, than to lose all constancy and direction.

In this context one can see why some doctrine of *Māyā* must continue to be a persistent alternative for acute minds. To render our discussion concrete it will be especially appropriate if we note how Mahadevan grapples with this problem.[1] It is also instructive to see what happens when this creative expositor of Gaudapada and Sankara gives his own interpretation of the relation of time and the timeless.

Mahadevan is impressed by the logical absurdities (made graphic recently by F. H. Bradley and McTaggart), with which we are faced when we try to think of the temporal world as an independently real, a self-sufficing, process. For example: 'If the whole of time flows, then past, present, and future, which are parts of time, must be simultaneous, which is absurd. The same absurdity persists if we say that the parts of time flow.'[2] Again, it is a contradiction to think of time, as we have been forced to do, as both a relation and not a relation. As Bradley says: 'If you take time as a relation between units without relation, then the whole time has no duration, and is not time at all. But, if you give duration to the whole of time, then at once the units themselves are forced to possess it; and they thus cease to be units.'[3] Mahadevan holds: 'In

[1] See *Time and the Timeless.*   [2] *Ibid.*, p. 51.   [3] *Ibid.*, p. 53.

the plenary experience, *Brahmānubhava*, then, time cannot be, even as in perfection imperfection cannot be.' Better then, to remain in the conclusion that, intellectually, time is 'a perpetual puzzle', and, 'like *māyā*, indeterminable'.[1]

What does it mean to say that, like *māyā*, time is indeterminable? It is to suggest that time, despite its intellectual contradictions, persists in finite experience, cannot be rejected, and yet must not be allowed to deceive us into acclaiming it as real. To use the old illustration: While the rope does indeed keep appearing to us, in certain situations, like a snake – so that we cannot say that the 'snake' is real or unreal – we must not be deluded into thinking of it as 'belonging to' the rope. However, we must grant that we should not see 'snake' if what we were perceiving was a 'stone' or a 'cloud'. It simply is 'indeterminable' what exactly 'snake' (*māyā*, time) is! Time exists, but is not real; it is unreal, but it is not a figment of the imagination. Still time is something which, hopelessly puzzling as it is if we try to think of it as real, can nevertheless lead us to deeper appreciation of what the Real is. Mahadevan seems to be striving not 'simply to dismiss' time.

Thus, he answers the question: What is the purpose of Time? with the suggestion: Time is 'to serve as the gateway to Reality'.[2] Time is not, as McTaggart said, 'the last enemy to be overcome', for it 'if properly approached, can be our friend inducting us into Eternity'. 'Time serves as the channel for all the orders of creation to return to their source, which is the eternal Brahman.'[3] Indeed, if in meditation we can see it as 'one of the principal forms of the supreme, immortal, disembodied Brahman', as the prominent 'subtle image' of Brahman, we shall 'cease to be time-bound'.[4] For we are not in time with its parts, but in 'the timeless', partless Brahman, our true Self.

The conception of Reality to which Mahadevan consequently introduces us must be clear if we are to see his alternative to creationism, on the one hand, and to Visishtadvaita, on the other. The important thing is to see that the 'created' temporal world of things, animals, and persons are not thrown into the melting-pot of the Absolute and dissolved. To say this would be to give their existence more reality than they ever had, for plurality cannot be granted reality. On the other hand, we must not think of the Absolute as a kind of Unity which gives no support at all to the differences between things and orders of being as seen in the

---

[1] *Ibid.*, p. 53.   [2] *Ibid.*, p. 53.   [3] *Ibid.*, p. 54.   [4] *Ibid.*, p. 56.

temporal world. True, the Absolute is never truly characterized by any part, or by any finite being – it is not this, not that! It is the full, distinctionless, changeless Unity in which all that is differential from 'our finite viewpoint', has some foundation. It is not as if the Absolute, assuming that it were to appear to another set of finite beings, could appear as something completely different or 'supporting' differences totally unlike what we 'know' them to be.

The truth to bear in mind is that the 'distinguishing marks' of things, as we see them partially, are not, because we see them partially, to be asserted as true characterizations of Brahman. Again, any description of Brahman, even as Bliss and Consciousness, is not literal but symbolic. But this does not mean that any characterization would be equally supported by the Absolute. The Absolute in its complete being is knowledge *per se* and for this 'state' we use the word 'bliss', the highest of our value categories. But Brahman 'in itself' is one undifferentiated reality surpassing even our highest categories of value, truth, and existence – without at the same time equally supporting all possible descriptions. Thus, to 'define Brahman as being, consciousness, bliss, is more adequate than to define it as the cause of the world'.[1] Also, to say that Brahman is the originator, sustainer, and destroyer of the world, while having 'no purport of its own', may serve to lead us nearer to Brahman but not as close to pure non-dual 'Being, Consciousness, Bliss'.

No one can gain any insight into the motives, the reasoning, and the conclusion of such Absolutism without responding sympathetically to a peculiar majesty in the vision, thought, feeling, and actions of its great exponents. Such Absolutism is not a way of 'getting away from' the world; it can provide a wiser way of living in the world where time and change corrupt when they are misconceived as real and are allowed to engage final commitments. The difficulties of creationism, the demands of logic, and what are felt to be the revelations of the profoundest spiritual experience, will continue to make Absolutism a persistent alternative for the metaphysical and religious spirit.

But if one is to accept such Absolutism because it corners the mystery of the relation between the Infinite and the finite, one is given pause. There are, indeed, difficulties in creationism. Yet, to introduce *māyā*(or *avidyā*) to account for the fact that the One does appear as many, is to provide a 'veil' which, however diaphanous

[1] See *Time and the Timeless*, p. 74.

to Brahman, simply does not help us to give any account of what we experience. Because we recognize that at some point the metaphysician must stare at stark mystery, we must not impatiently turn our backs on the hypothesis of *māyā* as an obscuring fact which necessitates the differentiation between time and eternity. But is it possible to accept a principle of obscuration, of nescience, of *avidyā*, in a world whose essence is said to be pure Consciousness? In any case, *māyā* hides the Absolute from us sufficiently to force us to ask: Why, if we can never know the Absolute as it is, should we have confidence in the criterion we have been using to characterize Reality as a timeless, distinctionless, plenary Experience? Why should we trust such a criterion more than any other, if owing to this indeterminable veil of *māyā* the Sun of Being and Becoming is in fact enshrouded by fog? Even to say that the fog gives way in 'realization' is to suggest that it disappears when we as subjects and agents disappear – or that 'we' never know that perfection.

The upshot in theory and practice is that we are forced to resolve our problems in the finite world without any real direction 'from above', despite promises to the contrary. We are not saying that we have no idea of 'perfection', but rather suggesting that the one we have in terms of timeless Unity may be challenged. In any case, as long as we introduce an obscuring factor to account for the limitations of time and change, we seem to be introducing a metaphysical 'power' which spells doom for both the trustworthiness of our notions of time and of the timeless. For us *māyā* or *avidyā* obscures both the Absolute and the finite. Indeed, it gives us no legitimate light at all by which to define the obscurity. It may be well, then, to look farther before making up our minds.

III

Ramanuja, the great critic of Sankara and exponent of Visishtadvaita, is especially interesting for a Western creationist theist. For he rejects *creatio ex nihilo*, on the one hand, and the impersonal, distinctionless Brahman, on the other; against each perspective his line of argument is not dissimilar to what was suggested above. He will not yield the unity of the Absolute: he insists that finite persons and biological and physical beings are inseparable from the Person, God; and that God, indeed, is the substance of every being without being exhausted in any of them; 'creation' and 'destruction' are not ultimate but are differentiating states of the immanent Person without whom no finite being can be or become.[1] The world of distinctions is not due to *māyā*, but, far from being independent of, actually constitutes the body of, God who includes it within his transcendent Unity. He agrees with the Advaitin that God is not this and not that, but holds that '*neti, neti*' does 'not deny the finite, but denies only the finitude of Brahman'.[2] Srinivasachari quotes Ramanuja:

> But, according to our views, Brahman has for its body all sentient and non-sentient beings in the subtle and in the gross state. In the effected as well as in the causal condition, it is free from all shadow of imperfection, and is an infinity of perfections. All imperfections and suffering and all change belong not to Brahman, but only to the sentient and non-sentient beings which are its modes. This view removes all difficulties. [And Srinivasachari continues:] How the absolute divides itself [*Sic!*] into finite centres may be a riddle of thought or a mystery, but that it does so is a fact to the *mumukṣu*.[3]

Expatiating, Srinivasachari says:

> Brahman with the creative urge wills the many and becomes manifold. It is the absolute that externalizes itself into the end-less variations of space-time and embodied beings by entering into matter with the living self and energizing it. . . . Effectua-tion is not an illusion or a self-enveloping process of reality, but it reveals the inner purpose of divine nature and enriches spiritual life. . . . The essential nature of Brahman is, however, pure and perfect, and is not affected by these changes.[4]

Finally:

> Brahman is not the 'infinite' in the sense that it is quantitative endlessness or the infinite that is conditioned by the finite, and is therefore, finite, but it is the infinite that dwells in the finite with a view to infinitizing the self . . . and giving it the eternal value of *mukti*.[5]

[1] See Paul D. Devanandam, *The Concept of Māyā* (London: Lutterworth Press, 1950), p. 124.

[2] Srinivasachari, *ibid.*, p. 107

[3] *Ibid.*, pp. 80–1. Note: This is the same recourse an Advaitin has for accepting the mystery of a distinctionless Absolute.

[4] *Ibid.*, p. 83.   [5] *Ibid.*, pp. 86–7.

Clearly, Ramanuja is attempting a philosophical synthesis which will save both the Appearances and the Absolute. With the creationist he would protect moral freedom and individuality, and with the Absolutist he would defend the immanence of the Infinite and its changeless perfection in the name of both logic and religious experience. Moral evil in the world is the product of finite freedom which is not to be dissolved in any doctrine of *karma*; natural evil would be seen as good if we knew enough.[1]

The very essence of Ramanuja's thought, and the problem, is the insistence that there is nothing wrong with saying that the finite self is a 'substantial mode having focalized being or uniqueness',[2] that 'Brahman is self-related and is at the same time the Inner Self of finite beings without being affected by those imperfections'.[3] His point is that 'otherness' of beings does not have to mean hostility; and that distinction does not necessitate externality and exclusiveness. To say that 'the absolute exists in the finite centres of experience as their ground and ultimate meaning'[4] is not to forsake 'differentness', for 'the infinite is itself and not its opposite. It excludes the other and is yet invaded by it'.[5]

We must simply confess that our own lack of insight, no doubt, makes it impossible for us to treat such statements as more than a juxtaposition of ideas. We refer specifically to the contention that the individuals can be foci or differentiations of the Ultimate and yet have independence and freedom. We also have in mind what seems to be the mystery of mysteries, that the Infinite is finite and yet infinitizes the finite 'within' him. The Visishtadvaitin, seeking to avoid the non-difference of the finite and the Infinite, must mean by finitude something different from infinitude. If he does, then, whether he starts from the finite side or from the Infinite, to be finite must involve something other than the Infinite. On the other hand, moving from the Infinite perspective to the finite, something radically new, some novelty, not intrinsic to the meaning of Infinite (in the sense of completeness) is involved.

Yet this sheer novelty is what the abhorrent idea of creation, for all its difficulties, does bring into prominence! The doctrine of creation, despite the attempts of some adherents to move toward the Advaita and Visishtadvaita perspective in order to soften the mystery of 'coming into being', does involve the mystery of the *how*, as we have said. But the doctrine of a Creator who transcends

---

[1] Cf. Srinivasachari, *ibid.*, pp. 168–80.   [2] Srinivasachari, *ibid.*, p. 75.
[3] *Ibid.*, p. 86.   [4] *Ibid.*, p. 115.   [5] *Ibid.*, p. 118.

and yet sustains, preserves, and yet guides (consistent with free will), the finite persons he has created, does 'save' both the Infinite and the finite persons, and it does allow for interaction at many levels of intimacy. But there is still another problem which haunts all three perspectives which we must articulate.

IV

Creationists, Advaitins, and Visishtadvaitins make one assumption that remains unquestioned, and which they protect at a price so costly that it may be time to question it. The assumption is that, whatever else may be involved, we must recognize that the eternal perfection of the Absolute Experience, or of the Personal Brahman, however intimately related to the waxing and waning of the temporal process, must not be infected by its imperfections. We have already suggested that even when a thinker comes to the brink of introducing any change into the Ultimate, he may well be driven back by the question: Whence would a change in the Ultimate come? '*Ex nihilo, nihil fit*' he exclaims. Furthermore, if the Ultimate is ultimate, there is no other being from which change in its own being could be initiated, no other being to which we can look for addition to, or subtraction from, what is.

Let us agree that insecurity would haunt the human spirit if some coming into being and going out of being is allowed into the Ultimate. Nobody can glibly turn aside this gnawing doubt. Therefore, such attempts as we have outlined must be made before considering an alternative. Nevertheless, even granting that creationism 'saves the appearances' or 'corners the mystery' better than the other alternatives, it joins the other alternatives in operating from such a fixed notion of what a Perfect Being or an Absolute Experience must be, that no other alternative is taken seriously.

However, as it seems to us at this stage, a Creator in no way affected by his creation, an Eternity unaffected by the time that somehow manifests it, involves such difficulty that we are willing tentatively, at any rate, to consider an alternative set of propositions.

First, then, we set aside, for reasons given above, the view that perfection must involve changelessness and timelessness. We suggest that Reality can be the kind of dynamic, active, changing-and-yet-continuing Unity whose nature it is to be creative and continuing. We shall not argue this thesis here, for the position needs the kind of elaboration given by the outstanding recent exponent of idealistic Personalism, E. S. Brightman, in *Person and Reality*.[1]

Second, we can find a limited model for this complex-unity-in-continuity in the experience of the finite person. It has been said, of course, by Eastern and Western philosophers, that the person's experience of succession is impossible without a permanent underlying soul-substance. It is this model of the person that has been the microcosm for the macrocosm. But our suggestion is that we do not need an underlying soul-substance to 'hold experience together'.

We actually experience ourselves as dynamic activities-in-unity. Each of us is not a mathematically discrete point. Our present, immediately experienced 'saddle-back' of *durée* is in its unity the very interpenetration of sensing, wanting, feeling, remembering, thinking, oughting, aesthetic and religious sensitivity which analysis abstracts out. But each of us *is* the unity of his activities. Instead of being non-temporal, the 'I' is omnitemporal. We point to it as an experienced temporal unity which is never beyond time, but actually has the ability to maintain its unity, according to the 'laws' or 'order' of its own nature, as it selectively interacts with its environment. Again, the fact of finite experience is that 'I' am able to be continuous in my conscious and self-conscious activities. Deep sleep, dream-experience, the unconscious, need further exposition, of course, but without leaving the realm of concrete experience, we can hold firmly to the fact that 'I' is not a collection of experiential items, but a unity of varied activities which does maintain continuity ontologically and psychologically in the midst of its world. The metaphysical contention is that it is so created and sustained.

Third, if we use this model of the person – not an unchanging soul which, like a string, holds together the beads of experience, as an enduring active unity whose very nature it is 'to affect and be affected', and yet not lose its obvious capacity to stay unified within its environment, we may have a better model for the Universal Being than the eternalistic one. The model is an Omnitemporal Creator.

Fourth, 'perfection' would now not mean completeness of the

[1] This book, edited by Peter A. Bertocci, in collaboration with Dr Jannette Newhall and Robert S. Brightman (New York: Ronald Press, 1957) argues the thesis that all reality is of the nature of persons, the temporal unified person, who energizes in Nature, and finite persons created with limited autonomy by Him. This view strengthens basic contentions of Bergson and Whitehead.

sort that leaves no room for change; nor would it mean sheer alteration, a maze-like going on and on without any controlling direction. It would involve comprehensive unity and growth, the kind of creativity which continually re-creates in the world consistent with the past creation but not victimized by it. The mystery of *how* remains, but as we have suggested, this is a legitimate mystery. God, on this view, would be the Creator-Sufferer-Lover, persuading, in many ways, finite persons to enter, as completely as their natures allow, into the tragic-joys of compassionate creativity. Much more, of course, would need to be said to make this view more intelligible, as well as to substantiate it in the light of observable facts of natural and human history, but we must move on to what may be the most difficult suggestion, which is at the heart of all the rest. (See Part IV below.)

We must make a right-about-face on the matter of coming-into-being and going-out-of-being; and we must stop the see-saw of reducing one to the other. Why not take seriously the possibility that, in the world as we observe it, there is both continuity-in-being and going-out-of-being? Is it mere *naïveté* to say that when, for example, I press the switch and the electric light goes off, *that light*, just gone off, is no longer existent as *that* light? True, electrical energy, luminosity may continue to exist, but, to repeat, does it make any sense, logically or otherwise, to deny that the particular light that went out, actually did *go out of its being as that light*? It is a fact that another press of the switch and the light will go on, but not *that* light of a moment ago.

To generalize, the world, including our experience as persons, seems to exist with much going-out-of-being and much coming-into-being, 'within' a larger context of continuing-being. Why *must* we say that the continuing omnitemporal Being *is* timeless or unchanging – especially if we then must face the problem all over again of understanding how the timeless and unchanging can affect or effect change and yet be unaffected by it? What seems to be clear is that the essential problem in creativity, coming-into-being-along-with-continuity, is a 'problem' if we start with certain presuppositions about what Reality and God *must* be! If we are willing to consider a model of reality which, if you please, accepts creative-change-in-continuity as the pervasive fact not only of existence but, with proper allowances, of Reality, a new metaphysical vista opens before us.

CHAPTER XIII

AN IMPASSE IN
PHILOSOPHICAL THEOLOGY

Paul Tillich, in many respects the Thomas Aquinas of our time, is my example of the impasse in much recent philosophical theology. Kant gave eloquent expression to the problem that occurs when cosmological and teleological considerations are advanced to prove the existence of an absolutely necessary Being, an ideal without a flaw. Yet he insisted that no other ideal could satisfy intellectual or religious requirements. Tillich accepts the requirement of certainty, and draws from a preconceived ideal of God the conclusion that unconditioned Being cannot possibly be one being alongside others. Nor can unconditioned Being be understood in terms of any symbols that are derived from any existent that is, by definition, partial.

But if there is no adequate way from man and world to God, why should any man's description of the route from God to imperfect man and the world be trustworthy? Can the standard of truth be different for the voyage from God to man than it is for the route from man to God? I try to show that in fact Tillich cannot deliver the certainty, and the God beyond God, which his system promises. In so doing I try to reinforce the need to argue for a conception of God allowed by the total evidence in human experience.

An impasse in philosophical theology: of its reality I have little doubt, and I shall illustrate it by referring to certain aspects of reasoning about rational philosophy and theology in Immanuel Kant and Paul Tillich. That we must find a way out of this impasse I also believe, and I shall make some suggestions that may be relevant to the predicament caused by the impasse.

I

'If anything exists, therefore an absolutely necessary being exists.'[1]

[1] Immanuel Kant, *The Critique of Pure Reason*, ed. Norman K. Smith, London: Macmillan, 1956, A605, B633. (All quotations will be from this edition.)

Thus Kant summarizes the cosmological argument. The cosmological argument differs critically from the teleological argument because it appeals not to the particular properties of the world but solely to the fact that something – anything at all – exists. Kant, as is well known, contended that the cosmological argument cannot move from the existence of a necessary being to that of a perfect being without borrowing gratuitously from the ontological argument. The conclusion of the ontological argument is that a perfect being *necessarily* exists.

We are not concerned with the relations of those arguments here, except to suggest that Kant had really no doubts on one point. If one is to speak of God, he must speak at once of an absolutely necessary being and of a perfect being – in a word, a union of being and perfection, the *ens realissimum*.

As he evaluates the cosmological argument on its own, without aid of ontological reasoning, Kant is bothered by the fact that since the cosmological argument is not based on particular properties of existence, it cannot aid us at all in achieving insight into what the characteristics of a necessarily existing being (who must in Kant's mind also be a perfect being) can be.[1] *Nothing in existence* can give content to the idea of what a necessary being would be like; and this is enough to disqualify the cosmological argument.

What needs special notice here, however, is that Kant is reasoning with two very different assumptions in mind, one concerning knowledge, the other concerning what God must be. Proof, or knowledge, means absolute certainty, or demonstration, or apodictic certainty. Thus, as Kant specifically says, we could 'postulate the existence of an all-sufficient being, as the cause of all possible effects'.[2] But postulation involving an admissible *hypothesis* falls short of what is required, so Kant concludes that 'unconditional necessity . . . is for human reason the veritable abyss'.[3]

Nor does Kant raise the question whether this union of perfection and necessity is the only possible meaning for the word 'God'. He does not even consider changing the requirements of knowledge from apodictic certainty to reasonable postulation, and his model of God creates the very impasse his own words so eloquently express:

The transcendental idea of a necessary and all-sufficient being is so overwhelmingly great, so high above everything empirical,

[1] Cf. A606, B634.   [2] A612, B640.   [3] A613, B641.

the latter being always conditioned, that it leaves us at a loss, partly because we can never find in experience material to satisfy such a concept, and partly because it is always in the sphere of the conditioned that we carry out our search, seeking there ever vainly for the unconditioned.[1]

Such an abyss yawns between the empirical and the unconditioned that Kant emphatically says that no empirical synthesis can provide 'an example of any such unconditioned', or 'the least guidance in its pursuit'.[2]

What strikes one in this reasoning is that the case for empirical guidance is lost before it can even get off the ground. If we grant that we can find no example of the unconditioned among the conditioned, but go on to ask whether some analogy to it might be suggested from experience, Kant says that we cannot find 'the least guidance in its pursuit' among the conditioned. Why? Because he is so convinced that the concept of a necessary, perfect being is 'so overwhelmingly great' that nothing in the empirical could ever be 'material sufficient to satisfy such a concept'.[3] So much for the cosmological argument.

The same demand for absolute certainty and the same conception of God as the union of being and perfection (of a certain sort) lies behind Kant's treatment of the teleological argument. Yet here another side of Kant is revealed in the justly famous passage:

This world presents to us so immeasurable a stage of variety, order, purposiveness, and beauty, . . . that all speech loses its force . . . and our judgment of the whole resolves itself into an amazement which is speechless, and only the more eloquent on that account.[4]

And then, continuing in cosmological vein, he continues:

The whole universe must thus sink into the abyss of nothingness, unless, over and above this infinite chain of contingencies, we assume something to support it – something which is original and independently self-subsistent, and which as the cause of the origin of the universe secures also at the same time its continuance. . . .[5]

[1] A621, B649.   [2] A621, B649.   [3] A621, B649.   [4] A622, B650.
[5] A623, B651.

Finally, evaluating this empirical vein, Kant allows himself an almost unrestrained eloquence when he says:

> Reason, constantly upheld by this ever-increasing [teleological] evidence, which, *though empirical, is yet so powerful*, cannot be so depressed through doubts suggested by subtle and abstruse speculation, that it is not at once aroused from the indecision of all melancholy reflection, as from a dream, by one glance at the wonders of nature and the majesty of the universe – ascending from height to height up to the all-highest, from the conditioned to its conditions, up to the supreme and unconditioned Author [of all conditioned being].[1]

Indeed, Kant goes so far as to say that he has 'nothing to bring against the rationality and utility of this procedure' and has 'rather to commend and further it'. Still, he cannot approve its claims to 'apodictic certainty and to an assent founded on no special favour or support from other quarters'.[2]

Let us take our bearings amid this conflict between the apodictic and the empirical. From the empirical, Kant makes clear, all we can hope for is support for 'a belief [not knowledge in Kant's sense] adequate to quiet our doubts, though not to command unconditional submission'.[3] It is when we seek to raise the teleological argument to apodictic certainty that we realize that it can be no more than an introduction to the ontological argument.[4] In view of such definite condemnation of the demonstrative nature of the teleological argument, no wonder that scholars, much as they may call attention to his praise of teleology, seem to have minimized Kant's commendation of this teleological approach as the best suited to the *ordinary human reason*.[5] Indeed, what are at war in Kant are two conceptions of a good argument for God: one that commands unconditional submission and one that falls short of this, but yet quiets doubt.

That Kant's way out of the impasse favours the absolutistic ideal, or unconditional submission to a union of being and perfection, is clear. For while granting that analogical reasoning from productions to their Author[6] is allowable, he concludes: 'The utmost, therefore, that the [teleological] argument can prove is an *architect* of the world who is always very much hampered by the

---

[1] A624, B652; italics mine.   [2] A624, B652.   [3] A625, B653.
[4] Cf. *loc. cit.*   [5] A624, B652.   [6] A626, B654.

adaptability of the material in which he works, not a *creator* of the world to whose idea everything is subject.'[1] Reasonable analogy simply cannot justify on empirical grounds 'the proof of an all-sufficient being'.[2] To say that God is 'very great', or 'immeasurable in power and excellence' falls far short of Kant's *desideratum*. For Kant wants to know what the being of God is in himself, and not what he is in relation to us as observers. 'To advance to absolute totality by the empirical road is utterly impossible.' And the final coup is given in the sentence: 'Physico-theology is therefore unable to give any determinate concept of the supreme cause of the world, and cannot therefore serve as the foundation of a theology which is itself in turn to form the basis of religion.'[3]

I would call attention once more to Kant's controlling preconceptions. If Kant had simply wanted to argue to a supreme being, he would have patiently asked what in fact a supreme being 'proportioned to the empirical evidence' would be like. But here he goes even further. He adds to his conviction that a necessary God must be perfect (in the classical sense) the contention that only such a God can form the adequate theological foundation for religion. In so doing Kant illustrates the impasse that faces absolutistic thinking about God. On the one hand, he assumes that the word 'God' can be used only for a being who is complete or perfect and thus religiously adequate. But on the other he complains that nothing in the experienced world can possibly provide a basis for proving that such a God exists. As Kant says, 'In all ages men have spoken of an *absolutely necessary* being, and in so doing have endeavored, not so much to understand whether and how a thing of this kind allows even of being thought, but rather to prove its existence.'[4] What we do, hints Kant, is to think that the concept of absolutely necessary being which we 'at first ventured upon blindly' can be exemplified, when in fact it cannot.

Is there a better way, in Freudian terms, to establish the 'future of an illusion'? What Kant has shown is that this classical view of God, because it initially refers to a kind of being whose necessity is 'not supposed to be derived from anything external'[5] is by that very fact not identifiable by anything outside of itself. Every time we try to move from existence to it, we confront an abyss – *and we cross it only by forgetting how different from anything we experience a necessary being, self-sufficient, and without any defect, must be.*

Yet, fascinatingly, while Kant concludes that such a supreme

[1] A627, B655.   [2] *Loc. cit.*   [3] A628, B656.   [4] A592, B620.   [5] A502, B620.

being is speculatively a mere ideal, he insists at the same time that
'it is *yet an ideal without a flaw*, a concept which completes and
crowns the whole of human knowledge',[1] an ideal that cannot be
given up as the religious and theological ideal. In the light of this
ideal, and a demand for apodictic certainty, he decides that the
cosmological and teleological arguments can prepare the mind for
theological knowledge but never give it. Can it be – this is my
question – that what Kant never saw is that such an ideal of knowledge and God do have serious flaws if they lose validity for us the
moment we touch the earth of finite experience?

Can it be that philosophical theology must be immobilized before
the impasse: the only God worth knowing and worshipping, nay,
worthy of being God, is a Being of whom we can in fact find no real
trace in existence? Or, can it be that the only God to whom experience testifies is not God? Let us see what happens when Paul
Tillich faces the impasse, or at least the obstacle, which Kant set
forth so clearly for those who would move either way: from the
finite to the infinite or from the perfect to the imperfect.

II

Tillich agrees with the essence of the Kantian critique of the traditional arguments. Nor does he set aside the 'ideal without a flaw'.
How then establish the reality of such an ideal if neither speculative
nor empirical arguments can justify it? By backing out of the
impasse and making a new beginning; by realizing that there can be
no rational arguments *for* God because God is the foundation, the
presupposition of, rationality. 'God is the presupposition of the
question of God.'[2] Reason cannot find God because it presupposes,
rather than proves, his existence.

Though treading well-packed ground, let me elaborate Tillich's
meaning as I understand it. For Tillich, as for Kant, knowledge
means certainty. But certainty in knowing can never be achieved,
he contends, if the knower is separate from the being he is presumably to discover. If the Being to be known is in no way identical
with the knower, there can be no assurance that the knower can
ever find what that Being is. If the knower and the object to be

[1] A641, B669.
[2] 'The Two Types of Philosophy of Religion', in *Theology of Culture*, ed. R. C.
Kimball (Oxford, 1959), p. 13. I am restricting myself to this essay because it
focuses sharply on the issue before us, but Tillich's *Systematic Theology*,
especially I, 108 ff. and 235 ff., could also have been used.

known are ontological strangers, then should the knower even
accidentally meet the Being he seeks to know, he would pass him
by, unable to recognize him, for they meet only as strangers.

In theological terms: if man in discovering himself does not
discover God, then God can only be reached on the basis of con-
jecture and probability. If man is searching for what is in no way
identical with him, he will always be in the condition of a stranger
meeting another stranger. Again, if God and man are not united
in Being or if the Being man seeks to know is outside of, or external
to, man's own being, there is no way of knowing that any meeting
is not merely accidental.

We must pause to emphasize that the knowledge situation is put
in absolutistic terms: either certainty or scepticism; either identity
or basic estrangement. Nothing else will do. In the last analysis a
philosophy of religion or a philosophical theology that is not based
on the ontological method will be philosophically and religiously
bankrupt. The most the cosmological-teleological approach to God
can do, Tillich agrees with Kant, is to help reconcile religion and
secular culture once the ontological approach and method can
undergird religion and its authority.

This ontological approach, however, must avoid the pitfall of
the ontological *argument* by radically reconceiving what is at stake
when we presumably argue for God. For, again, if you have to tie
God and Being together by some logical or cosmological evidence,
you can never be sure that what you are using as your cognitive
life-line can reach or fasten on to God. Kant used the moral
experience to link man and God when the other bases, including
religious experience, failed. For Tillich, anxious to avoid scepticism, no other model of knowledge will suffice than ontological
identity of some sort. And mystical experience gives content to his
model. We must review his analysis.

With Augustine, Tillich argues: '*Veritas* is presupposed in every
philosophic argument, and *veritas* is God. You cannot deny truth
as such because you could do it only in the name of truth, thus
establishing truth. And if you establish truth you affirm God.'[1] It
is not clear why truth must be God, why, in other words, to find
truth is to find God, but Tillich's aim is clear. For now one can say
that God (truth) is the presupposition of the question of God; that
'God can never be reached [meaning "certainly reached"] if he is
the *object* of the question, and not its basis'.[2] 'Psychologically, of

[1] *Ibid.*, p. 12.   [2] *Ibid.*, p. 13.

course, doubt is possible,' adds Tillich, following Bonaventure,
'but logically the Absolute is affirmed by the very act of doubt,
because it is implied in the very statement about the relation
between subject and predicate.'[1]

Thus, by a different route, we return to the epistemic base of
Tillich's system: the human search for any truth – for God, for
the nature of Being – cannot even get started unless one presupposes that the searcher and the object of his search are in some
sense one; an unbridged chasm will for ever yawn between subject
and object unless both subject and object participate in a Being
that is known without mediation. But the knowledge-situation is
saved not by an abstract argument that justifies new abstract presuppositions; it is saved by an adequate phenomenology: in the
knowledge-situation as *given*, subject and object are in depth
identical. This is why Tillich says that the ontological argument
for God is falsely called an argument. There is nothing to argue
about, for the ontological argument 'is the rational description of
the relation of our mind to Being as such'.[2] Again, Tillich is convinced that: 'Our mind implies *principia per se nota* which have
immediate evidence whenever they are noticed: the *transcendentalia,
esse, verum, bonum*'.[3]

Yet even now we shall miss Tillich's thrust unless we realize that
we are not talking about *a* truth, or *a* being, or *a* value. We are
concerned about the very ground for seeking any truth, any being,
any value. This is the ultimate ground for Tillich's more specific,
pervasive contention that God cannot properly be God and be
thought of as a being, however great, among or alongside of other
beings.

Finally, and to summarize: that the same Kantian 'ideal without
a flaw' dominates Tillich's thinking both about the nature of
knowledge and the union of being and perfection in God, is evident
in the statement: 'Only in the Unchangeable can be found the
prius of all goodness'.[4] Tillich differs from Kant in establishing
the ground of the ideal in 'the mystical element of Augustine's idea
of ultimate evidence'.[5] Remove that element and in one way or
another you find yourself trying to prove that God exists in the
same manner that a stone or a star exists. On this empirical, cosmological-teleological route you can never go further than ideas of
of God as the best explanation of man's general experience. The
way out of Kant's predicament, then, is to focus on the ontological

[1] *Loc. cit.*   [2] *Ibid.*, p. 15.   [3] *Loc. cit.*   [4] *Ibid.*, p. 14.   [5] *Ibid.*, p. 20.

principle in the philosophy of religion, namely: 'Man is immediately aware of something unconditional which is the *prius* of the separation of subject and object, theoretically as well as practically'.[1] It is *this* awareness, not of some object, but of the unconditioned 'as an element, as power, as demand',[2] that grounds all other inferences. And Tillich expresses this given 'unconditioned certainty',[3] this ontological awareness of the unity of the unconditioned and the conditioned,[4] by saying that man participates in a Reality or Being to which even the term *highest being* or *ens realissimum* will hardly do justice.

We have seen that Kant, disillusioned by rationalistic argument, was yet greatly attracted by cosmological and teleological 'preparations'. Tillich, once he has established the power of Being, is now free to trace the manifestations in the cultural and natural universe.[5] This cannot be emphasized enough. But we misconstrue the order of approach – with serious consequences – if we try to use the finite world to trace our way to the unconditioned.

From this whole analysis there results one serious religious consequence for the very definition of faith. *Faith* for Tillich never means the volitional acceptance of assertions about God that are probable but can never be fully verified. Faith never means a cognitive risk, a theoretical leap of some sort to the existence of the unconditioned. Existential risk is incurred when specific manifestations of the unconditioned are felt to be worthy of ultimate concern, but no risk is involved in the faith that is grounded in given ontological awareness.

III

We are now ready to analyse what I am calling an impasse in philosophical theology. If we begin with the view that God to be God must be perfect in the classical sense, then there is no passage from the world, including man, to God. By definition the majesty of God is such that no reasoning based on human experience in the world can ever penetrate the abyss between man-world and God. Any cosmological-teleological reasoning, furthermore, fails not only to fathom the nature of God, but falls short of the ideal of logical or ontological certainty. God being defined as *ens realissimum in this sense* and knowledge being defined *as this kind* of certainty, no passage from man-world to God meets either the philosophical or

[1] *Ibid.*, p. 22.   [2] *Ibid.*, p. 23.   [3] *Loc. cit.*   [4] *Loc. cit.*   [5] *Ibid.*, p. 27.

the religious ideal. This is one side of the picture, well illustrated by the aspects of Kant's and Tillich's thought as treated above.

But if the way from man-world to God is thus closed, is there a way from God to man-world that will meet the ideal of knowledge? Subtle and strenuous attempts, illustrated so acutely, I think, in Tillich's thought, have been made to keep the way open. But it seems clear that since man and nature are imperfect there is no way by which a perfect being can manifest itself *in its perfection* either in man's knowledge or in nature. In other words, 'ideals without a flaw', religious or epistemic, block passage either way. Why is this? *Because there is simply no way of knowing how close any human idea or experience is, or is not, to a God so defined that in every respect his nature for ever transcends our reach.* On this view, probable knowledge is never adequate; by definition an abyss will continue to extend from wherever we may have reached to the ideal!

To be more specific, if, as Kant argued, even the grandeur of the order of man-nature could not be trusted to take us to the flawless ideal, then no matter how much men achieve in nature, no matter what order of goodness they might exemplify, the distance between their state and the flawless being of God is still infinite. Take this line of reasoning seriously and you cannot even say that a mind inspired by the flawless ideal discerns the dim outlines, or the footprints, of a flawless God in nature and man. Any confidence that it discerns even dimly *should be undermined by the realization that it is imperfect and cannot know how imperfect it is*. Flawless Being, God above 'God', is by definition such that no matter where we look for his outlines, we are like Mary Magdalene, seeking to find our Lord where presumably he is not to be found. Thus, in what follows, I hope to show that in fact this 'ideal without a flaw', far from being flawless, simply does not in fact deliver what is promises, and that it is time to discard an ideal of perfection in being and in knowledge that is so deceptive and in fact so unilluminating.

IV

Let me, then, re-emphasize that the exponent of the flawless ideal in fact works with a double standard. By definition, or by assumption, nothing less than certainty will suffice when he comes to assert that his flawless God exists. But the moment he begins to tell us what that God is like, he is forced to use symbols, or to use analogies, which, however critically developed, fall short of certainty. He may be the first to admit that since analogies are born on earth and take their shape there, they can never spiral to heaven. He may emphasize and re-emphasize that nothing, nothing – be it prosaic or symbolic – nothing we say about God can be taken as final. But does it not then follow that in actuality the cognitive guidance we have is less than certain, and that we therefore have no more than the probability initially despised in the flawless ideal of knowledge? Do we in fact have more than the very probability that Bishop Butler wisely called the guide of life? Despite the assurance we are given that the flawless ideal, the 'God beyond God', exists, are we, in making the choices we make daily, warranted in assuming that our best ideal, symbol, or analogy, is relevant to the flawless ideal?

Nay, not even probability is trustworthy on this view. For however firmly supported by its earthly foundation, our probability can never reach, or ever know how far it is from, the flawless Being or ideal. If this is so, what is the cognitive value of urging initially that I am saved from ultimate uncertainty by a primitive awareness of God? Have I not been subjected to what might be called *the fallacy of specious assurance*? Is my situation not like that of one who is told that he has money in the bank but finds that he can never really draw on it with assurance for collateral?

Hence, we may ask: can we actually say that the foundations of religion will be shaken unless we enjoy indubitable knowledge of God's existence? Even here, as I see it, the certainty we are given with one hand is withdrawn with the other. To say that God certainly exists seems all that we can desire until it occurs to us that the assurance tells us nothing about his nature. Do we know beyond doubt that a *certain kind of God* exists? Do we indubitably know something about his nature and indubitably know his relation to other existents? If, for example, we are assured that God is ultimate Being, can we be equally assured that God is creator of the world and man? Can we be equally assured what creation means as over against any other kind of dependence, for example, participation in Being?

In other words, must we not stop asserting 'God exists' without also specifying the kind of God we have in mind? The question is never simply: Does God exist? but always: Which God exists? And this means that we need to define what we regard to be the essence and the attributes of that God, in a way that differentiates his nature and attributes from those of any other being.

And here quite clearly the impasse looms for the absolutistic theist. For even though he may have ontological certainty of God, the moment he tries to clarify what God is, and is not, he is compelled to depend for such knowledge on contrast and comparison with what we know empirically and with less than certainty. Even if he says, 'We can know what God is not, but we cannot know what God is', he has put himself in the position of rejecting, on his view of the flawless ideal of God and of knowledge, what might be advanced on experiential grounds. Does the absolutistic theist actually, then, have any guidance to give, if he denies that our best can be an adequate index to God's being and nature? For even if *he* tries to argue that a particular quality we find in our world does characterize God, he is faced by the impassable barrier which he has discovered to exist between the conditioned and the unconditioned. Whatever guidance may seem to be afforded by his ontological procedure is logically untrustworthy on his very premises. He assumes a similarity, a participation between the conditioned and the unconditioned that we can know only from our end, and cannot therefore suffice to define God or Being.

To make matters worse, there are some absolutists who hold that what is in experience may be in every way contradictory to what God's nature is. But if our goodness is God's evil, if our contradiction is God's consistency, then are we not barred once and for all from any knowledge of God's nature? What does it really mean to say that God is everything we and this world are not? No matter how much we say that God is not this, not that, for such statements to take on any cognitive content God at some point must in some sense be continuous with what is given in finite experience. Otherwise we run the risk of making God totally irrevevant.

In sum, philosophical theology has no point of orientation if the assumed supremacy of perfection of God's nature is such that it bears no determinable resemblance to the nature of conditioned being. Whether we start from God's end of things or from the man-world end, there is no way for philosophical theologians to justify their assertions unless they assume some continuity between the particular kind of God they propose and the world and man as they exist. If I am correct, the impasse we face if we insist that a flawless God is known with flawless knowledge is this: The moment we specify what we mean by God, we are forced in our epistemic situation to say that God is thus and so only in likelihood or probability. We promise certainty of God's existence, on the one hand, but can warrant no more than probability about his nature and his relation to man-world. But if we start with an absolutistic presumption about the flawless ideal, even our probability becomes improbable. For by definition we have lost any common ground for supposing that our best probabilities have any relevance to God's real nature or our relation to him. This means that the promised benefits of certainty beyond risk turn out to be more risky than the probability that can be built by carefully organizing the rich variety of experience with a view to discovering which way of thought and action promises more theoretical and practical advantages in the human situation.

If such probability seems shabby in relation to what, for example, is promised in Tillich's system, we might press one consideration. Tillich promised a mystically based absolute certainty of Being as saving man from the scepticism of mere probabilities. But he is the the first to insist that the moment we start expressing or describing, or referring to Being by symbols, even our best will be inadequate. Thus, a religious, epistemic heaven with its certainty is there; but an angel with a flaming sword is also there to bar access to all who approach bearing symbols on their breasts. What final epistemic good does it do, then, to insist on an ontological method that keeps knowledge and reason from floundering among the probabilities when in fact any symbol that is to guide us must receive its warrant by careful and imaginative analysis and synthesis of human experience?

What we learn, then, from the absolutistic impasse is that the very attempt to assure ourselves of an absolutistic model of perfection either in Being or in knowledge ends in failure. We may try to avoid scepticism in the epistemic situation by construing man's relation to the universe in such a way as to guarantee the results of good reasoning or penetrating self-awareness. We may insist on an inner link of ontological immediacy at the depth of our being so that we can live with our epistemic probabilities and moral anxieties. Yet on these same terms we have no real justification for trusting our probabilities; scepticism comes back with a vengeance. For while we assure ourselves of a religious situation in which God is met, not as a stranger but as the centre of our being, we then find that we can never be sure, even on the best results of our experience, that our best is not a stranger to his perfection. There simply is no way to extirpate uncertainty from knowledge, or possible epistemic estrangement from our relationship to whatever is ultimate. We see in part, we know in part; we experience only as *we* experience.

V

The alternative route philosophical theology must open up is implicit in what has already been said. We can only build from where we are, and realize that our lines of evidence, namely, our own varied experiences (including religious experience) and the related levels of nature, will never lead to an ideal without a flaw in the absolutistic sense. But what we lose in certainty we gain in a more realistic assurance based on the experienced foundations for the probabilities we live by – we measure the probability of our conclusions by the nature and quality of our evidence. Nor need we assume that God, if we can then reach him (and whatever his nature may be), will be a stranger. He may turn out to be our partner, a comrade who has been working and is working even as we work, whose nature can be more completely discovered as we come to appreciate the relationships in which our being is linked to the different dimensions of power within and beyond us.

I would further urge one more theoretical and practical reason for avoiding the absolutistic impasse. Attempts, in one way or another, to rise above it, or to get around it, have made for a mere patchwork in philosophy and theology. Theologians and philosophers of this persuasion have developed all kinds of theories as to how the flawless ideal could be related to the imperfect world they have already condemned in advance. For instance, once you have stark, unchanging, unconditioned perfection on the one side, and a changing, contingent, imperfect world on the other, then, since man somehow is to be related to both sides, bridges have to be built that always break down the moment perfection and imperfection are to join. For how shall we know how far the finger of God is from the reaching finger of man?

Why not, then, face our situation as it is without delivering *ultimata* as to what perfection in knowledge or religion must be? The impasse that we have been discussing is caused by two presumable ideals, one of knowledge and one of perfection. It would be interesting to speculate as to what would have happened if Kant had been willing to replace his ideal of knowledge as certainty by the claims of 'ordinary human reason', to use his term. Such reason guides us by correlating evidence in relation to some postulate or hypothesis that we use to help us the better to see the connections and meaning of the varied data we have available at any given stage of life.

Kant himself said, as he considered the evidence before him in the teleological argument: such reason can be 'constantly upheld by this ever-increasing evidence which, though empirical, is yet so powerful' that we can quiet our doubts even if we cannot reach conclusions justifying the unconditional submission deemed necessary in the logical or ontological approach. We recall that Kant, dominated by the ideal of truth and of Being without a flaw, could not take seriously the idea of a cosmic Architect suggested by critical analogy. Had he been able to disabuse himself of fixed preconceptions as to what God must be like, he might have patiently worked out the idea of God that the cosmological-teleogical considerations allowed. More specifically, had Kant been able to entertain seriously the possibility that cognition in general, and in religion and morality specifically, did not require demonstrative certainty, or unconditioned submission, he might have correlated moral, aesthetic, and religious data with the cosmological-teleogical considerations he himself pointed to: 'the world as presenting to us so immeasurable a stage of variety, order, purposiveness, and beauty . . . that our judgment of the whole resolves itself into an amazement which is speechless and only the more eloquent on that account'. Kant might have used his great powers and outdone the narrower empiricism of Hume's Cleanthes in considering what kind of 'something' it is that is 'original and independently self-subsistent, and which as the cause of the origin of the universe secures also at the same time its continuance. . .'.

It is not my purpose here to present a specific alternative argument for a certain kind of God. My concern here is to urge that nothing keeps us from the kind of study – phenomenological, analytical, or otherwise – of the different dimensions of experience and of nature (sensory-perceptual, moral, aesthetic, religious, and logico-mathematical) that does not force their possible uniqueness and autonomy into some arbitrary plan. The time has come to stop arguing from fixed positions based upon the supposed deliverance of any one kind of experience, be it sensory, moral, logical, or religious. For example, we should no longer tolerate the patchwork that results when we set up the supposed fixed demands or presuppositions of religion, or some type of religious experience, against the supposed obdurate demands of 'philosophy', or of some scientific or theoretical truth.

Again, to know ahead of time 'what God must be to be God', leads us only to a Procrustean attitude toward the interpretation of both nature and other possible existence. Finally, to set natural theology over against revealed theology, or theological philosophy over against philosophical theology, is to invite all over again the taking of either-or stands for one or the other, and to encourage the cutting and fitting that results from trying to meet the requirements of the predetermined model of 'nature' or 'God'. As long as this goes on, both sides continue in a theoretical and psychological cold war, in fear lest the other side will gain some advantage that will arbitrarily impinge on its own God-given rights.

VI

It is now obvious that I have been attacking the kind of *methodological imperialism* that results when any one aspect of experience claims for itself a veto against what it holds to be usurpers of its authentic prerogatives. But, please note: I have not been doing so on strategic grounds – important as it is especially in the modern world that the different phases of culture, let alone different cultures, keep in sensitive interaction – or, to use the current term, 'in dialogue' with each other. Two, more fundamental, reasons motivate me.

First, I take it that the basic concern of man as man is to be as sensitive as he can be to the qualitative variety and range of human experience in the world. To be sensitive to them is to appreciate them first for what they are in themselves in their own possible uniqueness and inner complexity, to see them in their variety, and then to consider how they are, or can be, related to each other. Religious experience, for example, has been sensitively described in more than one mood and mode: the feeling of absolute dependence, numinous creature-feeling, the dark night of the soul, lostness, nothingness, despair, anxiety, forgiveness, salvation, *satori*, *mukti*, union, participation, over-againstness, I-thou, or oceanic feeling. Any thinker will need to make up his mind as to which description is most adequate, and he will make allowance for psychological factors in his own historical upbringing that influence his interpretation. But, I ask: Will he not do well, the moment that he sees that his interpretations have consequences for his moral experience, or his aesthetic, or sensory-perceptual experience, to hold final decision in abeyance until he has worked out what relationships, what conclusions are justifiable, in their light also? If he does not, he is not simply being offensive to reason, but he is being offensive to the totality of claims that make him the person he is. Whatever system he develops must keep sensitive to new factors and new relationships: no curtains or walls must be set up in order to protect truths however hallowed by one traditional interpretation of his experience, or by seemingly crucial factors in the present and the emerging future.

A man's task as a man, as a thinker-appreciator-actor, is to seek not only the ties that bind but also to mark the discontinuities in his experience and in nature. With these in mind he seeks to come up with the working postulate that will guide further appreciation, thought, and action as responsively and co-responsively as possible. In so doing he cannot assume that he is, or is not, a stranger in the world as he comes to know it; neither wishful nor anti-pathetic thinking must keep him from sensitivity to as many phases and facts of experience as he can appreciate, or from being compassionate to all who share the search for truth and the fuller involvements of compassion.

Nor will he move from the fact that every thinker finally makes some commitment or other to the conclusion that he is justified in his own commitment. Somewhere, sometime, he must confront his own deepest commitment with those of others, with a spirit that honours them and the very purpose of dialogue, the willingness to listen, and to make whatever sacrifices the conversation and relevant evidence suggest. Otherwise a new relativism and a new scepticism take over, however piously cloaked in candour, or in the name of the truth to which he must 'witness', or which he must bravely but humbly profess. For, after all, his underlying conviction, underlying his own profession, let alone the dialogue or encounter, is that the reality to which he would witness is real for others also. Must then his guiding faith not be: If I patiently unravel and keep responsive to the dimensions of my own being in interaction with my total environment, I can come to a commitment that will bring me and others to deeper appreciation of at least the nature and grounds of our agreements and differences? Please note that I am not assuming that all evidence must be earthily empirical; but I am pleading that priority and ultimacy be not given antecedently to any one area. 'Let us reason together' must apply to our dealing with the different facets of our own experiences.

My second reason for attacking methodological imperialism has been given in the above analysis of what seems to me to be the historic impasse in thinking about God. When I try to get out of the realm of probabilities by setting up, on whatever grounds, absolute requirements for perfect knowledge, or faith, I soon find myself back in probability. I find that I have been a victim of *the fallacy of specious assurance*. That is, when I sought concrete guidance from the assurances which my certainties, beyond analogy and beyond symbols, presumably were supposed to give, I found that in fact I was forced to take my eyes off the certainties and go back to critical analogies and symbols from which I was supposed to be delivered in my search for reality. These symbols and analogies move up from imperfection and partiality, for there is no way down from perfection; they represent human ways of relating the data to the problems we face in given historical-cultural situations. What this means for me is that in fact I have no choice but to guide my life from probability or likelihood, by postulates or hypotheses that clarify my relationships between the data gathered in relevance to our problems of thought, appreciation, and action.

I have come to believe, as I have set forth elsewhere, that by this route of growing experiential coherence, an argument along the lines of what Tennant[1] has called 'the wider teleological argument', can help us to see human nature in relation to the world in which it arrives, survives, and grows in a way that brings man, the world, and a certain kind of God into dynamic, creative interaction. This particular argument may be inadequate, but it does have the advantage of preserving the possible mutual support and check that the different facets of human experience may contribute to each other, and it keeps alive the conversation that takes seriously the possibility of conversation.

Do I hear someone exclaim: 'But human beings cannot worship a hypothesis, however reasonable it may be. A hypothetical God cannot take the place of the living God.' The answer, of course, must be: no one is being asked to worship a hypothesis; he is being asked to worship the content of the hypothesis; in this instance that our being is tied with all other beings in a certain way to a certain kind of Creator-Being. But instead of prescribing in advance what worship presupposes, it may be suggested that the God to whom we are tied by the different dimensions of our being and his

[1] Cf. F. R. Tennant, *Philosophical Theology*, Volumes I and II, and P. A. Bertocci, *Introduction to Philosophy of Religion*, New York: Prentice-Hall, 1951.

world can indeed be worshipped with the whole of our being and in different modes. In this sense one can agree with Whitehead:

> The power of God is the worship he inspires. That religion is strong which in its ritual and its modes of thought evokes an apprehension of the commanding vision. The worship of God is not a rule of safety – it is an adventure of the spirit, a flight after the unattainable. The death of religion comes with the repression of the high hope of adventure.[1]

[1] *Science and the Modern World*, p. 192.

CHAPTER XIV

FREE WILL, THE CREATIVITY OF GOD, AND ORDER*

In this essay I return to a defence of free will against a strong critic, in order to leave little doubt about the way in which a creative will works its way in the finite person. By examining the act of creation in the person we can, contrary to denials by traditional theists, establish an experiential basis for the claim that God creates *ex nihilo*. Creation by God does not nullify the autonomy required by the experience of human will within the order of Nature.

What emerges from such considerations as those advanced in these essays is a temporalistic conception of man, the world, and God: the Creator-Person remains the omnitemporal Person, transcendent of, and immanent in, his creations, and in the orderly changes related to them. Persons, creating and fulfilling their natures; persons, challenged, supported, and threatened by the patterns and possibilities of order and disorder in the interrelated realms of fact and value – such beings are a microcosm of the macrocosm expressing the creative goodness of God.

There is an underlying assumption in this essay. It is that no adequate philosophical account can be given of the physical, the biological, or the divine realms of being without considering how human nature is related to them. Man, I am suggesting, is to be studied not as 'another instance of Nature', not as an instance of divine Being, but as the kind of being he is. He may then be related to other beings. This does not mean that, when this relating is done, man may not turn out to be another instance of God or Nature, or both together. But it does mean that the question of relationship cannot be judged before analysis of man's own experience of himself.

Hence, in what follows, limiting myself to the nature of human freedom, I shall attempt to describe free will on what seems to me

---

* This essay is an altered version of a paper delivered at a Conference on the Self in Western and Eastern Philosophy at Wooster College in April 1965.

to be its own terms. I shall then consider whether this analysis throws any light on the conception of divine creativity and natural law. I shall press the question: Can it be that in human freedom we have an enlightening analogy for divine creativity?

I

Quite understandably, philosophical discussion of will has concentrated on whether human will can be assigned any degree of freedom; and theological discussion has been affected by a concern to establish human freedom and autonomy as the ground of human responsibility for moral good and evil in the world. My main concern here is not to debate the issue as to whether there is free will, but, assuming limited freedom, to ask the further question: What is the activity of freedom? That is, what does free activity introduce that would not be achieved without it? Yet because talk of will (human or divine) as 'free' suggests arbitrary action to many psychologists, ethicists, metaphysicians, and theologians, it will be wiser to quell that fear, if I can, before proceeding to my main concern.

C. J. Ducasse's description of will illustrates not only his usual analytic insight but what seems to me to be an unjustifiable concern lest human 'free' will bring sheer arbitrariness into the life of a person. I take advantage of his analysis to deal briefly with this preliminary hurdle.

To assert 'free' will, says Ducasse, is in fact to assert not freedom of will but 'freedom to act as one wills'.[1] If my arm is neither shackled nor paralysed, 'I can' means that I am free to raise it or not as I will:

. . . under present circumstances, volition by me to raise it is sufficient to cause it to rise; and, to prove that such volition is sufficient now to cause this, I need only make the experiment: I do so and up goes the arm. . . . In sum, man, within limits, i.e. in some circumstances and in certain respects, does have freedom to act as he wills.[2]

I take no exception to this, nor to much of what is to follow. I quote the important passage:

[1] C. J. Ducasse, *A Philosophical Scrutiny of Religion*, New York: The Ronald Press, 1953, p. 369.
[2] *Ibid.*, p. 370.

. . . man's freedom to act as he wills, which we have shown he certainly has sometimes, does not, even on the occasions when he has it, in the least imply that his volition, which causes his act, is itself uncaused. The fact is on the contrary that the volition is itself determined – caused to occur – by some motivating factor, for instance, by some end in view which it will serve, or by the superior attractiveness of one of the alternatives open, or by some other consideration. My volition to raise my arm a moment ago, for example, was determined by my aim at the moment or prove that such a volition would, in the circumstances then existing, suffice to cause the arm to rise.[1]

Perhaps I am making too much of a subtle shift of emphasis from the more introspective and phenomenological account of the former quotation to the interpretative one of the latter. It is one thing to say that I am free to act as I will under certain circumstances, that I feel free and find myself, often at least, able to left my arm. But it is not the same as to argue, what I do not introspect, that the volition which causes my act is itself determined (caused) by some other factor in my life. This may be the case, but only some consideration other than what I introspect would lead me to say this. Among these would be the consideration Ducasse advances in the following passage:

Indeed, to suppose that one's volitions are not determined – either by one's past experiences, or by one's tastes . . . or by the sort of situation one is in at the time, or by one's beliefs as to right and wrong, or by the difference in the consequences one believes would follow from choice of one rather than another of the courses of action one can embark on if one but wills – to suppose, I say, that one's volition is not determined by any of these considerations nor by any others, is not to be supposing that one's volition is then free and responsible, but on the contrary that it is completely fortuitous, purely random, and therefore, wholly irresponsible. For to be acting in a morally responsible manner means precisely that the volitions causing the acts are being responsive to – determined by – such considerations as those listed above; and to treat a person as a morally responsible being means to be assuming that punishing or rewarding him for something he has done, holding out to him

[1] *Ibid.*, pp. 371, 372.

threats or promises if he does certain things, pointing out to him the probable effects of alternative courses of action, and so on, will be effective in shaping his future volitions on relevant kinds of occasions . . . the true opposite of determinism is not freedom but pure fortuity, absolute chance.[1]

Now if I saw the situation as Ducasse sees it – either caused freedom or pure fortuity – his analysis would determine my choice of theory. But I read one meaning into 'being responsive to' – and another into 'determined by' – other factors in my life as a morally responsible agent. 'Determined by' suggests that what leads to the final act are the inner and outer considerations and circumstances I would choose to approve and which I would oppose. Still, I should wish to grant that 'having freedom of choice never means that one can do anything whatever which one might will to do. The variety of alternative acts which one can perform if one but will is always limited, sometimes more and sometimes less so.'[2]

Nevertheless, granting that the course of action in given circumstances is influenced by the nature of those circumstances and also by the particular total set of dispositions, past experiences, and purposes operative in me at the time, what happens is that my willing at the time (not what Ducasse calls my total 'volitional nature' at the time) is itself an added factor in the situation I move into. Professor Ducasse anticipates my preference for saying that circumstances influence (rather than determine) volitions, and he would explain it perhaps by the hypnotic effect of the words 'free will', and by my 'gratuitous' assumption that determinism and free will are mutually exclusive. It would be nothing but silly banter for me to retort that there is a gratuitous assumption that free will must involve fortuity. What might be more helpful is to argue that inclinations, dispositions, circumstances do not have their full effect on me, wherever there seems to me to be an alternative, until I approve them as part of the process of working out the particular choice I make. The important point is that I am determined because I, in part at least, affect what will determine me – and not I am determined by factors within and without.[3]

---

[1] C. J. Ducasse, *A Philosophical Scrutiny of Religion*, New York: The Ronald Press, pp. 372, 373, 374.

[2] *Ibid.*, p. 375.

[3] Apart from the moral apprehensions Ducasse has, he is also concerned to undermine the theological contention of those who like myself urge that, if men are free to any degree, God cannot make, create, man free and morally good at

It will now be clear[1] that while there is no denying that man has limited freedom, there is a factor in willing that is neglected in Ducasse's analysis which is affected by his conviction that any other view equates free will with pure fortuity. I have tried elsewhere,[2] and in part because of such considerations as Ducasse has advanced, to dispel this legitimate fear by a distinction between will-agency and will-power. Here I can simply suggest the view that I have in mind, and which will serve as the basis for analogy with divine creativity.

II

Willing, as I would phrase it, is a distinctive phase of the total activity that comprises personal being. To be a person is to be a complex, non-summative unity of activities: sensing, remembering, perceiving, thinking, feeling, emoting, wanting, willing, oughting, and aesthetic and religious sensitivity. The argument here does not depend on agreement about the exact nature of these activities (other than willing). For the main contention is, minimally, that to be a person is (a) to be at least a unity of these activities, and (b) that these activities, while they are assigned different names, are not different parts in an assembly that constitutes a person. To be a person is to be a unity of such activities, a unity defined by what

the same time, since the last choice must be man's. Ducasse, however, urges: 'freedom and goodness are no wise incompatible: man could perfectly well be free to do evil if he wills, or good if he wills, and yet be such that in fact he never prefers the evil but always the good'. (*Ibid.*, p. 378.) In this passage, and when he continues 'an omnipotent creator certainly could have implanted moral goodness in his creatures, for moral goodness is goodness of intent, goodness of will – charitableness, compassion, kindness' (*Ibid.*, p. 378), Ducasse overlooks the particular meaning of moral goodness such thinkers have in mind. It is not what man wills but that he may or may not will either a presumable good or a presumable evil, in view of his innate and acquired disposition, that is in mind. Had God created him with a native intent to goodness, or with an invariable goodness of intent, the very meaning of man's moral goodness, or badness, disappears. The intention in such views is not so much to exonerate God from man's evil acts as to see what it means to say that man is free for God (as the sequel will further explain).

[1] For fuller treatment of Ducasse's view see his masterly *Nature, Mind, and Death*, LaSalle, Ill.: Open Court Publishing Company, 1951, Chapter II.

[2] See *Introduction to Philosophy of Religion*, New York: Prentice-Hall, 1958, pp. 223–39, and *Free Will, Responsibility, and Grace*, New York: Abingdon, 1958, and 'The Moral Structure of the Person', *Review of Metaphysics*, Volume 14, No. 3, March 1961, pp. 369–88, and also *Personality and the Good*, co-author R. M. Millard, New York: David McKay, 1963, Chapter 8.

these activities actually do and can do.[1] To will, then, is for the person to act in a way that can be discriminated introspectively from other personal activities: 'the person wills' is the accurate mode of speech; 'the will' is nothing other than one kind of, one dimension of, personal activity.

To say this is to emphasize that the will is not side-by-side, as it were, other phases of personal activity. Willing, as a certain kind of activity among the total activities of the self, simply cannot take place out of connection with the other activities and structures of personality. To neglect this fact is to invite fears about arbitrary acts of will. But another distinction must be drawn if we are to see more specifically why it is that willing does not bring sheer arbitrariness into the life of a person.

The distinction is that between will-agency and will-power. The person can will (will-agency) without fully accomplishing the objective he has in mind. When the person succumbs to temptation we say that will-agency does not have power (will-power). The distinction between will-power and will-agency cannot be absolute, since an agency that has no effective power at all would be nothing at all. Yet the distinction points up the fact that will-power is the effective difference made by will-agency within the total situation the person confronts at a given choice-point in his life. Thus, the student who chooses to study after having formed bad study habits, may well find that his will-agency makes little headway, that is, that he has little effective power over the habits formed. Yet for him to make no headway does not mean that he has no will-agency at all, or even no will-power at all. The act of willing does have some effect, however little, against the formations in personality that render it 'powerless' to break the habit.

To this extent we can agree with Professor Ducasse that no person wills arbitrarily, that is, that a person cannot en-act anything at will (will-power). We can also agree that he never wills outside the total context of his native and acquired capacities, that he is never impervious to the environment that impinges on him at choice-point. But what must be added to any concrete account of choice is that any behaviour or conduct in which will-agency is present is caused by many factors including the will-agency. A

[1] For our purpose here we may also neglect the question whether the 'total' person is conscious or unconscious. Yet, I should want to insist that what we know about unconscious activities we can know only by inferential analogy with the conscious.

person at choice-point often does not know ahead of time exactly how much his will-agency can accomplish. Nevertheless, will agency as felt is will-activity; it is not want-activity or thought-activity, or ought-activity; nor is will-agency the by-product of other activities exclusive of willing. Will-power, however, in a given situation is the by-product of all the factors involved in the matrix of activities, including willing, that constitute the total person-personality.

Indeed, a person's personality is the unique, more or less unified, acquired joint-product of the person's activities as they interact with the total environment. The person learns or acquires a personality that expresses his mode of interaction with his environment. Yet a person as an originative unity of activities is never exhausted in whatever degree of acquired unity his personality has; the person always lives and acts on, through and in his personality: hence the composite word 'person-personality' for a person at any moment in his career.[1]

III

Assuming, then, that will-agency is free within limits, but not arbitrary in a specious sense, we may ask: In what does the achievement of freedom consist? As has just been suggested, the person in willing does not act in a vacuum. The person does not will to will; he wills to think or not to think; or he wills to pursue what he acknowledges to be right or wrong. Moral freedom is the personal will to exert oneself in favour of, or against, what one believes he ought to do. A person uses his freedom to favour or oppose a situation in his personality-environment-matrix that his willing at this moment of choice did not choose. For example, will he now, faced with a problematic situation, pursue thinking that is self-consistent and related to the available evidence, even if he knows that the conclusion may be displeasing to his own past sentiments and those of others whose esteem he treasures? Let us assume that he can will to think about the situation. Yet his willing does not create the structure of logic and of reasonable thinking; nor does it create the evidence to be taken into account. What, then, does his

---

[1] 'The Psychological Self, the Ego, and Personality', in *Psychological Review*, Volume 52, No. 2, March 1945, pp. 91–9; and 'Foundations of Personalistic Psychology' in *Scientific Psychology*, ed. B. B. Wolman and E. Nagel, New York: Basic Books, 1965.

willing do? What difference does it make? What does it create, if anything?

Our point is critical; the person in willing (will-agency) does not will new basic capacities into being; it takes advantage of, or it is confined to the activating of 'givens' in its total person-personality. For example, willing certainly does not create the evidence or the rules of thinking. Nor does it at any given moment create the emotional sentiments that may be disappointed as they make themselves felt in a way that can make straight thinking more difficult. New thoughts flood in, and new feelings may come into play that would have been inconsequential otherwise, but we cannot say that willing creates these thoughts or feelings. For only thinking activity can think thoughts, and only according to implicit laws of thought; only emoting-activity expresses itself in one form of feeling or another; and only feeling-activity can take specific forms of feeling; only sensing capacities can experience sense-data. Willing, it seems clear, does not alter the basic activities of the person, or the basic rules by which they, once active, are governed, or the basic concomitants that come raining in upon the choice-situation from learned 'structures'.

All the more, then, what does human willing do? If it does not act out of relation to other activities and structures, unlearned or acquired, is there anything left for willing to do? Yes. Willing at least makes possible changes in the constellations of factors involved in a given choice situation. For example, by holding some factors in a situation in focus (or in action) when they, left to themselves, would cease being active, it changes the outcome that would otherwise have ensued. It makes a difference whether thinking can be kept thinking about the evidence, whether sentiments are kept from becoming the focus of the situation or dominating the associative process. In a word, the minimal difference willing seems to make is one of keeping some factors in focus and operative and 'shutting off', or decreasing, the power of other factors that in turn would be more effective if willing favoured them. To illustrate, if I will to hold on to the hot plate that is paining my fingers, I am keeping in focus the thinking of the goal: 'this plate must not be dropped' and favouring the feeling and other states favouring that goal, and thus refuse to allow the experienced reflex 'drop hot plate' from being fully enacted.

I do not suggest the above as a complete account of a very complicated situation; there are many more focal and peripheral factors (conscious and, probably, unconscious) that no doubt have an effect in my conscious matrix at any one point. But could I articulate all of those adequately, I doubt that the basic description just given would be abrogated. Willing is at least that activity of personal effort which, far from producing the situation with which it is confronted at any decision point, does create a situation that would not have ensued had the decision not been made to hold firm to certain activity-contents as opposed to others. This willing is free in so far as it is not the sheer outcome of a confluence of present and past forces now operative in person-personality. But its intended effect is to alter the existent situation in accordance with a goal decided upon at that point.

IV

We have been speaking in minimal terms reminiscent of William James's doctrine of fiat. I am no surer than he was of 'how' all this comes about. But, undaunted, I wish to go on to say that, if I read the situation aright, to will is to create. I use the word 'create' and give up the words 'change' and 'alter' because I have a specific kind of change in mind, namely creative change. Creative change is more than the actualizing of potential, although it presupposes both actuality and potentiality in the creator. Creative changes is a change in a situation that would not have taken place if the situation had been allowed to 'unfold' or to drift, as it were, with the outcome being no more than the consequence or outcome of interacting factors left to themselves. Creative change produces, in other words, an alteration that might well not have occurred, and, as far as we know, would not have occurred, without an activity that entered the situation in such a way as to allow a result to take place that simply would not have ensued without effort expended to this effect.

Accordingly, a person is here held to be creative in a given situation in so far as he wills in that situation an end that (ethical or not, aesthetic or not, reasonable or not) would not have taken place until he so willed (and exerted that amount of will-power). Willing, to be sure, always is willing in a personality context; but when willing takes place, it (will-agency) effects results believed to be possible in that situation but results that so far as we know would not have occurred if the willing did not endure until the end was achieved.

Much is involved in what we have said that needs further explication. But the situation to keep before us is nicely described by Professor Wilmon H. Sheldon when he says:

> The only genuine cause is one with a power quite its own, underived from what precedes, deciding so far quite by itself what it will do. Hence, when we reason in isolation, but we are reasoning and not feeling![1]

Sensitive to the dynamics of reason, feeling, and willing he continues:

> . . . Unless there were urges, lures deep or shallow, temporary or lasting, native or acquired, each with its own magnetism, there could be no choice made, no reflection as to which is better or best. And these lures stand on their own feet, actual given trends in the individual make-up. Reason doesn't create them, though it may discover them. . . . Nor does will create the lures. . . . The act of will, like reason may discover new goods, but their goodness is not created by the act. Will may indeed focus attention on this or that lure, letting its force be felt so strong that its opposite lure gradually recedes from the scene. We can by our free choice let the delights of the flesh so dominate our life that the appeal of the finer and more lasting goods disappear below the horizon.[2]

What, then, is the thesis being suggested? Willing, far from operating in a psychic-biological vacuum, is the effort of the person to deal with the given factors in a choice-matrix that would follow a line of least resistance, as it were, if the person had not directed them in the light of a new task. Willing, on the other hand, could not create the new task were thinking impossible, or were there no dispositions and trends in the total matrix of which it is a part. Willing does not take over the function of thinking, of wanting-desiring, of pleasing or displeasing; it constructs neither the laws of reason nor the intrinsic functions and sequences of emotions. Willing is like a parent who cannot be a parent without children, and who must accept certain brute facts about their actual and possible natures. However, since the parent has energies left that are not exhausted by his children, he is free to manage what they

---

[1] *Rational Religion*, New York: Philosophical Library, 1962, pp. 16, 17, 18.
[2] *Ibid.*, p. 18.

present to him in ways they cannot manage by themselves, and in ways still open to him.

Nothing less is involved, it seems, than to realize that the person, were he simply a composite of feeling, emotion, brute sense-data, oughts, and rational activities, could not will. When a person wills he does not become the senses, the retentive capacity, or the desires, or the sense-data, or the memories, or the sentiments. Yet in willing, when he is successful, he is able (will-power) to control these raw materials in the choice-matrix so that while each contributes its share, each further enters into conduct, into the formation of character and personality, in a way it would not, as far as we can tell, if left to itself. What is new as a result of a will, or its creative act, is not conduct in which there is no emotion, reason, memory, obligation (or something other than these), but those components of each that now constitute the person's purpose (good or bad).

Indeed, in this context, we can say that the character and personality of a person are the partial result of creative will – they are not mere changes or alterations – in the sense that they constitute the kind of unity – the degree of orchestration of dispositions and capacities – that express the self-conscious purpose of the person. In particular, a person's character is a creation of the person because, and to the extent that, he has been able to bring into being – not something which is neither desire, nor thought, nor obligation, but – something that is new, from the point of view of that person's past and present. This new partial creation, this new orchestration, was not impossible in view of actualities and potentialities in the choice-matrix; but it now exists because willing has sustained and controlled one possible focus rather than another. For example, fear that could easily express itself in cowardly flight is kept from 'taking over' the conscious matrix even as other emotions like sympathy, anger, and respect, are allowed to play a larger part in an act of courage that was cautious as well as daring.

v

Is it too much to say that such creative change involves positive addition to, and subtraction from, what is? Is there not illustrated in human personality the production of a change that brings into being new qualities and formations of character and personality at the expense of others? While I grant that it would not be an accurate description to say that willing brings into being the constituent emotions, memories, and thoughts, that it would not be accurate to say that willing merely follows the contour, trend, or dynamics of the unattended constituents, I do suggest that willing does produce something new. For willing sustains activities that might have ceased, and it activates and directs trends that might have been ineffective.

How often in our lives actions that are begun by impulse are continued when impulse is dead. For example, an act that begins in sympathy for another may still be continued when sympathy is gone (and an act begun by willing may continue from sympathy). Something new takes place which cannot be predicted from past or present experience, which would not take place if the person did not will action in a given situation toward a goal or end that he envisioned.

A very clear instance of willed creation in human experience is, I think, the formation of character. Something new comes into being as a person develops his character, and in two senses. First, some character-trait might never have come into the world without his willed purpose. Second, what was given at choice-point is directed into new channels, into directions or formations never known before or reached in a particular personality. Such creative change is not mechanical change involving new juxtaposition of pre-existing parts; nor is it emanation or the evolution of potential. It is the bringing into being of something which, once created, may be interpreted as the 'lawful' bringing together of parts at some points, and 'gradual' evolution at others. But did we actually find this in human experience, or are we foisting upon human experience 'models of occurrence' that may indeed fit the physical and biological world but may well be questioned in the light of what seems to take place in personal being?

For, in personal 'growth', in the 'development' of character, the situation, however difficult to 'comprehend' unless we use physical and biological analogies outruns those analogies. In human willing something envisioned as desirable and possible in a choice-situation is chosen and willed into being by the person. Furthermore, in human experience we may build from what we are, actual and potential, but we don't even know what the potential of the actual is until a new stride is made. Once the stride is taken, once the bridge from the 'potential' to the actual is built, we look back and think we can see the development or the phases that 'made' the 'new order' that was brought into being. And of course there were potentials and parts involved, and they are included in what was created. Yet can such analysis keep us from granting that a person's character, at every stage in his development, is a new fact in the horizon of his life?

To repeat, a good or bad man – be he a Socrates, a Jesus, a Gandhi, a Hitler, or the heroes and criminals of everyday life – is a creation; each person, in part, creates himself – literally. Such persons show what man can become only because by firm efforts they raise structures that take them beyond the foundations and the raw materials granted them. After they create their particular new forms of life, we are able to talk about these new stretches of thought, of aesthetic, moral, and religious sensitivity, as lawful as if they were just waiting to be realized. In fact they probably were not 'hidden'; they simply did not exist, at least in the specific form in which we now see them. Such creations are not arbitrary, because they were built in the context of a pre-existing situation; but they were not built 'out of' it, as far as we actually know. Yet they became, they came into being because of an effort that moved whatever did exist to become new in form, quality, and pattern.

To summarize: I am trying to get at a fact that defies articulation into any of the usual forms of intelligibility, of logical or of 'technical' reason. We claim to understand the ticking of a watch by taking it apart, seeing how each part functions, and then putting it back again. We claim to understand the growth of a good man by showing how this good man is a fulfilment of past and present potential. Such analysis and description does not do full justice to what actually happens in willing a character into being. I am urging that in the very nature of our experience and development of character, in so far as it is willed, we have a stark, brute kind of event that defies analysis into logical connection, temporal connection, mechanical connection, and even telic connection of the sort exhibited at the biological level. In the creative event to which I have been pointing, something comes into being because of willed effort that we say must have been 'there' potentially, but this is *ex post facto*, only after the creative event has taken place. This fact, I think, needs more attention than it has received in the past. For as far as we know in such instances, the reach actually exceeds the grasp, and we need to be warned about explaining the reached as a 'lawful' development from a supposedly latent past. At least this last assumption may well need to be given up in the light of what we actually experience.

Why not simply hold to what is given, the fact of creation as being the outright addition, increase, positing, of something new that is 'like' the old but not the mere developing of the old. The good man is, if you will, the man generated, not simply regenerated; the new man is built not on the old man, but with the old man taken into account. There are, no doubt, limits to freedom or to creation, but this is no reason for supposing that Socrates' taking the hemlock, in the spirit in which he took it, is not a new fact in his life, and in the history of the world. It is related, but nevertheless created; once created we can look back at the created, and often we discover its filament with the past. But the filament now there is there because it too was created. It too is part-product of willing by a being who knew not whether his fiat would realize his goal – and then finds that it did! This is freedom; this is creation in human experience, at the very core of what we hold precious in life, moral achievement.

VI

Does this analysis of human freedom and creativity afford any light at all on the problem of God as Creator? I am referring to the theistic hypothesis that God is a creator *ex nihilo*, a doctrine that has been so difficult to understand that great minds have preferred metaphysical monism or absolutism to theism.

For the purpose of this paper, I set aside the question of the ontic relation of the physical and biological realms to God, and limit myself to the question whether a doctrine of creatio ex nihilo, once carefully defined in relation to finite persons, and once its theoretical intent is clear, is as unbelievable and unintelligible as critics have held it to be. But why, in essence, has such a supposedly unintelligible doctrine as creatio *ex nihilo* been advanced?

The main ground for holding that God creates *ex nihilo* is to emphasize the fact that God has delegated freedom to persons, that persons are not ontologically part of God, however close their interaction with him may be, and however intimate their dependence upon him for quality in their lives. The doctrine is intended to interpret the fact that persons are free within limits, that no one else, including God, can be responsible for their own free activity. God as creator is responsible for their being free; but since the order of Nature's structures dependence upon him for quality in their lives. The doctrine is intended to interpret the fact that persons are free within limits, that no one else, including God, can be responsible for their being free; but since the order of Nature's structures depends essentially on him and not upon man, God is responsible for the consequences of man's willed choice. If men are free in this sense, they cannot be foci, or centres of God's centre, or the energizing of his being, however, their interaction with each other and with God be conceived.

But if men are free in this sense, with limited but definite delegated creativity, the whole metaphysical model of persons as modes of the divine Whole, as centres of complex Being, must be given up. For this model ultimately carries agency in all of its possible and actual directions back to Being as the One Source of all that is. In place of this model of parts-in-whole, we need to substitute the model of purposers-Purposer, that is, a model suggested by a moral system or community of persons. Even closer would be the model of an orchestra of moral agents, in which finite purposers, rooted indeed in an interactive network they themselves do not create, are yet free to cooperate with the creator-conductor, and to choose within limits different for effectively expressing their own freedom.

However, the importance is not so much in the model but in the metaphysical conception that it seems to me it seeks to develop. For what is involved in saying that persons are not part of God is that in some sense they are beings that God added and adds to all that is. Persons are no part of, nor do they emanate from, the rich effulgence of his being. They are independent, but not self-created, agents.

It is this fact and this kind of system, then, that *creatio ex nihilo* stipulates. The doctrine that free persons are not part of God but created by him does not mean that God takes nothing (little bits of nothing, as one of my students said) and makes something out of it. Impossible, no doubt, to imagine, or even to conceive in purely logical terms, this doctrine does mean that where earlier there had been non-existence (no Socrates), there then appeared Socrates, a new being – never as such existent before he was born – and that he then took a hand in his own further development in relation to God, as he formed the character and personality that took the hemlock.

But the question persists: Whence would such sheer novelty, such addition to all there is and has been, come? I confess I have no answer if I take the usual lines of trying to imagine how a

Socrates came into being from an earlier stage in which, even granting him being in the mind of God, he simply was not the existent
that made his Apology for philosophizing before the Athenian
judges in 399 B.C. All I know is that if I take the evidence at hand,
a new fact, a different quality of existent, came into being, developed, chose to die for his convictions that he should obey God and
yet not undermine the state or leave Athens for Boeotia.

If I am told that this fact was already among the possibilities in
God's mind, I would grant it. But I would still urge that what still
defies imagination and logical conception is the how of transforming that possibility into actual existence. In other words, I
grant that the *creatio ex nihilo*, of Socrates or anything else, cannot
be explained if we demand that explanation must involve explaining
how sheer novelty can be added to what already is, if we use as a
pattern of explanation either mechanical know-how or logical
implication. Logical implication simply will not do, for finite freedom cannot be implied by a total network of logical relationships.
And mechanical know-how is simply not forthcoming when the
problem is to account for the kind of novelty that is more than the
assembling of parts into a new combination.

VII

I am suggesting that in a doctrine of *creatio ex nihilo* we have
cornered an ultimate fact of being that must be the basis for other
explanation but is itself not explicable. And this fact of existence is
not at odds with human experience, and especially that of forming
character. For this reason we must turn to the claim that theists
themselves have been all too ready to grant. Nowhere in experience,
many theists have claimed, do we have an instance of *creatio ex
nihilo*. All human creation, for example, deals with materials
already at hand, and this surely does not apply to *creatio ex nihilo*
which by definition means that God has no Platonic co-eternal
stuff, for example, which he persuades to take on desired form.
Theists have been wont to argue that in this instance it should be
understandable that man, the created, should not find, in himself
or in the created world, empirical ground for such a doctrine as
creatio ex nihilo.

But this is the very point I am challenging, and which, hopefully,
the earlier analysis of the concrete meaning of freedom supports.
For if human freedom is at all like what we have analysed, it does

involve adding qualities and dimension to personality that simply were not there, and would not be there now, apart from the free act. Similarly, *creatio ex nihilo* on the part of God need not involve, I suggest, anything essentially different from what is given in our own experience, although there are differences of details beyond human imagination and conception. Why do I say this?

Because it seems to me that whenever, anywhere, there is addition of novelty, when a real difference appears, the problem of *creatio ex nihilo* is on our hands – if it is a problem at all. But I also suggest that it is a problem only if the philosopher insists on trying to explain how novelty comes into being instead of conforming his theory of reality to what is given in human experience. Whether God creates, or finite persons create, there is added to what is already present. Specifically, for God to create free, finite persons is for him to bring into being, in connection with what is given in his own being, something that could not come into being, and would not come into being, without his effort. Granted that God not only creates new beings but sustains them in a network of relations hidden from our knowledge, can there be any ontological difference in the act of creation? It matters not what the how of creation is, for what is involved, whatever the how, is the novelty resulting. And for this our own acts of will, in bringing new actualities into being in our own life, provide the nearest and perhaps the best example we have in experience of what it means to say *creatio ex nihilo* (be it human or divine). At least, this is the suggestion here.

Can it be that in our thinking about this whole matter of creation we have been more affected than we realized by an understandable fear comparable to that we found in the interpretation of human free will – a fear from which a more complete and radical empiricism could save us? This theoretical fear is represented in the presumably profound epigram, *ex nihil, nihil fit*. All that this means is that nothing is nothing, and nobody can make something out of it. But the contention here is not that nothing makes nothing, or that anyone, God or man, makes something out of nothing! In the world of our experience new qualities and existents come into being that are not reducible to recombinations of the old; and some things go out of being, whatever residuals are left. For these data there is no clearer description than one that points up the fact that there is something added where there earlier was nothing of that specific quality; that there is now nothing of that quality where there earlier was something.

This fear would be justified did we mean that in the beginning there was nothing, nothing, nothing, and then, behold, one day something came into being. What I actually experience, to take my paradigm, is that I, a person, exist and that I can, at certain points at least, not merely alter my being but bring into existence what was not in being until my effort made it possible. Creation presupposes some existent, and presupposes that existent as agent. Analogously, the existent, God, did not come from nothing, and he does not bring something into being out of nothing.

Thus, on the cosmic scale, when we say, 'In the beginning, God,' we are saying that a certain kind of self-existent Being was able to bring into being, create, new beings; he himself did not come from nothing, and he made or makes nothing from nothing; he created and creates – period! In a word, creating is a kind of change produced by a kind of being who pre-exists his creative act and is co-existent with his creative act, that is, maintaining his own identity as well as sustaining the creative process toward its goal, and to its goal when he is successful.

If we follow all of the actual data before us, therefore, and keep the creator and the creative activity related to each other, we shall find that our fears are ungrounded as far as what is given in experience is concerned. A finite person may himself die in the midst of creating, but the cosmic Person, as here assumed, is self-existent and continuous with all creativity, his own and that delegated (as to human beings). In short, what can be experientially grounded is the assertion that there is an originative structure able to create some sort of order. On this note we can turn to the relation of order and creativity.

VIII

It is unempirical, I have urged, to separate the creative act from the existential context in which it lives. And it has been argued that human creativity while adding to what is, (*a*) works in relation to the matrix of what is given up to the creative moment, and (*b*) is affected by the kind of opportunities and obstacles constituting the matrix. Put it this way: there is always some structure, some order of being, as the necessary, although not sufficient, ground of creativity. Let us illustrate at the human level.

The sensing, remembering, thinking, feeling, wanting, oughting, and appreciating of a finite person – each of these activities has a structure and order of its own that constitutes the inner, continuing base for a person's creativity. But though necessary, each activity is not the sufficient support for the creative act itself. A person wills within the structure of abilities and dispositions which their flexibility allows; and he wills in an environment, social and physical, that has structures and possibilities of which his creative act must take account.

If, for example, I say: 'I will forgive another person so that he and I can participate in a fellowship that neither of us knew before', I find myself confronting emotional dispositions and traits both in myself and in the other person that will, according to their own order, offer obstacles and opportunities with which my will to forgive must work. But my will to forgive does not 'emerge' or 'emanate' from my own past dispositions and present structure. To the extent that I succeed in forgiving, to the extent that the other person cooperates in the formation of the new fellowship, to that extent we are creatively willing into being a new order.

If this is true, we may say that to be creative, whether the act eventuate in good or evil, is to begin to build another order that bears some relation to the old order. The order may be shortlived and may not be able to resist pressures from its surrounding world. In the instance at hand, for example, my enemy and I may find in the initial stages of our new relation that hostilities are greater than anticipated, and even insuperable. Creativity, in other words, is initiated within, and presupposes a structure of order, a personal being, who remains to follow through as he confronts other orders of being, as they will to build a kind of stability that was not there before. No order, no freedom; no structures, no creativity. This means that our actual product of creativity or existence will always be a joint-product of what has been and now is.

We need always to keep in mind that in human experience when we create we never create what bears no relation at all to what already is. For example, in thinking we cannot create a logic that allows us to disregard consistency; and in emoting, we create no kind of emotion totally different from familiar kinds – we do create another emotional quality. Hence, there is little actual ground for fear lest the creative freedom we have will create discontinuities – arbitrary and fortuitous – in the structural givens of our lives.

On the other hand, if we do insist on structural discontinuity with the past, does this justify the contention that what we have called creation is not sheer novelty of the kind designated by '*ex nihilo*'? No. For to be continuous does not mean that there is no creation but only that what is created has characteristics in common with what has already occurred. The fact again seems to be that while we never know in advance exactly how much the creative process will actually accomplish, we discover, once the creative act has accomplished its purpose or any part of it, that we can often trace some continuity between the new accomplishment and the old facts! What the existence of continuity proves is not that there is no creation, but that much creation, at least, is related to some order already established. And the fact of continuity can also be understood ultimately in terms of some purpose that is being worked out in and through events that are creative.

IX

Finally, does this notion that creativity involves the addition of something new, without disregarding the order already established, help us to understand divine *creatio ex nihilo* when this involves the physical and biological realms of being?

Broadly speaking, *creatio ex nihilo* is compatible with the view that living or organic processes are not reducible completely to inorganic events. The reader may not be inclined to grant this, and, with such discoveries as DNA in mind, prefer to think of the living as another level of the physical. Bur such disagreement as to the point of discontinuity between the realms of matter and life is of no real significance for our purposes here. More important is it to keep the differences between what goes on in a stone, a starfish, a bone, and the frontal lobe of a brain from being neglected. Philosophical analysis here must be impressed not only by the broad differences between the inorganic and the organic, but by different classifications of entities within each realm. (If, for example, it should be the fact that different types of 'physical' entities do have properties markedly distinguishing them from other 'physical' beings, the philosopher may well ask how it is that such different beings constitute an order of physical nature – even before he faces the question of the addition of 'living' beings to a 'physical' realm.)

In any case, a doctrine of *creatio ex nihilo* is far from embarrassed by realms characterized by similarity and difference, or by continuity and discontinuity. If certain realms of being (such as the 'physical') seem to be the necessary but not sufficient ground for new developments (the biological and mental), a theistic doctrine of creation can accommodate both regularity in change and creative novelty. For the theist can hold that a cosmic Person has the kind of unified structure that can purposely create orders of being, both in consonance with his own nature and possibilities.[1]

The theist's main contention is that to talk about God creating the world *ex nihilo*, is to talk about a Being whose complex, unified nature it is to be creative also, creative in relation to his own given ontic structure. The very fact that, once the creative activity has taken place, it may be seen as a relatively continuous and even predictable order of change, itself testifies to the fact that, as Creator, God is not arbitrary in the vicious sense, but creates in orderly steps and humanly understandable fashion, with a purpose in view and in relation to givens of his own nature, as well as of the state of the created world.

Thus we press the underlying analogy, reminding ourselves of Plato's warning that in cosmological matters we are in the realm of the probable only, and that we are not here presenting the argument for such a God. God is the kind of unified being who, in creating, is himself involved in and affected by the additions (and subtractions) he makes, although such continuity-in-novelty as there is seems clearly to indicate that his nature is not exhausted in either change or creation. For to be a creator, as human experience indicates, is to be a creator within a certain structure that maintains itself in and through the creations that reflect the structure that maintains itself in and through the creations that reflect the structure. God as a Person, as Creator, is non-changing. But what he creates, the quality of his own experience, will be affected by, but not controlled by, the created world.

The underlying model for reality, suggested by personal creativity, has other far-reaching possibilities. Perhaps the time is ripe to stop thinking of change and creativity against a background of permanence. Creativity-and-Unity, Creativity-in-Unity, here is the ontological fact that for ever marries creativity and continuity.

[1] On other metaphysical grounds I would prefer the hypothesis that what we know as the space-time world of sense-perception is integral to the activity of God, and not 'outside' of His being. But such a personalistic, idealistic, view of the space-time world aside, I would urge in any case that the space-time world, in so far as it manifests related orders of change, may well be expressing the purpose of God's inner nature, including his capacity to create again and again. For God to create either an independent space-time world, or to be involved in the graded, orderly interrelated levels of changes as aspects of his own being, is for our purposes here not critical.

Instead of wondering how anything can be added to all there is, *ex nihilo*, we must acknowledge the category of categories: reality is a Creative Order, yes, analogous to, but not reducible to, the creative order exhibited in the finite person, If we conceive of God as the Creator-Person – both person and creator at once – what fact of existence, in the scientific, moral, aesthetic, or religious realm have we actually disregarded?

PART 4

RELIGION AS CO-CREATION
WITH GOD

CHAPTER XV

THREE VISIONS OF PERFECTION AND HUMAN FREEDOM

At the heart of a man's worship is his vision of excellence. The traditional theist's conception of God's perfection does not differ significantly from that held by the monistic Absolutist, once allowance is made for the fact that the Absolutist does not grant *creatio ex nihilo*. The Absolutist – and Paul Tillich and Martin Buber are recent examples – struggles valiantly to save the individual from being absorbed in the Absolute, but, as I see it, fails.

Yet, has the theist not been much too enchanted by the absolutistic notion of perfection? Has his difference with the Absolutist on the nature of creation, human and divine, actually affected the way in which he conceives the *quality* of the human-divine relation? The essays in this section probe in an elementary way the difference which creation, by God and man, make to a doctrine of excellence.

The thesis of this first essay, elaborated in the next two, is that the flight from Change to Permanence, from Conflict to Peace, from Insecurity to Security is all too seductive. Even naturalistic psychotherapy is seduced by a notion of fulfilment that idealizes spontaneity rather than freedom. My basic contention is that if to be a person is to become creatively, if to be a person is to have the courage to become (to alter Tillich's 'courage to be'), then the quality of self-fulfilment for both God and man must reflect the nature of the tip-toe experience of freedom.

'No science can be more secure than the unconscious metaphysics it tacitly presupposes.'[1]

I. FREEDOM-BEYOND TENSION

Perfect being is complete being; it is self-sufficient being; it is eternal, unchanging Being. Within it there are none of the dualities, complexities, and tensions that disturb even the highest moral,

[1] Alfred N. Whitehead, *Adventure of Ideas*, p. 157.

aesthetic, and theoretic experience of men. And nothing on land or sea, no aspect of human life, can illuminate the nature of that Perfection. Perhaps in the depth of religious ecstasy there is vouchsafed to the finite subject an ineffable experience of the Real that reaches so far beyond all the other thrusts of life that it becomes the moment of excellence, the climax toward which all other moments must point, and for which all other satisfactions must prepare one, if a person is indeed to 'know' the vision beatific.

What a galaxy of philosophers and mystics the world over have expounded this view of Perfection and of human freedom! In India, Sankara in the eighth century B.C. articulated the ageless vision of many Indian seers. The Advaita and Visistadvaita facets of the dominant Hindu philosophic-religious tradition develop aspects of the vision; but they do not contest the final vision of the Ultimate One and of liberation from human bondage; nor does the Buddhist critique of the Hindu vision, or the Zen-Buddhist development, so far as I can tell, leave the essential core untouched.

On the other hand, while the Judeo-Moslem-Christian religious visions, East and West, differ in turn at important points, they do not tamper with the ultimate vision of splendour. The Greek heritage – Parmenides, Plato, Aristotle, and the Stoics for example – fused with Jewish and Christian insights to create the dominant Christian conception of beatitude in Plotinus, Augustine, Aquinas, Spinoza, Kant and Hegel. Despite the difference between these many stars in the firmanent of world-civilization, the unifying vision is that *the Real* (whether arrived at by a strict concatenation of logical judgments or by the disciplined control of sense, desire, emotion, and will, or by both together), must be such that in it all the imperfection of partial human judgments, key-hole visions, and temporary loves and excitements, have no place. In the ultimate Ocean of Being there are no currents and no waves, for that Ocean flows nowhere but in some sense draws all seas, rivers, and streams of being into its unchanging Completeness.

So much in this vision of perfection seems to relieve the tension in logical, moral, aesthetic, and religious striving. There must be, says the logical mind, some one comprehensive *truth* in whose Meaning all other meanings are implied – the logical limit of theoretical intention. There must be, says the person amidst the struggle for a greater good, an All-Good that at once fulfils and puts an end to striving, a Perfection that moves not from want but from fulfilment. There must be, says the artist, a kind of Being that enjoys as the very fabric of its being, the strands of form that inspire aesthetic experience and creation. And, pervading all of these, is that oft-felt psychic yearning to be embedded and anchored – so satisfied that one feels no more wanting and grasping, no more coping and no more tension.

There is no doubting that this view of Reality, this perspective on finitude, seems to set every human pursuit and yearning in a cosmic setting that at once gives our changing lives a source and an objective. Without this Vision of Excellence men have felt uprooted, suspended between one oblivion and another. For without this Ultimate no envisioned good is caught up in a greater splendour and completed in a way that is fortified against all insecurity, change, and boredom.[1]

Indeed, without turning to these more sophisticated appeals for this kind of Ultimate and human freedom as fulfilment-without-tension, we could have taken cues from those psychologists and psychotherapists who stress the need for tension-reduction in human motivation and personality-development. As they see him, man is born into the world as a helpless infant, with needs he cannot himself fulfil, and with conditions to meet that are not the less obdurate because he cannot understand them. The development of his own abilities takes place slowly and with uncertainty, and the individual is forced constantly to depend on forces and persons outside of himself. At no point in his struggle to develop himself is there assurance of his own adequacy; and at every point there is the thrust of the accident that maims, the disease that kills, the natural catastrophe that destroys even what his best effort has built.

No wonder, then, that man cries for relief from the cycle of conflict, made temporarily endurable by interludes of need-reduction or by friendly ties, by the sleep that 'knits up the ravell'd sleave of care'. No wonder he yearns for the security of a 'Heaven'

[1] It is tempting to stop and underscore the philosophical objections that have been raised to this view of the Real. Basic have been the refusals to accept (a) the theoretical impasse confronted when the Unchanging is said to undergird change, without itself changing in the least, and (b) the moral impasse in which the individual person presumably 'found himself' by losing his identity completely. The reader is referred to Bergson's *Creative Evolution, The Two Sources of Morality and Religion,* Whitehead's *Religion in the Making* (and other works), and E. S. Brightman's *Person and Reality* for philosophical analyses that suggest a new perspective on change and the unchanging. In my *Introduction to Philosophy of Religion* and *Religion as Creative Insecurity,* an interpretation based on these other metaphysical perspectives is suggested.

in which there will be love without suspicion and care, of a 'Nirvana' beyond the seduction of desires, of a final state in which the self has been emptied of anxieties intrinsic to finitude.

As we know all too well, there is the High Road to Security, and the Low Road to Security. The first leads Pilgrim to self-discipline and a rigour which, accepting obstacles and insecurity as a testing-ground, moves on to the fulfilling joys Beyond; a strong man hammers at the gate of Heaven. There are other human beings who get lost before they find the High Road, or cannot accept its rigours. They drown their insecurities in bibulous ecstasies and temporary excitement, they drug themselves against sensitivity to the pain from within and threat from without, they cut their expectations to the requirements of the group in which they find both security and anonymity.

But both Roads are roads which lead *away from* suffering, despair, conflict; they lead *from* insecurity *to* Security. A cautions and calculating Epicurean, wishing to avoid the monotony and dullness of the Low Road, will not be caught in the chain of vulgar habit as he seeks the more refined pleasures of friendship on the aesthetic and intellectual plane, and he will be too wise, too 'smart', to involve himself in social responsibility. Fearing to be duped by false hopes, he is nevertheless forever fearful of disappointment, as long as he lives; he hopes that in death there will be Peace.

In every day and civilization the number in this group is legion. In our day even in the educated classes there are those who give themselves to variations on this Epicurean theme, moving from aestheticism to the 'graces' of refined social gatherings. For, some of them would say, they have learned much in a 'scientific' age about cause and effect; they know that there must be a cause for their discontents that is blocking the smooth flow of feeling as they would like it. But they have never found a purpose, since purpose has been ruled out of their causally controlled world. For them, accordingly, the Jamesian 'expulsive power of a great affection' is a dream of a wistful, ancient world – and, anyway, it sounds too much like a responsibility which would bring on new anxieties.

With these on the Low Road to Security those on the High Road would expostulate: You do not choose wisely or realistically. For the profoundest aesthetic experience still depends on some object external to you, the sturdiest kinship with your friends and lovers is still subject to the accidents of finite experience. As long as you make these and other human ends final attainments you will keep on risking the shattering of yourself. Rather than seek to preserve yourself against shattering, why do you not stop idolatrizing your individuality? There is a deeper *spiritual law of causality* that, once the conditions are met, will carry you to an indescribable experience of freedom. It has its own way of convincing you of a Security beyond all insecurities – it is one that paradoxically cuts the very roots from which insecurity grows, attachment to selfhood and its ultimate inanities.

II. FREEDOM – IN FULFILMENT

The curious thing about freedom as fulfilment-beyond-tension, especially on the mystical view, is that fulfilment means the loss ultimately of individuality, or at least a development beyond the stage of individuality in any of its known forms. The second view of perfection and freedom is naturalistic in its presupposition. It employs a bio-morphic model of fulfilment. While no simple model can be imposed upon the mystic, there is an important difference between the way in which he thinks about fulfilment and the way in which it is conceived on the bio-morphic model. For, in the latter, fulfilment means the *real*-izing of a potential for growth to the point of self-completion – as is exemplified when a seed becomes an oak, or an infant becomes a man. In this developmental process what is postulated is an immanent principle of growth that, if frustrated, leads the organism to illness, disease, and death.

For the mystic, on the other hand, the purpose of self-discipline is to reveal the Self, a Self within 'selves' which the 'world', *maya*, the life of desire and sense, and self-absorption, has veiled. Yet it is this immanent Self that ultimately is the only source of lasting nourishment – a Self that is not the individual self. On this view, self-realization ultimately means self-immolation in the Self. It is this that is denied in the bio-morphic view which would insist on an immanent process of individual growth that is never self-transcendent. On this bio-morphic view, stressed in different ways by Freud, Adler, Horney, Fromm, Maslow, Sullivan, Rogers, there are in every individual forces which need to be understood, liberated, freed from rigidities imposed from without, or by arrested development. Thus, if 'freedom' for the mystic is liberation from finitude, freedom for these psychologists means freedom from every obstacle to 'becoming a person', to use a Rogerian phrase. *What a person can become, he ought to become.*

The important difference is that the process of individual becoming is never to cease in some peak moment of ecstasy. Yet, interestingly enough, the problem before each individual is the same: to break the shackles of self-protective individualism and unleash the universal man[1] that is in him, to achieve freedom to unite his energies for complete self-fulfilment. But in the bio-morphic view, the individual is to fulfil himself, never by losing himself but, by dedicating himself to growth-in-communion on the one side, and to growth-in-responsibility on the other.

In so far as religious mystics stress outgoing love and compassion (in the preparation for awakening, realization, or communion with God) they can expect support from such psychotherapists; but the support fades away to antagonism the moment non-natural Being is introduced as the Source of inner process or its goal. The human is naturalized and socialized (not societized); he has no superhuman or supernatural roots. Human blessedness here is at best the kind of vigour that comes from fulfilment which is able to 'accept' decay and death when it can no longer resist them. The 'free man's worship' is reverence for the creativity that lies within him as a child of Nature. As Fromm puts it,

> . . . the notion of freedom of the fully developed person is that of recognizing reality [Nature] and its laws and acting within the laws of necessity, by relating oneself to the world productively by grasping the world with one's own powers of thought and affect.[2]

What are we to say about this view? Bluntly, *it does not go far enough in catching what might be called the peculiarly moral nature of individuality.* Concerned to overcome 'metaphysical dimensions', it places man in Nature as a growing being, in the biological sense of growth as realization of potential into full performance of function. And, in extension of this conception, it sees him as an active fighter against disabling, protective conventionality (automatic conscience) in order that the universal dimensions of his natural being can be heard (the humanistic conscience). Thus in Fromm's words again:

---

[1] See Fromm's essay in the second section of *Zen Buddhism and Psychoanalysis*, ed. Erich Fromm, P.T. Suzuki, and R. DeMartino, New York: Harper & Brothers, 1960, p. 107 ff.

[2] *Ibid*, p. 90.

Well-being means to be fully related to man and nature affectively, to overcome separateness and alienation, to arrive at the experience of oneness with all that exists – and yet to experience *myself* at the same time as the separate entity *I* am, as the individual. Well-being means to be freely born, to become what one potentially is; it means to have the full capacity for joy and for sadness or, to put it still differently, to awake from the half-slumber the average man lives in, and to be fully awake. If it is all that it means also to be creative; that is, to react and to respond to myself, to others, to everything that exists – to react and respond as the real, total man I am to the reality of everybody and everything as he or it is. Well-being means, finally to drop one's Ego, to give up greed, to cease chasing after the aggrandizement of the Ego, to be and to experience one's self in the act of being, not in having, preserving, coveting, using.[1]

In a word, if the mystic model seeks security by 'awakening' to selflessness, the naturalistic model seeks 'freedom' by becoming one's complete self. Many metaphysical issues hover around us here, but it is to the notion of creativity and freedom that I would direct attention.

For the creativity and freedom that seems clearly in mind here is the creativity and freedom of spontaneity. The creativity is the opposite of conformity, and the freedom is the opposite of deformity; and both notions are meaningful only in relation to the goal of fulfilment of potentiality that comes when there is no longer an obstacle. And I would not for a moment deny either this biomorphic model of freedom and creativity, or the mystical, but note that 'fulfilment' and 'security' are common aims.

III. FREEDOM – AS CREATIVE TENSION

Phenomenologically speaking (and some would say, existentially speaking) there is a kind of freedom that is not 'beyond tension' and qualitatively different from spontaneity. To believe in it is not to deny the other two in every respect, but to insist that it is the unique centre of the distinctive human struggle and must be kept central in any attempt to describe human beatitude. What is this freedom? It is a freedom felt by a person in the midst of conflict and at various levels of his existence. For example, a person wants

[1] *Ibid.*, pp. 91, 92.

to eat and he wants to be slender; he wants friends and he wants to dominate every situation; he wants to save money and he wants to buy many things; he wants security and he wants to be brave. Such conflicts may be between immediate wants and remote gains.

But, on this view, a person's life is not to be conceived as a field in which affective-conative forces meet to affect each other, and in which the strongest of these forces wins, with the person simply witnessing the conflict and the consequence of the struggle. The person does not feel torn between conflicting wants, he does feel tensions that threaten to resolve themselves in a way he does not approve, and often he is impotent against them. But that is just the point. It makes sense to say that 'he is overcome'. Evidently he had a preference, he had an approved goal, and he was eventually overcome. In other words, he *was free* up to a certain point, at least, to influence what was happening, even though the goal he approved was not gained.

To put the essential meaning of this moral freedom positively: a person is free to initiate in any situation some course of thought and action, however limited its final success. His freedom is felt in the conflicting and tense situation that is transpiring, and he feels it as a power to influence to some extent the course of action that is his very life. Whatever happens to him and in him as a result of inheritance and learning is one thing. But how the person 'sets himself' in favour of the alternative he approves (correctly or incorrectly) is also a factor in the situation. Standing in the midst all the cross-currents of conflict, the person initiates some line of action that would not have been taken otherwise.

It should be noted that without denying that there are 'causal sequences' in the life of the person, this view of freedom does square with a significant phenomenal fact in personal experience. Correctly or incorrectly, we all *feel* responsible for many of our actions, and when we do, we do so because we believe that we can exert a decisive effect on what happens. *In this sense we feel creative.* That is, we can add to, subtract from, and to some extent *transform* the course of events, so that what transpires cannot be said to have just happened to us or 'developed' in us. Whether this view be finally correct or not, it certainly alters the picture of the human situation.

For freedom now means creative tension. From the moment he can seriously think of alternatives a human being lives not simply amidst the uncertainties of internal development and external circumstances. *He lives in the uncertainty of his own creativity.* On any view of finitude, the person cannot know what his potentialities allow him to do. But on this view growth or decay will be affected not only by the 'natural' processes at work in the person, but by his own initiative. His initiative cannot add to his basic capacities, it cannot change his past; but his free initiative is a critical factor in what happens when there is a meeting of factors in any choice-situation. He can accelerate his own destruction and structure his own growth within limits. His vote may not win the election but his vote counts, and, what is more, it counts for him. He is insecure because he is creative. The personality in the light of which he chooses tomorrow is being built by the forces that play within him today as affected by his choice today. To be free is not simply to be free *from* obstacles or free *for* developments; it is to be free to influence development.

For some thinkers such a view of 'freedom' would render life so chaotic as to be unendurable. For, they would urge, it would seem that the most carefully ingrained characteristics would always be at the mercy of an 'arbitrary' will. It should suffice to allay such fears to recall that the person who wills here wills within his ultimate potential. Furthermore, he cannot escape the causal sequence of structures and dispositions that have been acquired, including those his past free choices have influenced. To urge this is not to take away freedom but to formulate more accurately the more or less determinate-indeterminate situation that is the matrix of creative insecurity.

In other words, when I become I become *myself*, as the biomorphic model would demand. But I *myself* choose to become what my self allows, on this moral model. Growth does not simply take place in me, but I transform the growth-potential according to ideals and goals I approve. I am not only responsive and even provocative; I am creative in bringing about what I shall be; I am responsible within the total, uncertain limits of my capacity. My very being at its growing point is its creativity in-tension.

IV. PERFECTION AS CREATIVE INSECURITY

It is this insistence that to be a person is to be a creative, responsible agent in becoming that is at the core of the theistic denial of pantheism or Cosmic Monism or Absolutism. This is not the place to elaborate on a particular view of God, but I must point out consequences that even traditional Christian theists have been unwilling to accept. But no less than another vision of excellence is at stake.

For the traditional Judeo-Christian-Moslem theist has on the one hand held a vision of God's excellence as fulfilment beyond tension. The existence of human freedom of the kind defined here has kept him from holding that the finite person is ever absorbed into the One or that the personal self is ever emptied into the Ocean of Being. Yet he has not, as it seems to me, been willing to accept the full consequences of God's creation of finite creators. For to the extent that finite persons are created with delegated freedom, capable of directing and transforming their natures, according to their own decision, within limits, to that extent could God himself not be 'beyond tension'. This does not mean that a person can realize his potential without becoming aware of the ties that bind him to other people and to Nature (bio-morphic model), and to God. But it does mean that a different quality of inter-personal relationship is involved in the definition of perfection. Let us see what this means.

The Cosmic Person, in creating persons, freely limited his own power by delegating responsibility. Take this fact seriously and it seems clear that God places creative autonomy before security of outcome. That is, the moral self-direction of persons, at the possible cost of moral prodigality, is more important than security-in-fulfilment-beyond-tension or the fulfilment-of-spontaneity. There is no escaping the conclusion that as long as we human beings can purposely hurt one another needlessly, to that extent, the quality of the universe, including God's involvement in it, is affected by our creativity. God is not beyond change and even suffering. To be sure he suffers only as a being of his dimensions can suffer, but he suffers in a sense never contemplated by the mystical and traditional theistic notion of excellence. For his being is not fulfilled in the sense that all that is *worth* being is at once, once and for all, within his grasp in a non-temporal eternal moment (*totum simul*); and he is not necessarily 'beyond' all deficit.

Is this a vision of excellence? Is this perfection? For many minds such a view is a contradiction in terms. It may be; but it may also be that a new vision is born when we grasp the full significance of creative, moral freedom. This vision cannot min-imize the *cosmic fact*, creative freedom, finite and Divine. In it there is insecurity, for wherever there is freedom there must be uncertainty of outcome and incompleteness of possible being in some degree. To say that God created persons free within limits is to say that men and God are partners, and co-creators. This means that history, finite and divine, is always to some extent insecure.

But it also means that the issue is not security *or* insecurity, but creativity and the kind of insecurity it entails. It is a creativity in which men stand upon their feet before each other and before God and take up the responsibility for forging the ties that will develop a community of fulfilment-in-love – a community that is bigger than any self but never bigger than concern for every individual self!

But, does not fulfilment-in-love mean unison, love of Self in a higher State? Not in this view. For the essence of God's love for man consists in his willingness to create co-creators and to accept the consequences of the delegated freedom of persons. For God to love is to grant individual freedom to develop one's own nature within a realm of order; for men to love each other is to accept and improve the conditions of each other's creativity. The course they undertake will be fraught with imperfection and struggle. Any 'union' will be one of common purpose, not of unified being.

But why think of this kind of creativity as perfection, as beatitude or excellence? This is hardly the place for dogmatism, but a value-judgment is involved: There is no greater good than to be involved in such creativity. To be fulfilled at the expense of such creativity (and the resultant insecurity) is not to be fulfilled in the best way possible. Can we find any experiential confirmation of it?

In the very fact, we suggest, that every worthwhile experience in life is the richer when it involves creativity of the agent or persons involved. Consider the nature of cognitive values, of social values, of aesthetic values, of economic and political values, of character values, and, above all, of affiliative values, and of religious communion. Do any of these reach their climax without persons who are willing to face hardship and insecurity in order to approach the respective goals? Take away the adventurous thrust, replace it with a foregone conclusion imposed from within or without, and you sacrifice not only zest in living but the peak experience of what I am calling 'creative insecurity', or the creativity which involves insecurity in its movement to a better objective. If we think of insecurity as the *bête noir* of life, as the experience which must be reduced to zero, do we not court the insecurity that comes from fearing insecurity as such? And, what is more important, do we not miss the peculiar joy of responsible creativity?

Clearly a new conception of 'peak experience', to use Maslow's term, is involved, and a different view of beatitude. It claims for itself a deeper appreciation of what is involved in the love that goes beyond compassion, even to forgiveness. In forgiving love a person reaches a new high in creativity, for to forgive is to involve oneself in a redemptive process the consequences of which will remain uncertain.

For there are special conditions and challenges involved if one is to forgive another person who has purposely used his freedom to destroy cherished values. A special compassion is called for in a relationship in which another has purposely alienated himself and purposely destroyed the values one holds dear. The temptation is to stop such destruction now at the cost of the other's life (and it may be that this is sometimes necessary in extreme emergencies). The uniquely creative compassion, forgiveness, accepts the challenge of doing everything in one's power to live with the destructive person, not in terms of the evil he has purposely created, but in terms of the good that can be achieved.

Indeed, in a world in which persons are free to do what they believe best, there will be the inevitable tragedies of cross-purposes among equally conscientious person who disagree about the directions of freedom. In this world both compassion and forgiveness, moving beyond the calculations of justice, must be the realistic order of the day. Those who have accepted the call to live unto forgiveness will know the quality of suffering, the heart-ache of disappointment, but they also know the peak experience of creativity in dedication to growth of community. But they also know the beatitude of creativity in small gains and even in failure, and they prefer this 'peace that surpasseth understanding' and 'not as the world knoweth' to any fulfilment that gets beyond the reaches of communion-in-freedom. On this world-view the highest beatitude is the comradeship of free persons dedicated to creative love. For in their pursuit of the love that redeems they are in communion with the cosmic Person who shares his creativity, his suffering, and his joy with them.

Maturity of personality, maturity of religion, on this view, means not 'a flight of the alone to the Alone', not an emptying of self to Self, but a disciplining of self so that one may continue to be a co-operative participant in the eternal purpose of creation and growth of persons.

Discerning readers will be asking the question that must indeed be asked. Are these three visions of perfection and human freedom exclusive of each other? Must the psychologist choose between them? Several comments may be justified.

It is important for the psychologist and psycho-therapist to be as clear as he can about the 'unconscious metaphysics' he may be tacitly presupposing. In this paper, without exhausting the alternatives, we have barely indicated that there are differences in the underlying conception of the human-cosmic predicament, involved in, and affecting the definition of freedom. To talk about freedom is to talk about man and his situation in the cosmos, and to make all-important value-judgments about its desirability. The ideal of personality in the back of our minds is at stake.

But what must be especially interesting to the psychologist is that these three visions of excellence and freedom are offered as true descriptions of human experience. In the last analysis the definition of the ideal takes root in descriptions of what happens to human beings. I, for one, am sure that we fluctuate from one to another, at least unwittingly, that we use analogies from actual experiences of those freedoms to move to the 'ideal' freedom. But which of them is the norm for human beings? The answer here must be given by each person on the basis of his most comprehensive reflection on values and his resulting world-view. From this perspective the other two will represent different stages perhaps on the road to the ideal.

My own present commitment is that the naturalistic and mystical view, as presented above, common in this demand for fulfilment, would be more adequate to the person-in-becoming if they allowed for the creative insecurity that makes 'courage to become' the essential issue in self-development and mature personality. As for the world-views and visions of excellence, their accreditation must involve metaphysical reflection that does not neglect the psychological aspects here considered.

CHAPTER XVI

RELIGION AS THE PURSUIT OF CREATIVITY BY GOD AND MEN

Creativity? Yes! Security? Yes! Insecurity? No! This, in some sense, has been the mixed response of religious and non-religious minds through the ages as to the essence of perfection. This mixed response also permeates much contemporary adoration of creativity without asking what the costs may be. We admire Prometheus but abhor his fate.

I am grateful to the Association Press for permission to reprint the second chapter of my book, *Religion as Creative Insecurity*. In this chapter, I press the conception of creative insecurity as the life-blood of a religion that is in earnest about the creativity of God and the freedom of persons. To be creative is to be insecure – let us face it! But let us also glory in the fact that this insecurity is the insecurity of creativity. It is this peace that 'surpasseth understanding'.

I. CAN A GOOD GOD ALLOW EVIL?[1]

He looked me square in the eye, and his eyes were flames of indignation. 'Your God is a fool!'

Thus spoke a university student. He was not 'another cynical, callow youth'. I knew him well enough to recognize his passion for social justice. It was moral earnestness which led to this eruption, and it is only fair that I summarize the rest of his case.

'You tell me', he said in substance, 'that God knew that men would oppress other men, that men would consider it great fun to see other men torn alive by lions in a Coliseum, that they would feel victorious when they systematically killed six million Jews, that they would take advantage of each others' weaknesses in every conceivable way, in slum, in sweatshop, and in segregated schools – you tell me that he knew that this could and probably would

---

[1] A portion of this chapter appeared in slightly different form in *Motive*, 1956, under the title 'Is God a Fool?'

happen; you tell me that he could have avoided this by making men differently, but that, nevertheless, he did make them as they are, capable now of exploding the very earth in each others' faces. Sir, I repeat, your God is a fool!'

Many students I have known have been less forthright, but they have been equally decisive. I can still feel the surprised and indignant incredulity of the negro college girl whose every word accused me of moral blindness when she said: 'How can you say that God is just when he knew what having a black skin would mean to so many human beings?'

At moments like these I am glad that there was a day in my own life when I too was similarly overwhelmed by 'man's inhumanity to man', for I now can feel with such students and be glad that their sense of fair play speaks, no matter how misguided. But, if I were now to be equally forthright I would say, with equal passion, I suspect, 'Any other God *would* be a fool!'

And, I would continue: 'If God made man so that he could not hurt others, if God had made man in such a way that he could never choose to create a slum, a concentration camp, and an atomic inferno, he would be unworthy of the name, and certainly not worthy of the worship of a *mature moral person*!'

The issue is now sharply joined. And as the three italicized words emphasize, the argument turns on what we mean by a mature moral person. When the student said he thought that God was a fool if he could prevent the evil men did to each other, but did not, what was he really saying? He was saying that he could not understand how any Being could be morally justified in allowing a situation to occur which could eventuate in the kind of suffering, and the amount of suffering, which human beings inflict upon each other. What he was denouncing was my conception of what made life worth while. When he attacked the idea of God he was really asserting his own set of values, by which God was falling short.

What is the premise on which I base a defence of the God which my student so indignantly rejected? It is the conviction that God's fundamental purpose for man's life is that man should be free to use his God-given abilities to do good, or to do evil. It was not God's purpose that man *do* evil, but it was God's purpose that he be allowed, that he be free, to do evil. This would mean that man could oppose God's purpose and actually use his God-given abilities to work against His own will as far as those abilities allowed. God, in other words, did not make men as a puppet-maker creates his puppets; he did not make them to act 'on the strings' which he alone controlled.

There is a sense, of course, in which men are puppets. Men, like puppets, can use only the capacities which constitute their nature. But they are unlike puppets in two important ways. In the first place, they are not just 'made', once for all time, but their capacities develop, and the course of the development depends in good measure upon the choices they themselves make. In the second place, they are not compelled to develop their capacities in one direction only, to one foreordained conclusion. No man is forced to develop his mind to its utmost capacity. What is more, he does not have to come to one and only one conclusion. Or, even had it been ordained that he come to a certain conclusion, he would not be forced to do anything about it! In a word, God presumably could have made man like a machine that smoothly operates, with all its power, only in one way, and only when the proper button is pressed. And man could therefore have been a kind of automatic machine, with compassion and good will 'built in', who would interact with his fellow men but never hurt them. On the view I am expounding, however, God believed that it was better not to preordain such compassion.

Having said this, I can hear the student cry once more: 'But why? Why make persons in such a way that they can hurt themselves and each other, if you can help it? Surely, we would consider any man a fool who made his children so that they could destroy each other, if he could avoid it? Why change this verdict when it is God, who, presumably, could have done otherwise?'

We are back again! But we are now nearer to the basic issue. Would we condemn such a father? I think the answer is clear: *Yes, provided that in making it impossible for his children to hurt and destroy each other, he at the same time made it impossible for them to have other experiences which make life worth while.* The argument thus will turn on the answer to another question. Let it be clear that neither the student nor I are 'for' suffering; we are both 'against' it! But the assumption in his thinking is that one could avoid this suffering without making impossible 'the things that matter most' in life.

The fundamental issue, then, does not immediately concern the nature of God. It concerns the nature of significant human living. We must ask two questions. First, what experiences in human life make living worth while? And, second, so far as one can know, can we enjoy these experiences without at the same time confronting the risks of falling into evil ourselves, and of hurting others?

The issue is so important that I restate it. I am suggesting that we cannot be clear about what we mean by God's goodness until we become clearer about the nature of the good in human life. Many thoughtful persons doubt the goodness of God because they disapprove of what they see in human beings who are his handiwork. In so doing, they are judging the actions of man and of God by a standard of goodness which I think should be rejected. In any case, we cannot be clear in asserting or denying: 'God is good to man', until we decide what it is that, so far as we can tell, makes life good.

Let me then state what I think makes life worth while, or good. Here I can do little more than suggest a line of thought which is not merely my own. I have been especially influenced by what seems to me to be the best in the Graeco-Judeo-Christian tradition – in other words, in the thought and action of Socrates, Plato, Aristotle, the Stoics, the Hebrew Prophets, Jesus, Paul, St Augustine, St Francis, St Thomas Aquinas, Spinoza, Kant, and Hegel. I could, of course, mention others and I must not give the false impression that even these men are all on one level of agreement, or greatness. I mention them because, in one way or another, it seems to me that each has put a finger on what it is that gives human life dignity and worth. And, without mentioning names, I shall make use of certain rewarding trends of investigation and thought in recent psychology as I make a detour to the central question of what constitutes God's goodness.

II. WHAT MAKES HUMAN LIFE WORTH WHILE?

We need to be loved

So many are the meanings of the word 'love' that I almost hesitate to say that human life would not be worth while without the *experience of love*. But no other word in our language will better indicate the area of life I have in mind. Love comes into our lives in different ways, reflecting the degree of maturity we have at the time. But, and this will be my thesis, love comes into our lives as the protector both of our freedom and of our security. To tell the story of love in each of our lives is to tell the story of how we developed our capacity for our freedom and security. It may be that in what follows I can clarify my meaning enough to justify my conviction that no other good in life is greater than love, for love at its best is at once the expression of our creativity as human beings and the protector of our creativity.

Most of us have known the love of mother and father. Their love was there before we knew what it was. We learned the meaning of our own emotions in the context of their responses to us. We learned what our states of anger, of fear, of gratitude, of jealousy meant, in large part through the way they dealt with us when we experienced these states. They taught us what sounds to leave out of our baby talk, what syllables to accent, and which of our enunciations would communicate to others what we were wanting and thinking. Bit by bit, by their example and direction in most of the emotional nooks and crannies of our lives, we learned what emotions we should prefer, and how we were expected to express them or any thoughts we wanted to convey. Listen to the little girl scolding her baby doll, notice what it is she scolds the doll for, mark the punishment doled out, and you will probably find the girl enacting her conception of mother's and father's tactics with her.

As each of us grew older we put those values on things which our parents (or those who stood in their place as guides), put on experiences; and we even came to evaluate ourselves in the light of what we thought was their evaluation of us. In inexpressible ways we were dependent upon them, and, more than we realized, we fitted our actions to the patterns which we thought they would approve. In fact, our sense of security and self-confidence grew in accordance with our conception of how well we were pleasing them. Of course, I am assuming that in these early days we were fortunate enough to have parents who cared about us and who did not treat us like furniture, to be kept clean and in its place.

Our dependence upon parents and others was due to the fact that we were not born with the capacity to take care of ourselves. For most of us our behaviour, as we matured, was not fixed in one pattern. As human infants we were wonderously flexible. But this very flexibility was the source of our dependence upon mother and father. And if mother and father knew enough, and 'put their minds to it', they could have gone a long way toward making their flexible infants become little automatons – not to say well-tamed circus animals almost unerringly responsive to the crack of the whip or the tone of the voice.

Anyone who has seen the child who dares not leave its mother's side, who breaks into tears at the slightest reprimand, and flushes with pleasure at a kind word, knows how far this process of 'training' can go. Now, if this child had simply the capacities of an animal, or if it could not soon observe that other persons do things differently, or realize that mother herself is quite inconsistent at times, the damage done by such training would be negligible (as with animals). For the less ability and flexibility a person has, the better, perhaps, it is for him to live 'in a rut'. The point is that parents who train the plastic abilities and emotions of their children into certain grooves are – like the tamers of circus animals – not interested in the child for his own sake, but only in controlling what will happen to him. They may even plead that they are anxious to avoid trouble, both for themselves, for others, and for the child. Indeed, they are interested in the child's doing the 'approved' thing.

Such training, and the motivation behind it, seems very sensible on the surface, for it prevents wrongdoing and encourages safety. We should all agree, no doubt, that some actions, especially those that concern his own immediate physical health and that of others, must be demanded for the child's own sake. But the real problem in child training is the same problem we must face if we are to answer the question before us. Do we train the child just for the sake of training him, or do we teach him so that he will preserve and increase the possibilities of value in his life? Do we teach or train him so that he will, as soon as possible – and this applies even to basic safety habits – participate in the training he needs? At some points, to repeat, parents who care for their children and for the safety of others, cannot allow certain patterns of action (such as running across the street at will, or indiscriminatingly throwing stones). Furthermore, when the child cannot possibly understand or anticipate the consequences of his own behaviour, the parent must accept the responsibility for the child's action. But does the parent who cares for the child's development not try as soon as possible, and as much as possible, to reason with the child and show him why these precautions are to be taken? In sum, must the parent who loves his child not try to understand how the child, with *his* nature, can best participate in the guidance of *his* own action in a way to increase the good and prevent unnecessary harm?

We have been outlining the basic predicament which every parent and child faces in order to make clear two meanings of 'good' and 'love' which are frequently confused. What we mean by a 'good' parent and what we mean by 'love' in this parent-child relation depends on whether we think that a parent is being good to his child if he does not allow that child, within limits, to take part in the decisions which affect even his own health.

Must love not protect freedom?

I am assuming that a loving parent and a good parent desires the good of the child. And I am asking: Can we, then, believe that a parent loves his child if he is concerned only about his, the parent's security, or only about the security of others, with the result that the child has no share in deciding about actions involving him which he can understand? Does love for child mean that the child must be made to feel dependent upon the parent for safety even when, probably, much of that safety could be left in the child's own hands? Does being 'good' to a child mean making sure that he will always do the approved thing whether *he* approves or not?

Everyone must make his choice here, and I must state my own and try to defend it as preferable to the alternative. I cannot accept a definition of either love or goodness, in terms of obedience at the expense of creativity, or even in terms of safety for all at the expense of freedom. *To be good to, or to love, a human being cannot mean safety for any of us at the cost of freedom and creativity.* One might love an animal, or an infant, before he has any ability to anticipate the future or learn from the past, by providing for safety only. But here freedom and creativity are not lost, for there is none to be lost. The moment any being can be self-conscious enough to know what is happening to him, and the moment he begins to be able to apply his experience for the sake of new experiences, it becomes my duty, as I understand love, and as I understand goodness, to help *him* to understand to the utmost of my ability and of his capacity, what it means to be a self-conscious being who can help and hurt himself and others.

We must pause to draw out some implications of accepting this meaning of *goodness* and *love* toward another. I am parting intellectual company with anyone who says that when we are dealing with persons who can be aware of some (at least) of their motives, or when we are dealing with persons who understand some (at least) of the consequences of their actions, it would be an act of goodness and of love on our part, to encourage them to do only what *we* thought was good for them and for us. I am not blinking at an important fact. Many of our human relations are complicated by the very fact that we differ with each other about what is right for us. And I do not deny that each of us has an obligation to do his best to prevent others, who act in accordance with their conception of goodness, from enacting laws which go against our own convictions about what is good. Yet, which of us, on reflection, would prefer to have agreement at the expense of freedom to stand for our convictions? We are forced, once more, to ask which values we put first.

What, in short, is the pearl of great price, for which, if we had to, we would sell, or *should* sell, all our other jewels? It may be obvious to the reader now that I would choose *creativity* as the experience which I treasure for all of us. Where there is no respect for creativity there is no lasting goodness. There is no love where there is no creativity or respect for creativity. This means that no matter how safe I think I am making a human being, I am not making him safe *as a human being*, unless I (and he) make it safe for him to be creative! For me to love a person is to do everything in my power to encourage him to be creative! To love him is to risk, if need be, some goods for the sake of greater goods; to love him is to risk them myself, and to allow him to risk them for the sake of growth. More must be said, as we move on, to define more adequately what creativity involves, but nothing will be said to contradict what seems to me to be a great paradox of life – that to be creative means to be free to take risks; to be creative means to be free not to be safe. Yet to be *safe* and to *stay* at the top of my humanity I must respect creativity *in* myself and in others.

Could God be good and not allow creativity?

Can we now go on to say that *if we reason from our experience*, there would be no meaning to talking about a good God if that God could grant man creativity but did not? Later we shall have more to say about whether God can be held to our best human standards. But now I shall simply say that if we are to use the word 'good' for God in any sense that can have meaning for human beings, we must be able to point to something in human experience that God's goodness resembles to some extent.[1]

---

[1] The question of the grounds for attributing goodness to God is discussed more extensively in my *Introduction to Philosophy of Religion* and in a manner more directly connected with the theme in 'Can the Goodness of God Be Empirically Grounded', in Chapter 10 above.

Let me be more specific. I am saying that so far as I can see, goodness toward man means allowing him to be creative. And any being, God or man, who sponsors creativity must risk 'man's inhumanity to man'. In creating man *for creativity* God conferred upon man, *so far as human experience testifies*, the noblest of goods. Indeed, as I see it, the very meaning of God's love for man consists in his having allowed men, within their limits, to participate in their own development. But because so much evil has occurred owing to the use and abuse of human creativity, because in our own day we may use our creative ability to annihilate each other through nuclear and bacterial warfare, we must continue to ask ourselves carefully whether creativity is in fact worth it.

When I ask myself why creativity is so essential to goodness and love, I find that I cannot escape three interrelated facts of life: First, that no other good in human life is as good as it might be, if it is not pervaded with, or related to, creativity. Second, that without creativity we actually lose other goods. Third, that creativity, though it involves risks to all concerned, is less of a risk for human beings than any other value or good we prize. It is this assertion, that no other good in life is as good as it might be without creativity, that each of us must justify by looking into his own experience. It may help us to understand our experience, if we examine the problem most of us have with our experience of love.

Is it enough to be loved?

It is probable that when most of us think of love we think of being loved. The theme song in our lives, from infancy on, has been 'I want to be loved'. Love has meant approval, affection, security; and the younger we were, the more important it was to gain love. The fact that we begin life in complete dependence upon the care of others, the fact that in our earliest days we want and need more than we can get with our own abilities, soon creates in us a yearning for security which we translate into the hunger for love. We learn all too soon that when others are affectionate toward us we can 'wangle' things so that we get what we think we need. And before we realize it, we are already at the point where we not only need love, but *demand* it! That is, we now want love not simply because we like affection, but because we can use it as a means of ensuring our getting what we want when we want it.

The more we were allowed by those who 'loved' us to *use them* to get what *we wanted* (even though we could have gotten it ourselves), the more have we found ourselves afraid to lose such 'convenient' love; for as we grew older we still had these want-habits, but, alas, no confidence in our own capacity to gratify them. In other words, this process of 'being loved' leaves us with much self-*gratification* but actually little self-*satisfaction*. Life itself, we see, teaches us that our very attempts to use others for gratifying our needs force us to become needlessly dependent upon them. We find our wants growing; yet our abilities to satisfy them have not been trained to grow. In demanding 'love' we were asking others to act for us, though we ourselves did little or nothing for ourselves or for them.

In this way, then, love which is interested only in 'security' turns out to be insecurity – and insecurity without creativity! We simply cannot take insecurity out of life by putting the emphasis on 'being loved', for 'being loved' does not call into play our whole natures, and leaves us with a devastating sense of helplessness. Once our whole nature is taken into account, we realize that if each of us is to grow, if each of us is to develop, *there must be insecurity in our lives.* What we actually learn from experience is that the demand for security at the expense of one's own activity in growth does not take us very far in solving the everyday problems each of us faces. To be a person is to need growth, and to grow is to break with the past without knowing exactly what the future will bring.

Can love be prudential only?

To be sure, this narrow *prudential love* we have been describing seems better than positive ill will, because it puts the emphasis on 'playing it safe'. Prudential love does not intend to do harm; it is really based on fear of change and the desire to preserve what is good. But the prudent lover, concerned as he is to save what is good, never acquires the wisdom to see that a person simply cannot stand still. Therefore, he does not see that the problem of life is not so much a matter of preserving good and 'keeping everything safe and sound'. Life calls for creating new goods. Personality growth demands that we preserve only that part of the present and past which can be used to create the new goods for which each new situation calls.

For example, every sensitive parent is tempted – as a part of his parental responsibility, he may think – to prevent disappointment and sorrow in the life of his child. He 'hates' to see his child suffer; it disturbs his own 'peace of mind'. Perhaps the child will not be able to take the disappointment and sorrow without despair. Perhaps discouragement here may cause other difficult problems in the child's life! Why, then 'take the chance'? Why not prevent the difficulty from arising? Why not wait until the child is a little older and is 'better prepared' to take it. The parent may therefore 'fix things' so that the child either will not have the disappointment and sorrow, or he may try to take the real edge from them by counterbalancing them somehow. In so doing, by taking more responsibility himself, he has, in fact, avoided personal disturbance, though he may feel virtuous for having prevented possible evil.

I would not for a moment be understood to suggest that parents become irresponsible in this attitude toward the problems of growing persons, or that they overlook the possible dangers in allowing children to face situations more difficult than they have the capacity to bear. I consider it basic principle that persons do everything in their power to prevent situations in which children or adults are confronted with more evil than they can bear or turn to good account. But, as the illustration given above may convey, the parent who conceives of his 'love' for his child in terms of keeping the child (and himself) 'out of danger' is quite likely to underestimate the real possibility of growth in the 'dangerous' situation. Instead of asking the question, Why take a chance now? he might well ask, Why not face possible sorrow and disappointment now? Why not let the child develop here and now his capacity for facing – and accepting – insecurity connected with a potential good?

Is it not a fact that parents who would not dream of offence to their children do in fact insult them by lack of faith in their capacity to endure suffering? In most cases children 'bounce back' from suffering as rapidly as they do from physical illness – and especially when there is a sympathetic and encouraging parent at hand to help. The 'prudent' parent, confronted with the problem of whether to encourage the youngster to do something which may bring more grief than he realized, is more likely to emphasize the possible grief than the possible good! Since, actually, he himself fears suffering more than he cares to create good, he will prefer to put off the test. In so doing, however, he may well be keeping the child from developing the self-confidence that comes from knowing that he can accomplish uncertain objectives – or from knowing that he can take disappointment!

There is another ground for putting more accent on creativity than on prudential love. Much human disappointment and sorrow depends less on the objective situation than on the individual's 'level of expectancy'. It is the level of expectancy that determines the 'level of frustration'. The person used to 'success', the person who takes comfort and security as a matter of course, begins to suffer frustration the moment things begin to go wrong. It is pathetic, for example, to see human beings, who are fairly well off in every good that others can bestow upon them, feel so insecure because they hardly know what they would do 'if something goes wrong'. The cause for much groundless disappointment and sorrow is often nothing more than the person's own fear of insecurity. He fears that he cannot stand suffering, and this fear creates his situation of insecurity and frustration.

To summarize: prudential love, love which emphasizes safety, is actually not safe! To 'play safe' is not to be safe! Prudential love is actually wrong in its calculations, because it does not face all the facts of life. None of us can keep things from changing. Our problem is to analyse change, including physical and mental change, and transform it into growth, into creativity. And to do this we must move from prudential love into creative love – that is, the love which lives in changing situations, accepts the facts in every situation, but does its utmost to transform the total situation into one in which persons will have another kind of security, the security of growing fellowship or community.

The need is to love, not to be loved
The meaning of creative love is by no means easy to define, since there is no formula for it. It is not correct even to oppose it to prudential love, as if it were not concerned with the preservation of the person. It is rather guided by a different, more inclusive ideal of what the good life for a person is.

Let me repeat that our conception of the nature of a good life is often shaped by our experiences as children in which safety is a necessity. Furthermore, since the dependence of children upon parents is necessarily so great, it is all too easy for any child to grow up demanding love as a basis for his security. This very dependence brings forth as the theme of life: I want *to be* loved. That an infant and a growing child need love is, of course, not to be deplored. Nor should the child's need to be loved be denied, for it springs from his inner nature, as well as from the uncertainty he fears when love is denied, or supplanted by indifference or hostility.

But our question is, Should the need 'to be loved' be allowed to dominate the conception of what makes life good? If the love that is showered upon children is one which simply caters to their wants for comfort, or if the love is given on the condition that the parent's demands be acceded to in slavish or never-questioning obedience, then the child does develop the conception of love as a prudent self-protective device to be used to manipulate people. I shall never forget the college sophomore who exclaimed: 'All the love I have ever known was an emotion used to get control of people.'

To generalize: in the human situation, where insecurity is always present, we can understand the use of 'love' as a way of achieving security. Much recent psychology has emphasized this 'need for love', without pointing out clearly that the need is *to love* as well as *to be loved*.[1] So much has been said about conflict and frustration as a basis for nervous disease and maladjustment that many persons are now more concerned about avoiding conflict and frustration than they are about encouraging frustrations which are in the line of growth. It makes a critical difference whether we think of the happy or good life in terms of love as 'security' or as adventure in the sharing of life. In fact, there is no more serious maladjustment than that involved in a person's thinking of life only in terms of *being loved*, for now the emphasis is on his own security and satisfaction at all costs. And this, far from bringing security and satisfaction, actually encourages insecurity and dissatisfaction for all concerned. It is therefore sad to see parents denying themselves so that their children will not have to 'suffer' as 'we did' – implying that they themselves had never been loved enough!

Once again, I am not deploring the spirit of sacrifice for another's good. But I am deploring personal sacrifice which is blind to what seems to me a basic fact about human existence. We can provide basic physical conditions for safety and security, but we cannot ever provide mental security for the person who is unwilling to face, as responsibly as he can, situations which necessarily involve uncertainty and insecurity – simply because they involve him in growth! In such situations the only 'creative insecurity' there can be consists, not in the feeling that everything will come out well, but in the conviction that no matter what happens, one can and will fight for the good.

It is hard to put this kind of security, this *quality* of life, into

---

[1] I am glad to note this more constructive emphasis in the works of G. W. Allport, S. Blanton, Erich Fromm, Paul E. Johnson, A. H. Maslow, Rollo May, A. Montagu, Carl Rogers, and P. Sorokin.

proper words, or to keep it from seeming like the spirit of bitter defiance. But what, in our calm, best moments, do we hope for ourselves when we confront uncertainty and hardship? Is it that we be delivered from this evil, if the alternative be more evil for somebody else? One thinks of the soldier confronted by the morrow's battle. Does he desire to be spared? Of course! But does he not also fervently hope that he will be able to *keep himself in control* during the moments of stress? If he is spared, but has not met his trial valiantly, his relief for his physical safety is spoiled by his realization that he has not won the inner battle of creating the spirit of self-command.

Character is the inner core of 'security'
To put is sharply: What person feels more 'secure' than the person who knows that he will not quail in the midst of danger! What man is freer in spirit than he who knows that suffering alone will not deter him from doing his best in the face of evil? We human beings are, in the last analysis, manacled by our own fear that some evil will happen to us for which we are not prepared. The fool acts as if he could not be overcome by evil; the coward will give up every other good thing he has if only he can be spared evil; the mature man is never free from danger but is confident that he will not cringe in panic even before an evil which may destroy him. The mature man does not see his life only in terms of what can happen to him, but also, and mainly, in terms of whether he can maintain his ideals. The meaning of his life comes home to him as the creative effort to live up to his ideals without flinching.

Again, we know in the last analysis that our characters are the one thing we can and must create for ourselves. What is our character? It is our will to live by our ideals, 'sacrificing' whatever is needed to realize them ever more completely. And we know that our character is the fortress that we must build by our own efforts, since every stone in it must be lifted out of our own thoughts and desires, carefully selected by each of us, and kept in place by our own wills under the stress of siege.

I know that there are those who will feel as they read these last pages that I simply do not understand, in my 'liberal' optimism, the real dynamics of life. There will be the psychoanalysts and psychologists who would say that I have learned nothing from depth psychologies which should have taught me that the fundamental dynamics of human life work not at such conscious levels of 'will' and 'reason' but in the unconscious forces. But I certainly do not deny that unconscious factors are present in the situation each person confronts as he strives to fulfil his needs creatively. Yet I insist that every person must ultimately carry on the battle of his life, with whatever insight he can gain, in the conscious vanguard. I do not for a moment disclaim that there are forces in his environment and in his unconscious which can help him to win his battles. This is part of the reason for my 'detour' into an analysis of adequate parental love.

Still, however 'moralistic' it may seem, the fact is that sooner or later, if a person is to be selective in growth, if he is to choose as well as he can which way 'his soul shall go', he must face the insecurity explicit at every critical point of personal growth – such as these considerations: Shall I be kind to someone who does not like me? Shall I work hard for a goal I can realize only several years hence? In all such battles, self-insight and a permissive unconscious will help tremendously. But is there any more pathetic fact, in our times, than the plight of persons, supposedly enlightened by 'dynamic' and 'depth' psychology, who think that no creative choice is ever open to them, and that if only they could understand themselves adequately, and then have 'emotional blocks' removed, they could enjoy self-actualizing lives?

Curiously enough, I would probably also be accused of optimistic and austere 'moralism' by some Christian thinkers of fundamentalist, existentialist, and neo-orthodox persuasion. If depth psychologists would be concerned by my seeming neglect of the unconscious, these thinkers would say that I have too much faith in man's ability to 'pull himself up by his own bootstraps'. In a word, I have overlooked the need for God as revealed in Christ and the dependence of the human being 'on him' for redemption and strength. Later I hope to say more about this, but here I would want to say that if it be 'moralistic' to emphasize human freedom and creativity, then I am indeed moralistic. In any case, if our analysis is correct, it would seem to be God's will that we accept our freedom and use it creatively. However, to emphasize creativity is not to deny human dependence upon God, but to praise God for creativity rather than for security! The creative person is certainly no less dependent upon God than he is upon his unconscious or his human environment. My emphasis would be on what God and man can do *together*.

I would not be misunderstood. There are other things in life that are precious, such as health and knowledge, beauty, fellowship with God, and the joy of loving – without them life would lose much of its savour. But we know that all of them depend to some extent upon good fortune. The one thing that depends upon us alone, and the one thing which undergirds the other blessings, is our unflinching and constant determination to develop these other values despite the insecurities that surround them.

MUST NOT A GOOD GOD CREATE AND SUPPORT CREATIVITY?

It may now be clear why I said that if God had made man so that he could not hurt himself or others, man would not be a morally mature person. What makes life most meaningful is not the security provided for us by mother, father, society, or God, but the creative effort which can penetrate into every nook and cranny of our lives. We have seen that for human beings security at the price of creativity means dehumanization. The love for security which forfeits creativity is a snare which turns men into cringing animals and generates a hate of which animals themselves are incapable. If we are to keep the blessings which being human makes possible, we must do so by accepting the risks of being human, and of creatively disciplining ourselves to suffer, whenever need be, for a greater good. It is because we, too much of the time, think that we can preserve our goods by hugging them to ourselves, it is because we conceive even of love as guaranteeing serenity, that we are in fact inhuman to ourselves and to each other. Persons who are not willing to help each other to be creative, persons who are suspicious of the creativity which seems to endanger their present good, live by putting up barricades between people, and they do all in their power to weaken the creative urge in others. But when persons live in a way that seeks to protect the freedom and creativity of others as much as possible, they find new reaches of goodness in their lives, and do not increase the insecurity of life foolishly.

Nor is the reply complete to the person claiming that a God who values for man such creative adventure is a fool. We certainly must not deny the awful reality of the evil men do to each other. We cannot minimize either the cheap little tricks which men play on each other or the wholesale frauds by which they cheat each other. We shall not belittle the frightful toll which fear, hostility, and aggressive feelings take every day in anxiety and nervous tension. We shall rather urge that men are in fact cruel to each other largely because they misconceive the conditions of their own deepest satisfactions. It is their exclusive demand to be loved, to be secure that keeps men tense and uses up their energy without actually providing the only security open to them as men. They do not see that the condition of human security is creative insecurity. They never see that creativity does not endanger the other blessings of life overmuch. After all, creativity creates other values, otherwise it would become pointless. But there is no value more significant than creativity itself – that is, the freedom to use one's own abilities to help bring into being what one believes to be good.

If this be granted, we repeat that any Being who would be good to man would endow man with as much creativity as would be desirable in the kind of world he inhabits. He would not be deterred from granting man creativity because man might abuse it and cut down his own creativity and that of others. If we believe that freedom to create within limits is the pearl of great price, we would morally condemn any person, finite or infinite, who would choose some other goal than freedom to create. In a word, if I were to be as blunt as my student was, I would say, 'Any God who rejects creative freedom for the sake of other values, is a fool.'

CREATIVITY DEMANDS DEPENDABILITY

There is, however, another aspect of creativity not stressed in our discussion. The simplest observation of daily life will serve to bring out the fact that our freedom and creativity are always tied in with some regularity. Indeed, if we could not expect regularity, our creativity would be worthless, and we would not exercise it. If the pen I moved across the page did not move in accordance with my will and with what I have learned in the past to expect from fountain pens, ink, and paper I would soon give up the attempt to write. I choose to use my fountain pen because I want the uninterrupted flow of writing and the stability of script which form past performance I know it will give me. But the moment I choose the pen, I am free to write only with pen properties. If I choose pencil, I am restricted to other properties. Any choice I make is a choice which develops me in the act of choosing but restricts me to some sort of regularity. I would not know what to do otherwise; and would remain immobilized until I could anticipate some conclusion to my creative action. I would, for example, be discouraged from developing the habit of kindness or honesty if I felt that I would be just as tempted to be dishonest after years of effort as I would had I not developed the habit in the past. *To be free to choose is to choose which regularity one wishes to take advantage of, which regularity to create.*

If this is true, then whether God chooses to create or whether man chooses to create, creation can achieve anything only by using stability for its purpose. Any creative agent preserves any specific creation only by sustaining regularity in that creation. To go even a step further, we cannot know what creativity can actually achieve unless what is created does endure and does make a noticeable difference to other things. We cannot, then, escape from the fact that creativity must work within 'poles'. At one pole, creativity destroys itself if it is tied for ever to only one channel and one rigid manner of acting. At the other pole, freedom or creativity can do nothing worth while unless it creates the dependable.

One other example may help us to see concretely the paradoxical way in which the creativity in our lives must always risk itself in the very act of using regular means to express itself. A person who drives a high-powered automobile can achieve speed and distance with greater comfort than one who is limited to an average car. But both persons achieve freedom in space by restricting themselves to the laws of their vehicles and each pays a different price for his achievement. They conquer space by allowing themselves to be controlled by the physical energy which governs their automobiles. The heavier car that gives more road-comfort makes demands other cars do not make, and anyone who has elected to drive such a car elects to be conformed to its action. He gains the freedom it gives him by accepting all the risks that it exposes him to, and he cannot accept one part of the mechanism without accepting the other.

We turn, once more, to what it means for God to endow man with creativity. If God was to allow man creativity, he had to involve it within the stable structure of man's capacities, and within a world of order which man could understand and use for purposes of creativity. But, to protect creativity, the same man who can understand the laws of nature enough to contrive machines must also be allowed to use them to destroy life. The man who can understand the cause-and-effect relationships governing the human body and mind has to be allowed the freedom to torture the minds and bodies of men. Furthermore, God himself has to live with the man he has made, and with all the consequences of the 'cars' which express man's creative use of his endowments. Both the purposes of God and of man are affected by man's use of his creativity. God is the creator of co-creators, for man does not create outright – that is, the very possibilities of creation. But man is co-creator with God; and God is implicated in the creations, the good and the bad creation of man. Likewise, man as co-creator with God has to accept the consequences of the order within which God must work if man's creativity is to exist at all.

Our total discussion, accordingly, moves to the conclusion that to call God good is to say that God created persons whose creativity was a crucial consideration. Any creativity, in turn, would be limited within, but not bounded by, regularities in man's nature and in the world about him. Man, above all, could demand to love or to be loved (or both); and either choice would release certain effects in his own nature and in that of others. God and man both would have to begin where these consequences made their impact. The human father, we have suggested, does not, at his best, seek security at the expense of the creativity which is basic to every profound human satisfaction. The divine Father, in respect for human creativity, accepts many consequences which he himself would not will, but which cannot be avoided when they follow from human volition. In God's willingness to do all in his power to help men develop their creativity, we find the supreme nature of the Love which we begin to know when we, too, love creativity more than security.

Finally, whatever else we may believe about Christian doctrine, whatever else we may think about the nature of Jesus and of his relation to God, it seems to me that there is a core of meaning in his death upon the cross which we cannot escape, and which is crucial, I believe, to Christian thinking. That meaning goes beyond even the realization that both God and man suffer when men in their moral confusion and self-rightiousness crucify the innocent. The Cross forces us to the new, pregnant awareness that to be divine is to accept as creatively as possible full responsibility for, and the consequences of, human freedom. The Jesus who in the wilderness, before beginning his ministry, refused the beguiling securities offered by Satan, the 'son of man' who, having 'no place to lay his head', yet could see and serve God in fisherman, tax collector, and prostitute – this was the kind of being who *could* 'endure the shame' of the cross with a spirit which gives new poignancy to the poor words, 'creative insecurity'.

CHAPTER XVII

THE GRACE OF GOD AS DISCOVERED THROUGH FREEDOM

What meaning can the grace of God have for a temporalistic personalism? Can so strong an emphasis on the irreducible person and his creativity, coupled with the insistence that there is no loss of personal identity in religious experience, make possible an adequate theory of religious grace?

The answer is important. For whatever else religion gives – on any view of God – it releases unique power, born of the hope and faith that man, by virtue of the relation he has to the ultimate Ground of being, is never completely lost or forsaken. Will the emphasis on personal creativity and love, as expressed in the preceding chapter especially, be compatible with the even more persistent theistic theme that man is lost without the help of a God who never forsakes him?

The discussion in this chapter is couched within the framework of Christian concern for defining the means of grace. The stress is once more on what must not be effaced in any doctrine of grace. It is by no means an adequate description of the transforming power which lies at the centre of the experience of God to which so many Christians testify.

This chapter originally appeared in my *Free Will, Responsibility and Grace*, now out of print.

In a very limited way we have traversed with seven-league boots a vast area. In the first part of this discussion it may help if we remind ourselves of the ground covered so far. Actually, we have been trying to gain insight into the meaning of the love of God by analysing the structure of the good as human beings can experience it. It has been urged that no greater love could a Creator have for man than to give him the freedom to be a creator also. Whatever else God willed to make of man, it was his will evidently that man should have a crucial part in shaping himself. Man can be a co-creator with God; he may align his life with God or he may create against God. Indeed, the delegated creativity of man becomes the crucial source of good and evil for both God and man.

But, if our analysis is correct, God allied to freedom in the structure of man the feeling of moral obligation, a persistent imperative to the best a human being knows. Man is not compelled to be his best in any choice situation, but he is not allowed to go against the best he knows without a gnawing sense of guilt. When he does his best, on the other hand, he experiences the satisfaction of moral approval, which is blessedness even in the midst of the agonies of anxiety! Again, when a human being has done what he felt to be best, and it turns out later that it was not the best, God has made possible at the very core of his nature the blessedness which gives creative significance to his life. 'Here I stand, I can do no other.' Is this not God's way of sharing in our willingness to be as creative as we can? Indeed, does he not say: 'This is my beloved child, even if I am not (completely) well pleased!' So much God does, shall we say, in accordance with his *general providence* for man in also providing for a stable world in which man's needs and capacities may be challenged and grow toward fulfilment.

But does not God make his will known to mankind more specifically? Has God not stipulated the directions in which man must go if his freedom is to be fully creative and if his sense of moral obligation is to realize the best? In the last chapter we tried to give more explicit content to the central Christian claim that it is God's will that men love and forgive one another. It is not within the province of these chapters to analyse the grounds for this claim. But I believe that there are reasonable grounds for asserting that man has direct experiences of God, and that the Judeo-Christian tradition, culminating especially in Jesus' consciousness of God, has illuminated man's relation to God and God's relation to man. I have suggested, however, that these direct experiences of God cannot be taken as final revelations about God, man, or the good life without being evaluated in the light of the rest of human experience.

If Jesus' life and claims have validity they have it because the values of such living and the truth of these claims is re-established in the criticized experience of persons. Jesus' own realization of the love of God, his own conviction that God was at work in his life revealing the nature of God's loving care, do not represent a transaction made once for all in the course of history, except as it happened to the person Jesus. In a word, God, in and through

Jesus, was able to do what he had been trying to do for every man, and what he is still trying to do in the lives of many men. While I hesitate to put such an important matter so baldly, I must say, so that my general orientation may be clear, that in Jesus a creative process, which is the essence of God's love, was illuminated in a unique way. Through the force of that life and death at a given time in history other men saw more clearly what God is trying to do with man. The *Logos*, the essence of God's relation to man and the world, was able to become flesh in a way that actually did change history.

I, for one, would not know how to read the moral history of Western civilization without the impact of a life and death which led men to say that here, supremely, God was showing what man could be if only he would indeed co-create with God. I could not explain the course of my own life were it not that the life and death of Jesus made possible a resurrection in my own. This cannot be the place to develop an adequate Christology but to make clearer how it seems to me (whatever else may also be said) that God has been at work and is at work in the lives of men. Men find God in religious experience, and Jesus found God in religious experience, which is another way of saying that God was able to work in their lives in ways not open to him through the rest of their experience (which evidences his presence in different ways).

Again, however, what I would urge is that we do not know the truth or the full implication of the religious experience for human lives by reading off, or having implanted in us, some final commandment. Indeed, the burden of the last chapter was that we have done less than justice to the Christian faith that men should love one another until we have shown what more concrete patterns of value in human persons must be sought by that love. The Christian intuition, or 'revelation', if you will, that it is God's will that men should love one another, is an incomplete revelation at best without the most careful analysis of the kind of personality a loving will ought to create. God's giving of himself to and through the general providential order of nature, God's making of himself available in and through religious experience, God's work in and through Jesus, is incomplete until every human life achieves the symphony of values actualizable in that life. We do disservice to God when we clamp his creative work into fixed, detailed affirmations, or when we are satisfied with pious generalities which need cautious but courageous elaboration if they are to be truly helpful. To me, again, it seems almost tragic that much Christian thought has been so anxious to emphasize its uniqueness, so anxious to remove the taints of 'modernism' and 'liberalism', that it has not accepted the help that can be given by scientific and philosophical analyses. The task before contemporary Christianity is not to hug its own purity, or even to use the insights of others, but to find a *new whole* which is more completely rededicated to God.

Such a new whole, already hinted at, can be made more specific if I suggest, in outline, the view of man which then emerges. A human being, on this view, is not an animal with rationality added. He is not a mere plastic set of needs and wants, which allow him more possibility than animals enjoy. He is not an animal with more choices, made possible by his capacity for self-conscious reflection and symbolization. He is not an unconscious wasteland of non-moral desires insecurely tied down by a superego which automatizes the prudential bargaining of his ego with the surrounding culture. Nor is *homo sapiens* a creature who is one-third animal, one-third man, and one-third God, full of anxiety about the monstrosities which may be produced from such a union.

Could I here develop the thought further, I would urge that we have been seduced by our evolutionary conception that because man emerges from a tree of life in which all other creatures are animals, we must not think too highly of him, of his rational function, of his will, of moral obligation, of religious experience, but see these as ultimately superimposed on an unstable animal or unconscious base. Man, on this 'evolutionary' view, is to be conceived as a being whose more plastic needs and greater abilities forced him to develop a culture. On this view, human personality, will, obligation, even logical functions and ideologies ultimately are formations moulded by processes of acculturation.

Such a view, I believe, misconceives the nature of man by thinking of his human nature as something emerging from and added to animal structure. However, many persons, unsatisfied by this conception, were subject to the seduction of thinking of man as a fallen god. Man, they said, may be an animal, yes, but he is also a god, for the spark of the divine in him is his hope and his despair. Man is a limited creature of space and time, but he is also a spirit disturbed by eternity in him; he is a self-transcendent being, forever goaded by stirrings which show that he is a denizen of two worlds, the eternal and the temporal. Yet despite the fact that there are many who propose this view as the pervading biblical view, we may wonder whether such views actually do justice to man. Should we keep on trying to think of man either as a higher animal or a fallen god? It seems to me that if we do we take our eyes off man himself and fit him either into a cosy divine economy or into a constricted scientific scheme.

The thesis I would defend is that man is what he is, neither animal nor god, that his society is neither that of an animal bewildered by new plasticity and capacity, nor a lost paradise. Our approach must see man as he is and not fit him into schemes either of evolution or of salvation. Man is not a complicated animal body; he is *his* body; man is not a partially divine mind; he is *his* mind; and to say that he is indissolubly mind and body seems to me to create more problems than it solves. Man must be seen as he is, a particular type of complex being, with certain kinds of activities, certain kinds of yearnings and cognitive capacities, and other functions which characterize him whether or not they characterize any other being, atom, God, or animal.

Following this procedure, and focusing on man as he experiences himself, we would suggest that man is a creature whose desires even are none of them like those of animals when seen *within the context of his whole being*. The very fact that man can think, that he feels obligation, that he can will, that he appreciates beauty, is stirred by the holy – these facts transform even his most physical demands for food and water, making them different from those of animals (as far as we can know). A man needs and wants to eat, but he may fast in order to think, or experience the holy, and he may starve in order to protest against injustice. On the other hand, the kind of willing, the choices open to man, are those of a creature that has the kind of desires man has along with the sensitivities to goodness, beauty, and holiness.

In other words, when God created a human being, at whatever point of time, with whatever biological or spiritual forebears he might have, he did not add to an animal, any more than he added to dust the spark of the divine as the biblical myth put it (although this way of stating it might serve some purposes). God created a kind of being *in toto*, *a new Gestalt*, with potentialities which we human beings later, as we try to understand them, are likely to see in the light of prior stereotypes. If we start by believing in God then we say: 'God made him, so he must be conceived of as so and so.' If we leave God out of account and start with physical and biological evolution, then we say: 'Since man emerges from the animal, he must be conceived thus and so!' What I plead for, perhaps too rashly, is that we see man for what he is and, if anything, ask what light *his* nature throws, along with the physical and animal world, on the structure of reality.

As a matter of fact, our knowledge of animals does not grow significantly unless our insight into man grows. Much as we may think that we better understand one *by* the other, all our knowledge – of man, animal nature, God – actually grows *pari passu*, and we constantly borrow analogies from one or the other to illuminate some particular problem. We simply cannot go *from* animal to man, or *from* man to animal, or *from* God to man, or *from* man to God without inviting distortion. Thus, man is neither God nor animal; he is neither sinner nor saint. He is a complex, continuant unity of human desires, human will, human cognitive capacity, human aesthetic sensitivity – a being who feels a moral imperative to create in the best way he knows, and is often invaded by a creature-feeling, to use Otto's term, or an objective Presence, to use James's expression. The Christian faith, for reasons not here in question, defines this presence as a loving Person who creates man and cares for him. We have tried to understand what it means for God to love man, and we have urged that God's love is expressed in allowing man to be creatively free, and in setting forth, in the structure of man's capacities and potentialities, the conditions which would lead man either to creative self-fulfilment or to a fretful, self-destructive demand for security at any cost.

Having reiterated and, I hope, set our central theme in focus, we can now look more squarely at a very difficult problem central to all significant religious living, and especially to the Christian perspective, namely, the problem of individual as contrasted with general grace of Providence.

Let us turn first to the facts of non-moral evil, that is, to the burdens which human beings often have to bear owing to physical infirmities, owing to natural catastrophes which destroy their homes and their loved ones and leave them helpless and in despair, beyond any repair that other human beings can effect. These evils are called non-moral because they are not due to anything which the person involved has done. Which of us, for example, has not had the experiences of seeing a loved one seriously ill, or afflicted by a problem which outreached all the resources at our disposal?

In such circumstances have we not found ourselves praying: 'Oh God, our Father, grant him special strength to bear this burden, and keep him from bitterness and despair'?

Here, in the very natural petition of a concerned and compassionate person, we see the root, I think, of the conviction that surely God will grant special power for special burdens. And the person so afflicted may himself pray for special power, for special insight. Such petitions, obviously, are born of dire need and stress and come unreflectively; but when we do reflect upon them we note the assumption that a special burden calls for emergency power and that the God is good enough to create us, who knows our frame, will not forsake us in special time of trial.

If such are the roots of the doctrine of special grace, what do the facts of human experience seem to be which justify the Christian conviction that such grace exists? Is it not the stubborn and crucial fact that persons who have had unusual burdens, who have faced tremendous obstacles, who have appealed to their God for help, have indeed found what seemed to them new strength to carry their burden, a renewal of hope and faith which, if it did not remove the mountain, at least helped them to climb it? Let me circumscribe exactly what I am asserting. For I am aware of the dark night of the soul, of the unanswered petition. Yet this absence of help would not even be mentioned were it not for the fact that the rule seems to be that the 'sincere prayer of a righteous man availeth much' – which I interpret to mean that the earnest and honest appeal of a conscientious person seems as a rule to unlock energies not otherwise available. And my main contention is that every religion would die of dry rot were it not for the continuing testimony of religious people that 'I could not have done it without God's help'.

I am not interested at the moment in various psychological ways of explaining this fact – as long as the fact is not explained away; for if psychological study can show how this takes place, hallelujah, we know more about how God works in human life! The fact is that the faith which led to the appeal to God – namely, that God was willing to help his creatures in need – was the key that turned the lock and opened the door to special grace! And, I repeat, the heart of everyday religious living, Christian or non-Christian, is that beyond the general grace there is the special providence to the specially needy. Religion ultimately lives and thrives by vital conviction that we are not alone in our attempt to do good and overcome evil. The religious man, even after he has taken into account his own ineptness, may never understand why some of his petitions for power seem to hit a stone wall. But in the last analysis, he lives in the persistent conviction that God is good, and with him in the struggle to grow.

I have purposely introduced the problem of special grace by reference to non-moral evil rather than sin because I suspect that if persons did not believe in special grace to deal with non-moral evil they would have little ground for belief that they could be helped in overcoming sin. Sin, however, is a much more complicated concept, and we must try to define it within the Christian context of man's relation to God as his loving creator.

Let us consider, all too briefly, what it involves. In the first place, sin is evil due to human choice; it is moral evil, that is, evil which takes place because man wills it. If there is no free will, there is no sin. If this is so, a doctrine of original sin – a sin one is born with – simply does not make any sense. For one is not responsible for what he inherits; he is responsible only for what he does with what he inherits in so far as it falls within his sphere of freedom. Thus, whether it be in the Christian or any other context, sin refers to evil originating in the free use of human ability. The only Christian view of sin which could make empirical sense, then, is that sin takes root in the human abuse of freedom toward God, man, and nature.

But the Christian view of sin is more specific than this, for it seeks to define not only the general basis for sinning but the essential root of all sins. And it, therefore, asks us to recall the basic relation of man to God in some such terms as these: Assume that God and man are not simply in the relation of Creator to created, but in a relation where the Creator does everything to help man to realize himself, short of denying his limited freedom of choice. Thus, the order of nature is dependable, there are the many values available to human effort, and intimate fellowship with God is possible – the basic situation in the Garden of Eden myth. The Creator is not treating the created person as a thing; the relation between man and God is one of *responsible responsiveness* to each other. Man as created knows that his existence and the good things in life are not his creation but made possible for him and his brethren. The relation of God to man is one of outgoing, self-forgetful care, not concerned with prerogatives of power, but with mutual concern for creativity.

When man is aware of this continuing providence of God but then cuts the tie of mutuality between himself (created creator) and the Creator-Person, how does man feel, and what are the consequences? Once more, when man, free to co-operate with God in creativity, rejects God, when a man, instead of grateful acceptance and response, turns away from God and tries to act as if he himself were the only source of goodness, something drastic happens. It happens, not because God now purposely and vindictively sets out to punish his ungrateful prodigal son, but because the fundamental structure of goodness, from God to man and man responsively to God, has been violated. It happens because man shuts God out of his life as far as possible and goes on to use the order of nature and his fellow man for his own purposes as if he were the Creator and not the created.

Assuming all this, what would happen when a man thus makes himself the privileged centre and demands that all else be a means to his own security? Put in subjective terms, men feel a special quality of moral guilt, which they have called sinfulness. 'Woe is me! for I am undone.' Moral guilt comes with the realization that man has broken the bond of trust with the Source of all good. He has denied his own dependence and has made himself lord. He has not (like Abel as opposed to Cain) responded gratefully to God, to his world, and the rest of God's creatures. Sin involves guilt and a peculiar sense of unworthiness.

To repeat, men who feel sin have an experience which, I suggest, is possible only where a relation of personal trust is destroyed; they have proved unworthy of that trust. They have broken the will of God which purposed love; they feel naked, alienated, estranged, and are overcome by a quality of moral remorse (as well as anxiety) which goes only with the breaking of a trust. Put in objective terms, a sad, nay, a seemingly hopeless state of affairs now exists; for they are not only estranged from God, they have not only cut the line of communication from their end, but they have lost confidence in their own worthiness and their own power to live up to the relationship of trust.

In these leaky words I have tried to suggest the unique relation between man and God which defines the human predicament in the essential Judeo-Christian perspective. I have purposely tried to define it in generic terms, for it seems to me that the 'sense of sin' is a quality of experience we feel in our human relations when we break a trust of generous love. The man who has broken, by his own act of infidelity, the line of confident responsiveness between himself and his wife knows the quality of remorse indicated when a personal tie of trusting love has been cut. Let a man believe, as the Christian believes, that God loves him, that he owes all he has that is good to God's love. Then let that man betray that trust. He will feel that he no longer has any right to 'belong' to a family of trust. And what is more, he will feel the anxiety implicit in the new situation his action has created, as well as the moral guilt. He has cut himself away from God, the creator, the lover, the source of good. He is lost!

Can we say that the history of Judeo-Christian doctrines of the Messiah and of the Atonement is the attempt to interpret the total meaning of this situation? Is not the one thing which all doctrines of the Atonement are grappling with that which I would make central here, namely, that man, once he has cut himself away from God, feels impotent to renew the right relationship between himself and God by anything he himself can do? I cannot deal with any specific doctrine of the Atonement here, but if I am correct in analysing the situation in which man, by making himself central, comes to feel lost and impotent, what is called for is an act of forgiving love on the part of God. In his sin, man feels cut away from his Source of Good; and nothing he can do can bridge the gap completely. What is called for is some redeeming action from God, which may indeed repair the breach between man and God. Thus an adequate doctrine of redemption becomes religiously fundamental. We restrict ourselves here to one phase which may be within my space and competence.

I have stressed the fact that men under special burdens found themselves needy of special strength to bear these burdens. But the weight of sin created, for reasons just suggested, a unique situation. For the sinner suffers from a different burden; it is one created by his own abuse of freedom. In sinning he has not only hurt others, he has not only 'come short of the glory of God', but he has shown himself capable of doing this himself. As long as he has this 'dreadful freedom', this will continue to be possible. And the result will be a weaker and weaker man. What can be done in this woeful situation?

For much Christian ethics, therefore, the focal problem has become not so much a matter of defining the ideal of personality, but that of discovering help for the sinner who finds his ideal, especially that of forgiving love, far beyond his own strength. Thus the apostle of Paul, in a passage which has had much influence on Christian thinking, confesses: 'For the good that I would I do not: but the evil which I would not, that I do.' How many Christians have felt the agony of a Paul or an Augustine as they contemplated the cherished ideal, noted their own disobedience to it, felt the remorse of sin, and the despair of ever being able to repair their wicked ways! And in this desperate situation, what was it that gave them courage and inspiration to go on? It was their conviction that God not only loved them for the good that they did and could do, but that God was willing to forgive them, so that though their sins were as scarlet they could be as white as snow.

For how many millions of Christians did Jesus' life, and especially his death upon the cross, become either a literal or symbolic expression of the fundamental conviction that the power of sin in man's life need not destroy him, that God was the forgiver, and that any man who would believe that God forgives is redeemed? What I wish to stress, once more, is this central conviction rather than different interpretations of it, namely, that though man had broken the trust and was unworthy, God himself stepped across the gap created and welcomed the prodigal son home and assured him that the past was forgiven. I wish to highlight this fact, for it seems clear that it is in this faith that the weakened sinner finds the inspiration and confidence to re-form his life. In other words, if the God he has forsaken and abused believes in him enough to reinstate him, if he can feel again that he 'belongs' and can participate in God's blessing, if God is not merely his judge but his redeemer – then he may indeed have hope.

In this way, it may be clear, the doctrine of general grace has now been supplemented by a quality of forgiving grace which reaches out to each individual sinner and says to him: 'No matter how much your abuse of freedom has destroyed, both in your own life and in the lives of others, no matter how much good has been sacrificed because of your wilful misdeeds, your sinning is forgiven. Go, and sin no more.' I repeat, here is a fundamental fact about the dynamics of love in the lives of sinners which Christianity has always made crucial, and which at long last much recent scientific psychology, especially in the thought of Carl Rogers, H. S. Sullivan, and their followers, is making central as a basis for therapeutic procedure. That is, there can be no redemption without establishing a co-operative relation of encouraging sympathy and appreciation between counsellor and patient. This relation results in renewed confidence and belief in one's power to be creative. Thus Carl Rogers writes:

If I can create a relationship characterized on my part:

by a genuineness and transparency, in which I am my real feelings;

by a warm acceptance of and liking for the other person as a separate individual;

by a sensitive ability to see his world and himself as he sees them;

Then the other individual in the relationship:

will experience and understand aspects of himself which previously he has repressed;

will find himself becoming better integrated, more able to function effectively;

will become more similar to the person he would like to be;

will be more self-directing and self-confident;

will become more of a person, more unique and more self-expressive;

will be able to cope with the problems of life more adequately and more comfortably.[1]

If this can happen between counsellor and patient, what is possible between God and sinner?

Where does the problem occur? It lies in what seems to me are two incompatible claims made frequently by Christian thinkers. The first one, which we have ourselves stressed, is that man in his own freedom abuses his creativity. If God is to respect man's freedom he cannot keep man from sinning. The second, incompatible, belief comes in the assertion that man cannot of his own will, but only by the grace of God, break the chains of sin. But one would then suppose that the God who, in respect for freedom, would not weaken the will to sin, should not, in respect for human freedom, strengthen the will to recover from sin. I see no way out of this sheer impasse. If God cannot interfere with my freedom to weaken, to sin, neither can he interfere with my freedom to turn back, to repent, to amend or not to amend. To put it concretely: the prodigal son freely wasted his father's endowment, without interference

[1] From *Becoming a Person*, lectures delivered at Oberlin College by Professor Rogers in 1954 on the Nellie Heldt Lecture Fund.

from his father, and, let it be noted, in Jesus's story at any rate, that the prodigal son must start back by his own volition, in the faith that his Father still cares for him. But to many Christians this would seem to give man too much freedom, or suggest more confidence in man than is justified. The result is that God's help in seeking recovery from sin and in realizing the ideal is made crucial. But can we have it both ways?

Once more, in defining the nature of free will, we said that freedom meant that the will in its choice is not *caused* to do what it does either by any force outside it, or any force within it. If the will now is said to receive its direction and strength from God, then it is no longer free, and man is not himself responsible for his return to God. The doctrine of special grace, thus conceived, ends up by making incompatible claims, and Christian thought cannot but be embarrassed by this state of affairs.

Thus a careful thinker like George Thomas seems to me to be in a serious quandary when he says on the one hand, in Augustinian terms: 'Where the sinner is "formally" free to choose good instead of evil . . . he does not have the power to choose the true good so long as he is dominated by love of self. . . . But unless there is a radical reorientation of his will, he is not likely to resist temptation.'[1] For if the sinning person cannot reorient his own will but God does it for him, or gives him power to do so, then it is God and not man that is responsible. Again, Thomas says that though man is 'not under the necessity of sinning in every act, he is threatened by his failure to overcome his sin and by his alienation from God and from his neighbour'.[2] Therefore, unless man can by divine grace receive a power not his own, he is doomed to failure. But does this not mean that divine aid must transform man's will in as causal a fashion as, someone might say, a secretion in the glands causes a change in will? If man's will is to be free from causal change by mother, father, or society, must it not also be free from causal change by God?

If this is a real quandary in Christian thinking, how can it be avoided? It is here, I suggest, that the distinction between will agency and will power may help. It will be recalled that we indicated that will agency is free to choose within limits, that will agency is always free from causality, but is itself creative cause!

---

[1] *Christian Ethics and Moral Philosophy*, pp. 191–2. Used by permission of Charles Scribner's Sons.
[2] *Ibid.*, p. 197.

Here we would insist that God does not and cannot change the will agency of a person, be he saint or sinner. To do so is to deny human freedom and responsibility.

But it will also be recalled that will agency always works within the limits not only of the total inherited self, but also within the habits, the attitudes, the sentiments and traits which constitute the personality at any one moment. The *power* of will agency, or will power, it was suggested, is a by-product of all the causal factors, including will agency itself, operating in a given situation. Thus, the power of will can be affected by the factors operating upon it from within the context of personality and from beyond.

Can our quandary be relieved, therefore, by the suggestion that God does not turn the will *as will agency*, but that God can be a most influential factor in a person's life without tampering with his will agency? Let us be clearer about what is being suggested here. I am not saying that I know *how* God affects a life, no more than I know *how* my love of my children affects me, and their love for me affects me! But I do know that my life would be different if they did not love me and if I did not love them. The 'how' of God's effect on a person is not the issue here. My concern is rather to suggest a doctrine of freedom and responsibility consistent with the fact that I am helped by what others and God do for me.

It would seem that what I become, *when I choose*, depends upon what doors in my life I open, as it were. I know that when I think and believe and do my best to act in certain ways I am often surprised at what the consequences are. My act of will agency often allies with itself, or finds allied with itself, many factors in my life and in my world which I had not realized were there or available for me to use. Accordingly, the doctrine of specific grace, on this view, means *not that God turns will agency and somehow alters it by giving it more power*, but that when will agency freely turns to God for renewed strength, in humble faith in God's forgiveness and good will, forces are let loose in the life of that personality which his own free will now can readily accept, and allow to work for the greater good one feels obligation to at the time. But this help, this grace, is not forthcoming apart from a self-committing act of will agency.

A simple illustration may suggest the analogy I wish to draw. As a teacher I can affect my students in the classroom in a general way: the same words are there for all of them, but it is up to them to listen, and they must decide what to think of what I say. Let us call this the stage of general grace or providence in my relation to my students, a grace which showers the same basic order of words on all students present. But supposing one of my students, of his own free will, follows me to my office and asks further questions there? I can, then, without turning his will agency, be allowed the opportunity to make other suggestions relative to his particular need. Again, it is still 'up to him' what he will do with my suggestions, but at least I have a stronger opportunity to influence him, and without infringing on his freedom. For I become a larger factor among the forces which will influence what finally takes place in his life. I can help him and be more of a power in his life because I want to be, and because he is willing to commit himself to me. Thus I influence his final will power but not his will agency. That remains free!

May I then draw the analogy to the religious situation, with the reminder once more that the exact dynamics are even less clear there than in interaction between man and man. The prodigal son, let us say, uses his free will agency to turn from God and from his responsibility to his fellow men. In so doing, in accordance with psychological laws instituted by God, he develops habits of mind and feeling which will have to be contended with, if and when he decides that his way of life should be changed and that he should return to his father and brethren. In other words, the self-love which he has chosen will not readily dissolve once he contemplates his wickedness and yearns to 'belong' once more to the fellowship of creative love. Then, indeed, he may cry: 'That which I would, I do not!' For the *power* of his will agency is now not great enough to overcome the life which has been habituated to self-love, and which is even now constantly tempted to go on loving itself instead of trusting in others and in its own capacity for goodness.[1] But let such man be willing to believe in God's willingness to help him bear his burden; let him be willing to believe that God yearns for him to become a stronger person; let him be willing to believe that God will not hold his past against him; finally, let such a sinner turn to God and be willing to bear the cross he has laid upon his own shoulders – and what will he find? The Christian experience here is the answer! The 'Hound of Heaven' will not let him go!

[1] See Donald H. Rhoades, 'Does Psychotherapy Deny Self-Denial?' *Pastoral Psychology*, February 1956; Smiley Blanton, 'The Price of Love's Denial', *Pastoral Psychology*, April 1956; and Carl Rogers, 'Becoming a Person', *Pastoral Psychology*, February and April 1956.

The change will not always be easy, and the cross will not be light. But somehow, step by step, power comes into his life because he has set his face toward God.

I might buttress my argument by appeal not only to the general experience of mankind, but to the psychotherapeutic process contemplated by a growing list of contemporary psychologists such as Carl Rogers, G. W. Allport, A. H. Maslow, Rollo May, Erich Fromm, H. S. Sullivan, Paul Johnson, and others. The dynamics of unfailing care, based on sin and repentance, as practised by Alcoholics Anonymous are also relevant. Referring, however, to our ordinary experience, it is a fact, is it not, that a man's life can be changed by the persistent and wise care of a wife who convinces him that she accepts him as he is and for his potential goodness? Indeed his free will agency may at first spurn her love, but the wiser and more persistent her love is, the harder it will be for his will agency and for the other factors in his personality seeking self-actualization, to keep him in the bitter security of selfishness. Lovers do not change each other's life by taking over each other's will agency and turning it. Each appeals to a multitude of factors in the other's life which join the creative tendencies within each life and thus influence the final flow of feeling and action toward greater mutual understanding and common purpose. If our social and physical environment can become factors influencing the final will power of our lives because *we take at least the initial step* in assessing that environment and allowing it to affect us, surely God, without infringing on will agency, can, at our request, enter our lives with the result that we find it possible to do what we could not otherwise do. The grace of God does not annul the will, as agency. But as each of us, sinners, turns penitently and gratefully to our Father, we find him already coming toward us, anxious to welcome us back into the fellowship of love.

I may be mistaken, but I am at a loss to see where such a theory misconstrues the essential experience of life. The facts are that the weak have found strength to bear their infirmities, and the sinners have found new courage and confidence through their faith that God loves and forgives with a view to continuing the creative purpose in each life. Adequate theory must explain the facts and not explain them away.

But theory, it seems to me, to be adequate must take full acount of those factors in human life which make for health and fulfilment. If our underlying theory is correct, it must recognize that human nature is open to sin because it is open to creative self-development. Such creative self-development will always involve insecurity, and a man may be unwilling to accept the conflicts and anxiety of insecurity as he must face it in the natural world, in the development and action of his fellow men, and in his experience of God.

When a man tries to protect himself against insecurity by preferring an immediate seeming good to a greater remote good, by choosing his own security at the expense of mutual security, by protecting his creativity ungenerously from the demands which the needs and sins of others make upon it, he cuts himself away from the central Person whose very being is creative love. When man thus cuts himself away, when he piles up evils in his own life and in his society, when he makes the creative work of God more difficult, he is on the road to his own deeper insecurity and the undermining of his moral and religious power. At this point, when he comes to himself, he may in self-pity seek for someone else to carry the burden of his sin, for someone else to carry his guilt. The God he now seeks may simply be the God who would grant him security against further sin. But this will not do, either. For each must bear his own cross as a responsible person; and each person, if he is to be fulfilled, must live in commitment to a growing fellowship of love. Thus faith in God will not be that God bear his burden *for him*, but that God will help him to accept the evil and the good in his life, and to make the most that he can make of himself, within the community of love. Nor will his concern for his own sin and for his own good be so great that he will forget his responsibility for the good and the evil in the lives of his brothers. For God can use an adequate sense of sin and a humble acceptance of responsibility to others as one of the significant ways in which human lives are regenerated. The Christian community thus becomes a fellowship of freedom through grace, a growing fellowship of fruitful freedom as each person strives to accept the responsibility for the best orchestration possible of values in all human lives, a fellowship in a constant creative insecurity in which men and God move forward in constantly renewed ties of love and appreciation.

CHAPTER XVIII

WHAT MAKES A PHILOSOPHY CHRISTIAN: A LIBERAL SPEAKS

In the first part of this final chapter I state a fundamental conviction which pervades, as the reader, no doubt, has already noted, every chapter in this book. I might call it 'philosophical liberalism'.

Liberalism never suspends judgment at one point: the person will best come by as much truth as is humanly possible by refusing to allow non-negotiable demands on the basis of any one aspect of experience, no matter how convincing or invincible that experience is psychologically. To be reasonable is to be sensitive to the possibility at one area of experience may turn out to be more authoritative than any other. But even this cannot be discovered unless reason does examine and relate each dimension of human experience to the others.

Reason, in this liberal sense, is the person at work knitting together, as far as possible, what seems to be the witness of his experiences as to his own nature and the possibilities open to it in the total environment. Such liberalism is no flight from conclusions. It is a search for the conclusions that matter most because they are related to as much as possible.

Of course, one cannot deny that every man has some guiding faith – I have just stated what mine is. But from the fact that none of us is as impartial as he would hope to be, it does not follow that any one guiding faith or commitment is correct. It is ironic that the realization, 'we all have underlying commitments', which stems from opposition to a philosophic and theological relativism leads back to a new form of relativism. It is not enough to be clear about the faith one lives by; nor is 'being committed' likely to create a community inspired by responsible love. The liberalism that is recommended here may make one a poorer Christian if this means holding that a final revelation has been given, but it might make him a better Christian in so far as it suggests that Christian love means taking the beliefs of other persons, Christian and non-

Christian, as manifestations of God's response to man – until there is ground for concluding otherwise.

It is my thesis that there is a legitimate way, and an illegitimate way, in which a philosophy can be Christian – just as there is a legitimate and an illegitimate way in which a philosophy can be materialistic. Since much depends on what is conceived to be the role of philosophy in the affairs of men, I shall begin by defining what I conceive to be the purpose of philosophizing. I shall not define what I take the word 'liberal' to mean, but let this become evident as the discussion proceeds.

It is not the task of the philosopher, as I see it, either to create, or to legislate for, reality. To philosophize is to seek that description of reality as a whole which is true, or as near the truth as anyone can get. The complete philosophical truth is beyond the reach of any human being. Each philosopher is one kind of existent, surrounded by many other kinds of beings, none of which he knows completely. The philosopher's initial act of faith is no different from that of any other person who believes that somehow he can discover 'the things that matter most'.

What is unique about the philosopher is an additional act of faith that sets his task off from that of other men. He believes that the only adequate way to find the truth is to gather all the data he can, from every corner of the world of human experience, and ask what contribution they make to the meaning of the whole. I call this an act of unique, philosophic faith and I shall show later why this is an act of reasonable, as opposed to blind, faith.

What I would emphasize, therefore, is that the philosopher cannot *as a philosopher* arbitrarily deny the witness of any aspect of experience, as if he had some prior insight into the true and the false. Let us assume, for a moment, that a philosopher said: 'But I do have a prior insight based on a logico-mathematical process of analysis.' He could immediately be asked: But can you show me that this process is intrinsically superior to a perceptual-aesthetic approach? What can the philosopher answer? Surely, not that there is some *prima facie* superiority which his logico-mathematical intuition has over the *prima facie* aspects of the perceptual-aesthetic. Any claim the philosopher makes that is arbitrary cannot be made in the name of philosophy; any truth-claim he makes he must justify only by showing that it takes better account of the rest of experience than any counter-claim. The philosopher can test the claims and counter-claims of the moralist, physical scientist, artist, or mystic, only by understanding their relations to each other and by a *review* of the experiences upon which those claims are made.

The philosopher is not less needy or desirous of belief than other men. He does not begin his investigation in a cultural vacuum, or without conscious and unconscious commitments and convictions. As a human being he stands with his fellow men *in mediis rebus*, trying to discover what makes life worth while, and committing himself to what his past experience, training, and human intercourse have led him to believe is most meaningful. What makes him a philosopher, then? It is his willingness to subject every one of his beliefs, as far as he can, to criticism in the light of counterclaims made by others who emerge from their experiences with different results.

For him as philosopher, *any* belief, his own, or anybody else's, *any* belief, religious or non-religious, moral or immoral, and no matter how sincerely advocated or vigorously deprecated, is, as such, neither true nor false. Any belief or disbelief is subject to further criticism the moment it is seen that some other experience suggests different conclusions. This is to say that the philosopher takes every experience and belief seriously, and looks upon it not with green, suspicious eyes but with a determination to understand its testimony.

Thus, the underlying critical faith of the philosopher is that the more data he acquires, the more varied the evidence he can sift, the more likely he is to find the truth. His scepticism, if it lies anywhere, lies in his unwillingness to assume that any one part of his experience, sensory or non-sensory, logical or non-logical, religious or non-religious, can dictate, from its vantage-point exclusively, what its own complete meaning is, let alone what the meaning of other experiences is.

II

It is now time to ask: Is not this faith, that the whole of experience is more to be trusted than any part, arbitrary? The philosopher must confess, I concede at once, that he cannot prove ahead of time that this faith will be victorious. If there were nothing more to say, the philosophic claim that the whole will lend more insight than the part, would indeed be as arbitrary as the reverse claim.

But the philosopher can defend his claim by the actual experience of all human beings in the search for truth. He can point out that even within any one area of experience, be it religious or non-religious, no one experience is allowed to speak for all the rest. In what area of experience, do we not find conflicting interpretations of the supposedly same thing. How do we then proceed? Do we not accept that version which is consistent with the larger balance of experiences in that realm?

Again, in the name of no one experience can another experience be discredited. Any one experience as such cannot be tested by another, for every experience is what it is. But when any one is interpreted in a way that theoretically discredits the possibility of other experiences, which I, or someone else, is nevertheless having, what procedure do we follow? We certainly do not allow the first interpretation to legislate for other experiences upon which it is not based! Every experience has a right to face and be faced by its accuser. Assume that I believe a man is honest. Assume that I later find him to be dishonest about political affiliations. I certainly cannot conclude that the man, as a whole, is honest. But if I allow my first 'discoveries' to stand for the whole, I am discrediting other 'discoveries'. To generalize, if our procedure in any one realm of experience leads us to judge any one moment, or any one portion, of it by the remainder, why should we not adopt this procedure for all experience, and seek to correlate the evidence, or data, or 'revelations', of any realm of experience with the others?

We may now summarize the philosopher's predicament. He asks: What is the structure of the reality in which I live and to which I must conform my feelings, volitions, and thought? He does not know ahead of time by what avenue his best evidence will come, whether it will be through logic, or through sense, or by way of the moral, the aesthetic, or the religious (or any other) consciousness. These facets of his consciousness provide him, *prima facie*, with different types of experience and his total response in each is freighted with suggestions (to say the least) as to what the nature of the world beyond himself is. His own nature, his cultural background, his own experience with life up to the point that he consciously sets out to philosophize, will no doubt create a predisposition in him to favour some area of experience more than others. His fundamental commitment, to trust the suggestions which accrue from the interweaving of all of his experiences, will force him to reconsider suggestions from any one experience or area of experience. A philosopher stakes his life on the thesis that he is more likely to find the truth by trusting (until he has strong grounds for not trusting) the whole of his experience as the inlet to the truth about reality. Perhaps he is being too sanguine about the potentialities of the whole. It may be that some one area is the highway to reality. He should realize that he is taking a calculated risk in thus trusting the whole rather than the part.

There is further justification, however, for considering this risk a better one than the alternative risk that some one part would be the more revelatory. If the philosopher decides to inspect every area assiduously, and then relate it to all the rest of his experience and knowledge, he may by this very procedure, discover that some one experience or area is more trustworthy than all the others. But if he assumes, in advance, that some one area, or some one type of experience, constitutes the exclusive highway to truth about reality, then the interpretation of other areas of experience is subordinated, without continued interrogation, to the preferred one. This is what happens, for example, when the naturalist makes the logical and experimental organization of sense-experience the highway to truth and expurgates, on this 'public basis', the supposedly 'private' insights of the religious consciousness. This is what happens when the religious consciousness asserts its insight as the authoritative source of truth about the nature of reality and morality. In both instances there is more trust in some area of experience to the condemnation of another realm; in both there is a lack of faith, if you will, in the essential validity and possible harmony of all the areas of experience as co-operative avenues to truth.

It should now be clear that the philosopher, as I see him, is not an anaemic sceptic, anxious to clip the wings of angels, with shears sharpened on the grindstone of logic, while his more red-blooded brother in the fields of either science or religion, keeps close to the real facts and issues of life. He is a man committed to the fundamental trustworthiness of human experience as a whole; he is a man committed to the self-discipline of belief by faithfulness to all of the data at his disposal.

I have purposely emphasized the function of the philosophical man because I have wished as far as possible to avoid the historic debate between philosophy and religion on the one hand, and philosophy and science on the other. I see no philosophical basis for hostility to either religion or to science, and consider much of the debate to revolve around a *methodological dogmatism*. I am here decrying such dogmatism, and this, I believe, it is the essence of liberalism to decry.

Nor can the liberal dissociate the active, volitional components in the total process of knowing from the others. At the same time, he cannot assume that in knowing we take a series of photographic shots of a completed reality which our knowing in no way affects. More should be said on this matter, but I am simply suggesting pitfalls into which we easily fall whenever we cut up the knowing process into isolated parts or responses, or when we cut it off from the constant *inter*action with the challenging and nurturant environment. The person as a whole is at stake in acting and in knowing, in hoping and in despairing, and he cannot escape the human predicament of relating himself cognitively, emotionally, volitionally, and appreciatively to a world which will always transcend his understanding.

Yet if a man justifies his belief by referring to the mysteriousness of the universe, does he do more than expose his *naïveté* and immaturity as a person? We live within processes which are indeed mysterious, and will never be completely understood by us. But as long as we are alive in a mysterious world, and alive *to* it, we are forced, by the very fact that we are still alive and thinking, to assume that its mysteriousness is not intrinsically hostile to us. A philosopher does not deny mystery, but he does not glorify or stand in awe of mystery as such. He approaches it as part of the human necessity to adjust to it, with the purpose of better understanding exactly where the mystery lies. As Whitehead once said in class; the purpose of philosophy is not to reduce or dissipate all mystery but to corner it.

III

In this context we ask the question: What makes a philosophy Christian? My answer would be: A philosophy is Christian in the sense that the philosopher, facing the mysteries of existence with all the responsiveness of which he is capable, and correlating all of the data available to him, including his own experience, comes to the conclusion that the essential insights of Jesus, about God and man, are true, and that the wise person will seek to guide his responses to God and man in the light of Jesus' teaching. In 'the light of Jesus' teaching' here means not that he will conform in some mechanical manner to what he knows of Jesus and his teaching, but that he will seek to explore these insights and to implement them for his own life and for his neighbours. A Christian philosopher, on this view, is not a person who takes his own experience as a Christian, or the experience of the Christian community, as the *undeniable given* by which the rest of human experience is to be interpreted. He is a philosopher who, whatever his previous commitment and experience, Christian or not Christian, finds as a result of investigating the total claims of experience, that what he conceives to be the Christian view of the meaning of life actually throws more light on the nature of the whole than any other.

Obviously, it cannot be a purpose of this paper to defend any particular set of Christian tenets. It goes without saying that there simply is no definitive answer as to what *the* Christian view of life is, any more than there is a definitive answer as to what *the* materialistic or *the* idealistic view of life is. I can simply assert my own conviction that a Christian philosophy, in the most generic sense, goes beyond belief in a metaphysical spiritual Principle which unifies and gives direction to the structure of things, to a more specific conception of this metaphysical Being. The Christian metaphysical Being consciously binds all beings together by the norm of love. In a word, I believe that any philosopher would have a right to call himself a Christian if he believed that the fundamental purpose in the world is a process of conscious Love – love, joyous and creative, love, suffering and redemptive. He in addition would believe that this conception of creative, long-suffering, and redemptive Love, as the only means by which men can fulfil themselves and find proper fellowship with God, was made clearest in the consciousness which Jesus had of God and in his main teachings as we have them. What I would emphasize, as critical and essential in the Christian view, is that quality of fellowship between God and man which makes self-giving and forgiving love imperative and normative. I believe that such a conception of the fundamental structure and norm of all being provides a crucial insight which enables us to see all the rest of experience with a minimum of distortion, and on these grounds I would consider myself a Christian philosopher.

I suspect that this view of the matter will be subject to two related criticisms. I may be told that I do not adequately recognize the fact that in Christian experience there is witness to a revelatory intrusion into history. The critic's argument might run something like this: 'A Christian's belief is based on an event which at once sheds light on the nature of the universe and human existence, and also gives the person who commits himself to it the power to achieve a quality of sacrificial love for God and man which is not possible otherwise. What must be admitted into the purview of philosophy and theology is an initiating act or event which, momentous for human motivation, cannot be assimilated into the categories of human conceptualization as these apply to the remainder of human experience.' At this point much might also be added about the limitation of intellect, about the 'pride of reason', about the 'offence', about the essential mystery, which is beyond reason, about the suspension of rational ethics. 'Christian religious experience', it might be urged 'has an autonomy which must forever resist attempts to consider it "one among others" in any way which would detract from its unique supremacy. Attempts to do this, as liberals have presumably done, have led to the watering down of the Christian revelation, to making God a human hypothesis. But we cannot judge God's way by human ways. We simply must not arrogate to man powers he does not have; we must be aware not only of the deficits in human nature but particularly of the inordinate selfishness in this nature.'

I am sure I cannot do justice to the issues intertwined in such a rejoinder to me. But it seems to me that the essential issue is methodological and criteriological. What I conceive to be the essential liberal objection to such contentions, and, in any case, the one which I would want to advance, has to do not so much with the claims themselves but with the problem of validating these claims. As I see it, there is no *a priori* objection to such claims, and there is no denying that these claims are rooted in human experience. The question, however, is this. How does one know all these claims are true unless he has carefully analysed them in the light of the rest of experience? If one is to make such claims responsibly, and as one sincere man among other sincere men, does he not need to face squarely the fact that contrary claims are made *within* the realm of so-called Christian experience? Many conflicting claims are made in the name of Christ, and if one seeks to find unity at all, he will find it difficult beyond asserting a theistic outlook. The stubborn facts are that claims are made for the Christian faith which leave one wondering what that faith comprises beyond the reference to the historical figure of Jesus.

The liberal then – as I see him – does not set out to water down an experience. After all, no experience as experienced can be diluted. But it is the liberal's respect for all experience as a guide to truth which makes him weigh carefully every experience and see experiences in their relation to each other. There is nothing in his method which precludes the possibility that God invaded history in Christ, but he and any other thinker must ask: On what grounds do we say God is in Jesus in a unique way – that is, what other experiences can live in *koinonia* if such a view is taken? Is the view of God envisioned through a given view of Jesus consistent with the views of God envisioned in the experiences of other moral and religious men?

When claims are made in the name of Christian religious experience which have to do with moral and aesthetic issues, and with cosmological issues, such as the relation of God to the world, then such Christian claims must enter the arena of appraisal and be judged by their capacity to solve both theoretical and practical problems. This means, for example, that natural morality and natural theology cannot be excluded from the attempt to decide what the truth in religion is, especially when there are conflicting views of what moral standards, and what conception of God, are supported by religious experiences. Unless the Christian, or any other religious believer, is to hold dogmatically that processes in the human being and the natural world can provide no evidence concerning the existence and nature of God, then what we know about human nature, what we know about its moral possibilities and achievements in interaction with the non-human world, may well be used to help arbitrate the differences between different views of God suggested by religious and Christian experience. The minimum use of natural theology and natural morality, let alone aesthetics, would then be to complete the conception of God felt to be revealed in religious experiences.

It would be a curiously distorted view of God, let alone of life, which maintained that the God who reigns over man and the universe does not show himself in them. Yet one of the most disappointing concomitants of the theology of the last quarter-century is its anti-metaphysical scepticism, a scepticism it shares, curiously enough, with its arch enemies, positivism and pragmatic naturalism. Yet if there is any doctrine which the religious believer can hardly afford not to reaffirm, it is that God is in his world and is to be found at work in it. Otherwise his religious affirmations must fail to keep contact with, and be relevant to, the other enterprises of God-made man.

At this point I shall be reprimanded, no doubt, by those who hold
that there is no truth in the moral-aesthetic nature and experience
of man apart from its being infused or permeated by experience 'in
Christ'. It is I, the liberal, and not the neo-orthodox theologian and
existentialist, who is separating God from man. For am I not
suggesting that we can know man's moral structure and imperatives
apart from his relation to the divine initiative?

Here is another large issue which is too important for even
summary treatment,[1] but I cannot avoid pointing up the issue.
What I should want to insist upon here, again, is the avoidance of
methodological inflexibility. It may be that there is a radical
discontinuity between the standard of moral judgment as found in
Christian witness and non-Christian experience. But this cannot be
asserted without full appreciation of the continuities of experience.
It may be that the best in moral experimentation without belief in
God does suggest a standard of love illustrated by the heroic in all
ages and in all places. But do we proceed most carefully when we
allow the either-or of supernaturalism or naturalism to gain control
of our interpretations of experience in such a way that the experiences of men fall apart in exclusive classes? Why not, in our thinking, realize that critical reflection on moral experience and experiment, *including moral experiment with religious experience*, may give
sounder guidance than either so-called religious morality or
naturalistic morality. No complete moral criticism of life can
possibly avoid careful appraisal of the possible revelations given in
religious experience and therefore in Christian experience. Yet I
find such high qualities of moral dedication and insight in so many
different sources and persons, believers and non-believers, that it
seems to me arbitrary and, in any case, hazardous to allow religious
moral experience to dictate to non-religious moral experience or
vice-versa.

I am purposely avoiding certain critical epistemological issues
here, and stating a methodological and criteriological point which
I regard as fundamental. The single most vexing question in this
area remains: Is the Christian moral insight dependent on his
religious experience, or is the Christian experience interpreted in
the light of the growing moral insight? Dogmatism in favour of a

[1] See Peter A. Bertocci, 'A Critique of Ramsey's *Basic Christian Ethics*',
Crozer Quarterly, 29, 1952, pp. 24–38.

naturalistic or in favour of a supernaturalistic interpretation of moral experience is hardly in order where difficult issues are involved. I prefer here to begin with the fact that certain insights and experiences of value are within human experience and to interpret the world in which man finds himself in the light of these experiences. To say that these experiences come from God does not in itself establish their validity or invalidity for human action. A crucial consideration in my thinking is that the source of a moral insight is in itself no guarantee of its relevance or irrelevance to human experience. What makes any value experience worth obedience is its capacity to protect, better than any other, the totality of other relevant values, including creativity, in human experience. I would also argue that when men believe that the values to which they can give obedience are rooted in the structure of the universe itself, they find the greatest incentive for living in accordance with their ideal. But important as the motivational problem in ethics is, the even more important question is that of establishing an ethical ideal which does not arbitrarily neglect the different phases of human experience for which it becomes the norm.

v

It may serve to clarify some of the orientations suggested thus far if I relate myself to several of the contentions in Professor Casserley's masterly book which I did not read until I came to this part of my deliberations. Casserley states that the real question he asked himself when he began to write this book were influenced by the fact that

> I was already a believing Christian with deep-seated metaphysical tastes and interests. The questions which my experience of life propounded to me were these: 'What must be true about the world of man and human language in a world in which the Bible and metaphysics are both valid'? 'What must be true about the Bible and metaphysics separately if it is possible for the same person to devote himself to each of them without tearing his mind and soul in two'?[1]

I find in Casserley no anti-metaphysical or anti-intellectual scep-

[1] J. V. Langmead Casserley, *The Christian in Philosophy*, New York: Scribner's Sons, 1951, p. 184.

ticism. He is willing to follow Kierkegaard's warning against mere objectivity but he insists that if men 'are to find the truth at all they can only discover it through being profoundly and personally themselves, through exploiting the opportunities and possibilities of their own unique point of view to the uttermost'.[1] For him subjectivity actually leads to objectivity, since he believes that 'the man is profoundly himself who will find within himself a craving for the objective'.[2]

I find myself in hearty agreement with this statement in so far as it concerns the psychology of belief and *one type* of motivation for philosophy. I, too, began my philosophical reflection as one kind of believing Christian. Indeed, my reflection and interest in philosophy gained momentum as I tried at first to save my adolescent faith from the contradictions I found within my version of it, and from conflict with a growing understanding of the world and human nature. But at every stage of further development it became crucial to distinguish between the psychological genesis and the *psychological convincedness* of my profoundest beliefs, on the one hand, and their *logical validity and truth-value*, on the other.

I do not for a moment deny that there is, and must be, an act of commitment involved psychologically, and, I would say, morally, in the venture of living for what one believes to be ultimate. I do not for a moment deny that in my life there are psychological roots of belief far deeper than I may realize. But because I know this, because I know that my ultimate stand is influenced by more factors than I may be fully aware of, I deem it an act of Christian charity, let alone of basic obligation to my fellow men, to do all in my power, in Casserley's admirable expression, to learn to live with such a high degree of subjectivity that my passion for objectivity is not smothered.

There are, of course, many times in my life when I have nothing else to trust but my subjectivity, but the ground for trusting such subjectivity to take me into action which affects others is the confidence that much that began in me as subjective conviction turned out to be objective, that is, common to me and my fellow men. There is a world of difference, in the realm of truth, between psychological certitude and epistemological certainty, and the presence of one does not guarantee the other.

As I see it, therefore, the continuing task of any human being

[1] *Ibid.*   [2] *Ibid.*

who would protect the world against raising his own idiosyncrasies into standards of revelation, is to demand that his private and vital certainties be subjected to the criticism of other human beings and the vital certainties in their lives. In the moment of philosophizing, when the purpose is to subject my psychological certainties to reflective consideration of all the available data, my conviction must be seen as conviction which may be wrong. If I start as a particular type of Christian I must be willing to become another type; and I must be willing to give up my Christian belief altogether if it is not coherent with all the facts.

These general remarks about the ground of belief, however, must not hide the more objective epistemological sources of difficulty. The difference between Professor Casserley and myself, I think, stems from the conclusion he draws from his analysis of religious experience as he believes the Bible presents it. As he sees it: 'For the Christian, the Bible is a mirror of both personality and history, and it is to history and self-conscious personal existence, as he discovers them revealed with unparalleled clarity in biblical religion, that he turns for the analogies most requisite and necessary to his metaphysical needs, with the maximum of expectation and the minimum of disappointment.'[1] The issue, however, lies not in the fact that a Christian metaphysician uses analogies from the Bible, but how he knows that we have here an unparalleled mirror or revelation of both personality and history. Again, I myself find the Bible and Christian experience a rich source of suggestion and analogy, let alone of experience that appeals strongly to me psychologically as a person with a certain type of emotional and moral temperament. But my more fundamental loyalty, not simply as a philosopher but as a person among persons, must be to the search for that fullness of experience which includes coherent interpretation. I must not allow myself, as a person, to be bound even by the riches of biblical experience. Why? Because the very process of knowing what the Bible means, and what its truth consists in, forces me to relate it to other types and versions of experience.

We are thus led to the basic theoretical point of difference between us. It is Casserley's contention that metaphysics and philosophy in general cannot do justice to the logic of the Singular. Since the God encountered in biblical experience is the one being

[1] See Peter A. Bertocci, 'A Critique of Ramsey's *Basic Christian Ethics*', *Crozer Quarterly*, 29, 1952, p. 225, and see pp. 252, 253, 260, and 182.

of his kind, the highest of all beings, it is impossible to define God and religious reality in the discursive terms and universals of ordinary language and philosophy. What we are forced to do is to use paradox to express what we know. The 'singular demands singular expression, and only paradox can achieve genuine singularity of expression'.[1] The traditional ways of conceiving of God, by negation and analogy, themselves involve paradox, so that the paradoxical way of knowing is fundamental.

One might well agree with all this. But the questions I have been forced to ask myself are as follows: Can one express a truth in paradoxical form, let alone interpret the paradoxical, unless he sees it in a non-paradoxical way? Can the paradox have more than individual value unless it succeeds in communicating to others who have had an experience similar to that to which the paradox applies? Without doubt, in experiencing we always experience the unique, the unrepeated, the different in some sense; and I would agree also that we can move only by negation and by analogy when dealing with concrete experience. But, as we perform the paradox-ical act of trying to express what is not an expression but an experi-ence, what is our real problem epistemologically? Is it not that of knowing which paradox, which negation, which analogy, is more acceptable in the light of the variety of experience? I see no way of choosing the proper paradox unless I can decide which interpreta-tion, which paradox, is first more coherent within the realm of Christian experience. There then follows the task of considering whether this paradox does justice to the remainder of experience, religious and non-religious, coherently understood. As a metaphys-ician I do not object or protest paradox simply because it is paradox, but I criticize any one in the light of all other plausible aids to knowing. Of course, I must realize that if there be a highest reality none of the relations and terms which I draw from other restricted realms will do. But this will not disturb one who like myself seeks to test beliefs by the criterion of *growing, empirical* coherence rather than dictate the structure of reality. It is when paradox, or one paradox, is held up as beyond reasonable criticism, or as true regardless of the reflections it throws on the rest of experience that my total person protests.

Finally, it may be, as Casserley says, that 'the truth about all history is not equally revealed in all history'.[2] But the Christian who is also a philosopher, that is, a human being who is trying to

[1] *Ibid.*, p. 182.   [2] *Ibid.*, p. 235.

enlarge his insights by as much experience as possible, must be willing to subject this claim to the evidence. His philosophy is correct not because it is Christian but it is his Christian philosophy because it is the best interpretation of experience he can find. A Christian philosopher may indeed take the 'person-historical' level of human experience 'for his metaphysical departure', just as a philosopher of physical science may take the impersonal, mathematical or sensory realm as a point of departure. But neither, *as a philosopher*, must protect insights in this realm from exposure to the deliverances of every other realm of experience. Pre-philosophically a person can be anything he finds himself being. Post-philosophically he must learn to discipline himself to the new light gathered in his exploration of the whole of experience.

INDEX OF AUTHORS

INDEX OF SUBJECTS

GEORGE ALLEN & UNWIN LTD

Head Office
40 Museum Street, London, W.C.1
Telephone: 01-405 8577

Sales, Distribution and Accounts Departments
Park Lane, Hemel Hempstead, Herts.
Telephone: 0442 3244

Athens: 7 Stadiou Street, Athens 125
Auckland: P.O. Box 36013, Nortcote Auckland 9
Barbados: P.O. Box 222, Bridgetown
Bombay: 103/5 Fort Street, Bombay 1
Calcutta: 285J Bepin Behari Ganguli Street, Calcutta 12
Dacca: Alico Building, 18 Montijheel, Dacca 2
Hong Kong: 105 Wing on Mansion, 26 Hankow Road, Kowloon
Ibadan: P.O. Box 62
Johannesburg: P.O. Box 23134, Joubert Park
Karachi: Karachi Chambers, McLeod Road, Karachi 2
Lahore: 22 Falettis' Hotel, Egerton Road
Madras: 2/18 Mount Road, Madras 2
Manila: P.O. Box 157, Quezon City, D-502
Mexico: Serapio Rendon 125, Mexico 4, D.F.
Nairobi: P.O. Box 30583
New Delhi: 1/18B Asaf Ali Road, New Delhi 1
Ontario: 2330 Midland Avenue, Agincourt
Rio de Janeiro: Caixa Postal 2537-ZC-00
Singapore: 36c Prinsep Street, Singapore 7
Sydney N.S.W. 2000: Bradbury House, 55 York Street
Tokyo: C.P.O. Box 1728, Tokyo 100-91